A
PLA
IN THE
SUN

Bill Cope and Mary Kalantzis

A PLACE IN THE SUN

re-creating the Australian Way of Life

HarperCollins*Publishers*

HarperCollins*Publishers*

First published in Australia in 2000
by HarperCollins*Publishers* Pty Limited
ACN 009 913 517
A member of HarperCollins*Publishers* (Australia) Pty Limited Group
http://www.harpercollins.com.au

HarperCollins*Publishers*
25 Ryde Road, Pymble, Sydney, NSW 2073, Australia
31 View Road, Glenfield, Auckland 10, New Zealand
77–85 Fulham Palace Road, London W6 8JB, United Kingdom
Hazelton Lanes, 55 Avenue Road, Suite 2900, Toronto, Ontario M5R 3L2
and 1995 Markham Road, Scarborough, Ontario M1B 5M8, Canada
10 East 53rd Street, New York NY 10022, USA

The National Library of Australia Cataloguing-in-Publication data:

Cope, Bill. 1957– .
  A place in the sun: the Australian way of life.
  ISBN 0 7322 6522 3.
  1. National characteristics, Australian. 2. Pluralism
  (Social sciences) — Australia. 3. Australia — Politics and
  government — 1990– . I. Kalantzis, Mary, 1949– . II. Title.
305.0994

Printed in Australia by Griffin Press Pty Ltd on 79gsm Bulky Paperback

5 4 3 2 1   00 01 02 03

CONTENTS

PROLOGUE

Australian Days at the Turn of a Century

Linda rings us up from the Northern Territory. She works at Batchelor College and her husband Mark works on a cattle property nearby. Ordinary Australians, we've been friends for years.

'What on earth's happening to our country?' she wants to know. 'What's got into everyone? What does it all mean?'

These were Pauline Hanson days, *Mabo* and *Wik* days, days when some Australian political leaders and media voices were priding themselves for having lifted the veil of 'political correctness' and for having removed the guilt of 'black armband' history.

'Freedom of speech' and 'a timely debate,' they chose to call it, except nobody seemed to be feeling good about this newfound freedom, not even the complainers. The litany of complaint seemed relentless, with no optimistic alternative, no relief; only vindication and martyrdom, victimisation and demonisation, the creation of a disparate group of scapegoats — so necessary when blame needs to be allocated.

Multiculturalism, we were being told, creates ghettoes. Indigenous people are dividing the nation into separate tribes. We are being swamped by Asians. The Labor Party has been hijacked by the ethnic industry; it has been corrupted by ethnic branch-stacking. The Aboriginal industry is creating privileges the 'Aussie battler' doesn't get. We are not really a part of Asia, so why should we have to trade our history for our geography? Multiculturalism gives ethnic communities billions of dollars that they don't deserve. Native Title creates two laws; it divides the country by race, into black and white; it is taking away our land. We are giving our country away to foreigners because we are not protecting our industries against foreign competition. Our cities are blighted by Asian crime and Lebanese gangs. Aborigines are about to own eighty-five per cent of the continent. An Australian republic is a dangerous lurch into the unknown. Asian countries are more discriminatory than we are, so why should we have open immigration? They protect their industries more than we do, so why should we have free trade? Migration must be stopped because we are becoming overpopulated. The traffic has slowed down to a crawl and our water is undrinkable. The country is falling apart.

These are questions and claims that create fear and distrust. But we need answers, not accusations; understanding, not glib assertions.

'Why are they accusing us?' Linda asks. 'Why do they want to hurt us again?'

Linda's people, the Rak Mak Mak Marranunnggu, won the lands back through a Native Title claim between 1991 and 1995, and have other claims still in the pipeline. Linda is trained to train teachers at Batchelor College, has a Master's in Education from Deakin University, and now she's recording her mother's language. There are only ten speakers of Rak Mak Mak Marranunnggu left. Linda's husband Mark is an Anglo-Australian, originally from Victoria. Now he's working to rebuild the Rak Mak Mak Marranunnggu lands as a pastoral station for the community, for their children; getting rid of a century of exotic mimosa pigra bushes that have almost taken over parts of the property.

'We've got to do something.'

Linda just wants to get on with her life. An ordinary Australian life.

— • —

'I can't stand it.'

Another friend had called us, this time from Perth.

'I don't feel comfortable anymore, I don't seem to belong to this place.'

And yet she does belong. This is where she was born and this is where she has built her life. She's done really well, works for an airline, has a nice house. You'd think the material things of life would be paramount — jobs and taxes, costs and benefits. But her agonising was now about identity, about belonging, about being Australian.

She has her Anglo-Australian husband's name, which, you might think, would mean she blends in.

'...but you don't look Greek,' people say, as if she was needlessly saying she was Greek, just to make them feel uncomfortable. She could disappear into the crowd, but why should she have to?

'We're becoming a spiteful, mean country: Anti-Aboriginal, anti-immigrant, anti-Asian, anti-multicultural, anti-republic, anti-the-outside-world.'

'I can't recognise the place. I'd taken things for granted and now I have to defend them on every side. What I have always felt emotionally, now I have to turn into words.'

— • —

'This doctor, he said Australia has to reduce its population to twelve million. Otherwise nobody will survive. Migration is destroying the environment. Australia is all deserts, poor soils, no water.'

We were at a relative's seventieth birthday, having lunch with her in Sydney. She'd seen Tim Flannery being interviewed on daytime television, talking about population problems. As an ecologist, best selling author, and Senior Research Scientist at the Australian Museum in Sydney, his was the voice of authority, the voice of apparent reason.

Rational arguments, insidiously rational it would seem, creating fear and apprehension.

'How could that be? We have given so much. We have worked so hard. We have been good farmers and looked after our backyards. Do they want us to go? What will they do next? Kill us?'

She had come to Australia as a twenty-four-year-old with two young children, worked as a cleaner in a psychiatric hospital, learnt English without ever attending a class, bought a home and planted a luxuriant garden of Sydney subtropical profusion.

Her son is a bricklayer; that's part of the reason his skin is darkish, working in the sun all day. On the job, his mates are from all backgrounds. They are all building homes, and their lives, together in Australia.

'Why blame the Asians or the Aborigines? It's like the way we're called wogs. Are they really ripping the country off? How could that be true? What are we doing now that's so different? How have things changed?'

— • —

A climate of fear and apprehension generates questions which require answers.

The group of elderly women — ordinary Australians — were sitting, attentively, in an ordinary suburban hall. They wanted to continue to learn, not vegetate in their retirement. They wanted to keep up-to-date by talking about the things that were changing in their society. So they had asked along a guest speaker to talk about multiculturalism because they wanted to understand it.

'It's about respect, about feeling at home without having to deny who you are, about recognition . . . ' the speaker said.

The silvery white heads nodded in understanding as they listened to the explanations about what they needed to know. Born of an era when politeness was a virtue, these women were determined to be decent and give their guest speaker a respect that was proper.

They had already asked their questions and were ready to listen to the answers.

Over tea and scones, one of them commented, 'I'm ashamed of what's being said. These people are my neighbours, and we get on . . . '

It's a question of how you keep the neighbourhood neighbourly.

— • —

The crowd spilled out of the doors of the Town Hall: hundreds of people — ordinary Australians — there for an Indigenous Reconciliation meeting. They, too, had asked questions and found answers which satisfied them.

A welcome from the traditional owners, a Native Title trivial pursuit game and speeches all around — Indigenous people, older Aussies and newer immigrants. They had come together in their numbers to express a faith in history's road to fairness and redemption. Ordinary folk, old and young, besuited after work and bethonged after a steamy summer school day.

Not much had been said about why the people were together there that night. That was understood.

— • —

A time like this was the reason why we decided to write a book like this.

The media spins the tales that make us feel at home, or not. They tell us the daily stories of our communities and our nation. They provide us with images of the world against which to measure ourselves. It's their story board. Unfortunately there's not always a lot of truth or balance in the stories.

Pauline Hanson was a great story for a while: powerful stuff, the stuff of controversy and headlines. Good fare to stir the 'little Aussie battlers,' good fare to fuel 'debate.' She told us that Aborigines had got too much and that Asians were swamping Australia. Now that's news, the attraction in the repulsion, juxtaposed with car accidents and civil wars.

Immigration and Indigenous rights are things we should debate, the more respectable commentators were also saying. These are serious issues, and Pauline was sort of half right. It's just a pity she was such an unaccomplished messenger, they said.

For the media, stories without complaint or derision are not stories at all. So we end up with a jaundiced view of who we are, and our future.

Then the populist politicians in the mainstream parties pick up the thread. They, too, are in the business of peddling stories — stories that will bring Labor voters over to the conservatives, or conservative voters over to Labor. Any story will do, for winning votes is their game, less than saying things that might make us true to ourselves, true to our country and its history. No wonder politicians are held in such low esteem.

This is how we ended up living in an atmosphere of complaint, oppressed by a presence of gloom, struggling against an undercurrent of blame.

Yet this is not the Australia most of us know and love. This is not the truth of an ordinary Australian life.

At century's end, there is a gap between who we really are and the images of Australia that are circulating in the media or that make up the populist pap peddled by many of our politicians. It's an unnecessary gap and an unflattering one. It is also a worrying gap which can only create division and distrust. It is a gap based on legitimate questions that need responsible answers.

— • —

Getting off the plane at Sydney airport, we are at the beginning of our journey, off to meet *Charlie Perkins*, the first of the thirty-four people we interviewed for this book. The airport is packed: men and women in suits hurrying to make connections, travellers struggling with piles of luggage, tourists from the ends of the earth. A melange of peoples, and experiences, and histories; all making journeys of one kind or another.

We have flown in from Melbourne, a city built from the wealth of the nineteenth-century gold rushes by people from all over the world, people who had made the journey hoping to make good in a new country. The lucky country. Australia Felix. A country in which the difficult promise to immigrants of a new life in a new world created other difficulties for the Indigenous peoples who were its original owners.

We are starting out on a journey to capture the sensibility of a nation, at a difficult and ambiguous moment, at a moment of self examination — examination of our immigrant origins, of the relations between immigrant and Indigenous peoples, of our location in the world. We want to talk to people; we need to understand.

This book describes our journey into the Australian Way of Life. It is a book of optimism in which we have tried, with the help of the Australians to whom we spoke, to bridge the gap between the pessimistic public rhetoric and a more complex and reassuring reality. It's about the place we have made for ourselves in Australia, a place of progress yet hesitancy. And it's about what we can still be if only we can keep faith in what has been achieved in this country, and see our way through this complex and ambiguous moment.

— • —

On our journey, we spent many hours talking with thirty-four Australians — Prime Ministers, captains of industry, politicians, leaders of Indigenous and immigrant communities. It was their ordinariness that interested us most, the everyday landscape of the Australian experience that led the people with whom we spoke to make an out-of-the-ordinary contribution. The conversations were mostly hopeful and only occasionally depressing. They helped answer the questions which are troubling our society, sometimes directly, sometimes indirectly.

Franca Arena: founder of the Australian Republican movement and first woman from a non-English-speaking background to become a member of an Australian Parliament; *Nick Bolkus,* Minister for Immigration and Ethnic Affairs in the former Keating

Government and longtime advocate of multiculturalism; *Bob Brown*, environmentalist and Australian Greens senator for Tasmania; *John Cook*, Managing Director of Berri, a large food processing company; *Mick Dodson*, Aboriginal activist and former Aboriginal Social Justice Commissioner with the Human Rights and Equal Opportunity Commission; *Alexander Downer*, Australian Foreign Minister since 1996; *Tim Fischer*, Deputy Prime Minister from 1996 to 1999; *Malcolm Fraser*, Liberal Prime Minister of Australia from 1975 to 1983; *Al Grassby*, Minister for Immigration in the Whitlam Government from 1972 to 1974, and the man who introduced the word 'multiculturalism' to Australia; *Bob Hawke*, Labor Prime Minister of Australia from 1983 to 1991; *Anthony Helou*, Mayor of the City of Moreland in Melbourne; *Don Henry*, Director of the Australian Conservation Foundation; *Jackie Huggins*, Aboriginal activist and member of the Council for Aboriginal Reconciliation; *Helen Sham-Ho*, the first Asian-Australian to become a member of an Australian Parliament; *Phil Honeywood*, the Minister for Multicultural Affairs in the former Kennett Government in Victoria; *Donald Horne*, public intellectual and author of possibly the most influential book about Australia, *The Lucky Country*; *Barry Jones*, President of the Australian Labor Party; *Bob Katter*, National Party Member for the far north Queensland seat of Kennedy in the Federal Parliament; *Mark Latham*, Federal Member for Werriwa in Sydney, former Prime Minister Gough Whitlam's old seat, and one of the rising stars of the Labor Party; *Joe Lo Bianco*, the Director of the National Languages and Literacy Institute of Australia; *Michael MacKellar*, the Minister for Immigration in the Fraser Government, who oversaw the beginnings of the first large-scale Asian immigration to Australia in a century; *Ian Macphee*, his successor; *Rod McGeoch*, a leading lawyer and head of Sydney's successful Olympic bid; *Margaret Reynolds*, retired Senator for North Queensland; *John Pasquarelli*, the former adviser to Pauline Hanson who wrote her now famous maiden speech; *Charles Perkins*, the first Indigenous Australian to receive a university degree; *Neville Roach*, the Managing Director of Fujitsu Australia and Chair of the National Multicultural Advisory Committee; *Philip Ruddock*, Minister for Immigration and Multicultural Affairs since 1996, and since 1998, also the Minister Assisting the Prime Minister for Reconciliation; *Con Sciacca*, the Labor Opposition's Immigration spokesperson since 1998; *Lindsay Tanner*, Federal Member for Melbourne and another of the Labor Party's rising stars; *Andrew*

Theophanous, Federal Labor Member for the Melbourne seat of Calwell in the Federal Parliament and longtime advocate of immigration and multiculturalism; *Anne Warner,* Minister for Family Services and Aboriginal and Islander Affairs in the Queensland Labor Government from 1989 to 1995; and *Peter* and *Cyril Wong,* founders of the multicultural Unity Party.[1]

These people are politicians, community leaders and captains of industry. Each of them is iconic, a person whose presence has shaped our recent past, influenced the present and created, in part, our future. Through their voices we have tried to distil the ordinary Australian-ness of what motivated them, and also the complexities, the ambiguity of their lives and times. What we discovered is that the important differences in the struggle to interpret our past and determine our future do not fall around party-political lines, around the old fashioned left/right divide. We asked people about immigration and multiculturalism — and we found supporters and detractors right across the conventional political spectrum. We asked about Indigenous rights and Reconciliation, and we asked about Australia's place in Asia. And again, the answers did not fit conventional political patterns. This seems to indicate a new shift — a new politics and new answers to the question of what it is to be Australian, which our political system and the public culture created by our media does not yet adequately capture or reflect.

Many of the people with whom we spoke also turned out to be, sometimes to our surprise, the first of their kind — as women, as Indigenous people, as immigrants. Some, tragically, had been thrown up into public prominence and then discarded in the cruellest and most confusing of ways when the tide seemed to turn or when another sort of 'new blood' was required. But despite this, their presence had made a difference. Others expressed views with which we might disagree, slightly or vehemently, but whose views are nevertheless founded in unsettling and occasionally tortured truths. In a time of uncertainty, we need to engage in these kinds of difficult dialogues, we need to participate in these kinds of compromised discussions.

As much as possible, we leave our interviewees to speak for themselves. Between the conversations, we interweave our own commentary. This takes various forms — historical narrative, background information, and analysis and interpretation of the issues.

— ● —

This book is about the promise and the difficulties of being a recently settled nation of the New World, and a nation that is barely a century old. But more about the promise than the difficulties, because in addressing the difficulties we have, as a nation, shown new promise — promise that was not even imaginable at the time of the creation of the Australian nation in 1901.

Yet at the beginning of our second century as a nation, we seem to be afflicted by a deep sense of malaise. There is a sense that the ever-evolving promise of what, in moments of optimism, we have called the Australian Way of Life, has stalled. We have failed to reach a settlement with Indigenous Australians to which a broad majority of Indigenes and settlers consent. We are reluctant in our republicanism. Our economic engagement with the world is becoming hesitant as globalisation becomes more insistent. We are increasingly anxious about immigrants and their diversity. Our integration with Asia is faltering. We have seen reverses in the project of increasing equality. Government has withdrawn the creative role it once had in a mixed economy. And we are failing to define our democracy confidently, and to tell citizens a convincing story about our collective achievements.

But in this book we don't want to dwell too much on negatives. Mostly, we want to speak optimistically about solutions, about the Australian achievement in transforming ourselves as a nation over the course of the twentieth century, and about the ways in which we have been creating a social contract as exciting, as forward-looking and as ingeniously pragmatic as any in the world. This is despite the backdrop of negativity and pessimism, despite accidental lapses in leadership and will, despite moments of bad faith, and despite moments in which we are more inclined to cast our eyes nervously back over our shoulders than to look forward with clarity of vision.

This book tries to tell the story of what we have been becoming, and what we could still be.

In telling this story, we want to correct misconceptions about immigration, about population and the environment, about the Indigenous presence, about multiculturalism and Reconciliation and about our national identity — misconceptions that have led to a mean-spirited and narrow sense of who we are. We also want to say that these issues are critical to our social and economic well-being. A robust economy can only be built on a robust society. A frayed society does a disservice to the nation's economic potential. It's not enough to get the textbook economic fundamentals right, and to dismiss vexing questions of national identity as needless social engineering or political correctness. We need to work through these questions. They are as much as anything questions of domestic and international economic self-interest.

The 'place in the sun' metaphor expresses the promise made to Indigenous people, immigrants, and indeed all Australians, the promise that Australia is a country which can provide opportunities for everybody. The way in which this promise has been offered has varied over the years. In the fifties and sixties it was development and assimilation — the idea that the development of 'Australia Unlimited' would benefit all Australians, and that immigrants and Aboriginal people could enjoy the benefits of living in the same way as other Australians. More recently there have been quite different kinds of promises: of unity-through-diversity, of indigenous self-determination and of ecologically sustainable development. Yet these newer projects have fallen into disrepair of late.

This is why it is time to re-evaluate the Australian Way of Life and the kinds of promise that might realistically, as well as idealistically, be made.

— • —

In this book, we address this question of the promise of the Australian Way of Life from three broad perspectives. Part 1 is an historical perspective. It compares the promises of the new nation at the time of Federation with the kinds of promises that can and can't be made a century later. None of the major promises of 1901 are sustainable at the turn of our first century of nationhood. So what can the new promises be? Part 2 is a geographical perspective, examining the difficult relationships between people and the environment in Australia: the relationship between the land and its settlement, including the question of the capacity of the land to sustain continued immigration; the conflicting Indigenous and settler claims to land ownership; and the location of the land, as a place nearer to Asia than anywhere else. Part 3 is a journey into the national sensibility at the centenary of Federation, and its moods of anger and optimism as reflected in the end-of-century debates about our national identity.

In this moment of complexity and ambiguity, our political, media and intellectual leaders are struggling to find messages of optimism, messages that convincingly inspire. Yet there are reasons for optimism, and these are to be found in the truth of the Australian people, the journey we have travelled through the twentieth century, and the journey we are still taking. We would like this book to provide confidence to those who maintain their belief in the development of a robust, just, outward-looking, pluralist democracy in Australia. We hope too that it might inspire our political leaders, community leaders and the captains of industry, to champion more overtly a multicultural, reconciled and internationalist Australia.

So, we have tried to make this a book of conservative optimism. We did not want to build utopian castles-in-the-sky, nor try to perform miracles of ideological transfiguration. Ours is more of a pedestrian kind of optimism. Yet it is utopian nevertheless, a utopianism of the possible in which we might speak of things we know we as a nation have done well and that we can do again. It is a story in which people manage to find ways of living together: Indigenous people living with settlers, and settlers who have travelled from the opposite ends of the earth, living with each other.

Its highest idealism is the ordinariness of making a safe home. The setting is days and skies, buildings and food, sunlight and rain; and the meaning of the story is no more, and no less, than everyday happiness.

PART 1

AT AN AUSTRALIAN WATERSHED

CHAPTER 1

A Place in the Sun

The cab dropped us off on King Street, Newtown, now one of the great streets of cosmopolitan Sydney. Restaurants and shops here represent every fine distinction of ethnicity; there are bookshops from old left to new age, a burgeoning gay community and pubs for every sexual orientation. Once mainly an inner city working-class suburb, Newtown today is a fancy place to live.

Charlie Perkins's house was never working-class; it is a mansion of a terrace house standing in a small neighbourhood of big houses, encased in a suburb of mostly small dwellings. Away from the steaming middle-of-the-day-Sydney heat of King Street, around the corner, past an old synagogue, down a street lined with huge old shade trees, we end up at Charlie's place.

He's on the phone and his wife Eileen answers the door. Heritage-hued walls display Aboriginal paintings framed in perspex boxes. The room is dominated by a massive dining room table that Charlie says is good for meetings when he works with the next generation of Aboriginal activists, fighting a struggle that it seems will be never-ending.

Charlie is an Australian success story, but his is not an easy or comfortable success. From the place where he was born — a police-run camp for Aborigines at Alice Springs in the centre of the Australian continent — it's a vast step to a city by the coast, this beautiful house, a smart car, successful children.

Eileen brings in a crystal jug of water on a silver tray and clears a space among the documents and photographs spread from one end of the dining room table to the other. She had been sorting them out, the story of lives with so much living, so successful and yet so difficult.

Charlie Perkins is an iconic Australian. He was the first person whose ancestry was of this continent to complete a university degree. The year was 1967.

'I was born on a police compound just outside Alice, you know. Next to the old Telegraph Station. I was born on the table where they used to send the messages. The Aboriginal compound, beside the Todd River, at the original Alice Springs.

'We lived up there till I was ten. I couldn't read or write until I was ten.

'And the things I witnessed around me, like, you know, we used to go into town on the back of a truck to the pictures, go in when the pictures had started and come out before the pictures finished, that sort of stuff. You really begin to wonder what's going on here. Why are we sneaking in so we don't offend the white people? Talk about a sordid picture of life. Made a great film critic of me, working out about a film without seeing the titles or the ending.

'And then we weren't allowed on the streets of Alice Springs after dark, which is very, you know, upsetting, and all my people sort of felt that.

'My grandmother was a full-blood tribal — my mother's mother — she wasn't allowed to talk to us. You got to keep a distance, you know, and we weren't allowed to talk to her in the language. But we used to sneak around at night and give her food. And this is Australia, yeah, this is Australia.

'Then this priest, Father Smith — an Anglican priest—was gathering up boys around town to give them a decent chance. Good intentions. But, in reality it was a "stolen generations" kind of thing, you know? My mother couldn't refuse. "We are going to take them all away from all of this and put them into a home and we'll educate them," Father Smith said.

'I was taken to St Francis House, Port Adelaide. I was denied my mother without my authority. Stolen generations. I was too young to say yes or no. I went down there because I thought I'd see the sea and when I saw it I would come back again. And I wanted to see a boat.

'I ran into the sea, took mouthful and said, hey this stinks, this water. It was salty. It had seaweed in it. I thought it was going to be fresh water. I'd seen a boat and then I wanted to come home again.

'No, I finished up down there for the rest of my life, my young life anyhow. Went to school down there and did nothing, learnt nothing. I just failed down there. I was there from the age of 10 to about 22 or 23.

'I charge the Anglican Church and I charge Australian society for denying me my youth. They deprived me of my youth. They took away from me the best years of my life.'

Father Smith made a kind of promise to Charlie and his mother. It was the promise of assimilation. When Charlie was born, C.E.A. Cook was the Protector of Aborigines in the Northern Territory. This is how he saw Charlie's problem, and the problem of the Aboriginal people:

> The Australian Native has, through the centuries, developed as a nomad, producing nothing, storing nothing, and relying for his survival upon Nature completely unchanged. At every point, therefore, his evolution has been under influences, the direct antithesis of those which have evolved the civilization into which it is now hoped to admit him ... If assimilation is to be successful, it will be necessary first to remould his character in harmony with the new social structure. To this end, he must be subjected to influences and stimuli which have evolved our own race. Sheltering him from these influences, out of considerations of compassion or philanthropy, can only convert him to a dependant parasite with little expectation of racial survival.[1]

So, the Anglican Church set about remoulding Charlie's character, in the hope of admitting him to white civilization. It failed in every way, says Charlie. His break was to become a star soccer player with the Greek and Croatian teams in Sydney. That was how he bought his first house. That was how he was able to go to the University of Sydney. And, far from being assimilated, he was to become a fierce advocate for Indigenous self-determination.

— • —

In 1967, the year Charlie graduated, the Minister for Education, Electricity and Native Affairs and Deputy Leader of the Country Party in Western Australia was Edgar Henry Mead Lewis. The world was changing. By a majority of 90 per cent, a referendum of the Australian people had voted to amend the Australian Constitution to remove racially discriminatory references to Aboriginal people. They could now be counted in the census; and the Commonwealth could now make laws relating to Aboriginal people — neither of which had been allowed by the Constitution since Australia became a nation in 1901.

In the spirit of the new times, Lewis issued a little information booklet for the people of Western Australia:

> All are agreed that, for the Aborigines to survive and prosper, this numerically small group ... should be assimilated ... Assimilation ... means that Aborigines will be allowed to choose to live as members of a single Australian community — enjoying the same rights and privileges and accepting the same responsibilities and loyalties as other Australians.

This was a promise that things would get better for 'the Aborigine,' a promise to make things better by making them the same. No longer would Australians 'see him as a mean, stoop-shouldered individual, living under dismal conditions in a dirty hovel, getting into scrapes with the police and someone to be shunned.'

And so, chapter by chapter, the booklet went through all the things that would be done to make assimilation work: improvements to education, housing, employment and health; improvements designed to give Aboriginal people the chance to partake in the Australian way of life.

On the cover of the booklet are Mr and Mrs Harold Little, who the caption tells us, 'study the plans of their new home in a Perth riverside suburb.' Harold Little was a well known Aboriginal footballer. Here was 'already ample proof in the achievements of Aboriginal families that assimilation is possible and is already taking place at an encouraging rate. They are regaining their place in the sun.'

Assimilation was a promise made, but not kept. Now, at the turn of a new century, Aboriginal Australia is still another country to the country of immigrants, a much poorer country without the average educational, health and housing standards that might be regarded as 'the Australian way of life.' For most of the land area of the continent, people are living in an Australia which is still, by any measure, a Third World country, a country of far, far Eastern Africa. Just past Eritrea, or Somalia, or Mozambique, and not that different when you look at the conditions of life.

And there was another promise made in the Lewis booklet:

Assimilation does not mean that Aborigines will necessarily lose their identity as Aborigines or their pride in their Aboriginal ancestry. It does not mean, either, that Aboriginal language, arts and customs should be allowed to languish. These can and should enrich the whole Australian culture.

This was a promise that couldn't be kept because the idea of assimilation wouldn't allow it to be kept. The booklet quotes Paul Hasluck, who was one of the careful thinkers, one of the earnest conservatives, in the postwar Federal Cabinets of Sir Robert Menzies:

For many years past, people have been rather nervous of using phrases about carrying the blessings of civilization for fear that they might be accused of cant or humbug. The world today, however, is coming around to the idea that inevitable change can be made a change for the better. We recognise now that the noble savage can benefit from measures taken to improve his health and his nutrition, to teach him better cultivation, and to lead him in civilized ways of life.[2]

'Better cultivation,' of course, meant that Aboriginal culture had been less than cultivated. 'Leading him to civilization' meant that his culture was not the stuff of civilization. Assimilation was never likely to work as something that fostered pride in Aboriginal ancestry or identity. Assimilation was a false, a misleading, an untenable promise. It was a promise that would not and could not be kept. To do so was, quite simply, impossible.

A different kind of promise would not be imaginable until the people of Australia were able to rethink the basic terms of the conversation — to rethink the concepts of culture, civilization and nation. Only then would it be possible to make a new kind of promise for a new way of life — a new kind of Australia which is open, tolerant and genuinely respectful of differences in history and experience. Three decades later, Australians are on the verge of that imagination.

CHAPTER 2

A New Social Contract

It is just one century since Australia became, in the words of its Constitution, 'one indissoluble Federal Commonwealth.' Federation was a great watershed in our history. A century later we have reached another great watershed.

— • —

Crossing a ridge — the watershed — a traveller comes to a new river system. Water flows into streams that run in another direction. The streams flow into a river that reaches the sea at another place. A watershed is the start of a new landscape. Metaphorically, it is a change in direction, a turning point.

In the flat, dry, ancient lands of Australia, watersheds are often stranger, more radical, yet less immediately obvious things than the geographer's definition allows. School atlases show the Great Dividing Range stretching the full length of the east coast of Australia: a watershed of continental proportions, like the Rockies, or the Alps, or the Andes, or the Himalayas.

The Queensland outback stretches endlessly, interspersed with small towns of greying fibro and corrugated iron shops and verandahed timber houses. Ghost towns with the odd splash of modernity such as a petrol station or a salesyard of bright green tractors. Communities suffering for their progress. Rural efficiency means unemployment and people moving out of a locale which was only sparsely populated in the first place. Mingela, Prairie, Muttaburra, Winton, Boulia. The traveller moves quickly past run-down Aboriginal communities on the edge of town, but they're not moving anywhere.

It's hard to tell when you are crossing the Great Dividing Range in outback Queensland, but when you do, and if you notice, you enter a landscape more radically different than the other side of any of the earth's other continental watersheds.

On the west side the streams and rivers rarely flow; and, when they do, there is no sea for them to reach. It is a landscape of great colour and contrast, a landscape in which you must adjust your horizontal perspective to think in terms of hundreds of miles from ridge to valley to ridge, and your vertical perspective to span from nothing to no more than a hundred feet. This is a place of enormous resource wealth, and a place of parallel and now ailing civilizations, black and white.

Australians today are travelling through enormous change, facing enormous challenges, reaching towards a new landscape of enormous possibility. This is a very Australian watershed. It's difficult to see if you are not looking hard, but if you do, the changes we have begun to make to our national landscape are ingenious and visionary, and the transformation we are undergoing challenges to the core conventional understandings of civic and cultural topography. Yet, in a very Australian kind of way, what we have been doing is down-to-earth, pragmatic and most of all, basically decent.

This watershed is nearby somewhere, you can tell. Although there is no obvious marker sign, it is a landscape of the future, a landscape yet to be discovered, a place still to be made fit for human habitation.

— • —

This is a time of high anxiety and great uncertainty. Piercing questions are being asked about the very basis of our social contract — the very way in which we agree to live together. Questions about the legitimacy of land ownership and sovereignty since the invasion of Indigenous Australia. Questions about our status as a nation, a nation which has taken a long time to shed its colonial heritage, a nation whose Constitution until century's end was still an Act of the Imperial Parliament in London and whose Head of State is drawn from the hereditary line of the British monarchy. Questions about our economic direction in the globalised economy of free trade. Questions about immigration and our cultural diversity. Questions about our destiny at the bottom right-hand corner of Asia. Questions about the responsibility the state holds to engineer greater social equality. Questions about the role of government in creating economic opportunities. And questions about the character and strength of our democracy itself.

All of these questions exist in an uneasy state of still-being-answered — fitfully, in bursts, with setbacks, more and then less and then more clearly. If a country is defined by the ways in which its people feel at home, if national identity is the stuff of mood and sensibility, and if a sense of comfortably belonging creates committed citizens, then you would have to say that at the turn of its second century Australia is afflicted by a deep unease, uncertainty and national ambivalence.

The only certain thing is that the answers to every one of these questions today have to be very different from what they were at the time of Federation in 1901. There is no going back, even if this seems like the easiest path for the mind to take. The foundations of our social contract have changed. We are not the people we used to be.

— • —

Looking back over our future's past, the first and most dramatic watershed in Australia's history was human habitation itself — the indeterminable millennia in which Indigenous peoples developed countries of their own in every part of this continent and created a civilization as dazzlingly inventive as any other on earth. The second watershed was what amounted to invasion for the Indigenes, yet was called 'discovery' and then 'settlement' by the newcomers, who saw their own actions from a different perspective. They began to arrive over two centuries ago, first to make a gaol and, only later, a life for themselves. The third great watershed occurred around 1901, when Australia became a nation, flawed admittedly, but nevertheless a single, self-governing polis, a nation for a continent. And now, at the turn of the millennium, perhaps we are at another watershed . . .

The country born of the third watershed was both a new nation as well as a nation in the New World. While both of these ideas are filled with promise, they are also filled with difficulty. The promise of a new nation is to create a society unencumbered by the shackles of tradition, the histories of oppression and the miseries of gross inequality. The migration experience captures this promise at a personal level — to travel to the ends of the earth and find a place that promises a new life, a better life, opportunities not available in the old country. And the New World has its own promise — lands and natural resources to be discovered, and developed, and exploited for human benefit.

The difficulty for a new nation in the New World is that it can't escape dealing with old worlds: with the old world of Indigenous civilization, with the old baggage of immigrants and settlers, and then with the rest of the world, as a nation still struggling to define a place and a role.

— • —

The first social contract of the Australian nation, created a century ago at the watershed of Federation, represented the terms of agreement for a new nation; a resolution of the tensions that bedevilled late nineteenth-century colonial society. Conflicts between capitalists and workers. Conflicts between white settlers and coloured settlers. Conflicts between Aboriginal peoples and their invaders. Conflicts between imperialists and Australian nationalists. The newly Federated nation of 1901 provided solutions to all these problems, solutions which were durable enough to last for at least half a century.

A contract for a nation, Federation was built upon great eight pillars — eight great principles, eight great social and political ideas:

1. *Terra Nullius* and Aboriginal Protection
2. White Australia
3. The British Empire
4. British Imperial History in Asian Geography
5. Protection for the Labour and Enterprise of the White Man
6. Social Security
7. An Active State in a Mixed Economy
8. A Unitary Democratic Nation

Mostly for the better, but sometimes for the worse, every one of these pillars has crumbled a century later. They have become irrelevant, or turned out to be dangerously destructive in totally different circumstances, or have even proven to be morally unconscionable.

— • —

The first pillar of Australian nationhood was *Terra Nullius* and the provision of Aboriginal 'Protection'. At the height of British colonial rule a serious effort had been made, if not always successfully, to ensure that Aborigines enjoyed certain rights; at the very least, these were the rights of people who had become British subjects by virtue of conquest. This tradition began with Governor Phillip's instructions to negotiate with the inhabitants of the continent when, in Sydney in 1788, he established the first British settlement in Australia. It was an approach that continued through to Colonial Secretary Earl Grey's instructions in the late 1840s that the colonies were to establish large-scale reservations for Aborigines so they could continue to provide for themselves. Grey also insisted that the pastoral leases, which recognised the expanding squatter settlement, were for pasturage only and that Aboriginal people had 'mutual' property rights.

By the time of Federation, however, everything had changed. The new Australian nation had developed a completely different way of answering the question of pre-existing Aboriginal occupancy. The case of *Cooper v. Stuart* in 1889 had established the doctrine of *terra nullius,* or empty land. Australia, according to this line of reasoning, had been 'practically unoccupied' before British settlement, 'without settled inhabitants or settled law.'

Meanwhile, Aborigines' rights as full British subjects were progressively removed by the increasingly independently-minded colonial legislatures. The Colonial approach had always been one of *laissez-faire*: of undeclared frontier war when Aborigines got in the way of the new settlement, including sporadic revenge expeditions such as the Tasmanian 'roundup'; but also leaving them to themselves when they didn't get in the way, and sometimes even the development of remarkably productive collaborations, for instance in the foundation of a pastoral industry on mutually owned lands.

The new 'native welfare' approach obsessively interfered in Aboriginal people's lives. This evolved into a system which institutionalised Aboriginal people on reserves — a system so authoritarian as to amount in many cases almost to incarceration. Aborigines were put into the same category as prisoners and lunatics in a society which was busily setting up 'modern' institutions to remove every manner of social evil and to keep these evils out of sight and, therefore, out of mind.

At the same time, 'mixed race' children were removed from the reserves and from their families. It was thought that interbreeding with whites would at least gave them a chance. For the remaining Aborigines, however, it was a matter of 'smoothing the pillow' of a 'dying' race — to quote a phrase in common use at the time.

As an inferior race and a primitive culture, modern rationality held they were destined to disappear.

So, by the time the Australian Constitution was drafted, Aboriginal people were only mentioned twice — both times negatively: in Section 51(xxvi), which prohibited the Commonwealth from making special laws for Aboriginal people, and Section 127, which said they could not be counted in the Commonwealth census. And, if this wasn't quite obvious, the first *Commonwealth Franchise Act* of 1902, explicitly denied the right to vote to 'aboriginal natives.' The former colonial legislatures, now States in the new Constitution, were left to deal with Aboriginal 'welfare.'

Terra nullius, racial segregation, removal of citizenship rights — this was the new nation's mostly home-grown solution to the question of land tenure and sovereignty.

Clearly none of this framework is sustainable a century later. Now it is unthinkable, immoral, impossible. Not even the maddest, most unrealistic, most racist and most rabid turn-of-the-twenty-first-century conservative thinker could advocate what had simply become an accepted fact by 1901.

The negative provisions in the Constitution were removed in 1967. The full right to vote for Aborigines was granted in the sixties and the compulsory 'Australian ballot' in the eighties, though in practice Aboriginal people still do not enjoy the same electoral rights and responsibilities as those enjoyed by other Australians because, unlike other Australians, they are not required to register their names on the Commonwealth electoral roll.

The High Court's 1992 *Mabo* and 1996 *Wik* decisions confirmed Indigenous property rights in common law. Not even in the convolutions and contortions of the 1993 and 1998 Native Title Acts did modern Australian legislators go so far as to deny the truth of Indigenous title, although they did attempt to restrict the practical enjoyment of the benefits of those rights by the Native Title owners.

So, too, the policy of Protection or separatism was replaced between the 1930s and the 1980s by assimilation, then integration, and most recently by self-determination.

These have been extraordinary reversals. The foundations for a completely new settlement of the conflict over land and sovereignty have been laid by the end of the Federation's first century. However, much unfinished business remains. We have still to have a discussion between Indigenous people and settlers that arrives at a mutually acceptable settlement. We still do not have a social contract that has moral legitimacy. We are, in fact, at a new watershed.

— • —

Charlie Perkins was at the frontline during these reversals in policy, witnessing the change in attitudes, the swing that began to change the terms of the Indigenous clauses in the social contract of Federation.

'Jim Spiegelman and I and some other students at Sydney University hired a bus. Student Action for Aborigines, we called ourselves. The Australian Freedom Ride, like the Freedom Ride that helped break the segregation in the Southern states of the USA.'

It was 1965.

'We had an anarchist, a communist, Liberal Party members, Labor Party members. We had Jewish students, students from every ethnic group. We just all took off into the blazing sunset without knowing where we were going to go.'

The bus reached Walgett, 400 miles north-west of Sydney. The Walgett Branch of the Returned Services' League had welcomed back Aboriginal servicemen one day in 1945, then they had banned Aborigines from entering the club.

The Freedom Riders stood outside the RSL holding up their placards. People couldn't believe what was happening.

'CIVIL RIGHTS FOR ABORIGINES.' 'WALGETT RSL SHOULD NOT BAN ABORIGINES.' 'CLOSE THIS CLUB DOWN.'

'These were not very startling sorts of things to say on posters, but I suppose they were revolutionary at the time.'

RSL members had to pass the protesters. They laughed. They spat. They tore up banners. Others were ashamed. Aboriginal people and white people gathered. All were there to watch.

'Arguments began to break out all over the place: not among our people only, but also among the Walgett community. White people were arguing with white people, Aborigines were arguing with Aborigines, Aborigines were arguing with whites. Friends were arguing with friends, brothers were arguing with brothers, fathers were arguing with their sons. It was sensational, the effect the demonstration had upon people on that hot day. All the hatred and confused thinking about race boiled to the surface and it was like a volcano exploding.'

The bus went on to Moree. Charlie tried to take nine Aboriginal children for a swim in the local pool. They were refused entry; prohibited by Council Resolution, the man at the gate told them. So the protesters held up placards again.

'RESCIND COUNCIL STATUTES AND DESEGREGATE SWIMMING POOL.' 'SOME IN POOL — WHY NOT ALL?' 'ARE YOU PROUD OF YOUR COUNCIL?'[1]

'I reckon that was the greatest catalyst for change, for dealing with racism in Australia. It got amazing publicity and an amazing reaction from people. A lot of Australians genuinely didn't know that those sorts of things were happening. The publicity had a real impact. The referendum was good, but it wouldn't have happened unless a thing like that happened before it.'

Three decades later Charlie Perkins is still at the frontline.

'We have got to the tail end of a generation that's a lost cause. They are people who were brought up with the idea that they own the country, they run the country and blacks are just second-class. And everybody else. The ethnic groups are second-class, too. It's either wogs or boongs, that's what you are if you don't fit into their own category. That generation is dying out rapidly.

'The new generation coming up is more discriminating in their discrimination. Before it was just blind stupidity: "Oh, the blacks are no good, and just stick the bloody bastards down the end of the road, that's all they are good for."

'Today they are not saying that, but the effect is basically the same. But at least they are thinking. They are thinking people and you can work with them, you can argue the point with them. The other people you couldn't.

'So I think we have come a long way in a very short space of time in terms of racism in this country. But we have the residue of these people still hanging on and they affect a lot of people.

'These are the people that are catered for by Alan Jones. They vote and they are vocal and they are predominantly from places like the RSL, the pastoral industry, the mining industry and these commercial enterprises that don't know. Just dumb bastards a lot of them, don't know anything about anything. All they know is that they have to sell four hundred bolts and fifteen nuts a week and everything else is just secondary.

'And as for John Howard — it's a time of so much promise, but really he hasn't got the intellect or the breadth or the vision to realise his place in history. He has precipitated all of what is going around us at the moment. He's caused it. He made the bullets and Pauline Hanson fired them. They used Hanson as cannon fodder and now she's gone. She was a sucker to have fallen for it. Yet again, she did answer a lot of problems in people's minds which I think the stupidity of the Labor Party allowed to happen. But I blame Howard more than anyone else.'

At another Australian watershed, we stand thinking about the terms of a new social contract.

CHAPTER 3

Great South Land

Helen Sham-Ho agreed to see us on a Sunday afternoon, in her office at Parliament House in Sydney. The place was dead quiet, hardly a soul around. Better to talk there, she said, than in a restaurant as we had suggested. This was the Chinese way. Speaking and eating were separate activities — this kind of speaking, anyway. She was right of course, so we talked first, and then ate, and kept talking until late in the evening.

You'd never know that Helen Sham-Ho is another truly iconic Australian — from the size of her office, or from her manner, or from the story she told. For a continent that sits beside Asia, so close to Asia, for a country where significant numbers of Chinese have lived for a century and a half, she was the first Chinese, even the first Asian, to win a place in an Australian parliament. The year was 1988.

'Australian' is a word now used to describe the citizens of a country and the people of a continent. It's a word Helen Sham-Ho uses to describe herself. The word means 'south' in the terminology of European mapmakers; *Terra Australis* it was in Latin, the language of Europe's early modern intellectual and scientific elite. Words for an uncertain place, way south of Europe, but just south of Asia. Very close indeed to Timor, established as a Portuguese colony in 1516 for its ready supply of sandalwood. Maybe the Portuguese were the first people to 'discover' Australia, or that's what so many old history textbooks used to tell generations of schoolchildren.

Much earlier, Yung Lo, Ming Emperor and founder of Beijing, probably also had an idea that there was a Southern Land beyond Timor. From 1405 to 1433 great fleets of imperial junks travelled to places as far away as the east African coast, to the Red Sea, to India, and to Java, Sumatra and Timor.

Timor, as the Chinese found out well before any Europeans,

was a source of the fragrant sandalwood they used for cabinet-making and incense. It is quite likely that Chinese boats would have reached Australia about the time they were in Timor, for the Chinese had an established pattern of sending ships out to find out about neighbouring areas. In 1879, a soapstone image of the Taoist god of long life, Shou Lao, was found one metre below ground in the roots of a very old banyan tree near Darwin, evidence perhaps that the Chinese had been there in the past. The banyan is not a native tree, itself brought to Australia from Asia, by somebody, some time before.[1]

The first recorded migrations of Chinese date from the thirteenth century. Emperor Yung Lo's fleets visited already well-established Chinese colonies in Thailand, Java and Sumatra. Over the centuries, Chinese continued to travel and to settle in other parts of the world. In the second half of the nineteenth century two and a half million people left — to today's Malaysia, Indonesia, Singapore, the Philippines, Vietnam, the United States, Canada, Peru, Cuba, the West Indies — and to Australia. The Chinese diaspora is now about twenty-two million. One million migrated to the US between 1960 and 1990 and many more have since. By 1997, nearly three hundred thousand Australian citizens or permanent residents had been born in Northern Asia, and a significant number of the half million born in South-East Asia were ethnic Chinese.

For Charlie Perkins's people, Australia is an old world, misnamed by the invaders because before the European arrival it was south of nowhere, and its 'discovery' is, for them, a meaningless concept. Everyone else lives in the New World, the world of diaspora — from the Greek word, literally a 'spreading.' An English diaspora, an Irish diaspora, an Italian diaspora, a Greek diaspora, a Chinese diaspora. The story of each of their old worlds is one of horror and departure. An estimated one million died of starvation in Ireland during the 'Great Famine' of 1845–1849 and one and a half million left; tens of millions starved in China in the second half of the nineteenth century. Millions fled the European War of 1939–1945 and the South-East Asian wars of the sixties and seventies. These people created new lives in new worlds, some under conditions more welcoming than others. They made many 'discoveries' and they became, more or less, citizens of somewhere else.

Helen Sham-Ho became a citizen of Australia.

'I came to Australia in 1961 as an overseas student from Hong Kong. I did an arts degree in social work at Sydney University.

'In those days people were just curious. They were very curious. I stayed with an Irish Catholic family while I was in high school, just under two years until I went to University. They were genuine and very sincere but they seemed to think I came from Timbuktu. I wouldn't call them naïve; they were very unsophisticated, in those days, in 1961.

'I never meant to stay, would never have been allowed to stay. But I ended up marrying an Australian citizen. I graduated, had two children and became a housewife and Australian citizen.'

— • —

The second pillar of Australian nationhood in 1901 was a White Australia and it stood for two-thirds of the century.

In 1937 the Commonwealth Parliament appointed a Board of Inquiry to investigate the potential to develop the Northern Territory, an area the size of the United Kingdom, Italy, Germany and France combined. The report was nothing if not mundane, talking about the kinds of agricultural uses for the territory, the minerals that might be found, and the kinds of ports and railways and towns that could or could not be built. And the population: 3,609 in 1901, which had only increased to 4,850 by the 1933 census.

That 4,850 doesn't include Aboriginal people, because the Constitution said they were not countable. The two-member board of William Payne and John Fletcher did, however, quote Chief Protector Cook's version of Aboriginal policy in their report, who had said that 'the ultimate objective of the policy is the conversion of the de-tribalised aboriginal in town districts from a social incubus to a civil unit of economic value, and in country districts from an unproductive nomad to a self-supporting peasant.'[2] This was the matter-of-fact policy, the policy of progress and development that had separated Charlie Perkins from his mother in Alice Springs.

There was, however, one point of high idealism in the document, and that was under the heading 'White Australia Policy.' Lest anybody suggest 'coloured' labour might increase the population and development potential of Northern Australia, Payne and Fletcher reported:

In the various schemes of development recommended throughout this report, we have kept in mind the need for the maintenance in its inviolability of the national policy of a White Australia. This is something which the Australian people regard as sacrosanct. All the states, all political parties, and all sections of the people are united in an ardent desire to maintain racial purity ... There can be no compromise on this fundamental principle. Australia is prepared to stand or fall on this great ideal.[3]

At the time Payne and Fletcher were writing, racial purity was a great ideal in other parts of the world, too. It was greatest perhaps in Hitler's Third Reich. By mid-century, however, when racial purity had been utterly discredited as an ardent desire, Australian governments found themselves struggling with the White Australia Policy. They wanted to continue its practice whilst knowing the theory was morally wrong.

Alexander Downer was Australia's Immigration Minister when Helen Sham-Ho arrived in Australia as a student in 1961. Another Alexander Downer, his son, was to be Australian Foreign Minister in another political generation. On the one hand, Alexander Downer Sr had this to say:

The aim of the Australian Government is to maintain the homogeneity of the Australian people in order to avoid the insoluble problems which arise from the inability of Europeans and non-Europeans in any one country to merge successfully into a single and harmonious community. In such an attitude there is not the slightest suggestion that Europeans are a superior race to others, but only a clear and frank recognition that there are between Europeans and Asians real differences of customs, culture, religion and economic standards which prevent assimilation.

Yet, on the other hand, Alexander Downer also wanted to say this:

To describe our immigration policy in such a sweeping generalisation as 'White Australia' is misleading. It imparts an innuendo of racial superiority, which in truth is absent from our natural attitude to foreigners. Few people are less conscious of race and colour than contemporary Australians.

Our troops fraternised uninhibitedly with Malays, Indonesians, Chinese and other Asians in the last war ... In the years of peace Asian visitors and students have been encouraged to come to Australia.[4]

And Helen Sham-Ho was one of those visitors. Downer and the Government in which he served were for the moment juggling two messages. The first was addressed to the settlers who, for the first half of the century, had been so convinced by all the social institutions mentioned by Payne and Fletcher that White Australia was the cornerstone of Australian society. Racial and cultural homogeneity, Downer assured them, was not under threat. The second message was addressed to a world in which the doctrine of racial purity was now repugnant. And Helen Sham-Ho's presence in Australia was itself evidence of that shift.

In truth, Downer and his government were fast moving away from the first message. Downer was reshaping what 'Australian' meant, and reshaping it in a way in which Helen Sham-Ho might herself become Australian.

Speaking to the Australian Institute of International Affairs in 1960, Downer mentioned the impact of the Colombo Plan which was bringing thousands of Asian students to study in Australia, of new Australian diplomatic and trade missions in Asia, of the South-East Asian Treaty Organization. These were evidence that Australia was creating a more positive sense of its place in Asia:

What we are doing is only a beginning; the pro-Asian momentum in knowledge, understanding and outlook must gather speed in the mutual interests of ourselves and our neighbours ... Does the wisdom of attuning our minds to Asian ideas and requirements imply that our future lies with Asia, that in fact Australia is an Asian country, that sooner or later to the unbroken stream of peoples pouring in from Europe there must be added a confluent flow from Asia? ... Part of our destiny may well be with Asia; if so, we must fulfil it spiritually, unselfishly, with shining enlightenment ...[5]

The path to shining enlightenment was perhaps to be an even more direct one that Downer might himself have foreshadowed. The Australian Labor Party deleted White Australia from its policies in 1965, the last party to do so. Downer's successor as Immigration

Minister, Hubert Opperman, announced limited Asian immigration in 1966, and the first large-scale Asian immigration to Australia for more than a century recommenced under the Fraser Government in 1976. By then, even the idea of assimilation and the goal of cultural homogeneity was being replaced by a very different kind of ideal: that of 'multiculturalism.'

— • —

In the first half-century of British colonisation Australia was primarily a penal colony, with its inmates reflecting the stresses and strains of imperial expansion and industrial revolution. They were the poor of England and unruly people from the fringes of the British Empire, who had been convicted for their misdemeanours in courts from one end of the Empire to the other. Of the 165,000 convicts who came to Australia, barely half were English people who had been convicted in England. The rest were mainly from the original colony, Ireland, as well as significant numbers from Scotland and Wales; about five per cent of all convicts sent to Australia were neither Anglo-Saxon nor Celtic. The records of the First Fleet, for instance, show that among the convicts eleven were 'negroes' and eleven were Jews.[6]

Attracted by gold rushes, floods of free immigrants began to enter Australia from around the mid-nineteenth century. Not only did they come from the different ethnic groups of the British Isles; they came from continental Europe and Asia too.

The nineteenth century was an era of unrestricted immigration and, by its closing decades, the majority of the immigrant population across much of the land mass of the continent was no longer from the British Isles. In northern Australia, South Sea Islanders, Chinese, Afghans, Malays and Japanese outnumbered whites. In the nineties, the Japanese set up their first consulate in Australia — in Townsville, as this was both the heartland of Japanese Australia and where they thought the economic as well as cultural centre of the emerging nation would be.

By Federation, Australia was the richest country on earth, with a per capita national wealth several times greater than its nearest rival, the United States. Federation, however, brought with it an enormous change in the pattern of Australian immigration. In settling the conflicts of late nineteenth-century colonial society, new institutions of social accommodation had been created: trade unions, the parliamentary Labor Party, and then a rudimentary welfare state and an industrial arbitration system that guaranteed wage levels and living standards for workers that were among the best in the world. For white workers, that is.

The White Australia Policy — capitalised, official, and shouted out loud with no sense of shame — was one of the pillars of the new social accommodation. White businesses would be protected from foreign competition that had the advantage of cheap labour. In return, white men would be paid enough to support not only themselves but a wife and family as well, to keep them in material circumstances that had come to be accepted as the Australian standard.

Although Australians were firmly men of Empire, this was one way they made themselves different from an Empire that had preached non-discrimination. An Empire which included so many coloured subjects could not discriminate against some in favour of others. So, in the closing decades of the nineteenth century, Australian colonial Parliaments were in constant conflict with London over the emerging White Australia Policy. This was one of the main things that distinguished Australians from the men of Empire, one of the reasons for creating an independent nation, one of the main threads of independent Australian sentiment.

In this way, Federation was a watershed in Australia's approach to immigration and settlement. The main items of legislation in the first sitting of the new Parliament were the *Immigration Restriction Act*, which was designed to enforce the White Australia Policy, and the *Pacific Island Labourers' Act*, which was designed to repatriate the South Sea Islanders who had been brought to Australia in the late nineteenth century to work almost as slaves in the sugar plantations which stretched along the East Coast from northern New South Wales to Far North Queensland.

Nor was it enough to be pragmatic. White Australia was also supported by high idealism and grand theory. Here is our first Prime Minister, Liberal-Protectionist Edmund Barton, speaking in Parliament in support of the immigration restriction legislation. This is the closest the thinkers in the new Australian Federation came to social philosophy or an anthropology of different human natures:

The doctrine of the equality of man was never intended to apply to the equality of the Englishman and the Chinaman. There is a deep-set difference, and we see no prospect and no promise of its ever being effaced. Nothing in this world can put these two races upon an equality. Nothing we can do by cultivation, by refinement, or by anything else will make some races equal to others.[7]

On the Labor side of politics, the side which had thought longer and harder about equality than Barton's people, the truth of human nature and history came out no differently. J.C. Watson was Labor's first Federal Leader, later to be the first Labor Prime Minister. He said that equality had its limits, and that limit was the colour of a person's skin. 'We never say that "all men are equal." No sensible set of men would ever say so.'[8]

What followed from this fortuitous agreement between the conservatives and Labor was Imperial Preference and Empire Settlement. This was an attempt to set up a society of white yeoman farmers, family producers in closely settled farms who exported their canned meat and dried fruit back to the Mother Country in exchange for industrial goods. As an economic set-up, it proved an abject failure. Decades later, Australia was an inward-looking country with a stalled population and in economic decline.

This brings us to our contemporary watershed in Australian nationhood and Australian consciousness. The borders of the nation have been opened further and further over the past fifty years. We went from 8 to 19 million people during the second half century of Federation — half of which is a result of immigration. Forty-one per cent of the population now have at least one parent born overseas.[9] Ours has become one of the most diverse societies in the world, and it is this diversity which has changed who we are once again.

The first concession to cultural isolationism and separatism was 'assimilation,' an idea which was first used in the late 1930s but which came into its own in the post-war decades. This was the idea that Barton could never have contemplated, for it meant that Chinamen — or Aborigines for that matter — could live with 'us.' But it was also an idea which was based on another cultural arrogance — that 'they' should, or even could, in time, become just like 'us.' The second concession, in the 1960s and 1970s, was the policy of 'integration,' in which some diversity could be tolerated, so long as the fundamental objective was to create a more or less homogeneous society. For the past two decades the guiding principle has been multiculturalism: the idea that a civic pluralism makes for greater social cohesion, and the recognition that diversity is our social as well as our economic and cultural strength.

Even after all this change has been going on, and for so long now — and even though there can be no return to White Australia — we are still hesitant to take our next step. Do we continue to be a country that is open to immigrants? This is, after all, the way we have been for all our history, apart from the half-century in which our Federation settlement tried to create a racially and culturally homogenous nation. Do we have the strength to contradict the spirit and the letter of the words of the authors of Federation, to say that we are now a nation proud to be of many races? Are we a people who can confidently say our cultural origins are many?

— • —

Australia promised a lot to its post-war immigrants. It was a time of optimism, a time of hope. Arthur Calwell was Minister for Information as well as Minister for Immigration from 1945–49. He was followed by Harold Holt, then Alexander Downer, then Athol Townley, then Hubert Opperman. These were decades in which Australia was to become a different kind of country.

Pamphlet after pamphlet promoted the benefits of migrating to Australia:

> This pamphlet tells you about your personal stake in one of the nation's greatest projects — the expansion of our population by sustained and planned immigration. Australia's future will be made by the Australians of today and tomorrow.[10]

At first the promotional material was targeted at the British:

> This country offers opportunities for a new life to all those who are not afraid to work. Australia welcomes her British kinsmen and women wholeheartedly. There are no prejudices, no social barriers, and there will be new jobs for skilled workers in the industries of her cities and towns, and for workers on the farms, in the forests and the mines and on the sheep-lands.[11]

Soon the idea that there were no prejudices was extended to include refugees from Continental Europe: Germany, the Baltic States, the Netherlands.

An average of eight hours sun daily! That's the proud boast of Perth, capital of Western Australia and on overall sunshine usually Australia's sunniest capital. But no capital in Australia has less than an average of six hours sun daily — winter, summer, all the year round. And when the sun shines in Australia it doesn't have to struggle to cast a shadow ... Men work in the open with bare arms and in shorts, without fear of cold or sunburn they cannot take ... children thrive in sunshine and the setting for healthy outdoor games ... men and women work indoors and know they'll get their share of bright clear skies when the week's work is over ... families thank the five-day working week for weekend sports and picnics throughout the year.[12]

Then the welcome was extended to Southern Europe: Italy, Malta, Greece.

Australia Is a Land Worth Planning For.
A Welcome Awaits YOU There.
... You will feel at home in Australia.[13]

After 1950, streams of students spent time studying in Australia under the Colombo Plan. They changed the look of university lecture theatres and inner-city streetscapes. Most went home. Some stayed, including Helen Sham-Ho.

'I became Vice-President of the Hong Kong Students' Association at Sydney University. I met a lot of Asian students and migrants at university. Only one in ten was a woman. I became a citizen by marrying my first husband, who was an Australian citizen. I graduated in 1967 and married in 1968.'

By then, the White Australia Policy had officially been abolished and a few Asians were being allowed to migrate to Australia. And by the seventies, the immigration net had been cast further afield, to the Middle East and Latin America.

Throughout these decades, the promise of the Australian way of life remained the same:

On the pier are a number of pieces of baggage. Stickers on them show their destination — Australia. At the wharf lies an overseas liner. Within the hour she will be casting off and heading through the tropics to the world's largest island-continent. Maybe YOU will one day be one of the passengers setting out for a new land, a new home and a new life.

Today, Australia is inviting people to become Australians
...

Australia invites you to share its future and help make it the stronghold of prosperity and freedom in the South Pacific
...

An old Chinese proverb says: "If you are planning for one year plant grain; if you are planning for ten years plant trees; if you are planning for a hundred years plant men." Australia is planning for more than a hundred years.[14]

'I started to get involved in the Chinese community whilst working as a social worker in a hospital,' says Helen Sham-Ho.

'I became a lobbyist, submitting for funding. But I never aspired to be a politician. It so happened I had a few good friends and they asked me to join the Liberal Party. So I asked them, what are the principles and what are the policies? I agreed with their answers: freedom of choice, reward for effort, individualism, family values. All these suited my own personal ideals, I suppose, my ideology.'

Helen's personal ideals were very Australian ideals. Australian ideals were the reason why she decided to make her life here.

'I got to know John Dowd in 1981, when I had to do a placement, a work experience placement. I was completing a law degree then. I did it here, in Parliament. John Dowd was the shadow Attorney-General. He was always close to the Chinese community. He had a couple of close friends who were Chinese and they often asked him to go to Chinese community activities. Even when I first knew him, he always said look, we might have different-coloured skins but there's no difference between us. John has always been very friendly to me. He was like a mentor to me. I graduated in law in 1985.

'And can I just tell you a very honest statement? I had never been to a Liberal Party meeting, you know, those branch meetings, until I went for preselection. It was John Dowd who approached me. The Liberal Party at this stage actually had a vision. We are talking about the mid-eighties and I suppose they said, look, Asians are increasing in number, so we need them in the Party and in Parliament.

'So I was actually approached to try for preselection. I knew nobody. And so for three weeks I worked very hard. Of course it is not only my own efforts. But that is how it worked in those days. They pushed me forward. It's like the Chinese saying really, I was in the right place at the right time with the right people. With the right people, that was the most important bit.

'I won number five position on the Liberal ticket in 1986. I was one of the few candidates to get preselected the first time. Not even John Howard did that. That's why I say I was lucky. I didn't know anybody.

'I got into Parliament in 1988 with the swing to Greiner. My slogan was "Vote for Helen Sham-Ho in the Dragon Year." Even some Labor Party members voted for me. I won ninety-nine per cent of the Chinese votes. I was the first Chinese candidate ever.'

Helen Sham-Ho resigned from the Liberal Party ten years later after John Howard refused to instruct the Queensland branch of the Liberal Party to direct its preferences to the Labor Party ahead of Pauline Hanson's One Nation Party.

'All the letters I sent, he never replied. I asked to see him. It was not till after my resignation, and then his office rang and said the PM has no time to see you.

'Howard never wanted to understand. He can never even say the word "multiculturalism". If they don't want to understand, then there is no way you can educate them. I've known Howard for a long time. You know how some people ideologically will never accept certain things. I think he is one of those. You know what I said before about the Australia I arrived in, in 1961. I think he does belong to that era.'

After the interview we drove to her husband's restaurant in Chinatown. The food's as good as the best in Hong Kong, people say, and Hong Kong's is the best. Helen shook her head. She said she felt she had wasted ten years of her life. Glad to be free of all that now. Not being told what to do. Not being used all the time.

'The Liberal Party have approached me many times since I resigned, and I have said, as long as John Howard is the Prime Minister, I cannot rejoin the Party. I can't.'

CHAPTER 4

Being 'Australian'

Sir Alexander Downer died in 1981. His obituary in the Melbourne *Age* said he was among the half-dozen or so South Australians this century to have been seriously considered by commentators as a potential Prime Minister:

> Sir Alexander was rich and lived like a member of the traditional English gentry ... With his English accent and manners, and what someone once called his Right-wing lifestyle, he seemed — to those who did not know him well — a personality more suited to nineteenth than twentieth-century politics ... When he took up his duties as High Commissioner in London, he and his wife bought a splendid early Georgian mansion named Oare House, with 52 hectares of woods and gardens around it, in Wiltshire ... There they entertained thousands of guests ...

Downer was a favoured son of the Anglo establishment and a child of a political dynasty; his father was Sir John Downer, one of the more active contributors in the Constitutional conventions of the 1890s.

But Alexander Downer, *The Age* obituary went on, 'was also a man of wide culture; an internationalist; a man with a warmth and a common touch, developed by the years in a prisoner of war camp; and one with surprisingly progressive political ideas.'[1] He was a man of Empire. Yet he knew Australia was destined to become a different kind of place.

Another Alexander Downer, representing the political dynasty in a new generation, reflected decades later on his father's character and contribution:

> I grew up in household where the arrival of a shipload of Greek immigrants was a cause of celebration ... When my

father returned to Australia [from Britain] in the mid-1930s the thing that struck him about Australia was how mono-cultural and dull it was. He wanted us to be more than a Manchester in the sun.[2]

Far from reinforcing a Manchester in the sun, Sir Alexander Downer was one of the people who changed Australian society forever and began to demolish the White Australia Policy that his father, Sir John Downer, had helped build. He knew Australia would become more closely interlinked with countries other than the United Kingdom, those of the Asian region in particular. His life was a bridge between the past and the future.

— • —

The third pillar of Australian nationhood was the British Empire. As much as Federation was about creating a new nation in a predetermined mould, it was also about being a part of the British Empire, an Empire upon which, it was promised, the sun would never set.

Henry Parkes told Australians to 'make yourself a united people, appear before the world as one, and the dream of going "home" would die away.' He was a dedicated Australian, a new nationalist, a founding father of the Federation.

Yet the same Parkes — Sir Henry Parkes in the world of Imperial honours — was also an Empire loyalist. That's what 'Australian' invariably meant to the makers of the Australian Federation. It was in truth a great vision:

My whole being trembles with an unuttered prayer ... that the whole of the British possessions may remain for ever forming parts of one beneficent Empire such as the world has never seen ... The North American Colonies will, I think, become more completely a Federal Dominion by some reform of their present Constitution. Our South African possessions may, with great care ... become also a cluster of states; and I can see no reason on earth why this comparatively great congeries of states should not unite with the mother country in forming an Empire such as has never yet been formed, and which would carry our language, our laws, our social habits, our literature, our great stores of science, to all parts of the habitable globe.[3]

It was in this spirit that the Australian people 'agreed to unite in one indissoluble Federal Commonwealth under the Crown of the United Kingdom of Great Britain and Ireland', to use the words of the preamble to the Constitution passed by the Parliament in Westminster and which became law with the assent of Queen Victoria on 9 July 1900.

A little more than half a century after Federation, however, the British Empire had gone the way of other empires before it. Even the idea of empire itself was to be made entirely redundant in an era when economic, military and political influence can be exerted without literal conquest or colonisation.

By the end of the twentieth century, the constitutional foundation of the Australian Federation in the British Empire has become nonsensical. Belatedly, Australia changed its national anthem in 1984 from 'God Save the Queen' to 'Advance Australia Fair' and, in the same year, the High Court became the highest court of appeal in Australian law instead of the Privy Council in the House of Lords. However, a century after Federation we still have for our head of state a Queen sitting on a throne in the old capital of Empire, and an Australian flag that includes the British Imperial flag in its corner.

— • —

Still another generation was added to the political dynasty when Alexander Downer the younger became Australia's Foreign Minister in 1996.

In the hall outside his office in Parliament hangs a huge school map of Asia, the sort that used to roll up like a blind in many an Australian classroom: durable cloth backing, big letters so the kids at the back of the class could read it, the countries in garish contrasting colours. The only difference is that, back then, the British Empire was all coloured pink — Australia, New Guinea, New Zealand, Malaya, India, South Africa, Canada.

The cricket's on, a sport that still neatly fits the ghost-map of Empire. Hardly anybody else plays it. So we sit on one side of the TV in the Foreign Minister's office, two mute advisers on the other. We sit in a row, an audience of five. His eyes jump backwards and forwards between the game and our questions.

'...and if you are referring to things I said about Pauline Hanson and One Nation: well it's wrong. I mean, you should not be judging people on the basis of their backgrounds or their ethnicity. You should not be creating an environment in a society where people are not able to live out the sorts of lives they want to live, an illiberal environment. If they want to live out an Asian cultural experience, or an Italian cultural experience, or an English cultural experience, what is that to me? I mean we shouldn't be meddling with them telling them how they should live.

'I suppose I am educated by my early experience. I mean, as a teenager I had a sense of Australia being a bit of a conformist place. There were pressures in Australia that required people to conform to certain norms which are sometimes described now as Anglo-Celtic norms.

'Not that I am opposed to Anglo-Celtic norms. I am as Anglo-Celtic as they come. But I am very much opposed to intolerance of individuality, and if people want to express themselves in different types of ways ... Well, that first of all is important to them in terms of their own self-development and secondly it does, as a matter of fact, create a much more attractive and interesting society, a place where you have a diversity of ideas and views. And through that process you generate a great deal more social, cultural and economic creativity. We end up with a much stronger society.

'...and the whole notion of keeping Asians out of Australia. I think Pauline Hanson did say that implicitly. You see, that is her sort of leitmotif.

'I know what it's about. It's about conformity. It's about making sure her notion of "Australian-ness" is Anglo-Celtic Australia. But Anglo-Celtic Australia is not all that Australia is about.

'She's on about going back. Well, I just can't stand all this "Let's go back in time" stuff. In any case, you can't.'

A gasp. Somebody's been bowled out. Australia versus England.

— • —

The fourth pillar of Australian nationhood was the British Imperial history in Asian geography. In the nineteenth century, British colonial possessions stretched across Asia, through India, Malaya, Singapore, Hong Kong and as far as a place called Australasia — the Asia of the south made up of New Zealand, Fiji, and the Australian colonies. In every case, native peoples were colonised, if not by the British, then by the Dutch in Indonesia, the Portuguese in Timor, or the Germans in New Guinea. Or almost-colonised, as in the case of China or Japan.

All bar Australia and New Zealand were decolonised in the twentieth century; only in Australia and New Zealand did the colonised fail to send the colonisers packing. So, from being a similar kind of place to others in Asia during the era of imperialism, Australia became a different kind of place to its neighbours in the twentieth century: a remnant society of colonisers.

Historian Geoffrey Blainey described what he thought was Australia's historical plight in the title of his book, *The Tyranny of Distance*. But distant from what? In fact, in the nineteenth century we were close to other parts of the British Empire. The careers of British colonial administrators, merchants or clergy easily took them from Calcutta, to Singapore or Hong Kong, to Darwin or Hobart.

The tyranny of distance is, in fact, a twentieth-century phobia; a tyranny of being different, of being fundamentally at odds with the historical drift of a region where the Union Jack and other imperial flags have been lowered, and where national stories now focus on the struggle of indigenous peoples for independent nationhood.

In the twentieth century, a self-consciously out-of-place Australian psychosis developed which has been the obverse of the tyranny of distance. It is the tyranny of proximity. The enemy of coloured labour and the so-called 'Yellow Peril' was conjured up in the White Australia Policy. The enemy of cheap goods was configured through Empire Preference in trade and protectionism. The Japanese enemy got as far as Australia's borders during the Second World War, and after this the enemy of communism kept the tyranny of proximity alive for a few more decades. This last enemy was called a 'Red Peril' rather than a yellow one; a politico-economic peril more than a race peril.

By the end of the twentieth century, Australia's circumstances have changed beyond recognition. Proximity is an impossible regret. Distance cannot tyrannise when three-quarters of Australian exports go to Asia-Pacific countries. Only seven per cent of Australia's exports went to Europe in 1996–1997, compared to sixty per cent in the 1930s. From 0.3 per cent of the population in 1947, the Asian-born had grown to 5.3 per cent of the population in 1998. 1.6 million Asian tourists visited Australia in 1997. Nearly half of the 1.5 million Australian tourists who travelled overseas in 1998 went to Asia. And the vast majority of the estimated 100,000 overseas students were studying in Australia in 1997 were from Asian countries.[4]

Feeling apart from our geography is now simply anachronistic. It is also bad business, bad diplomacy, and a bad national self-image. So is negative international publicity about the fate of the Indigenous peoples who were colonised. As is even the slightest hint of throwback to the racism of White Australia in our immigration policies or attitudes to Asian immigrants. As is the threadbare iconography and constitutional reality which today tells of no more than British imperial-ethnic regret.

— • —

Australia 3 for 151. The English are struggling.

'In any case, I don't think Australia is a society that should rejoice in just being Anglo-Saxon or Anglo-Celtic,' says Alexander Downer.

'Australia is a society that should rejoice in diversity. I mean this is of course what I generally think. What I specifically think as a Foreign Minister is that Australia is an Asia-Pacific country. What could be less intelligent than to transmit messages to the Pacific and to Asia ... it's the underlying theme of what Pauline Hanson is saying ... messages of hostility to all the countries that are around you.'

Like it or not, change was occurring. It was inevitable.

'If you take a sort of culturally elitist exclusive approach to the countries around you, well then all you are doing is exacerbating your security problems and potentially causing yourself economic grief. Well, it's hard for me to see how that's in the national interest. You asked me how I felt myself and just where I come from.'

'But you know,' we said, 'when your father was Immigration Minister this country felt very different. We were a country that was optimistic about the future, a country that needed many more people and went out looking for them. And he knew that sometime, this was going to include significant numbers of Asians. This was because of where we were. Now there's a sense of gloom — the environment can't take it, they'll take our jobs rather than contribute to our future ... Why the change in mood? What does it mean?'

He stared at the television set, maybe for as long as a run.

'Yes,' he said, '... and it's just a tragedy.' We asked him what he meant, and he didn't want to say.

'And did the Pauline Hanson stuff do us damage?' we go on.

'It's sort of blown over. Actually I think it was seriously exaggerated, how much damage it was doing. I think there is a difference between Pauline Hanson getting a lot of media coverage and the first Hanson Government being elected.'

He laughs. A ridiculous idea. An horrendous idea.

'I mean, I think of course, if a Hanson Government were elected, led by Pauline Hanson herself, it would do Australia immense damage — immense damage. But they didn't win any seats in the House of Representatives and there is a perception in Asia and the Pacific that Pauline Hanson has blown away.'

A man of natural largesse and easy generosity. Also a man with a responsibility to put the best spin on things. A travelling salesperson for a nation.

A nation hanging onto the results of a game of cricket and onto the edge of the largest, most populated continent. A nation that has not yet fully come to grips with the natural consequences of living in Asia.

Time for the next meeting, a Cabinet committee, East Timor on the agenda, working on that continental divide again. Alexander Downer hurries off, advisers in tow.

CHAPTER 5

Market Realities

Stylish offices in East Melbourne — minimalist designer furniture, handmade pottery with a modern Asian feel, abstract paintings of the landscape of remote Australia. This is today's corporate Australia. We are waiting in the conference room to speak with the CEO of a major Australian company of 1400 employees and thousands more working with contractors and suppliers. The company has a domestic market in which the product is a household name and now has ambitions to become a major supplier in Asia.

A serious-looking man walks in with a clutch of advertising material, videos and posters. Grey-suited and earnest, wooden even on first impressions. Definitely corporate. Vision and mission.

John Cook is the Managing Director of the fruit juice manufacturer Berri Australia. His company made a name for itself by producing a series of television advertisements after the 1998 Queensland election in which Pauline Hanson's One Nation Party won 23 per cent of the vote and took eleven parliamentary seats:

Orange: I hate the apples.
Apple: I can't stand the tomatoes. They're lazy and stupid.
Tomato: Those bloody strawberries. They're ruining the
  neighbourhood.
Strawberry: I reckon those pineapples have funny skin.
Pineapple: Can you believe lemon-lime? A mixed marriage!
  Disgusting.
  INTOLERANCE IN PEOPLE IS JUST AS STUPID.
  CELEBRATE AUSTRALIA'S DIVERSITY. BERRI.

The Australian Electoral Commission was upset, for a while. They thought the ads were unauthorised political advertising.

'So who are you?' we ask John Cook. 'Just what kind of Australian are you?'

'Okay. I guess maybe I am a different sort of Aussie. I'll tell you how. After leaving university, I had the opportunity to start working with the Kellogg company. And in a company like Kellogg, with operations all over the world, I was given the opportunity to expand in my skills, go to Japan and learn something more about Kellogg's overseas business. Inevitably working in somebody else's culture, your skill sets improve, your orientation, your attitudes towards things you once took for granted change quite rapidly, you know, on a market level.'

Actually, while he might be a different kind of Aussie to the Aussies of the past, John Cook's story is fast becoming a common one. It is the story of a generation of Australians who have travelled, whose work has taken them to live in other countries, who see themselves as proud citizens of a newly emerging kind of country.

'...you know, on a market level,' he says as he talks about the changes that have occurred in business. For earlier Australian generations, the generations of White Australia, 'on a market level' meant 'protecting' Australian products against outside competition. Whilst the White Australia Policy kept out dangerously different foreigners who would work for lower wages, great tariff walls were erected around fortress Australia to keep out dangerously inexpensive foreign goods. The idea was to build up domestic production for a domestic market, to make Australia self-sufficient, to protect Australian standards of living against inferior races who would work for less, produce more for less, and live in ways well below the standards of the Australian Way of Life. White people would keep themselves employed in Australia, so the argument went, by making for themselves locally all the things they needed.

Economics is always the stuff of race and identity, and the changing discussion about race and identity is, as much as anything else, a changing discussion about economics.

'Personally, the chance to go to Japan with a responsibility for a large part of Kellogg's Asian operations, and living in Tokyo, was very enriching. That experience led, for various reasons, to me being brought back as Managing Director of Kellogg Australia. There were probably a couple of reasons for that, not the least of which is that Kellogg's Australian operation at Botany in Sydney saw itself as an entity very independent of Asia. It had been a factory and an infrastructure built largely to satisfy the requirements of an Australian market. It hadn't occurred to anyone really to think about Australia in conjunction with Asia, just as a part of Asia supplying both Australian and Asian requirements from Australia. They brought me back as an Australian experienced overseas, with a mission to expand the Australian business. I think the company saw my experience as a great opportunity to enlighten and waken the employees' attitudes at Botany to the wonderful opportunities Australia had in being part of Asia. To break down the barriers . . . '

John Cook was on a corporate journey, a journey in which business promise, employment promise and the promise of economic futures for the whole country were rapidly changing. Indeed, he was one of the many business people who have taken on the task of changing Australian business, employment and economic futures and carrying everyone in their organisations along with them.

He came back to an Australia that was changing and new in another sense, a country where the productive backbone of places like Kellogg in Botany was made up of 'New Australians' — immigrants who had come from the ends of the earth to live in Sydney.

'Now, the Botany facility was like so many Australian companies, a mosaic of people. It had been built in 1928 and expanded most years since that time. When looking for new employees, invariably the people who were applying were so many of those who chose to come to Australia through the immigration programs of the fifties, sixties and seventies. When you actually walked the factory floors of Botany, you found seventy or eighty nationalities.

'So when you are talking about changing the mindset and the orientation of the Australian business of Kellogg, you are not only doing that in terms of the psyche of it seeing itself as an Australian organisation, you also had to do that with people who themselves had incredibly diverse backgrounds.'

Later he became the Managing Director of Berri. And then Pauline Hanson came along.

— • —

The fifth pillar of Australian nationhood was protection for the labour and enterprise of the white man. White Australia and trade protection came together as a matching pair of ideas and aspirations. In the mid-nineteenth century, at the height of British colonial rule, Australia was a place of *laissez-faire* economics and free trade. It was a place where immigration was unrestricted.

Through the Federation accord, high tariff walls were erected to protect the labour and industry of white men. After the class war of the 1890s, it was agreed that the state should interfere in the market for the mutual benefit of both classes. The material benefits of industrial arbitration, however, could only be afforded with the protection of high tariff barriers. It was only possible to replace the Kanakas —the South Sea Island labourers — on the sugar canefields of north-eastern Australia with better paid white labour if there was a tariff on sugar imports and a bounty on sugar production.

The Labor–Protectionist accord, a package of compromises to regulate the market, was for the benefit of a nation personified as 'Australians.' Tariffs protected, not the rights of man, but the rights of 'Australians.' They protected, not the working class or the ruling class particularly or separately, but both classes in a trade-off of increased wages for reduced international competition. Immigration restriction protected 'Australians' (white workers) from labour market competition and 'Australian' business people from the competition of enterprising 'aliens' on Australian shores. The interests of 'Australians' were to be put before the unrestrained forces of the market. The economy and society of national interest replaced the economy and society of *laissez-faire* and free markets.

Almost everybody was in agreement at the time, but not absolutely everybody. A certain Mr Howard — Bruce Howard a Member of the first Federal Parliament, one of the brandy-and-soda men of the old Anglo-Imperial ruling class and an inheritor of the Howard Smith shipping fortune — told another uncomfortable kind of truth:

> We talk very fluently, especially in one part of this House, about the equality of man. Whenever gentlemen who use that term very freely appeal to it, I always observe that it is to obtain some concession for the particular class which they represent ... 'The equality of man!' When we inquire 'What man?' we may be told 'Australians.' But when we attempt to apply the term in its broadest sense, as implying human

nature, we are met with the answer — 'Oh no, we draw an important distinction.'[1]

He was alluding, of course, to the Labor men on the other side of Federal politics.

'Australians.' This, then, was the key word, a word that described the new unity of nation. It was a word that fabricated unity by drawing a distinction, the distinction of what the nation had to exclude. To define their unity as a nation, 'Australians' had to define themselves against others of those lesser races who would work for less and produce things more cheaply, on-shore or off-shore. Equality was a concept for 'Australians.'

A century later, the Federation idea of 'Australians' no longer works because the economics on which it was based are, quite simply, utterly defunct. The protectionist accord worked for half a century, even if it worked in a way that led Australia into relative international economic decline. But it doesn't work anymore. And it can't work anymore.

Over the past half-century, Australia has progressively moved towards freer trade and an export-oriented economy. We try to stick to what we do better and cheaper than other countries, while buying from the rest of the world those things that they do better and cheaper. This is the simple lesson of the new, globalised economy. The increasingly influential international trade institutions, particularly the General Agreement on Tariffs and Trade, later renamed the World Trade Organization, have progressively pressured national economies in the direction of free trade. There has been constant haggling. Often there have been setbacks. But the trend has been inexorable.

The free market may be merciless. It may be unforgiving of industries and workers or cultures and nations that don't make the bottom line. But it is also based on a new kind of sensibility, a new kind of identity, a new kind of person: open, tolerant, flexible, outward-looking and cosmopolitan. These are character traits that are good for business in open global markets. The emerging sensibility of cultural pluralism has become an Australian virtue in another historical watershed.

Today the racism of the Federation accord is just plain bad for business. It is contrary to the economic interests of Australians. By the time we have realised this, 'Australian' means something very different to what it did in 1901.

— • —

Throughout the sixties, the *Sydney Morning Herald* used to produce an annual 'Australia Unlimited' supplement. The 1966 supplement was like any other year's; it brimmed with the promise of Australian growth, the promise to Australians of economic development and the translation of development into the standards of living of the Australian Way of Life. Commerce, Industry, Communications, Mining, Science, Youth; the list of headings went on, lots of pictures and lots of facts for many a school project.

Under the heading of 'Overseas Trade', Deputy Prime Minister, Minister for Trade and Industry and leader of the Country Party Jack McEwen told *Herald* readers:

> This has been a period of great achievement, of progress of which we can be proud; but in the ultimate Australian record, it will be an opening chapter only. New-found reserves of vast mineral wealth, rapid expansion of production capacity and continuing development of our trading potential could be among the chief ingredients of our future progress. It is a fact of Australia's economic life that progress and growth generate a demand for overseas goods and services: that our capacity for growth is closely related to our capacity to pay for imports. Australia is already a leading trader among the nations of the world. Its prosperity and security in the future will depend greatly on the vigour, enthusiasm and skill with which it continues to play that role.[2]

These were signs of the development of a new kind of economy, and a new kind of identity-in-the-world. In the era of high tariff walls, trade had been a matter of Imperial Preference. Australia was a source of primary products, the Mother Country a source of manufactures.

McEwen went on to speak of spectacular growth in Australia's trade with Japan. 'The more Australia exports, the more it can afford to import to nourish its growth. This is the moving force behind the considerable changes achieved in the pattern of our trade in recent years.' He also spoke of the decline in the share of Australian exports taken by Britain.

Having been a high tariff man in his younger years, McEwen spoke of how Australia was participating in the 'Kennedy Round' of trade negotiations as a part of the General Agreement on Tariffs and Trade. Australia, he said 'must continue to fight vigorously for better access for its produce in the markets of the world, and strive for better prices for many of its foodstuffs and raw materials. These are more than ideals. They are aims which we must accomplish if the generous promise of the future Australia is to be fulfilled.'

— • —

'Oh yes, there has been a sharp debate over McEwenism.'

We are talking with Tim Fischer, one of Jack McEwen's successors and leader of the former Country Party, now renamed the National Party. He was Deputy Prime Minister and Minister for Trade from 1996 until 1999 when he resigned from the front bench to spend more time with his family.

'He's not always accurately portrayed. Remember, Jack McEwen took this country from import volume restrictions and import licensing to the next stage, which was tariffs only. Now, as you move from that to the full-on Singapore free trade model, there have to be stages.'

We met Tim Fischer on a visit to Melbourne. He was staying at the Windsor Hotel, a huge, ornate stone edifice where, for a century, the members of the wealthy Anglo squattocracy have stopped over whenever they come to town.

But Tim's not quite of that class. He grew up in the bush at Lockhart in the often-parched Riverina, went to Boree Creek Primary School before Catholic boarding school, and still lives at Boree Creek. He's the son of farmers and a farmer still. And one of the first Catholics to be a member of the National Party, and one of the few to represent one of the conservative parties in parliament.

'German on the paternal side and Dutch on the maternal.' It's Fischer with a 'c'; we ask him about his family.

'Only third generation. My grandfather on my father's side came from Germany around 1890.'

It was not so easy to be German in Australia in the first half of the twentieth century, nor was it particularly advantageous to be Catholic.

'I guess there is always a range of factors that shape who you are. It was on a broad road to Damascus. And I realised from age 21 onwards — I was in Vietnam, Thailand and Taiwan during my military service — I realised it was a very fast-moving world out there and that Asia was very close to Australia. We were going to have to change to be a winning part of that equation. So I came to that view that Fortress Australia just was not going to be a ticket to anywhere for the Australian economy in the last quarter of the twentieth century.

'Yes, it's been a range of factors, along with a realisation that we'd be stimulated by the diversity of people born elsewhere in the world. And a natural curiosity on my part — I've always found it interesting to sit next to people on aeroplanes, on trains, elsewhere. Then, of course, my sister married a Frenchman, my brother married a Chilean and my other sister married an Australian, so we had quite a varied family background.

'Can I go back a bit? McEwenism is misused to justify a sentimentalism that reaches back to policies of the sixties. It has little enough going for it in an intellectual sense, but it has absolutely nothing going for it if you realise that McEwenism is in fact wrongly stated. Menzies and McEwen together signed the 1957 Japanese Trade Treaty. They had the Ruxtons of that era — Bruce Ruxton is the President of the Returned Services' League in Victoria and a staunch opponent of Asian immigration, free trade and any notion that Australia is a country of Asia — passing resolutions of no confidence, RSL congresses going absolutely berserk against Menzies and McEwen.

'But, here we are today, nineteen million people. We produce five times more than we can consume. Unless the complainers want four-fifths of their production to be scrapped, or dumped, we'd better have markets. And if we want markets, then we need to have a global approach.'

'So who are the Hanson people, the people who want to take a Fortress Australia approach, not a global approach?' we ask.

'I think they are people who resist change, people who are disturbed by change, people who feel undercompetent in the face of change, and who are especially anxious about their employment and economic prospects.

'But you've got to break them down further than that, though. Some are very ugly people. In any nation of eighteen, nineteen million people, you are going to get some with very ugly thoughts. It's like the KKK in America. And sadly, through a lack of education and broad experience and perhaps a good deal of economic suffering, they know no better. These are people who have very ugly mind-sets. But they are a minority of the Hanson people. The vast majority are genuine Australians, absolutely frustrated with their lot in life, and not happy with the rate of change being imposed upon Australia, and being imposed, in a sense, whether Australia likes it or not.'

And, we suggest, the Hansonites are not necessarily only on the country side of Australia's regional divide.

'I tend to agree with what you are saying because in fact Hanson performed just as strongly in some of the suburbs of Sydney and Melbourne and Brisbane as she did in pockets of disadvantaged country Australia. Out there in the bush you have farmers who are focused on their export efforts and fine-tuning their beef products accordingly, and their wool production, or opening B and Bs to snap up the international tourist trade going past. Equally you have others in the city who are in their nine-to-five job and don't think much beyond their pay packet and who resent the challenge to change.'

'And as Trade Minister at the time, what was your assessment of the impact of the Hanson phenomenon on Australia's trade?' we ask.

'Oh, we got hell. In the diplomatic circuit we had a lot of our competitors set up straw men. They went out of their way to see that the worst aspects of Pauline Hansonism were on the fax machines to some of the key people making purchase decisions.

'I don't think one tonne of iron ore or coal or dairy product was diverted actually. But I tell you that in the areas of individual decision, in education, in inbound tourism, absolutely there was an effect. Absolutely.'

'So, have they gone away?' we ask.

'No, they are still not to be underestimated. They are down, but they are not out.'

We got up from the huge old leather lounges in the upstairs foyer area of the Windsor where we had been talking, and Tim Fischer walked us to the stairs. Down in the main entrance, an Indonesian trade group was being welcomed to a function by members of the local Melbourne Indonesian community. The welcomers were resplendent in traditional clothing so spectacular that even the foyer seemed bland for a moment.

'That's assimilation for you,' says Fischer with a wink. It's a nice irony. It had been McEwen who first used the idea of assimilation as public policy in the late thirties when one of the few groups of non-British immigrants for a generation were allowed entry to Australia — Jewish refugees from Nazism.

— • —

'So, the million people who voted for One Nation in the 1998 Federal election, don't you think the big parties will shift their policies as they squabble to get their votes?' we asked Alexander Downer the younger. 'Look how both parties have shifted in the direction of protectionism,' we add.

'We haven't shifted on those things. We argue very passionately the Liberal Market Paradigm, and unashamedly so. The battlers? Yes, it is a problem. It is a problem but it is not a reason to change your policies — it's a reason to communicate better with them and explain the policies. There is no excuse in politics for pursuing a whole lot of bad policy just to get votes, because in the end bad policy will catch up with you. The Labor Party will find that out, they will. They're going nowhere now because they are just playing a political game, and whilst they may think that what they are doing resonates with some battlers, they are just losing people left, right and centre.'

We're talking here about economic nationalism as a cure to the insecurities of economic rationalism. It appeals to some of the middle ground of lower middle-class voters who are inclined to swing to the conservative parties when they are disappointed by Labor. In an earlier era, longtime Liberal Party Prime Minister Sir Robert Menzies called them 'the forgotten people.' In the era of global anxiety, conservative Prime Minister John Howard and the Labor Party alike call them 'the battlers.'

'I think there is, if you like, a constituency in Australia for economic nationalism, and you are quite right, you do identify the constituency of the people who have found globalisation hard going, have felt threatened by globalisation, in turn are likely to be attracted by what you might call "economic nationalism," extreme "economic nationalism." Nationalism has its place . . . '

He gestures to the cricket on the TV screen. Australia 4 for 225.

'. . . I'm definitely on Australia's side.

'But it's not being on Australia's side to pursue economic nationalism. It is not on Australia's side because education teaches you that really you will do this country untold damage, and it is a challenge for politicians to explain that to people. It is difficult and often painful to explain and, you are quite right, one of the issues that needs to be addressed is this whole question of how to manage society so that the losers from globalisation are protected and new opportunities are created for them.'

And the sense of pessimism? The loss in confidence? How do you deal with that?

'I had an experience over Christmas which I think confirmed to me what you are saying. We were down at the beach and my wife and I were invited around to dinner with this friend of hers and his wife and a couple of other people. He is a businessman, this guy, a bit of a devotee of economic liberalism I'd thought, though not a bit as it turned out. This guy was arguing that Australia was just in the most terrible state and this country was going so badly.

'I said to him, "Compare Australia with Malaysia." He said "Malaysia is doing much better than Australia." "Oh, hang on," I said.

'And he said, "Oh, apart from a bit of a problem with the Asian economic crisis."

'I said, "Look, before the Asian economic crisis, Australia's GDP per capita was four times that of Malaysia's."

'He said, "That could not be true, that is definitely not true."

'I checked it. It's definitely true. Four times that of Malaysia's, and he had this sort of sense that Australia is just going badly.

'It's manifestly false. As somebody who has travelled to something like sixty countries in the last three years, I can tell you, what he was saying couldn't be further from the truth. This is the easiest country to live in. I know it's got its faults. They've all got their faults. But why does he feel that way?

'He's negative because he sees negative stories on television. He comes home tired at night and sees stories of conflict. If you watch the commercial TV news, it's all about things that have gone wrong — you know, car crashes, road rage, burglaries, an old woman being beaten up in a shopping centre or something. And Pauline Hanson.

'The difference between your perceptions and reality is the difference between what the media reports and what it doesn't report. It reported Pauline Hanson. It reported everything she said and did.

'It just went on night after night after night, so why do I think there has developed a culture of complaint? Why do you think that there is suddenly a debate about whether multiculturalism is a good idea?

'I suppose the best defence you could make of the media is that they judge this is the best way of selling papers and television programs — conflict and negativism, disaster. That's why when you read the news there is a sort of massive overstatement, massive. And that's not an overstatement. How often can we say we have been at an event, we've seen something happen and we've gone home and we've seen it on the TV at night and we've thought "Gee, they're really blowing that out of proportion." Everybody's seen that.'

Trade liberalisation? Multiculturalism?

'It's a hard sell.'

— • —

But it seems to work as a fruit juice advertisement.

A collage of Berri workers' faces, and of workers doing their jobs in the production process, from the farm to the supermarket:

WHO MAKES BERRI?

[*Harvesting fruit image:*] 'It was back in 1964, I came to Australia and I stayed for the first five years here by myself, and then I went back to the old country and married my wife, and came back, and I've lived here ever since.' Tom Poulos, Fruit Grower for 27 years.

[*Trucking images:*] Levi Bouffon, Transport Operator.

[*Factory images:*] Joseph Aglasz, Berri Process Worker for 22 Years.

Diana Walker, Berri Lab Assistant for 6 Years.

Nick Halkadis, Berri Forklift Driver for 5 Years.

Effie Liambis, Berri Process Worker for 20 Years.

Adrian 'Doug' Rigney, Berri Forklift Driver for 14 Years.

[*Supermarket Image:*] Ho Niang, Berri Drinker for Life.

The names and the faces say it all: Asian, European, Aboriginal. A new Australia and new Australians all — the company, its customers, its orientation to the world. And this is just fruit juice, just business, just economics?

'Our business is based on fruits,' says John Cook. As a matter of fact.

'And many of the people who had chosen to migrate to Australia actually had those skills in the old country. It stands to reason that when our businesses operate in the Murrumbidgee Irrigation Area in New South Wales, the

Riverland in South Australia and places like that, then inevitably you will have a large representation of overseas-born employees as well as of the growers of the fruit we need to produce our product.

'The criticisms Pauline Hanson and her followers were offering were criticisms of the very essence of us as a company and us as a community.

'So this is why we made "Who makes Berri?"

'It's chock-a-block full of emotional content, chock-a-block. You've got people who love living in Australia. And they express it, with a view from the old country to the life in the new country.

'So you actually have to take it back to the people. They are proud of their lives and achievements. They are immensely proud of what they have done personally. They are immensely proud of what they are doing with Berri. They are proud to be serving Australia as well as sending more of our fruit juices to other countries overseas.

'The parallel is how we celebrate Australia's success with multiculturalism. Because we, the enterprise of Australia, have got things that need to be done, and admittedly it is more complex than just taking fruit and making juice. But the parallels and the imagery is exactly the same. I think it is just as appropriate.

'Looking at the fundamental tenets of One Nation and One Nation's sympathisers, the last forty or fifty years of immigration are now a period through which we have passed. Many people made decisions about their lives, and they cannot be undone. Society has changed manifestly, and in my opinion, and presumably that of the great majority of Australians, we have greatly benefited from that investment.

'They say we need to debate immigration and multiculturalism. But why do you need to debate something that has proven to be a huge success for Australia? And as a community trying to find a role in the broader world community, I find nothing but downsides imagining that this is an issue we have to debate.

'So, who am I? you ask.

'A very passionate Australian who has had the chance to live overseas and mix with the people who now are the new gene pool for Australia.'

One of the people in *Who Makes Berri?* is an Aboriginal bloke, we notice. 'So, what about the Indigenous question?' we ask.

'Yeah, a great guy, a lovely man. He was so proud to end up there in the promotion. Actually, we had reason to be in the Riverland soon after it was finished and we took it and showed it to all the people there. He just loved it. He was proud to support the Adelaide Crows in the football. He took his hat off to show me — he actually had the Crows emblem tattooed on his head. A real wild man. He wears his clan emblem on his head. He's proud to be Aboriginal. He loves being a member of Berri.

'You see, I can remember sitting at the dinner table in my grandparents' place in Mosman in Sydney, and hearing things. They didn't shock me, because it was part and parcel of what White Australia thought at the time. There were views on all sorts of ethnic communities.

'My grandfather was Chief Protector of the Aborigines in the Northern Territory which meant that he had a lot to do with the Aboriginal community and lots to do with the Chinese community. He had views on both communities.

'Yes, C.E.A. Cook.' The same C.E.A. Cook who was Chief Protector when Charlie Perkins was a child.

'So, there I sat as a young boy, for the first however many years of my life. You know how incredibly influential grandparents can be. And the things that he said ... maybe these things were a big influence on me.

'He was very much a frontiersman, loved to sort of bang away on those things. I find that exactly the same things motivate me.

'But then, look at the transformation. I don't think I have ever seen myself as being racist or bigoted. With my grandfather, maybe it was acceptable then, because that's the way life was. Most people were quite happy about having a White Australia Policy then.

'That's how I was brought up, and I have turned out to be a very different individual.

'My grandfather risked his life flying around the Northern Territory. Occasionally he was forced into making judgements about where little black children lived, with their parents or not. Now in the context of my grandfather's time and in the period of the thirties and forties, I am sure that he felt he was doing the right thing. But I as a parent I find it hard to reconcile myself with that.

'So, these were things that happened, and they touched our family.

'I think we as a community have got some atoning to do. People, our people, John Howard and others, have been saying that it wasn't us.

'And although it wasn't us, at the end of the day we did sit at those breakfast tables, we did sit there at those dinner tables, we did listen. And we're still having to listen today.

'If I had to listen now to some of the things my grandfather said back then, I would have to have a very heated argument with him. It is not sufficient to say it was yesterday, I wasn't responsible, end of story.

'Maybe this is some of the stuff we should be saying to the Aboriginal community.'

So, to answer the question 'Who Makes Berri?'; it's a lot more than people who just handle fruit.

CHAPTER 6

Creating Security

'In the end, it's all about the creation of happiness. That's what politics is about. It's what I'm about. That's what we're here for, to create happiness. A better life for people. So that they can enjoy their brief time on this bloody planet.'

Bob Hawke was in an expansive frame of mind.

'Sorry, I'm a bit buggered this morning.' That's how he'd begun. He and his wife Blanche been out the night before to a think-tank event, facilitated by one of the world's best-known business gurus.

'A bloody fraud.'

They were there with a top business person and his wife, a young Asian-Australian student … Half a dozen people. All household names in Australia.

'Depressing. Talking cliches. Might be nice people but …'

'Do you mind if I'm politically incorrect?' he asks, pulling out a cigar to get him going for the new day.

Cigars don't get much bigger than this. A Buddha statute on the desk, and a memo headed GOLF. Hon. R.J.L. Hawke, Chairman of the Board, retired.

'I really have to trace it back to my upbringing. I was brought up in the Manse.' He began by explaining where he had come from and the kinds of views he had developed.

'…and from my earliest days the concept of non-discrimination was instilled as part of my thinking. My father wasn't necessarily involved in the brotherhood of man, but I remember him saying to me all people are equal in the eyes of God. That's something that I've absorbed and genuinely believe. Discrimination on any grounds is something I've always found to be totally unacceptable.'

Born to the Manse. Educated at Perth Modern School, then on to the University of Western Australia. It was just after the War.

'Students were starting to come under — what was it? — the Colombo Plan. We were getting students there in Western Australia from Malaya, India, all over Asia. And I was appalled by the way most of them were treated. It was virtually a ghetto-type situation. I used to invite them home, go to their places and actually established the International Club there.

'There were lots of arguments at University. That's why I set up the International Club. I was appalled by the attitude of lots of people. And as I say, I brought them into my home and went to their places and actually went out of my way to try and raise the moral bloody consciousness, if you like, but I can remember, whether it was Asian students or immigrants, the language was basically that the Greeks and Italians were wogs and dagoes — that was the sort of language — and the Chinese were chinks and chows, and all that sort of thing.

'I'm not saying that I was the only one out. There were a lot of good people and decent people who had the right idea. But there were a hell of a lot who weren't accustomed to this and who didn't understand the dimensions of what we were starting.

'Then I went to Oxford, and of course, Oxford was a melting pot in itself. It wasn't just a WASP sort of situation. You had the opportunity to meet people from all over the world. You got an understanding of just how enhanced a community can be by having a variety of inputs.'

'So, what's happened fifty years later?' we asked. 'How do you account for the atmosphere today?'

'There's the other element now, and that's related to the "age of uncertainty." I mean, we're living in a time of more rapid and dramatic change than ever before in history. There's just great uncertainty and insecurity around. The whole of history shows that in those circumstances people listen to false prophets, and false prophets always have scapegoats.'

— • —

The sixth pillar of Australian nationhood is social security. The Federation accord was an attempt to create security and certainty for its people. After temporary successes in the great class conflicts of 1890–1894, *laissez-faire* capitalism had, apparently, lost the war. Capitalism was to be civilized, its sharpest edges blunted somewhat by the old age pension, the invalid pension and unemployment benefits. And as the century went on, the 'welfare state' was extended to include a myriad of protections: family benefits, medical benefits, and free secondary and university education. The key to security and certainty was the idea that the distribution of everyday material necessities should be moderately fair — fair among white men, that is, and to a lesser extent, white women.

Parallel to the 'welfare state', a system of wage regulation was established to restrain the free market for labour. A Conciliation and Arbitration Court was established in New South Wales in 1901. In 1907, Justice Higgins of the Commonwealth Court of Conciliation and Arbitration held in the seminal 'Harvester Case' that 'a fair and reasonable wage' should be paid, and that this was one which satisfied the 'normal needs of the average employee, regarded as a human being living in a civilized community' and supporting a wife with three children. And why not?

H.V. McKay's Sunshine Harvester Works in Melbourne made a product like none other in the world, and exported everywhere — from South Africa to South America. Under the new regime of fairness, and so that companies like McKay's could pay 'fair wages', high tariffs were applied to imported goods. In the words of Alfred Deakin, one of the architects of the Federation accord, protection 'aims at according to the manufacturer that degree of exemption from unfair outside competition which will enable him to pay fair and reasonable wages.'[1]

The accord was a great victory for McKay's class and, it would seem, a great victory for working people. A revolutionary victory, in fact, that would keep the threat of communism — real revolution — at bay during a century in which a third of the world's population took that journey. It was a very Australian kind of solution: to be fair but only in moderation, instead of creating the rigorous equality that was the dictatorship of the proletariat.

But the McKay story is also symbolic of what went wrong with the deal about fairness. From exporting large numbers of harvesters in the early 1900s, McKay's Sunshine Harvester Works went into gradual decline, partly because it shifted its focus to concentrate on the small, protected Australian market. The decline was not because McKay was paying his workers too much. Rather it was because tariffs allowed him to take much higher profits per harvester than his Canadian and United States competitors, and because McKay let his factory fall behind technologically and thus slip behind in its costs of production.

Protection made McKay a very wealthy man. Good profits could be made without having to invest in new plant and technology. Eventually the company was merged with Massey-Harris, a Canadian competitor. Later, the factory in Sunshine was shut.

A century later, the security accord of the Federation is dead and buried. 'Welfare' has become a dirty word. Increasingly, the user of public services is expected to pay, and citizens have become clients. The idea of 'mutual obligation' which underlies new approaches to social security such as the current 'work for the dole' scheme, and even official usage of the term 'dole', implies that people were getting something for nothing, and too easily.

The business of protecting wages because they are white people's wages is also over. If wages are high in Australia it has to be because we do things particularly well and with particular skill, because we do things particularly efficiently on the world market.

And we still talk fairness.

Our national anthem exhorts us to 'Advance Australia Fair ... for we are young and free.' These words are were written by Peter Dodds McCormick in 1878, and they became the national anthem in 1984. Australia Fair: the land of the fair go, of social security and fair wages.

But when McCormick wrote 'fair', he really meant fair skinned. At the turn of the century, one kind of 'fair' was a synonym for the other. 'Normal needs ... human being ... civilized community.' Justice Higgins meant 'fair' in both senses.

A century later, 'fair' can no longer be used as a race concept. It means something much broader — 'fair' as between the peoples of different races and creeds who have come to live in Australia, and 'fair' on the common ground of increasingly integrated world markets.

Yet we do still need a certain kind of protection, even if the protectionism of tariff walls is now counterproductive to our interests. We still need to create a sense of security. But it has to be on a different basis to the security created in the Federation accord.

As we dismantle Federation's structures of security, we tread into new and dangerous territories. Some nostalgically reinvent racism and trade protectionism in order to run away from the rigours of global competition. Some want to spend more on the police, to build a regime of 'zero tolerance', to maintain 'security' by force in a society of disillusion and disaffection, a society racked by psychological fault lines and physiological dependencies.

In order to be fair we need to nurture society, not to look after only those who are, at the moment, nationally or racially 'our own', but in order to make a globally outstanding contribution. Our merits must be those upon which all people can be judged: excellence, ingenuity and efficiency of effort and cost. This is what 'fair' means. Protection now amounts to unfairness — as Australian farmers will testify, for instance, when US or European subsidised products are dumped on world markets, products that are not produced there so efficiently or so well as they are here.

We also need a radical new conceptualisation of welfare and public responsibility. In this watershed, we are still struggling to find a direction.

— • —

Mark Latham is considered to be one of the bright young men of the Labor Party, struggling to solve age-old conundrums about capital and labour, to reconcile what any level-headed observer of the past two centuries might reasonably regard to be the irreconcilable.

The Howard Government's Treasurer Peter Costello jokes that the Labor Party is not an opposition, it's a book club. No policies, just an angst-ridden struggle to work out what to do next; that's what Costello means. Latham is a notable contributor to the book club, alongside Lindsay Tanner and Andrew Theophanous to name just two others.

Civilizing Global Capital: New Thinking for Australian Labor is the full title of Latham's recent book. Three hundred and ninety-one pages of dense text. Four appendices and plenty of serious conjecture: 'new macroeconomics', 'twin deficits theory', 'social capital', 'the Kaldor tax', 'demand side socialism', 'economic multilateralism', 'policy incrementalism', 'intergenerational equity', 'public universality', 'Australian statism', 'new collectivism'. These are the terms in the formula for a 'third way' when the other two ways — the unrestrained free market or the welfare state — seem to have ended in one kind of moral bankruptcy or another. It doesn't sound like a platform that will easily become popular.

Mark Latham's electoral office is in Campbelltown, on the fringe of Sydney's suburban sprawl. He's the Member for Werriwa,

Labor Prime Minister Gough Whitlam's old seat. On the book's back cover, Gough says that it 'is a fresh and thoughtful assessment of the means by which Labor might renew its program for social democracy.'

'I think it comes down to this matter of being multisituated, to have multisituated citizenship, and . . .'

'But really, what do you mean, tell us about yourself,' we say. The theory is in the book for all to read. It's something else we want to find out.

'When I think about my thirty-eight years, I grew up in a home where I suppose, especially on my mother's side of the family, Arthur Calwell's politics would have been the order of the day. Old Australia was their ideal view of the world. Monocultural, economically protected, you know, the basis of the post-Federation settlement. I came out of the old Australia, working-class Australia.

'I grew up in Green Valley, a public housing estate. I still live in the area and represent an electorate with people who are doing it pretty tough in our society.'

He's a man born into the working class, now serving the community into which he was born.

'My mother's parents would have been saluting Hanson right now. They were full-on White Australia, full-on protectionism, and full-on monoculturalism. They embodied the Old Australia of a "fair go," and the "fair go" was mateship, social egalitarianism, treat people as you find them, so long as the people were white Anglo-Saxon and more often male than female. They made up an egalitarian unit that excluded Aborigines and migrants and invariably women.'

'So what's changed?' we ask. 'What makes you different?'

'I still value those social justice ideals that my grandparents had. And I draw a lot of loyalty and identity from where I live, from my locality.'

'But through education I got to learn more about the nation, the nation's place in the world, and I've had the chance to travel. Through my twenties I got involved in politics, got involved in thinking about international citizenship, international trade. Thinking about loyalties and forms of identity in life well beyond the things that I saw as a child.

'It's almost like you've got to go from the local through to the global. You've got the widening circles of life's responsibility and sources of identity. It's the changing networks of friendship and family, community and work that we're all grappling with.

'This is the big issue. You need to give people the skills they need to allow their identities to cross social boundaries. So they're not just locked in the one form of identity or one loyalty, but are able to deal with life's widening circle of identities by having the trust, the education, the personal skills and experience that will allow them to situate themselves with many forms of identity and to understand that none is necessarily more valuable than any other.

'People also need to realise that they are always best served by co-operating and trying to put themselves in the shoes of another country. It's not a zero-sum game between nations. Nations can all derive benefits from the co-operation that comes out of the exchange of goods, investment, ideas, values, culture.

'We're not being called on to make a choice between local, regional, national and global. It's not as if it's only one flag I have to salute and only one alone. It's possible to salute many.

'So these are things about my own life, what makes me an Aussie as such, and well, I don't think you can think about national citizenship as the only form of citizenship now. I think we need to think about citizenship that is multisituated.'

That word again, something that seems to indicate a third way, in the flow of a life story this time.

And without prejudice towards the past.

'...but I still admire those "fair go" principles of my grandparents. Now we need to give them meaning within this widening circle of life's identities. Bringing these things together, past values as well as change, it's a tremendous thing. I maintain that a big number of people in my generation have done this and that a bigger number in following generations will do it.'

— • —

The seventh pillar of Australian nationhood was an active state in a mixed economy. In the Federation settlement, Australia developed a tradition of engaged government — another aspect of the turn away from nineteenth-century *laissez-faire*. It was a time of great national projects: the transcontinental railway, a telephone system, a people's bank, electricity grids, an international and a domestic airline, the Commonwealth Scientific and Industrial Research Organisation (CSIRO), and later, the Woomera Rocket Range, the Snowy Mountains Scheme and mass immigration. These were all the acts of an economically, socially and technologically innovative government. They were the acts of a carefully interventionary state. They were great and inspirational projects, owned by the people.

By the last quarter of the twentieth century, Australian governments had turned away from this tradition. State banks — and Labor Governments — fell through the eighties because of their poorly secured lending. The idea of a mixed economy has been replaced by the mantra of 'privatisation,' 'deregulation,' 'economic rationalism' and 'user pays.' The result is that Australian government is getting smaller. In 1998, Government expenditure in Australia was 32.6 per cent of Gross Domestic Product, down from 35.1 per cent in 1995. This compares to 46.9 per cent for Germany in 1998, 42.1 per cent for Canada and 39.8 per cent for New Zealand. The OECD average in 1998 was just under 40 per cent.[2]

This watershed, of course, is full of new dangers. For one thing, the race reaction sets in — why are we selling 'our' airline or 'our' trains or 'our' electricity company to 'foreigners'? — as the concept of protection takes another tumble.

Clearly there's also a real question of protection involved here. What happens if government gets too small to withstand unpredictable economic or geopolitical shocks? How small is dangerously too small? Who other than government will underwrite investments that are not immediately or self-evidently profitable?

The American boom at the end of the twentieth century was an accidental byproduct of the arms race and the Cold War. Computer and aerospace innovations were not created because there was a market for them, but rather for the sake of military objectives not immediately connected to that financial year's balance sheets. The innovations that emerged from the arms race later made a market for themselves. Here and there, ideas turned up which had enormous commercial potential — potential which was often barely predictable at the time of the innovation.

In a previous generation, Australian governments invested, hard and wisely, in innovations that were as inventive as any in the world — and as commercially practical. In this generation our public investments would have been in multimedia, biotechnology, sustainable development and education: that is, if we hadn't simply fallen for the 'market-always-knows-best' ideology. Government has lost the will to lead in a mixed economy.

This is not to say we should, or could, return to the Federation settlement. We have learnt from the eighties and nineties that privatisation can work, even if it involves selling the assets of the many and the poorer to the fewer and the richer. We might decide to sell successful enterprises when they become saleable but as long as the proceeds are used to reinvest. Privatisation in some cases may well be fine, so long as government does not use it as an alibi to abdicate its investing role, its role in economic leadership. The lesson we seem to be learning in this watershed, however, is that when government does abdicate, we will be left exposed to the casino of the free market and the paranoid delusions of race economics.

— • —

Mark Latham seems acutely aware of the danger of removing the pillars of the Federation settlement and the need to put something new in their place.

'You know Christopher Lasch's book, *The Revolt of the Elites*? Have you had a look at that? It runs an argument that I don't think my side of politics has adequately grappled with or responded to. The argument seems to be one of internalising the emotions of those who've been left behind by the change process, globalisation, the information age, the shifts in social values. To them, their emotions, their feelings seem to represent the only view of the world that's morally sound, the only one that's real.

'Meanwhile the elites are doing all these sort of things at an abstract, government level, at an academic level, at a media level, globally rather than connected to local communities. So the elites seem to be immoral, essentially. Self-interested and doing their own thing at the expense of the rest of society, at the expense of community.

'And that is a very hard sort of argument to grapple with. Helping people justify their emotions is never a broadening process, is it? I mean, the true basis of social cohesion today is to broaden and to allow people to situate themselves with different forms of identity and different forms of loyalty. If people just salute one flag, then that's not going to be a socially broadening cohesive process in a world of constant change.

'Conservative politicians like Howard and Hanson have cleverly been able to exploit this feeling. They are telling people that these changes are being shoved down your throat. Whether it's been happening in practice doesn't matter too much.'

— • —

Bob Hawke is less academic and more rhetorical.

'For Christ's sake, you've got to get into the minds of people. Do they really want to stay the same or do they want to change?

'Do the farmers still want to be driving a bloody mob of horses that are pulling a plough? Is that what they want? Do we want the wharfies to be down there breaking their backs lugging things? I mean, we should proud of the human genius.

'You have try to explain that the processes of change are not something to resist. It just strikes me as absurd. We should glory in the genius of the mind.

'One of the things I get annoyed about in this whole discussion is where good-hearted people blame it all on the economic rationalists. "So what's the alternative?" I say. "Do you really want to be economically irrational, for Christ's sake?" We've got to be economically rational, and socially compassionate and imaginative.

'You've got to be very committed, I think, to understanding the rapidity of change in the world, why industries are changing, and so we've got to have a workforce which is going to be continuously equipped and adaptable to handle the sorts of demands that go with being there in a competitive world. And it won't happen if you just sit on the education system of the past and say that's going to be right. The Howard Government's not serious about education. We've got to invest in education. Education creates security.

'As I was saying to that bunch of bozos last night, the problem is that mankind has suffered a sort of collective lobotomy. One side of the brain, the technical side, has flourished and grown in an exponential sense, and we should value that.'

He holds one side of his head, and then the other.

'What we should be worried about is this other side of the bloody brain. The social engineering and cultural side is sort of moribund, by comparison with the technological side. So the challenge is to glory in the genius of the technical side, and say, "This side gives us opportunities for a better life. Better standards of living, better quality of life."

'But for Christ's sake get this other side going. If the genius of the technological side is going to produce situations whereby we may not be able to have full employment in an historical sense, one that the market can provide, well then you might have to pay a bit more tax. So that a citizen who is qualified but can't get a job in today's market will go into the education system do or some sort of community work, but he won't be a second-class citizen.'

This is how Bob Hawke says you create security in the era of economic rationalism.

'I've always said to people, "You've got to get your time scales right." People never seem to be able to see that they are part of a stream and they sort of just think they're here, and everything is promoted in terms of here. But you're not. You're moving, you're evolving, you're changing.'

And to expand the time-scale? to expand the vision? to get a sense of the bigger picture? to get the cultural to align with the technical? and the social with the economically rational? we ask.

'I suppose knowledge is power. It is true, but knowledge is more than power. Knowledge is the basis of decency. When people understand things, they are much more likely to be decent than not. It's ignorance which is so much the parent of bastardry.'

He's still holding his head, both sides now. As if to dramatise the site of the greatest struggle of all, the battle of decency against bastardry.

CHAPTER 7

Citizens All

137,000 people, 45 per cent of whom speak a language other than English at home, born in 132 different countries. 474 Aboriginal people, 71 Torres Strait Islanders, 27 people who are of both Aboriginal and Torres Strait Islander descent.

These are the people of the City of Moreland, Melbourne, Australia. At the turn of another century. At an Australian watershed.

Moreland is 'a constant surprise as cultures and people meet and work together.' This is how the material produced by Moreland City Council describes the place, in the northern suburbs of Melbourne. The City was created in 1994 after the amalgamation of the former municipalities of Brunswick and Coburg.

It is 'the embodiment of a successful multicultural community.'

Moreland is a city of the world, a city of global cultural diversity. With 'direct access to Melbourne Airport and to the CBD and docks,' Moreland's 'multilingual workforce makes it highly attractive for manufacturers exporting to the world.'[1]

'One Community — Proudly Diverse' is the City's motto, replacing the Latin inscriptions to Imperial rectitude and enlightenment of a former era.

Behind Moreland's motto is a new conception of democracy.

The old state of liberal democracy assumed that individuals were identical, replicable, substitutable. Sameness made for community and cohesion. Moreland City is now saying another thing entirely about the nature of its democracy. Its main feature is community-in-diversity: people living together harmoniously because they respect their differences. Nor is its community defined by the boundaries of locality. Moreland's diversity is genuinely global in its scope. Local citizens are global citizens.

Anthony Helou is the Mayor.

'I was nearly 18 years old when I came to Australia. It was late 1969. Not only did I want to learn the language, I did not speak a single word of English when I came here. I also wanted to be with the mainstream. You know, if you live in Australia, you want to be Australian.'

Anthony Helou speaks English with an Arabic accent. As an Australian, in the mainstream.

'I finished high school in Lebanon. If I had continued my studies in Lebanon I wanted to study journalism, and become a freelance journalist.

'But when I came to Australia I didn't speak English. So I had to work in a factory, to start with.'

It's all a very Australian story, a story that's been repeated again and again since 1788.

'For nearly two years I studied English in the evening. Then I got a job at the Royal Children's Hospital, where I worked there for another three years.

'One day, somebody there told me, "Go back to your own country." I was working there as a pharmacy assistant. This was something I heard many times, "Go back to your own country."

'All the cleaners were Italian, the kitchen hands were Greeks and Yugoslavs, but the white collar staff were Anglo-Saxon. I usually ignored it.

'But this time I just got this fellow and said, "Listen, I want to talk to you. You have said it many times, but I want to tell you that I am more Australian than you are."

'He didn't know what I was talking about.

'And I said, "You were born here, you have had no choice about your nationality. But when I came here I had the choice to go to here, or Canada, or elsewhere. So I am more Australian than you, so just stop telling me to go back to my own country."

'He never said it again.

'If we live in Australia, why, why can't we say we are Australian? I am Australian of Lebanese background, there is nothing wrong with that. I grew up in Lebanon and if I ignored my cultural origin when I came here, I could just as easily ignore Australia as well.

'I came without my family, without a knowledge of English, with a great fear of the unknown. Now my family is here, my apprehensions have been conquered, and I am at home. I have become an Australian in my attitudes and my view of the world. But in so doing I have not abandoned my traditions, my faith, or my customs.'

This is why Anthony Helou regards himself as a part of the Australian mainstream.

'Nowadays, there are many parts of the Middle Eastern way of life that are increasingly part of mainstream life in Australia.'

And, still talking about the mainstream of Moreland, there are just 572 Indigenous people among 132,000, or .044 per cent of the total population. Many have no direct connection to the original inhabitants, the Wurundjeri people. Yet they are still at the heart of Anthony Helou's conception of the mainstream.

Moreland City Council has gone out of its way to make Indigenous issues a focus of concern and action:

> Council recognises: that Indigenous Australians were the first people of the land; ... that social and cultural dispossession has caused the current disadvantages experienced by Aboriginal and Torres Strait Islander Australians; the centrality of Indigenous issues to Australian identity; that Indigenous people have lost their land, their children, their health and their lives and regrets these losses.

Moreland is not front line territory in the battle over Native Title. Nor is Aboriginal poverty the in-your-face thing that it is in many other parts of the country. Mainstream Moreland does not really have to do anything about Indigenous issues — that's if you think of the mainstream as a statistical thing. But it does have to do something if you can think of the mainstream in terms other than by weighing statistical majorities against statistical minorities. So,

> Council supports: the right of Indigenous people to live according to their own values and customs; ... campaigns for rights, especially to land and native title to land.
>
> Council commits itself to: building a trusting, collaborative and supportive relationship with Indigenous groups; respecting identified Aboriginal sacred sites and special places; ... encouraging equity and access for all members of Indigenous communities to culturally sensitive services.[2]

'Yesterday is history, today is reality,' says Anthony Helou. 'Let's concentrate on the reality. Let's bring Aboriginals into our community and make them part of the mainstream.'

It's all part of the process of coming to grips with what the Australian mainstream really is, and really has to be.

We mention Prime Minister Howard's idea of the mainstream, which means the old 'Aussie battlers' who have been left behind by the minority interest groups that seem to be demanding all kinds of special favours.

'The Prime Minister and us here in Moreland, we are talking about two different things. When I said the mainstream, I meant the multicultural mainstream, not merely the Anglo-Saxon mainstream or the white mainstream. I am referring to a mainstream where the whole community is involved.'

This is all part of a larger discussion in which the very meanings of 'Australian' and 'mainstream,' and even the nature of our democracy, have changed.

'Over these thirty years, Australians too have largely overcome their fears of the unknown. We have embraced difference.'

— • —

The eighth pillar of Australian nationhood was a unitary democratic nation. The Federation settlement created a modern, participatory democracy. The franchise was extended to include women. The only place where women had been able to vote in the Constitutional referendum itself was in South Australia, but all Australian women were granted the vote in Federal elections by the Franchise Act of 1902. The last state to introduce the vote for women, Victoria, did so in 1908.

On top of this, from the 1890s members of the Colonial Parliaments, then the Federal Parliament, began to be paid. This meant that political representation became a practical possibility for anybody, and not just a duty — or a sinecure — for the rich. Participation then became a responsibility with the introduction of the 'Australian ballot,' or compulsory voting, in 1924.

The limits of liberal democracy, however, remained steadfastly race limits. The only Aboriginal people who could vote under the 1902 Franchise Act were those few who happened to be already enrolled for State elections. Coloured residents could not vote either, with the exception of New Zealand Maoris.

Over the course of the twentieth century, the race barriers fell. Aboriginal people acquired the right to vote in all State and Federal elections in the 1960s. Compulsory voting for those on the electoral roll did not occur until 1988, and even today not all Aboriginal people vote because they are not required to enrol, and many do not.

Towards the end of the twentieth century, however, we began to reach another watershed in the development of liberal democracy. This was the watershed of civic pluralism.

The foundational philosophers of modern democracy considered all citizens to be identical, interchangeable individuals. Rights and responsibilities were universal, which actually meant the same, precisely the same. But treating people the same, people whose histories and experiences are different, never creates equal opportunities, let alone fair outcomes. In fact, treating people the same means that some people get a chance because what's on offer works naturally in their favour, whilst for others what's on offer never works. It's an offer in name only, a way of leaving people out in reality, even though formally, on paper, they've been counted in. Opportunity in this case is a dishonest formality.

Civic pluralism is an extension of our participatory democracy. It transforms the very nature of democracy, and is evidence of a shift in the fundamentals of the Federation accord. By the end of the twentieth century, liberal democracy has come to mean something entirely different to what it had in 1901.

Consider Indigenous self-determination, for instance. This is an idea about sovereignty, both Indigenous and national. The idea is that within 'one indissoluble Federal Commonwealth' as described by the Constitution of the Commonwealth of Australia, it is possible to have parallel Federal structures representing Indigenous interests. This is because Indigenous interests are not the same. They are based on a distinctive history, unique forms of land tenure, and specific cultural traditions of self-governance.

Established in 1990, the Aboriginal and Torres Strait Islander Commission consists of elected regional councils and a national Commission. It is responsible for providing programs and services in Indigenous communities. Adding this arm of government does not reduce the cohesion of our democracy. Rather, it extends and enhances democracy by providing a forum for inclusion, a forum for belonging, a forum through which

Indigenous people govern their own lives. Having a whole group left out is no longer in the national interest. Being unable to look after yourself is no longer in the national interest.

Take the concept of multiculturalism, too. The 1989 *National Agenda for a Multicultural Australia* spelt out the principles of cultural pluralism. You can choose to live your life, maintaining traditions, living according to lifestyles that you have inherited or chosen, and enjoy the full support of communities of common affiliation. In turn, these communities are a locus of welfare responsibility, of cultural self-creation, of human concern. Here, too, the concept of democracy has been extended to mean cultural democracy.

Cultural pluralism appears all too often as fluff and tokenism, colour and movement, spaghetti and polka. In fact, it is a fundamentally new solution to the main cleavage in communities at the turn of the twenty-first century: the cleavage of identity and belonging.

Multiculturalism is a new kind of accommodation, a new kind of social contract. In a world where differences of ethnic origin, interest and affiliation and sexual orientation become ever more pointed, ever more in-your-face, we need a new agreement on how we live together. Multiculturalism is no less than a new kind of democracy.

Yet the reaction of the xenophobes is fearsome. In its death throes, the old world of racism and exclusion throws up ideologues who think we cannot work together as a nation unless and until everybody is more or less the same. Forces nostalgic for the democracy of Australia's past operate under slogans like 'One Australia,' 'Australia First' or 'One Nation.' In other parts of the world, the serious proponents of this same view put the theory into practice through programs such as 'ethnic cleansing.'

So, in this watershed the struggle continues. We are on the verge of a new democracy, and Australian ideas and institutions are among the best and the most effective in the world. Yet, everywhere you look, the footsoldiers of sameness have become the enemies of democracy, the creators of division, the wellspring of conflict and violence.

The outcomes for Australia, and the world, are unclear.

— • —

'Australia is like an orchestra,' says Anthony Helou. 'And our city is like an orchestra, with different players, different instruments. Each one is played differently, but together they produce a beautiful music. This is what makes our city so beautiful.'

Moreland is not just a beautiful place. It is a place where old ideas of democracy have been turned on their head.

As the Federal Government and many of the State Governments seem to have run very low on moral legitimacy, just as they seem to have lost the will to reinvigorate democracy and lost the capacity to listen and to lead, remarkable things are happening at the local government level in Australia. Perhaps that's because local government is so close to the people, and because there's a kind of truth to be found in the everyday experiences of the people.

The Council's Plan for 1998–2001 sets out to do no less than redefine 'Democracy and Accountability.' That's the title of the document. The City Council is 'your first level of government,' it says. Council 'represents its community in a host of State and Federal Government issues.' Its work is based on 'a vision of a democratic local government working in partnership with its diverse community.'

> The local government of Moreland is about working collaboratively with people to improve community life ... Leadership is required as a result of powerful local, state, federal and global issues that impact on the everyday lives of the Moreland community ... There is a clearly emerging challenge for local government, as the first level of the Australian democratic system, to provide stronger leadership on behalf of its citizens ... We believe in democracy and accountability and in providing a responsive, consultative local government in which our resources and programs will be fairly distributed across the full community.

This is how the Council is 'building a sense of belonging,' putting into practice the principles of 'fairness and distributive justice,' creating 'mutual respect for the diverse people and communities of Moreland' and 'nurturing a democratic culture' by 'giving residents confidence that their views and aspirations will be respected.'

And this is how Anthony Helou put it in his speech when he took up the position of Mayor:

'We are giving life to our principles of inclusion and acceptance, we are saying that all Australians can live the Australian dream and achieve great things in the Australian community.'

Yet, all is not well; there is no denying that. And Anthony Helou recognises it. 'Some parts of this country built and enhanced by waves of immigration are now rejecting that history,' he says. This is why Moreland City Council decided to act, to lead.

'Soon after the Hanson phenomenon had begun, we organised a series of public seminars. Over four hundred people came along to one of them. They attracted a lot of media attention and community interest.

'And because we are active in the community, because we address these issues of daily importance, Robert Maclellan, the Local Government Minister, started to call us the People's Republic of Moreland. So we appropriated the idea and put it on T-shirts. "PROUD TO BE A CITIZEN. THE PEOPLE'S REPUBLIC OF MORELAND." But we are not going to break away from the State of Victoria or Australia.'

In the era of ethnic self-assertion and national self-determination, this is a many-layered joke indeed. It is as if to say that differences do not mean any lack of loyalty to state or nation and that loyalty itself can have as many layers as the joke.

'So what's the make-up of the Council?' we ask.

'We have ten Australians,' says Anthony Helou. It's a perfectly complicated answer for the new era of civic pluralism.

'And their backgrounds . . . ?' We press him further.

'Yes, we have two of Greek background, one of Lebanese, one of Maltese, six of, you know . . .'

He hesitates for a second, and the Mayor's assistant chips in.

'I hate being called an Anglo-Australian, I am Celtic, with a name like Joseph O'Reilly.'

Scratch the surface and even the categories that describe differences, like 'Anglo-Australian,' force all-too-neat sameness upon us.

We remember him and he remembers us, from when he got us to write something for a gay paper, the *Melbourne Star Observer* — — it must have been a former job of his.

'You know, the biggest contingent at the Pride March the other day was Gays and Lesbians for Reconciliation,' he added. Scratch the surface and there are still more differences. And one kind of difference that wants to show its solidarity with other kinds. That's exactly how civic pluralism makes for social cohesion. Not by forcing sameness, but by recognising and respecting differences.

'Places like Moreland are wellsprings of hope. They demonstrate what is possible.'

— • —

So, the eight pillars of Federation no longer work for us. They no longer describe the principles of our association as a national community.

Something new is happening in this latest Australian watershed. And in the absence of national leadership, this something new is arising from the people. At the first level of government, the people are beginning to be represented by a new wave of leaders, people like Anthony Helou.

John Howard ('One Australia' — 1987) and Pauline Hanson ('One Nation' — 1997) belong to a once entirely respectable Western democratic tradition in which national identity is defined by sameness, and social cohesion is created through the various technologies of cultural conformity: exclusion, separatism, assimilation, and integration. The technology itself is not so much the point. It's the purpose that is fundamental. The end results of this seemingly respectable modern idea have often been hideous in the extreme: from apartheid, to forced assimilation, to ethnic cleansing, to death camps.

Instead, Anthony Helou and Moreland City Council are proposing a social settlement based on the idea of difference. This is a perfectly commonsensical idea, a conservative idea even. It is nothing more than a description of what happens in Moreland. It's also a dramatically new and innovative idea.

PART 2

LAND AND PEOPLE

CHAPTER 8

People for a Continent

Australian history, Australian identity and Australian futures are built on three fraught relationships between land and people.

One of these is between the environment of a continent that is mostly desert and the ninety-eight per cent of the people who have arrived to live here since 1788. About one million Indigenous people lived in Australia in 1788, and that population had, in all probability, been stable for millennia. Nineteen million live here at the turn of the twenty-first century, and the number is growing, although less rapidly in the nineties than in previous decades. For the past two centuries the constant question has been 'How many?' On one measure, Australia is the most sparsely populated continent on earth. Its population density is 2.5 people per square kilometre, compared to Asia's 73, Europe's 68, Africa's 21, North America's 19 and South America's 16.[1] On this purely numerical measure, Australia has been, and could continue to be, a place of enormous promise. Just as they have in the past, people might continue to make new lives for themselves on this land. On another measure, however, Australia is a vast, dry, fragile land. On this measure, some people argue that nineteen million people is too many, and that population growth should be slowed to a stop.

Another of the three difficult relationships between Australian land and Australian people is the now undoubtable fact that the two per cent of the population who have lived here since time immemorial are the original owners of the whole place. For a while, the conventional legal and historical wisdoms of the ninety-eight per cent were based on the idea that Australia was theirs for the taking, that it was, for all intents and purposes, an empty land to which they had come. These presumptions were always ideologically loaded — loaded by the war of conquest just as much as they were loaded by the palpable continuing presence of an ancient civilization. At the turn of the twenty-first century, the old presumptions are now so obsolete that they cannot be ignored or simply repudiated in words; they require no less than a complete revision of our social contract. It is no longer possible to imagine that this was an empty land. The recognition of that fact brings with it profound legal and moral consequences. It involves recognising that there are two fundamentally different relationships of people to this land, and that these overlap in ways which require new kinds of negotiation, new kinds of legal accommodation, and new kinds of imagination about the very meaning of the relationship of people with land.

The third of the difficult relationships between land and people is shaped by the location of the land itself and by the people who live nearby. Until about the middle of the twentieth century, Australians tried to create a place that was unlike its region. They tried to create a White Australia that was, to use the words of prominent early New South Wales colonist, William Charles Wentworth, 'a new Britannia in another world.' They tried to create a nation which was part independent and part vassal-state of the British Crown. They tried to make a country that was unlike its location in the world.

In practical terms, if not yet in the national imagination, this project was roundly defeated in the second half of the twentieth century. The bulk of Australia's trading and diplomatic activity drifted away from Europe to Asia and, in the most recent phase of that practical defeat, one million non-white immigrants and their children have come to live in Australia from the countries of the immediate region during the course of the fourth quarter of the twentieth century. A country that recently imagined itself to be narrowly British or, more broadly, European has found itself to be a country in Asia, and perhaps even, in some definitions, an Asian country.

— • —

John Howard led the Liberal–National Party Coalition to a landslide electoral victory in 1996. The conservatives had been out of government for thirteen years. In the election campaign, there seemed to be no striking differences between the policies of Labor and those of the Coalition on many issues, including the question of immigration — the number of people coming to Australia. The media called it the 'me too' election. On Native

Title, John Howard said 'me too' to Prime Minister Paul Keating. On the question of never introducing a Goods and Services Tax, he said 'me too' to Keating. On multiculturalism, he said 'me too' to Keating. So too, with immigration; Howard agreed with Keating that the numbers coming to Australia should be left at their existing levels. These were the Coalition's policies.

Once it had won government, the Coalition cut migration in 1996. And again in 1997. And again in 1998.

'Migrant Cut a Win for Hansonites.' 'Business Leaders Blast Immigration Cutback.' 'Migration Cuts May Please Hanson Camp.'[2] These were some of the news headlines that greeted the policy reversal. An *Australian Financial Review* editorial made its disapproval clear and was just as clear about the Government's motives in making the cut:

> The Federal Government claims it has reduced Australia's migrant intake for 1997–8 because of high unemployment. This is a nonsense argument that is no excuse for restricting Australia's access to the undoubted benefits of immigration. It is difficult to escape the suspicion that deference to the strident anti-immigration and anti-Asian views of Ms Pauline Hanson is behind the Government's decision.[3]

Each year, when the cuts were made, there were the usual supporters and objectors. Their appearance became predictable. But the division of opinions did not run along any predictable party lines. Immigration is not the stuff of easily understandable Left–Right, Labor–Liberal politics.

Each year, New South Wales Labor Premier Bob Carr came out in support of Liberal Prime Minister Howard. Here's how he opened the annual conference of the anti-immigration group Australians for an Ecologically Sustainable Population in August 1997:

> Australia has enormous difficulties because of the vulnerability of our soils, our water, and our vegetation ... We've got to dispose once and for all of the notion that Australia is an underpopulated continent, an empty continent waiting to be filled up. We're not in that position. In Australia the pressure of population is having a very marked effect on our capacity to provide a secure environment capable of sustaining the incomes of our people in the years ahead.[4]

It was a theme he'd been pushing since he became Premier in 1995:

> Sydney has been sprawling too widely and it has reached its
> natural limits. The city is losing a lot of its appeal ... I think
> we have been too ambitious in setting immigration targets
> beyond the capacity of the great cities to absorb ... What I am
> saying is that Sydney has reached its limits ... the nation's
> biggest city is bursting at the seams.[5]

And as surely as Bob Carr continued to come out in support of
the Prime Minister on the issue of immigration, year in and year
out, Victorian Liberal Premier Jeff Kennett would come out
against both Liberal Prime Minister Howard and Labor's Mr Carr:

> My policy has always been that I believe we should have more
> migration. This is a very large country [and] we have a small
> population.

This is what he said specifically about Bob Carr:

> It's just the most appalling thing I have heard in a long, long
> time, and he owes an apology to the community ... It totally
> underestimates the value of a multicultural Australia. In
> Victoria, about 24 per cent of our community is of ethnic
> origin. They are an integral part of our history, an integral part
> of our development and are certainly an integral part of the
> life of the city. I cannot believe that this is not the case in New
> South Wales. If Bob Carr said that, then he ought to apologise
> to the very large ethnic community in New South Wales.[6]

The *Sydney Morning Herald* was just as direct. Mr Carr, the
newspaper's editorial said, seemed to want to draw 'a metaphorical
cordon sanitaire around Sydney so that migrants are made to feel
unwelcome. This is sloppy thinking and sloppy politics. It will also
give encouragement to the rednecks and racists in the community.'[7]
The prior editorial had also pointed to an enormous contradiction
in Carr's policies, commenting that it was 'hard to reconcile ... the
Carr Government's recent decision to abolish dual occupancy
subdivision ... without being in a position to substitute it with an
alternative urban consolidation strategy.'[8]

— • —

Although Malcolm Fraser left politics and the Prime Ministership of Australia in 1983, he's still very busy, a workaholic some would say. A charity person at the helm of Care Australia, he also writes a newspaper column and still does Liberal Party business. Hardly retired, in fact.

A huge man, whose sharp-edged features were captured by the caricaturists as one of those statues on Easter Island. A man of the Australian political establishment — his grandfather Simon Fraser took part in the Australasian Federal Convention of 1897–98, and topped the Victorian Senate poll to sit in the first Federal Parliament. He's also a man not purely or simply of the establishment — his grandfather on his mother's side was Jewish.

Like any other day, Malcolm Fraser was booked solid and he had only an hour to talk with us.

'Migration has no proponents of any conviction in the Federal Parliament today. But in the fifties and sixties migration was an article of faith supported by both parties. Everybody knew that Australia had no future unless we could expand this nation.

'As seven million people we were indefensible. As twenty million we are probably still indefensible.

'And we all knew that migration created jobs. One of the reasons for high levels of employment was the high level of migration. All the local businesses knew the market was going to expand so they could invest and plan for an expanding market.

'You know, in the fifties we were bringing in, one hundred and fifty, one hundred and eighty thousand people [a year], maybe even a bit more, and we did it without too much difficulty.

'Now all the certainties about where migration will take us have gone.

'Of course, some people used to say we have too many wogs, we have too many Italians, we have too many Greeks. And then, when the next wave of migration came, all that was forgotten. Then we had too many of the last lot of arrivals, wherever they came from. This is how it was in Australian slang, if you like, but it wasn't really a deep-seated feeling. By and large, post-war migration was accepted by Australians, with some blemishes, but mostly with good humour and with a recognition that it was in the interests of all of us.

'Now we've got people like Bob Carr saying we're overpopulated.

'But when you look at population movements around the world, you know, if I want my grandchildren to be secure I would want policies which take Australia's population up to something between forty and fifty million. Then I think we could be regarded as a nation that counts, a nation of some substance. Our views would have much more weight. We would obviously have much more economic strength, more of a regional presence.'

— • —

Bob Hawke, who followed Malcolm Fraser as Prime Minister in 1983 and stayed in the job until 1991, was a high migration man as well. In fact, he was the last Prime Minister of the century to be a high migration man.

'After the war, here was this great country with seven million bloody people, and it was just crazy. We had this enormous opportunity. We were just about the richest country in the world. We were rich in resources, we had the physical space, we had the economic opportunities ...

'One of the things that led me to join the Labor Party, although I would have joined the Party anyway, one of the things that excited me about the Party, was the immigration program. I joined as soon as I went to university, in 1947.

'We were a big country, we could sustain many more people,and I thought Australia would just become a much better, more exciting, vibrant country with a large migration program.

'So that was one of my reasons for joining.

'Actually, there were two elements, the sort of, the moral-ethical one, if you like, and economic considerations as well.

'The aggregate statistics since the immigration program began back then ... you have to get people to understand the magnitude of it. We've had six million people come to this country, about five and a half million as immigrants and over half a million as refugees. And the population at the end of the war was just seven million. So virtually the equivalent of the population of Australia at the end of the war has come in as migrants since then.'

Bob Hawke's office is in a tower on William Street in Sydney, halfway between the city and Kings Cross, with sweeping views over Woolloomooloo, down to the harbour and across the Domain to the city. Perched up there, you get a sense that even in his political retirement he's still watching over all that's going on.

'But the optimism's gone today,' we say. 'Over there, Bob Carr says the environment won't take it.' The NSW Parliament is on the other is side of the Domain. 'And over there, Tim Flannery at the

Australian Museum'... On College Street, opposite Hyde Park. Flannery is a senior research scientist at the Australian Museum, a best selling author on the Australian environment and an active opponent of immigration. '... He says the carrying capacity of the country is probably only about twelve million.'

Australia's population reached twelve million in 1968. It reached nineteen million in 1999.

'Environmentalists, I would shoot them. They are the most selfish lot of bastards. They really are. I just find them appalling. They're supposed to be concerned for people. It's just selfishness, for Christ's sake.

'No, I'm in favour of a bigger immigration program for Australia.'

— • —

Back then, from the forties to the eighties, including years of both the Fraser and Hawke Governments, it was called a bipartisan approach. Both sides of politics, conservatives and Labor, agreed that migration was good for the country.

In 1945, 90 per cent of the Australian population had been born here, and another 8 per cent were born in Britain or New Zealand. Half a century later, 41 per cent of the Australian population was born outside Australia, or had one parent born outside Australia. 23 per cent are from are a non-English-speaking country or have a parent who was born in a non-English-speaking country.[9]

No other country has had a bigger migration program in the past half-century. No other country has experienced such a revolutionary transformation. The only possible exception is the state of Israel, which is a peculiar exception because it was a state created by migration, a state that didn't even exist until half a century ago.

Then something momentous began to happen half a century into Australia's great post-war migration program. It began in about 1992, although hardly anybody noticed it at the time. After half a century of sustained migration, the flow was slowed for the first significant length of time.

Between 1987 and 1991, average annual population gain through migration was about 140,000 — a relatively modest figure by the standards of the fifties and sixties, but still not far off the historical norm. Between 1992 and 1998 the average figure dropped to 88,000. In the second year of the Howard Government, net immigration fell by 17.4 per cent compared to the first year.[10]

Not that the Howard Government had made the move in the first place. The most significant shift was after Paul Keating took over from Bob Hawke as Prime Minister in 1991. Cutting immigration was a predictably old-fashioned Labor response to recession and high unemployment — whether or not it was a correctly judged and appropriate response is another matter. The Howard Government's action in leaving immigration low, and then cutting it further, was far more unusual, particularly for a conservative government. This was the first government in the post-war years to cut immigration to such low levels during a period of economic growth and declining rates of unemployment.

Meanwhile, unprecedented numbers of Australians were, and still are, leaving the country. Permanent departures, or people emigrating from Australia, rose from 18,100 in 1986 to 28,700 in 1996 and then 32,000 in 1998. They are the youngest and the brightest. About half are in the 20–39 age group; most are professionals, managers, or skilled workers. And there's an even more interesting category buried away in the migration figures: long term departures — Australians who are leaving the country for a year or more. Taken away from long-term arrivals, we come up with a figure called 'net movement'. In 1988 there was an increase of 123,000 in the number of people living in Australia as a result of migration and long-term movements. In 1998 the figure was a mere 45,300.[11]

In 1945, Labor Immigration Minister Arthur Calwell set a target of a one per cent annual population increase through immigration. For almost five decades, conservative and Labor governments alike have continued this tradition. At the turn of another century Calwell's target seems prescient indeed. Now, each year, one per cent of the world's population moves country.

In our region, other developed countries have substantial immigration programs. Singapore's is now nearly the same as Australia's, with a tiny land mass and barely one-seventh of the population. So is Hong Kong's. In 1993, the population of Hong Kong grew by 41,000 as a result of natural increase (the number of births less the number of deaths); by 1998 natural increase had halved, to 20,900. Yet the population increase as a result of people moving across the border had doubled, from 69,000 more permanent arrivals than permanent departures in 1993, to 136,000 in 1998.[12]

New Zealand and Canada's immigration programs have been around the one per cent level in recent years. Canada's immigration figure was 1 for every 143 of the population in 1998. New Zealand's was 1 for every 124 in 1997–8 and, in recent years, was as high as 1 for every 68 in 1995–6. Yet the Australian figures only amounted to 1 immigrant for every 253 of the existing population in 1998.[13]

So, even by the standards of historically, socially and economically comparable First World countries, Australia is doing something radically unusual.

And that's the point. The move away from immigration is a radical change. It's a shift in what we have normally done. It's very different to what similar kinds of countries are doing now.

The consequences are many. One is an inevitable slowing of our population growth. Fertility rates have steadily dropped through the nineties and are predicted to drop further. The trend in Australia is to population stability and then decline some time in the next few decades. So if John Howard and Bob Carr continue to have their way, Tim Flannery might be right. Some time in the future we could end up with a population of just 12 million people.

The number of people born overseas has already begun to decline. We have begun to head back to where we were before the great post-war migration program began, to a population that is increasingly native-born.

One result is that our ethnic diversity is now diminishing. If current trends continue, the overseas-born who are leaving the country will soon outnumber new arrivals. Some immigrant groups are even in decline. Our Italian-born population fell by 2.5 per cent in 1997 alone, and the population of those born in Britain and Ireland dropped by 6 per cent in the same year.

It sounds like a grandiose overgeneralisation, but our history could be boiled down to three key facts. One is the fact that this continent has been inhabited by Aboriginal and Torres Strait Islander peoples from time immemorial. Another is the history of migration and settlement since 1788. The third is the fact of our geographical location in Asia. Each fact, of course, profoundly influences the meaning of the others.

Today's level of immigration means that we've started to turn against the spirit of the fact that we are an immigrant and settler society, to shift our sense of who we are and what we are doing here in this land. We are ninety-eight per cent a society of people who made good by moving to this continent from the different ends of the earth. To pull up the drawbridge, to try to build a fortress Australia, represents a denial of our history and our identity.

— • —

Just after John Howard had announced one of the series of cuts to the annual migration program in 1997, Opposition Leader Kim Beazley spoke on ABC radio, saying:

> Well, what the Government has done is run foul of its own unwillingness to take a strong stand on the issues Mrs Hanson has raised ... And, as a result, they've left their position on immigration open to misrepresentation overseas, and open to the nonsense she was coming out with today.

'So, you disagree with the move?' the interviewer asked Beazley.

> Well, the numbers are around the points that we had there. We disagree with the increased emphasis on skills migration as opposed to family reunion. But these are all within the framework of a low migration intake which we put in place before we left office, so we can scarcely complain about it ... By and large immigration levels have been low, including under us, for the last five or six years.[14]

Here is the ensuing exchange between Howard and Beazley in Parliament:

> Howard: 'Isn't it the fact that the Opposition has not opposed the cut?'
> Beazley: 'Yes.'
> Howard: 'Yes, he says. Thank you. You confirm you have not opposed the cut. You support the cut. You are up here like a humbug. Thank you very much. No further answer required.'[15]

This reflects a new bipartisanship in a country very different to the one in which Calwell and Menzies, and Fraser and Hawke, used to live.

— • —

In February 1999, the Department of Immigration and Multicultural Affairs ran a one-day conference on Population and Immigration at Sydney University. It was opened by Howard's Immigration Minister, Philip Ruddock, who told the assembled hundreds — politicians, community leaders, academics — that the conference was an opportunity to explore the facts behind issues that had become highly charged with political emotion in recent years. He was, of course, referring to the rise of Pauline Hanson and the 'race' debate.

First up on the program was Peter McDonald, Professor of Demography at the Australian National University. 'In the absence of science, populism prevails,' he said in support of Philip Ruddock's appeal to objectivity. His objectivity is built on the solid foundation of a research project funded by the Department of Immigration and Multicultural Affairs.

Using a Powerpoint presentation to drive home his argument, graphs shrank or bulged as the assistant scrolled through the years. So what were the assumptions behind this exercise in science, this demonstration of academic neutrality? To illustrate his point, he presented the audience with three population scenarios: the One Nation zero net immigration scenario, the Howard Government's 'moderate' scenario, and the 'Beazley scenario.' This last scenario was based on a comment that Beazley was supposed to have made of the variety that runs something like '. . . if Australia had the population of Java.' So, the Beazley option was an Australia with a population of hundreds of millions — and this, surely, knowing Labor's ambivalence about immigration.

So what's the perfect answer according to the professor — the scientifically true answer? It's the one in the middle. Like ordering the right drink: small, medium or large. A reasonable person, a person who thirsts in moderation, would order medium. This is how an academic's 'scientific' demography tells us that John Howard's immigration program is the 'moderate option.'

And how was it moderate? Well, the Howard Government option takes us in the direction of a static population, which, the

Professor tells us, is what all sensible people seem to agree about now. It was moderate, because he says everybody now knows that the higher immigration program of the 1980s was a mistake. And it was moderate in that 'high immigration is unlikely to be socially sustainable' — that's a scientific way of saying that if there are too many immigrants in the population, we're going to have more outbreaks of conflict like the rise of One Nation. We can have some immigrants, but you can see what happens when we have too many.

For all its studied moderation, however, the position McDonald puts is a radical departure from Australia's actual historical experience. And it's radically different from what comparable New World countries like New Zealand and Canada are doing.

Next was Barney Foran, Program Leader, Resource Futures Program at CSIRO Wildlife and Ecology. The Department was funding them, too, to develop an Australian Stocks and Flows Framework. Stocks are the good things we have, such as the people who are already here, as well as oil, water, and arable soil. Flows are the things that take away from what we have, such as immigration, waste, sewage, and petrol. This leads us to three options: Economic Growth, Conservative Development, Post-Materialism. Once again, the moderate answer is the obvious one. The concepts are from the new book of another of the CSIRO's anti-immigration scientists, Doug Cocks, *Future Makers — Future Takers*.

In the fifties and sixties the CSIRO had an honourable tradition of working out how to get things done. It was always inventing ingenious new ways of living in the Australian environment. Today, the CSIRO is one of the key homes of the powerful anti-immigration lobby. It tells us how and why we can't get things done: the lack of water, the poor soils, the resources that are running out. Such is the mood of their new Australia, fast on the way to 'post-materialism.'

Next was Bob Birrell, of the Centre for Population and Urban Research at Monash University. He's well known as an anti-immigration lobbyist. Pauline Hanson's former adviser, John Pasquarelli, told us how helpful Birrell was as a kind of academic fellow traveller. Birrell told the conference that the Howard Government's cuts to family migration were basically a good idea. He talked about the drop-off in spouse applications since the rules had been drastically tightened. This meant that all those former applicants 'could not have been serious about the relationship.'

Then he explained how 'parents cost the Australian community a great deal of money.' He was counting the cost of immigrant parents, that is. No-one else in the community would ever have to consider parents as an option, as a cost to be calculated when deciding whether or not to have parents. You see, 'it's not a human right to have parents' — an astounding statement, because it clearly means we now live in a society in which one person's human rights can be very different to somebody else's. So, Birrell counted the costs of parents — which are actually quite low, given that immigrant parents are not entitled to the pension within ten years of becoming residents — but enumerated none of the benefits. No mention of the capital parents bring with them, nor the benefits of grandparents looking after young children, nor any number of other eminently quantifiable dollar values. Thus Birrell explained the reasons why the parent quota has been cut to five hundred per year. By mid–1999 the queue of parents eligible to migrate to Australia was twenty thousand long. That means a forty-year wait for new applicants, by which time they will almost certainly be dead.

When Birrell had finished, there was an eerie silence. Nobody clapped, even though there was a fair spread of the anti-immigration lobby in the audience.

The tone of the day captured the mood of the moment. Pessimistic, mean-spirited, whingeing. In the end, nobody feels like applauding. Not even the most ardent avatars of the culture of complaint.

— • —

When we saw him, Barry Jones wanted to set the record straight. He was an aggrieved national icon.

Jones is President of the Australian Labor Party, a former quiz champion with the reputation of being a walking encyclopedia. His latest book is *Barry Jones' Dictionary of World Biography*, and his photo is one of a dozen or so in the collage of faces on the dust jacket, along with Adolf Hitler, Jesus Christ, Marilyn Monroe, Winston Churchill, Mao Zedong and Mother Teresa.

Sydney Morning Herald journalist Paul Sheehan had recently published a book, *Among the Barbarians: The Dividing of Australia*, about how immigration is ruining the Australian environment, about the billions of dollars of taxpayers' money that is supposed to be spent every year on 'the multicultural industry', and how the Labor Party has been hijacked by ethnic lobby groups and 'ethnic branch-stacking.'

This is what Sheehan said Barry Jones had said when he addressed the annual conference of Australians for an Ecologically Sustainable Population in August 1997, the same one at which Bob Carr had spoken:

> The handling of it by the previous government was, I'd have to say, less than distinguished. Partly because, I think, immigration was seen as very important, a tremendously important element in building up a long-term political constituency ... There was a sense that you might get the Greek vote locked up, or, from other party-political points of view, you might get the Chinese vote locked up.[16]

'Barry Jones is an honourable man,' Sheehan said when he quoted Jones in the first edition of his book. 'He let the truth escape.'

So Jones responded, in a speech in Parliament. It was not what he'd said, he stated:

> The words attributed to me are a very rough paraphrase of what I said. As quoted they completely misrepresent my position.
>
> Sheehan used my remarks as the peg on which to attack multiculturalism and the ALP.[17]

In the second edition of *Among the Barbarians* Sheehan produced a record of what he says Barry Jones had actually said, both a transcript off tape (the text above) as well as a written text of the speech with Jones's handwritten amendments, which was virtually the same.

'Memory Loss Left Barry Wishing He Were Speechless' was the headline for Sheehan's reporting of the whole affair in the *Sydney Morning Herald*.[18]

This is why Jones was so keen to set the record straight with us. He pulls a folder full of papers out of his bag to back him up.

'So, what did you really say at that conference?' we ask.

'I was a mug to have gone to that meeting. Actually the person who was meant to have spoken dropped out, and then they asked me, did I want to talk about my report?'

In 1994 Jones had chaired the House of Representatives Long Term Strategies Committee inquiry into Australia's population-carrying capacity. The Committee's report came out under the title *One Nation — Two Ecologies*. As a country, we've been working on the various possible meanings of the 'One Nation' concept in recent years. The 'two ecologies' theme is somewhat more obscure. The committee meant that there were two Australias: arid Australia and arable Australia. Arable Australia is about the size of France and Britain combined. The rest of Australia is arid.

'...I said yes, and so I arranged to go up to Sydney. When I got there and I had this prepared speech ...'

He hands us a copy of the speech together with a copy of the indignant reply to Sheehan that he sent to the *Sydney Morning Herald* and which they never published. The sentences, even phrases, Sheehan alleges Jones to have used are not there in the text of the speech he gives us.

'...but where Sheehan was partly correct and I was wrong is that I had ground my way through writing my speech laboriously, and the speech actually represents a considered view. I thought he is quoting a whole lot of things I didn't say because it's not in my written speech.

'What had happened was that it was a half-hour speech and then they said, "We've got a really tight program. We're so glad you have come all the way from Melbourne, but we really only want about ten minutes or something." So they said, "Maybe you can talk around it." So I just sort of babbled on in a kind of free association ...'

Barry had realised what was going on at the conference by the time it came to questions.

'This guy got up and said, "Look, we are up to here with people relying on evidence, too many people calling for evidence, and it's about time we got back to some old-fashioned gut feeling." The reaction of the crowd was "Yeah, yeah that's right."

'I realised then that there was a distinctly Hansonite tone to the conference. During the speech I had tossed in — and I know I shouldn't have done it — a cheap jibe at her expense, and it just fell very flat. And I thought "There's something not quite right here."

'But what I found particularly disconcerting was the following Monday, I was in the Parliament and I saw Nick Minchin.'

Nick Minchin was Special Minister of State and later Minister for Industry, Science and Resources in the Howard Government. He's a friend of the Prime Minister, and also one of the closest of Howard's political fellow travellers. He's been given all the most ideologically sensitive things to do — like Native Title when he and Howard don't like the idea, and the job of organising the republic convention and referendum when he and Howard are both staunch monarchists.

'And Nick Minchin — he's not one of my favourite people — came up and he said: "It was a good speech that you gave on the weekend, I was interested in your speech."

'I think I had spoken somewhere else that weekend and I wasn't quite sure what he meant.

'So I said, "Which speech?"

'And he said, "The speech for Australians for an Ecologically Sustainable Population."

'Because it had been on the TV, I said, "Oh, you caught it on television."

'He said, "No, I was there. I've been a member for years." He may've said he was a foundation member, I'm not sure now.

'I said, "Normally I am very good at picking up people, and establishing eye contact, and I missed you."

'"Oh, I was sitting right up the back," he said. Next to Paul Sheehan.

'And I said: "Do your views coincide with the views of the All Highest?"'

Meaning Prime Minister Howard.

'"Pretty well," he said.'

'What about this book by Mark O'Connor?' we ask Barry Jones. 'It mentions you, too.'

This Tired Brown Land, it's called, with an introduction by Tim Flannery — the same names keep on coming up. In a small country like Australia, a handful of people in the intellectual, political and media establishment can create very powerful networks that profoundly influence government policy, that change the feel of the country and even influence the course of its history.

A bright red slash across the front cover of the O'Connor book says it's about 'how Australia's booming population is destroying

our environment and why discussion of this has been stifled.'
Between Paul Sheehan at the *Herald*, the conferences held by
Australians for an Ecologically Sustainable Population, and the
political pronouncements of Howard, Minchin and Carr on
immigration, it's hard to see how debate has been stifled.

In the book O'Connor quotes from a speech Jones gave at
RMIT University on 27 March 1996:

> I have maintained a judicious silence about some policies
> pursued by the outgoing government with which I disagreed.
> However, I will break my resolve a little to say that I was
> profoundly disappointed by the government response to the
> Report of the House of Representatives Long Term Strategies
> Committee on Australia's Population Carrying Capacity ...
> The draft government response was essentially 'No worries, we
> have plenty of room.' The specific environmental issues we
> raised were completely ignored.[19]

Barry complains that this is another gross distortion. He told us
he was going to write a letter to O'Connor, too, objecting to the
way his words had been used.

A couple of weeks after we had spoken, Barry sent us a copy of
the letter he'd written to O'Connor about misleading promotion,
and how the back cover claims the book is about the ways in
which debates about immigration have been stifled by political
correctness, but how he could find only one passing reference
inside to political correctness.

Barry Jones also tells us how angry he was with Nick Bolkus,
who was Immigration Minister at the time the *One Nation — Two
Ecologies* report was tabled.

'You're not from Kastellorizo are you?' Jones asks Mary.

Nick Bolkus's family came from Kastellorizo, a tiny Greek
island close to the Turkish coast. Virtually the whole island came
to Australia, among the first waves of Greek migrants. They're well
established now and very influential among the Greek
community in Australia.

'What annoyed me particularly is that having said to the PM
that we think this issue is too important to be left to the
Department of Immigration, Keating, to my rage ... ', he thumps
the table, '... gave it the flick pass to Bolkus and his Department to
prepare the Government's response. Well, it was obvious what the

Government response would be as soon that happened. Of course, they were going to say, "Look, there's nothing wrong with the way we are doing it, let's keep on doing that forever."

'I saw the draft response towards the end of 1995, some months before the election. It was completely dismissive. I was furious.

'I said, "This is completely unacceptable. If you release this report I will be obliged to attack it." So a compromise was reached where there was no government response at all.

'What had annoyed me particularly was that, in some ways, we thought the central recommendation was to say, "The population issue is too big to be simply left to a client department." And that's exactly what they wanted to do. They wanted to leave population policy with the Immigration Department.

'This is how you get the Hansonite view that says if you get a Department that is dealing with wog clients all the time, then the wogs will determine the way in which it operates.'

It's a fine line when you oppose immigration on environmental grounds, and accuse interest groups of hijacking the discussion. Jones has been getting into difficulties treading that line for a few years now. And it's hard to see how what he calls the 'Hansonite view' of the Immigration Department's population agenda differs in effect from Jones's own view that the Department cannot be trusted to handle population policy.

Later, when we were talking with Bob Hawke, we mention Barry Jones and his views on immigration.

He winces.

'Barry has the virtue that he can tell you the name of the fourteenth child of the second Duke of Hapsburg, what date they were born on and what they died of. And that may indeed be a virtue ...'

As it happens, Barry Jones's views won the ideological war within the Labor Party, at least in the short term. Had Labor won the 1998 election, Labor was going to abolish the Immigration Department and create a Department of Employment of Population — 'Population' meaning the kinds of things Jones and Carr, and Sheehan and O'Connor and all the rest of the anti-immigration lobby are talking about. This was one of several policy mistakes that helped Labor lose an election it might otherwise have won. John Howard had certainly blown it on race and immigration, but the Labor Party did not offer an unambiguous alternative.

After the 1998 election, Population was left with anti-immigration shadow Employment Minister Martin Ferguson, quite distinct from Con Sciacca's shadow portfolio of Immigration and Multicultural Affairs, presumably because someone dealing with Immigration could not be trusted to think sensibly about Population, and even though immigration is the only real tool you have to work with in a population policy.

Then, in October 1999, Ferguson was moved to the crucial Regional Development portfolio, but kept Population. Labor had just beaten Jeff Kennett in the Victorian State election nobody had thought it could win, and the main swing was in the bush. The Federal Liberals' Senate Leader, Senator Richard Alston, called the swing to Labor 'our own One Nation experience.'[20] He meant that the 'battlers' of regional Australia who may have swung to One Nation before had now swung to Labor. They were reacting against the pace of change and cocky big-city cosmopolitans like Kennett. With his particular spin on 'population' and support for an at least partial return to protectionism, Ferguson was Federal Labor's new man for the bush.

CHAPTER 9

The Nature of Australia

Con Sciacca came sailing into the office, a big, boisterous man with a meek adviser in tow. He had been warned that we had a reputation for being frank and tough on these issues. The minder was anxious. Con impressed upon us that he could be frank and tough, too. He could serve back whatever he was served.

As it turned out, we all did fine. The adviser only added the odd nod.

'I came here at the age of four. I've always taken an interest in immigration. I was appointed Parliamentary Secretary to the Minister for Social Security — Graham Richardson it was at the time — with responsibility specifically for migrant services in the portfolio. I held that position till 1994, when I was appointed Minister for Veterans' Affairs, probably the opposite if you like to Immigration.'

'So who are you?' we ask. 'What do you bring to public life?'

'I'm not a token ethnic, I'm Sicilian-born. I have been brought up with all the prejudices of the 1950s and 1960s. I have been brought up with the jokes about the twenty reverse gears in Italian tanks and the one forward.

'Yet I ended up becoming the minister who took the diggers back to El Alamein in Egypt in 1995, where my forebears had fought the Australians. My name appears as the person who unveiled a plaque commemorating the 9th Division at El Alamein where the Italians fought the Australians. The diggers who fought the Italians insisted that their minister, because he was Italian, go and see the Italian war graves of the people who had been killing them.

'That shows you what Australia is all about.

'Then I got defeated in 1996, in the big anti-Keating swing in Queensland, and when I came back in 1998 I got elected to the front bench, promoted to the position of Shadow Minister for

Immigration and Shadow Minister Assisting the Leader of the Opposition for Multicultural Affairs.'

'So what about this population issue?' we asked.

'Well, I happen to be a personal friend of one Mr Bruce Ruxton.'

Bruce Ruxton is President of the Victorian branch of the Returned Services' League. The media love him for the outrageous comments he always seems to be making about Aboriginal rights, multiculturalism, and gays in the military. He has a knack for indelicacy on any kind of sensitive topic you might like to bring up.

'In my capacity as Minister for Veterans' Affairs we became quite close. Yesterday he took me to lunch at the Melbourne Club. He reckons I am the first socialist he has ever taken to lunch. At the Melbourne Club, too.

'Nevertheless I discuss these issues with him and I can assure you he is nowhere near as right-wing and bigoted as people may think.

'The point I am making is this, I believe we need to talk to those people, if nothing else, to try to get the message across to them, and to try to turn them around.

'That is just not a platitude I am telling you. I have hit the ground running. Today is my eighth or ninth meeting in two days.

'And, whilst I, as the Shadow Immigration Minister can't sort of talk in terms of population ...'

That's Martin Ferguson's job, even though immigration is about population.

'... I will make the comment that I don't believe that it has been properly ... if you like ... that it hasn't been proven that this country ... I mean that those who argue the environmental side of what our population policy should be ... and how many people we should have in this country ... I don't think they have proven their case.'

Con's choosing his words carefully. It's not his role to be talking about population.

'The very fact that we don't lack for anything now with a population of nineteen million ... who wouldn't agree that we have got enough water or enough natural resources in this country to sustain our population? To me, it's a nonsense.'

Yet party discipline means following the party line.

A month after our interview he created a furore when he agreed with the Australian Chamber of Commerce and Industry that immigration should be increased by 45,000 places per year.

_ • _

Until recently, it was the commonly held view that Australia was a place where many people could live. It's the sixth largest country in the world, slightly smaller than the United States and more than twice the size of India.

On the centenary of the British settlement in Sydney in January 1888, the London *Spectator* said:

> There is every reasonable probability that in 1988 Australia will be a Federal Republic, peopled by 50 millions of English speaking men. [The republic will] approximate more closely to the Italian than the American type — that is, it will be democratic, but not hard ... The Australians, we conceive, with more genial and altogether warmer climate, without puritan traditions, with wealth among them from the first, and with the habit of communion with Europe, will be a softer, though not a weaker people, fonder of luxury, and better fitted to enjoy art.[1]

After the First World War, the dreamers in the Empire Settlement Scheme thought Australia might be a place where one hundred million people could live. In the 1970s, the report of the massive National Population Inquiry suggested a figure of fifty to sixty million.[2]

Until recently, there was only one exception to the general thrust of these predictions, and that was Sydney University geographer Griffith Taylor. Working in the 1920s, he claimed that Australia could not support more than 65 million people, and possibly only 20 million. This last figure is the one contemporary anti-immigration people now repeatedly seize upon. He's the original environmentalist, they say, the first person to see that there was a limit to the population that this country could take and that the limit is probably a low one.

In retrospect, Taylor's 20 million figure is the only one that is a complete nonsense. In today's global market, Australia feeds and clothes — to take just two variables of human sustenance — perhaps one hundred and fifty or two hundred million people.[3] From the point of view of environmental impact, it barely matters whether they are on-shore or off-shore.

_ • _

Bob Katter is another Queenslander. He and Con Sciacca are both from the heartland of Pauline Hanson territory. But Bob's not someone who has ever been known to toe the party line.

He's the National Party's Member for Kennedy, a huge electorate which starts at dripping wet tropical Innisfail on the coast and extends through the dry savannahland that stretches all the way from Charters Towers to Mount Isa and the Gulf of Carpentaria.

Bob looks out of place in the clean white modernity of Parliament House, though there are a few telling signs in his office: elegantly framed historic black and white photographs of a boundary rider on a horse, a farewell parade for troops going off to the Great War in 1914, and a huge crocodile strung up beside its hunter somewhere in Northern Australia.

While he gets us tea, he runs an excited monologue about what he's been up to. He's trying to get a kosher abattoir running in North Queensland. Who was he to comment on how people killed their meat? They probably reckon what we do is pretty strange, too. Anyhow, maybe they're right, slitting the throat of the beast might be a better way to die than being hit in the head.

He washed up some cups. His was a tin mug, chipped blue enamel on the outside and an inside, once white, stained with the dark grey-brown of tea and time. A bushman's kitchen, in Parliament House, Canberra.

'Don't forget that stuff about the peanuts ... and the petrol stations,' he boomed out to his aide. The aide's a real bloke in jeans with a smoker's voice. Taking care of business, electoral business, community business.

'So, who are you? What drives you? What makes you the kind of Australian you are?' It's been the opening question for all the people we interviewed to write this book.

'My Great Grand-daddy came out in 1870, you know, on one line of my family, my father's side of the family, and he was a hawker. He had a covered wagon and he became very rich. He was probably the most important driving force in building the port of Townsville. He got the first two big cranes.

'And your great-grandfather, where was it that he came from?'

'Mary, I don't know how you want to handle it, but I really don't like answering that, because I mean, you know, the ALP have always called my family Afghan camel drivers.'

It's the sort of nonsense that happens around the time of elections particularly. Some media person asked Bob the same question a couple of years back, and his response was, 'I'm an Australian ... '— of course —'... and you know who I am' — of course, because you're asking the question.

'My kids ask me, "Where did our family come from?", and I say "All over, forget about it, you know, too complicated," which is pretty right. You know, I mean, about six or seven different racial backgrounds.'

When Bob's Great Grand-daddy was hawking, the majority of the population of North Queensland was Aboriginal, and most of the minority immigrant population was non-white.

'North Queensland is like that. Down south they don't sort of get that about North Queensland. You know, the election where I made the remarks about the slanty-eyed ideologues ... '

During the 1996 elections, Bob Katter made his now-famous remark about the ideological trendies. A political furore ensued.

'... that was a direct quote from *Dr Zhivago*. I always thought it was a beautiful quote, but you know it was interpreted as some sort of racial remark. A couple of my friends of Aboriginal descent, they said, "You know we're all part-Chinese." They know I like them, but they thought I might have been having a go at the Chinese.

'I said, "I'm not having a go at the bloody Chinese, what are you talking about?" I was talking about the book-burners, you know, the bloody Spanish Inquisition, the Salem witch hunt, the McCarthy era.'

'And if people want to celebrate where they come from, their ethnic origins ... ?' we ask.

'No, no, I don't hold that against them at all. You know in fact I'm trying to get a picture of one of my forebears in the garb of the country where they came from. This friend of mine, he's got a picture of his grandfather dressed up in the full Chinese gear. I know there's a photograph of one of my forebears kicking around in that sort of stuff. One of my cousins has got it and I was going to get a copy of it. They don't look racially different to the average Anglo-Australian, I suppose.

'Far from being ashamed about it, on the contrary I'm very, very proud of it. But, you know, and this is where I think Mary, you and I sometimes disagree, I want to become Australian,

I mean, I absolutely love being Australian. I can never understand why they talk about cultural cringe. I can't see any reason to cringe.'

There's no disagreement, actually. We should all be able to be as Australian as we like, and that doesn't mean we can't recognise where we have come from. Identity is not a neat quantity, so that you have to take something away from being one thing in order to be something else at the same time.

'They say, "Why haven't you ever been overseas?" and I say, "Well, gees, I haven't seen the top two gorges on St Francis Station yet." You know what I mean?'

It's unspeakably beautiful country he's talking about, vast plains of surprise.

Before he moved into Federal politics, Bob was a Minister in the Bjelke-Petersen Government in Queensland — Minister for Aboriginal Affairs for six years, the longest serving Aboriginal Affairs Minister ever, he says.

'Back in 1987, Robert Ray was Immigration Minister and the migration intake was about 120,000 a year. So we put in a submission saying that we wanted 350,000 a year.

'Robert Ray said, "Are you going to provide jobs for them?" And I said absolutely, we'll take the whole 350,000. I said, "I'm not here representing my view, I'm here representing the viewpoint of the Queensland Government."

'I never give a speech now without going into the population thing. I ask, if we maintain our present growth, you know, the birth rate, maintain it where it is now, what would the population of Australia be a hundred years from now?

'Out of about ten thousand people I've put that question to — and I always put it at public meetings — only about fifteen people got it qualitatively right, never mind about precisely quantitatively right.'

'What's the answer?' we ask.

'Six million.' He said he had the reference, it was a demographer, a professor at Melbourne University.

'Six million, that's all the people that will be left in this country.

'Now if you say that you can't sustain the population, I just go into a catatonic rage.

'The Murray–Darling system produces half Australia's agriculture, half. It has got only twenty million megalitres of water. The Gulf country — and it's not even the super-wet belt along the coast that I'm talking about, around Tully or Innisfail, I'm talking about west of the coastal range — has one hundred and thirty million megalitres. And we have the rolling plains of super- fertile black soil stretching from Blackall, which is about one hundred kilometres north of Brisbane, all the way up to the Gulf country, and they're about six hundred kilometres wide. We could feed China from that plain, there's enough water and land there.

'Well, maybe not China, but certainly Indonesia. And I want to make this point, there are one hundred million people going to bed in that country tonight, in Indonesia, not hungry, but starving. Starving. I mean how can we hold our heads upright among the nations of the world?

'I mean this is absolutely a national disgrace. How could scientists, so absolutely lacking in scholarship and brains and intelligence, come out with statements like this country can't take any more population?

'If we developed the water resources for the Gulf country, we could bring a million to populate it, you know.

'Ernie Bridge and I, we put this statement together and I'm really pleased with it.'

Bob starts reading the statement he and Ernie Bridge wrote. It's in the form of a pledge:

That our country's great rivers should,
on their journey to the sea,
pay a small tribute to those people living along their banks.
That this great land of ours provides for its people
the opportunity of properly developing their talents,
both their natural assets and the great richness of character
that God has given each and every one of them.

'Bridgie is very inspiring, you know. A great Australian, a bloke of Aboriginal descent. A good-looking fellow, styles himself as a country music singer. He served as a Minister in the Western Australian Government.

'He was a little timid fellow when I first went in there but I saw him grow over the years, and now he's just gone out and become an Independent.'

That Australia becomes a bigger and more fascinating world,
a world of wonder, hope and excitement.
That we again unleash the wonderful aspirations
and dreams that took our forebears tens of thousands of miles
away from their homes towards adventure
and a new and bigger dream.
That we affirm again that we are the descendants
of a brave-hearted, enterprising and intrepid people.
That we are the descendants of a people who
faced a misery of hardship and oppression
and who in spite of it all survived and prospered.
That we are the descendants of people who looked out through the
narrow grimy window panes of the old world and
saw a clear, shimmering, golden vision
of what might be.

'I heard him give one of his speeches, so I added to it myself. That's how we came to write this together,' Bob says.

'I put it in the back of this document.'

Bob had recently completed a submission to the Commonwealth's Federation Fund proposing the construction of a dam across the Burdekin River at Hells Gates.

He gives us a copy.

In it there's a map entitled 'The Other Australia.' The continent is shaded in two colours, reminiscent of the two Australias of the Jones *One Nation — Two Ecologies* report. It's just that Bob Katter's message about the two Australias is the opposite of Jones's message.

On the map, one Australia is 'The coastal strip: 18.2 per cent of Australia's land mass, 25.9 per cent of Australia's water, yet 96.7 per cent of Australia's population.' The 'other Australia,' the 'unpopulated Lucky Country' of the inland consists of '81.8 per cent of Australia's land mass, 74.1 per cent of Australia's water, but only 3.3 per cent of Australia's population.'

CHAPTER 10

Sustaining a Life

'Australia's population debate, such as it is, is being conducted under a growing shadow, that of the world population explosion.'

Barry Jones was speaking at the Australians for an Ecologically Sustainable Population conference.

He went on to explain the 'revived interest' in the work of Rev. Thomas Malthus.

'In his famous *Essay on the Principles of Population* (1798),' Jones explained, Malthus 'argued that population tends to increase at a geometric ratio (each generation can double up), while the means of subsistence only increases at an arithmetic ratio (incrementally), and that the only constraints to population growth were famine, war, disease, infanticide and what he called the "vicious practice" of contraception.

'With world population at 5.6 billion and serious problems of water supply, inadequate soil for farming, and loss of wood for fuel and building, Malthus's predictions are starting to look more relevant,' Jones told the conference. It was a message that fitted in very well with the organisation's concerns.

In fact, everything that Malthus said has been proven to be wrong about modern societies. Population has tended to stabilise, and the birth rate drop. And technological developments mean that greater and greater quantities of the means of human subsistence are produced by fewer and fewer people.

The evidence to support this case comes from the Report of the 1994 House of Representatives Long Term Strategies Committee, chaired by Barry Jones, *One Nation — Two Ecologies*. World fertility rates have declined dramatically in the past forty years, from about five children per woman to around 3.4. This would have produced an extraordinary drop in population growth had life expectancy not increased just as dramatically, from 45 to about 65 worldwide over the same period. The result has been that, over these four decades, the annual rate of world population growth increased from 1.7 per cent initially to 2.1 per cent by the late 1960s. But it has since dropped, to take us back to 1.7 per cent today. And the drop continues. World population is heading towards stability, and maybe even eventual decline. Meanwhile, world food supply is keeping pace with population growth. Lack of food is a product of poverty, not environmental barriers.[1]

The conclusion of the *One Nation — Two Ecologies* report goes straight back to Malthus:

'The predictions of Thomas Malthus (1766–1834) in his famous *Essay on the Principles of Population* (1798) concerning the relationship between population and food supplies have so far been unproven.'[2]

— • —

Bob Brown — one of Australia's best-known environmentalists. He led the famous campaign to save Tasmania's Franklin River from being dammed in 1983. Today he's a Senator in the Federal Parliament representing the Australian Greens.

'I had a very conservative upbringing in the bush, came to Sydney in 1954 and for seven out of nine times the Queen drove around the streets, I was there, with millions of other people. My Dad had put a little flag in my pocket and lifted me up over the fence so I could see.

'I got this sense that there was an elite which you could do nothing but admire. But I came to realise that, of course, these are human beings who go to the toilet and are fussy about their food and don't make their bed sometimes and who really have a weight on their own shoulders because of the absurd fix they're in.

'My mother was off a dairy farm and my dad was a country policeman in NSW. I had a fairly conventional fifties upbringing.

'I went to Presbyterian Sunday School. I got the best marks in primary school. When I got into my youth I realised that the dogma I'd been taught which gave a simple prescription for life didn't work. The humble people of the world seemed to go backwards whereas the brash and egotistical went forward. And the world wasn't a fair place.

'Going right back, there was one experience that really burned into my mind as a kid. I went with my dad, who was a policeman, to the tip. He was serving a warrant on an Aboriginal man who was living in an upturned water tank, a galvanised iron tank with a hessian sheet across the front of it. And he said to my father, "You can't arrest a man in his own house." There were kids running around on this tip. We had no Aboriginal kids at the school I went to because it was a "demonstration school," a school for achievers. That incident on the tip shocked me to my core. That was back then in the fifties, when we were told that our way was the right way; the secure way and the narrow way.

'The other formative experience was that I found myself as a young homosexual with no-one to speak to at all, unable to even talk to my own family about it. We were all supposed to be a part of God's creation, but listening to the fulminations, I didn't fit the very narrow, confined definition of what was right and good in human beings. It was a matter of evil and a matter of shame.

'And so I went through a decade or two of absolute inner turmoil, including consideration of suicide, when on the outside I had everything going for me. I was zooming through university. I was going to become a doctor with a brass plate up in Macquarie Street. A specialist, with the North Shore residence, a Jaguar car, the whole works. To be successful in the fifties you had to be Anglo-Saxon, preferably Protestant, have a tertiary degree and be well-connected.

'But when you're told that you are a second-class individual and that there is nothing you can do to change it, you've got the mark on you, and it's a very difficult psychological effort to rise above it. It's almost beyond human ability to do that.'

It's the same with the race issue and the multicultural issue, with the struggles people go through about identity, we suggested.

'Absolutely, and it wasn't until I had done the round of psychologists and psychiatrists, it wasn't until then that I realised that I was part of the magnificent spectrum of natural diversity. It was something to be celebrated, not cured. I became determined through that experience that I would listen to what other people had to say, and would relate to people who themselves were ill with the weight of feeling second-rate, for whatever the reason.'

Bob did become a doctor, floated down the Franklin River in 1976, then left medical practice to become Director of the Wilderness Society, was elected as a member of the Tasmanian Parliament, and later became a Senator representing Tasmania in the Federal Parliament.

'It's been nearly a quarter of a century now,' working for the environmental movement.

Bob Brown speaks for values in which humans and the environment are more important than profits and the transitory gratifications of materialism.

'I left doctoring to become involved in fighting to protect nature. And I guess I have an anthropocentric viewpoint here. Other species on this planet have rights, but I believe that we as human beings can't survive in a happy, rounded-out way if we destroy the very thing we've come from, our own cradle of creation, the wild world. We put pictures of flowers on our wall, not pictures of chainsaws and bulldozers, because they do our soul good. Even in the cities we have window boxes because they're a remnant of nature which brings us delight. Why destroy what's left of that to build more tranquilliser factories?

'So I became involved in fighting for that. I always had this concern for the stress and turbulence of human life and the enormous bounty that nature lends to us all the time.'

Yet the good cause of the environmentalists can run into difficulties with the good cause of multiculturalism and those sympathetic to a substantial immigration program. Few causes are simply, or always, good.

So, what about this population debate? we ask.

'Mmm. Although ... I don't think that premise that immigration is bad for the environment has prevailed in the environmental movement. It's an argument over in the corner which has not had much impact.'

We mention Australians for an Ecologically Sustainable Development which includes John Howard's ally Nick Minchin among its number, the new CSIRO/Australian Museum environmental establishment, the Australian Democrats who provide the same environmental arguments for zero net immigration as One Nation, and the Paul Sheehan and the Mark O'Connor books which are now the most read environmental texts in Australia. We suggest that they might have prevailed.

Bob turns to the substance of the argument.

'Well, there are too many people in the world if you want to protect all the rest of the species' diversity, which I think is a great thing for human enjoyment into the future. We began the century with 1.6 billion people. We are going to end it with 6.1 billion people. It will tail off at somewhere at about 10–12 billion in the middle of the next century and start falling, and so I am optimistic about that. We've got to try and do the best we can to protect the rest of the environment until we get to that stage and it starts to come down.

'But to regionalise that and say, well, in our little corner, we are going to shield ourselves and not be part of the world community, is just daft. I want to be part of the world. I feel like a world citizen. This idea of pulling up the drawbridge, if you could — and I don't believe you can — is one of the worst manifestations of greed. And greed is the central problem with the global community at the moment. The difference between the haves and the have-nots feeds discrimination.'

— • —

Nobody would disagree that world population growth should be slowed down so it reaches a point of ecologically sustainable stability. It's just that there are no moral or logical grounds for running population-in-one-nation arguments, particularly from the vantage point of a country with such a phenomenal resource endowment as Australia. Population is an issue of world proportions, and that's the only way to see it.

Environmentalists have various formulae to describe the impact of humans on the environment. Usually the formulae are only applied to one nation.

Paul Ehrlich's formulation is I = PAT, or Impact = Population x Affluence x Technology. Barry Jones's committee used the CSIRO's formula I = PLOT, or Impact = Population x Lifestyle x Organisation x Technology.[3] Population always seems to come first in the equation. In the minds of the anti-immigration environmentalists, it's also the easiest and quickest fix. It's the main focus of their attention. And it's a purely a one-nation question, because in world population terms, people moving from one country to another is a zero-sum equation.

So, when they talk about population in these terms, they only mean the people who live locally; as if everything that is produced locally is consumed locally, and as if there's a simple relationship between the environmental impact and the number of people that live in that environment. It's a neat trick and a dishonest one.

Australia feeds at least one hundred and fifty million people. Some estimates put the figure as high as 188 million. It provides the raw materials to clothe three hundred million people.[4]

It provides the resources that produce industrial products used by hundreds of millions of people around the world. The list could go on. Doubling the migration program, or even increasing it tenfold, would make next to no difference to the environmental impacts of population — hundreds of millions of the world's population — on the Australian environment.

If the anti-immigration environmentalists really wanted to reduce the 'P' impact on the Australian environment, there is a simple solution which they could advocate, but which they don't. Stop exporting food, and stop exporting everything else that draws any of its raw materials from the Australian environment. This solution would have an immediate and wonderful 'I' effect.

In fact, if we play with the formula a bit more, there are ways in which we could reduce the local 'P' factor almost to zero. Let's stick to forms of employment like financial services and multimedia and ecotourism, let's sell these on the world market, and let's import all our food and other material necessities. Then we could turn everything except the footprint of a few cities into a giant wilderness and still have a vibrant and successful economy. In fact, we could increase 'P' quite radically and still have almost zero environmental impact. Mind you, we would be exporting the 'P' problem somewhere else. And that's the point: in the era of global economic integration, local population is nearly irrelevant from an environmental point of view.

In all the talk about 'P', immigration is the primary focus. This begs the question of what difference thousands or even hundreds of thousands of people moving from one place to another make. The answer is not much on the scale of the overall impact of 'P' — people beyond as well as within the Australian borders — on the Australian environment. And on a global scale, the only environmental difference in the zero-sum game of global population movement is as a consequence of immigrants improving their standard of living. Improved standards of living use more resources. In environmental terms, migration allows a few more people to live like we do. The anti-immigration environmentalists resist even this tiny shift to correct the global resource imbalance and, in so doing, preserve their accidental privileges as environmental haves whilst maintaining the relative penury of the have-nots.

When it comes to the 'T' bit of the formula, or the question of technology, much of the environmental damage that has been done in Australia happened in the nineteenth century when the population was just a few million and when there were far fewer exports than there are today. The problem was a technological one: how we related to the environment, rather than the number of people who were relating to it. Conversely, we could do less damage with many more people if we developed different relationships to the environment and new technologies of sustainability. It's the way we use the environment that matters far more than the number of locals who happen to be using it.

Indeed, much of the ongoing environmental degradation is happening in rural areas where population is in decline. The anti-immigration environmentalists focus the blame on the last few thousand migrants to have arrived, migrants who mostly settle in cities.

The Australian environment has a problem with introduced mammals, Tim Flannery, the fauna man from the Australian Museum, tells us. Certainly he sees humans as a major part of Australia's introduced mammal problem, but what about those other mammals, the 26 million head of cattle and 137 million sheep? By comparison, a few extra introduced human-immigrant mammals are a drop in the ocean.

Hopefully, too, the technological problems are not insurmountable. If what we are doing is unsustainable, we will just have to create technologies of environmental sustainability. This is not just a moral 'have to.' It's a practical and a business 'how to' as well.

Around the world, agriculture is becoming less of an attractive business to be in. There is an oversupply of commodities in the world market and prices are dropping, but we've stayed in the game and that's partly because we're using the environment more and more effectively. In the last thirty years, the volume of Australian agricultural production and exports has doubled, but the land area farmed has increased by only sixteen per cent. A CSIRO report on sustainable agriculture tells us that 'a general decline in regional net farm income has been partly offset by more efficient use of inputs, particularly land.' In the rangelands of Australia, 'less degradation seems to be happening now than in the past and many areas appear to be improving.' Meanwhile, 'soil erosion, measured by a dust storm index, has decreased in the past ten years due to changed farming practices which reduce the area of bare soil.'[5]

The news is getting better, but when immigrants are your focus, you don't want to hear good news about our relationship to the environment.

So, what's the truth of the land of Australia? Let's go back to Barry Jones's two ecologies. One Australian ecology consists of arable land, or land defined as 'having both soils and rainfall suitable for growing rain-fed crops.' This adds up to 787,000 square kilometres, an area approximately equal to the size of France and the United Kingdom combined. If arable Australia had the same population density as France, our population would be 79.6 million; the same as the UK it would be 178.4 million; the same as Japan 247.5 million; or the same as Java 750 million.

Furthermore, even arid Australia is not wasteland. Sixty-one per cent of the whole country is classified as domesticated land, which includes low-density grazing. This compares with 19 per cent of Indonesia, 14 per cent of Japan and 8 per cent of Canada.[6]

And, what's the truth about the urban environment? NSW Premier Bob Carr says that Australia should cut back its immigration program because Sydney is 'bursting at the seams.' Sydney is a mess, and one of the solutions Carr is suggesting is to cut immigration.

You mightn't notice it when you are sitting in a Sydney traffic jam, or having to boil Sydney water because it might have the giardia virus in it, but Sydney's population is growing at a slower rate than the rest of Australia. In fact, the two biggest Australian cities, Sydney and Melbourne, are decreasing in their shares of the Australian population. Perth and Brisbane, on the other hand, are increasing their shares.

True, many migrants do settle in Sydney: 158,000 between 1986 and 1991, just before migration was cut to its current level. But in those same years, 142,000 people left Sydney, including many migrants. They were leaving to live on the North Coast of New South Wales, or in Perth, or in Queensland. These are the places where significant population growth is occurring.

In fact, population is declining in large areas of Sydney, particularly the ring of old suburbs around the city centre, because fewer people are living in each household.[7] The problem with Sydney is not population growth. It's a failure to plan infrastructure, and the people who don't like the traffic jams and the dirty water should focus on just that.

And what's the truth about this so terribly dry continent? Even without any of the dams that people like Bob Katter and Ernie Bridge might suggest should be built, Australia already has more stored water per head of population than any country in the world, with the sole exception of Canada.

So, whenever anybody feels they have to do their population–environment sums, they should start with the figures which show that Australia has just one per cent of the Asia-Pacific population but holds 34 per cent of the land mass. Certainly they should end by explaining to the 99 per cent why the one per cent living on this massive, resource rich land have reached the point where they don't want to take anybody else.

— • —

Australian Conservation Foundation President Don Henry greeted us with a strange sort of cheeriness for someone who'd just been talking so gloomily on the radio about the fate of the Great Barrier Reef, attacking the Government and pointing to the dire consequences of neglect. A mild-mannered man but a consummate activist, he'd taken up the job some months before, after eight years as an environmental lobbyist in Washington D.C.

'Coming back to Australia, what I found quite ... shocking is not the right word ... you know your stomach goes in a knot when you see this kind of thing going on in your own country ...'

He was beginning to talk about the increase in racism reflected in the rise of the One Nation Party.

'... where opinion leaders, particularly in Government, but broader than that, people whose voices are listened to and heard around Australia, where they weren't standing up very strongly and immediately and saying, "Intolerance is not the way to go, it is unacceptable; it is against the Australian way of the fair go, it ignores our history, it ignores what we need for our future."

'It just struck me, having been in the US ... Washington is a very multicultural place, and a very divided society, between those who are poor and African-American, and those who are from a professional, wealthy, Anglo community.

'And understanding some of the history my wife's family went through: her grandfather's family was all shot in front of him in Latvia under Hitler, which was the end result of some of the most horrendous intolerance our world has seen. Then growing up in Kazakstan, as political prisoners in Stalin's Gulag.

'When you go and read the history of fascism, it started very gradually. I have a view that you have to stand up straight away, really early and really firmly and say, "This is out of bounds."

'Being in America I read a lot of American history, like *Bury My Heart at Wounded Knee*, fine works that really look at the terrible crimes committed against Native Americans; in America's case documented, but committed in Australia and poorly documented. And we're still trying to hide. At least it is out in the open and debated in America.

'So when I came back I just had a profound sadness inside of me to see what was happening in our country.'

We press him on the issue of population and the environment, and how environmental arguments are used to support One Nation's zero immigration policy, as well as the Australian Democrats' policy, which is the same.

'It's all a balancing act. And I am not an expert on this. I should dust off the Foundation's policy for you.'

Still, he's happy to express his own view.

'It's a matter of balance, what you do as a people to reduce your impact on the environment and how you live sustainably, as well as the responsibility. You've also got to look at the impact of your consumption and your activities around the world. It's not just local.

'What we hear in some of the discussions today gets everything mixed up. Arguments about how we can reduce our impact on the environment get simplified right down to "Look, that means no more people." And that is not correct. It is much more complex than that.

'My personal point of view is that immigration has enriched Australia. And the diversity is good. I can tell you from the friends I have in the environment movement. Steve Komono who's Greek, one of the lawyers who provided all the background legal work for the Fraser Island cases, for Cape York, for Moreton Island; for 30 years and free of charge. And some of the great wildlife photographers, like Olegas Truchanas in Tasmania. I often wonder what gave him that eye and that love for nature. I think perhaps when you come into something new you see it with fresh eyes.

'Likewise, getting to know and being involved with Kath Walker and some of the Aboriginal communities on Stradbroke Island. There's a real tenderness and closeness to the land, a spiritual connection. The land is also a provider of life, as I've learnt from Aboriginal friends showing me some of the things that are bush tucker. I feel very comfortable in it. Some of that comfort and liveability I have learnt from Aboriginal colleagues. I've learnt that this is not a foreign land.'

— • —

When the Howard Government made an eight per cent cut to the immigration program in 1997, a spokesperson for Pauline Hanson's One Nation Party welcomed the move. But Dr John Coulter, a former Senator and leader of the Australian Democrats and now a spokesperson for Australians for an Ecologically Sustainable Population, said the cuts did not go far enough. The Government, he said, was pursuing a course of 'deliberate scientific stupidity.'[8] The cut was 6000 people. The focus of attention for the environmental condition of the whole continent was plus or minus a few thousand people.

In all the discussion about population and the environment, there's much talk about immigrants and virtually none about short term entrants. They don't seem to be 'population' of the kind that raises environmentalist passions. In just one flash of time, September 1998, there were 454,800 people staying in Australia on temporary entry visas: 175,400 visitors; 117,000 students; 32,500 working holiday-makers; 39,700 long-stay business entrants and 9,100 short-stay business entrants.

Nearly half a million people. Nearly ten times the net population increase created by immigration. If the population–environment formulae are really accurate, let's just stop tourism, or overseas students, or business visitors. But none of the anti-immigration environmentalists are suggesting this.

Long-term arrivals to Australia, people who are not migrants but who are coming to live and work in Australia temporarily, grew from 98,800 in 1988 to 188,100 in 1998. In the year to 30 June 1998, business long-stay entrants alone were up 37.4 per cent on the previous year to a figure of 35,730 people.[9]

Such temporary entries are a rapidly growing amount. On current trends, half a million temporary entrants living in Australia at any one time could become a million in a decade. That's an extra half a million people added to Australia's population.

This is the trend everywhere in the world. People are moving, moving, and moving again; and an increasing proportion of the movement is temporary rather than permanent.

Looking at the immigration program numbers alone reduces still further the credibility of environmental arguments which attack immigration in the name of population. The fact that the zero population growth environmentalists focus on immigration tells us more about their true agenda than it tells us anything about the actual population of Australia.

— • —

These, then, are the dimensions of the first public discussions now taking place in Australia concerning the land and its people. At root, it's an argument about the size of the local population and the nature of Australia.

We have a conservative suggestion to make about the local population, and that is, let's stick with who we are. We should keep doing what we have been doing for a long time now. We are a society of immigrants and we should stay that way, because this is one of our virtues. Immigrants and their descendants are people of ambition, people who have chosen their destiny, and people who, by and large, are thankful to be able to enjoy the opportunities available in a new place, in the New World. This is our history and our character. It should remain our destiny.

Immigrants are also people who are able no less than any other Australians to appreciate the richness of the Australian environment, to see the place with fresh eyes rather than take it for granted.

So what are the consequences of this conservative line of argument for the numbers of people on the land? If we take this course, let's stay with an immigration program which is equal to the average size of the program as a proportion of the Australian population over the past half century. On average, the number of immigrants arriving in Australia each year has equalled 0.72 per cent of the existing population per year over the course of the second half of the twentieth century. With a current population of 19 million, this means that our immigration program today should be 136,800 per year, returning immigration levels to where they were in the late 1980s.

Then, let's take the forewarnings of environmentalists very seriously indeed, for population growth is a global environmental problem of enormous proportions. Then there are four things that we Australians should do.

Firstly, we should take an international leadership role on global population issues. The key question is, how can the whole world's population be brought to a position of stability, without prejudice to people's human rights to fertility and their power to choose the size of their family? Continued population growth in Australia is not at all incompatible with working towards this global objective. It's just a matter of redressing resource imbalances. No country under resource or developmental pressure could accuse us of hypocrisy or of having duplicitous motives.

Secondly, we should focus our energies on technologies of sustainability. How can we stay on our historic path of population growth and continue to raise our standards of living — standards of living which are premised upon continued economic growth — whilst at the same time moving towards environmental sustainability? To do this, we'd need to get organisations like the CSIRO back to investigating the mechanics of how sustainable growth can be achieved, instead of manufacturing prophecies of doom. This process would also require historic accommodations, compromises and collaborations between hostile camps — the farmers and industrialists on the one hand, and the environmentalists on the other.

Thirdly, as custodians of a disproportionate amount of the world's land and resources, we need to conceive our responsibility to ourselves as also being a responsibility to the people of the world. Our capacities to produce food and the raw materials for clothing, as well as our mineral and energy resources, are part of the common heritage of humankind. This creates a peculiar responsibility towards the many on the part of the few who, accidentally, are today's inhabitants of this land.

Finally, and this is where all three of the other challenges meet, we should contemplate the human and environmental conditions under which every person on the planet could achieve comparable standards of living. This is the truly 'big picture' question. Answering this will require enormous imaginative energy and technical ingenuity. This will be one of the huge and pressing questions of the twenty-first century, and we are as well-placed to be able to tackle it as any country in the world. It's an environmental question far more worthy of our attention than debating however many thousand people are getting off the plane in Australia, and staying here.

CHAPTER 11

The Lie of the Land

There are three large difficulties in the relationship of the Australian land to the Australian people. We have begun the discussion of land and people in the preceding chapters by examining the first of these difficulties: the tension between the numbers of people who are here and the nature of the Australian lands. In later chapters, we will examine the third of the land–people relationships: our geographical location a long way away from those people we have habitually imagined we are like.

For now, however, we will dwell on the second of the difficult relationships: the relationship of the people who left other Old Worlds to create a 'New World' in the antipodes, to the Old World peoples who originally occupied the land.

Discussions about the relationship of people to land focus almost entirely on the ninety-eight per cent of the population who are immigrants and the descendants of immigrants, and the prospect that these numbers will grow. Mention 'population' and you mostly start talking about the continuing history of immigration and New World settlement. Rarely do Australia's Old World peoples, the remaining two per cent, figure in discussions of the relationship of population to land.

The presence of the ninety-eight per cent, however, was established long after the presence of those who are now the two per cent. It's a statement of the obvious, but being after is not the same as being before. Those who are after always have to justify their relationship to those who were before, in a way that those who were before don't have to in reverse. Coming after means that a different kind of accommodation needs to be made with those who were here before. Immigration, the business of peopling the land, has inevitable historical and moral consequences that are often forgotten or ignored.

— • —

In the global story of befores and afters, in the world history of imperial conquest and colonial settlement, Australia is a strange place indeed. The Australian colonies were the only ones in the history of British colonialism founded without recognition of the land rights of the people who already lived there and without treaties acknowledging the fact of colonial occupation.

When the case of *Cooper v. Stuart* found its way from Australia to the Privy Council in London in 1889, Lord Watson came to the legal and historical conclusion that Australia was 'practically unoccupied, without settled inhabitants or settled law, at the time when it was peacefully annexed to the British dominions.'[1] This was the doctrine of *terra nullius*, or 'the empty land.'

Rarely in the history of colonialism was the slate of pre-existing human habitation wiped so thoroughly clean. *Terra nullius* removed, in one sentence, in one sleight of hand, the Old World peoples of Australia from the legal and historical record.

There were a number of supporting lies to give credence to this one large lie about the land. The place had, in fact, been occupied — absolutely, completely, practically — and the inhabitants had been settled here from time immemorial. They had elaborate systems of law, including land tenure. And the conquest had been far from peaceful. An estimated twenty thousand people died in direct conflict, and hundreds of thousands died of disease. Two centuries later, Professor Colin Tatz, Director of the Centre for Comparative Genocide Studies at Macquarie University, is even using the word 'genocide' to describe what happened to the Indigenous peoples of Australia. In its past treatment of Aboriginal people, he says, Australia has violated the United Nations Convention of the Prevention and Punishment of the Crime of Genocide, ratified by Australia in 1949.

Yet some of the immigrants and their descendants still don't like unsavoury words to be used to describe their arrival. Words such as 'invasion' or 'conquest' seem to indicate to them a 'black armband' view of our past: unduly pessimistic and self-doubting when we should, in fact, be glorying in stories of 'discovery,' 'exploration' and 'development.' Certainly it would be preferable to be able to think that something more agreeable had occurred, but not if this means continuing a blatant lie. Not if this means pretending that there was some residual truth to the *terra nullius* story of peaceful settlement.

The High Court of Australia overturned the legal doctrine of *terra nullius* in the Mabo decision of 1992. Since then, there have been two systems of land tenure in Australia, one based on the first fact of our history, and the other on the second. In the aftermath, there has been an agonising discussion about how to draw the boundaries between the older system, 'Native Title,' and the newer.

After Mabo, the *Native Title Act* of 1993 attempted to codify in legislation what the High Court had found, with the benefit of late twentieth-century hindsight, to be the old truth of English common law. Then the High Court's Wik decision of 1996 found that there were, in retrospect, overlapping native title rights on the pastoral leases that cover forty-two per cent of the continent. Following this, the Howard Government attempted to codify these rights in the *Native Title Amendment Act* of 1998.

The nineties were a decade in which Australia's state of one law, one people, one nation, was transformed into a state of legal and civic pluralism. On one side of the discussion stood Professor Geoffrey Blainey.

As a young historian, Blainey had made his academic career by writing commissioned histories of mining companies. He was later to become a significant economic historian of Australia. He sprang to wider public fame in 1984 when he warned that, for the sake of social stability, Asian immigration should be limited.

Blainey is one of John Howard's mates. In fact, he coined the term 'black armband history,' which the Prime Minister was later to use as a counterpoint to his more 'positive' view. Along with right-wing poet Les Murray, he was one of just two mates privy to Howard's first draft of a new preamble to the Australian Constitution, a draft that enshrined 'mateship' itself as a national ideal. Howard also put Blainey on the Centenary of Federation Committee, to make sure that we got our history right as we celebrated one hundred years of the Australian Commonwealth in 2001.

When Mabo and Wik came along, Blainey said he thought there was something fundamentally wrong with the very possibility of native title:

Native Title ... embodies a crusade against racial discrimination and yet it perpetuates a new form of racial discrimination: a nationwide form of land tenure based on race. [It is] 'racism' by almost every definition used in current political discussion in Australia [because] it sets up two systems of land tenure in Australia, and one of them is based on race. It is ridiculous to say that the Aboriginal society could have survived the way it was. What happened in 1788 had happened in most parts of the world ... thousands of years before the time of Christ. The Native Title Act tries to revive what is largely dead. The High Court [is guilty of] a deplorable misuse of history.

The basis of Blainey's objection is a broader objection to cultural pluralism. He's absolutely a one-nation man and rejects the view that diversity is generally a nice thing:

Multiculturalism is more than a snack bar. As a political and social basis for a nation it is not yet a proven recipe, as Yugoslavia, Fiji, Lebanon and a string of other disasters or failures reveal ... The past provides a warning to those who talk optimistically of the virtues of contrasting cultures living side by side. They should realise that the more pronounced the diversity, the higher the long-term danger. If Australia 'succeeds' in acquiring great cultural diversity in the next 30 years — and then experiences an outbreak of, say, Islamic fundamentalism or a decisive crusade by Aborigines for their own laws and a separate nation — today's multicultural policies will have a lot to answer for.[2]

On the other side of the discussion, the debate has left Australia's shores. The Howard Government's Native Title Amendment Act seems to be the last word from Australian authorities, for the moment at least. Now the question of land has become a matter of international law.

In 1966, Australia signed the International Convention for the Elimination of All Forms of Racial Discrimination. It was a timely move, coinciding with the official end of the White Australia Policy and the 1967 referendum that removed the racially discriminatory provisions from the Australian Constitution. Australia was improving its performance and could, with some confidence, report on these improvements to the international community.

With this began the process of submitting periodical reports to the United Nations Committee for the Elimination of All Forms of Racial Discrimination. Responding in 1994 to Australia's ninth report, the Committee said that progress was being made, that this was a good sign, and that there was, of course, still a lot more that could be done. Australia should continue to 'pursue an energetic policy of recognising Aboriginal rights and furnishing adequate compensation for the discrimination and injustice of the past.'[3]

The tenth periodical report was due to be submitted by 30 October 1994. It was not submitted. The eleventh was due in 1996. It was not submitted either. In August 1998, an Early Warning/Urgent Action notice was issued by the Committee. After examining submissions from the Australian Government and Indigenous organisations, the Committee handed down its decision in March 1999.

Its findings were damning:

3 The Committee recognises that within the broad range of discriminatory practices that have long been directed against Australia's Aboriginal and Torres Strait Islander people, the effects of Australia's racially discriminatory land practices have endured as an acute impairment of the rights of Australia's Indigenous communities ...

6 The Committee, having considered a series of new amendments to the *Native Title Act*, as adopted in 1998, expresses concern over the compatibility of the *Native Title Act*, as currently amended, with the State Party's [Australia's] international obligations under the Convention ... [P]rovisions that extinguish or impair the exercise of Indigenous title rights and interests pervade the amended Act ...

11. The Committee calls on the State Party to address these concerns as a matter of utmost urgency ... [and] urges the State Party to suspend implementation of the 1998 amendments and re-open discussions with the representatives of the Aboriginal and Torres Strait Islander peoples with a view to finding solutions ... which would comply with Australia's obligations under the Convention.[4]

Geoffrey Blainey was talking racism, but so was the United Nations Committee for the Elimination of All Forms of Racial Discrimination.

Despite the whirlwind of change — Mabo, the 1993 legislation that covered Crown lands, then Wik and the 1998 legislation that added mutual ownership rights over pastoral leases — there's an extraordinary sense of failure. The one-nation people like Geoffrey Blainey will probably never be happy again because the tide of history is running so thoroughly against them. However, nobody who supports the general drift of the changes thinks they are satisfactory or that they will hold.

'It is terrible. It's very embarrassing,' says Charlie Perkins.

'We're the first Western nation ever to be dragged before that Committee. It's the special committee that looks at atrocities, massacres and racial discrimination. There we are, lined up with all these lunatic-type countries where brutality happens every day, you know, in Kosovo and all those places. There we are, side by side with the worst nations ever, having to answer the case against us for racism and human rights abuses in this country against Aboriginal people.

'I think we are heading towards a breakdown in our relationships that we have never seen before in this country.'

— • —

Talking with Mick Dodson, the former Aboriginal and Torres Strait Islander Social Justice Commissioner with the Human Rights and Equal Opportunity Commission, we heard the same fears being expressed.

'We're in the same company as bloody Bosnia, Uganda and Equador. Australia's the first-ever Western democracy to be called up in front of the UN for human rights abuses.

'This government is two-faced about it. They say, we'll adhere to international standards so far as trade and commerce is concerned, but human rights is a domestic concern only.

'It will do this country a lot of damage. And it's not just a question of doing damage in the future. A lot of damage has already been done.'

Mick didn't have too much time to talk, an hour at the most. He was off to a reception for Gerry Adams, the Sinn Fein leader. Adams had finally been allowed to visit Australia, even though he'd been to the United States a number of times and met President Clinton, where he was hailed for his role in the Northern Ireland peace process.

At last the Australian Government had allowed him a visa, but Prime Minister Howard was still not going to meet him, even though Federal Opposition Leader Kim Beazley and Victorian Premier Jeff Kennett would. Adams was also going to meet a group of Indigenous leaders whose claim to sovereignty over the lands of Australia was older than Howard's people, and older than either of the Catholic or Protestant claims to Ireland. Mick Dodson was going to be there.

We start with the same questions we'd asked the others we spoke to for this book.

'What makes you the person you are?' 'What motivates you?' 'What kind of Australian are you?' As the words came out, we realised what lame questions they were.

'My history ... ? My people's experience isn't exactly a happy one. I came from a very impoverished background ... a fringe-dwelling existence. Anybody with a modicum of compassion or intelligence, or both, should be able to clearly see that there's been great injustices done and that continue to be done.'

He wasn't suggesting we lacked intelligence or compassion, but it's hard for the descendants of immigrants to get started on these issues with Indigenous people without a sense of unease about how to start. It's even a question of whether there is anything more that can be said.

He spoke slowly, deliberately.

'Up until 1996, for the first time, we had Government at a national level that started to listen to what Indigenous people had to say. They were starting to accept certain things had to be done to redress the injustices of the past and to actually confront our history as a nation.

'But I think the present National Government is very much determined to stay in power, whatever the cost. They've cynically exploited racism.

'Any Government who can pass racially discriminatory legislation, not just once, but a number of times, and then seek to defend it as being something fair and honourable, makes you wonder about the rest of the country.

'Of course, there are good people who've stood up to the racism, particularly with the Native Title legislation. I think the majority of people are decent, but there's also this racist streak that runs through Australian society.

'Australia is built on a fundamental act of racism. I mean, we are invisible people. Our societies didn't exist here. Our civilization, our culture, our languages, our land-holding systems were thought to be not only unworthy but non-existent. I think that's the challenge for Australia. Keating got close, I think, but there's really been no national leader, political leader, who's been prepared to deal with it.

'Whoever coined the phrase "the land of a fair go" must have been bloody deaf and blind and stupid. In the last few years it's certainly become a greedier, more selfish place.'

Since the Federal Government decided not to renew Dodson's contract as Aboriginal and Torres Strait Islander Social Justice Commissioner, Mick Dodson has been working in the Indigenous Law Centre at the University of New South Wales. The Centre had won an ATSIC contract to write their submission to the UN Committee for the Elimination of All Forms of Racial Discrimination. Mick was one of the submission's authors.

'And being silent is not an answer. And I don't know if we're getting anywhere at the moment. Some things have changed. Some things haven't. Some things have gone backwards.'

The University of New South Wales is one of the legacies of sixties and seventies boomtime confidence. A scramble of huge, sharp-edged tower blocks, tombstone-like monuments to brutal scientific truth and academic dispassion. The Indigenous Law Centre is at the top of one of the tallest blocks. The windows start at waist height, and Mick's desk is under the window. So, here's the profile of an Aboriginal man, and from this angle you can't see the worst excesses of Sydney architecture, including the university. Looking across Randwick Racecourse and the tops of the trees of suburban Sydney, it seems like you're looking over a rolling subtropical jungle, lurid green, with the city skyline touching black storm clouds in the distance. A man in the environment, and, as the clouds close in, the city in the distance appears almost as a pictorial and historical illusion.

'Well, you know, they talk about partnership and talk about it in the future. But we're never ever considered equal partners. With Native Title, Howard came into the room and said, "This is my plan. We don't care what you think about it. This is what we're going to do."'

The plan was the so-called 'ten-point' plan that was the basis for the Native Title Amendment Act of 1998.

'There was no attempt to legitimise their process even with so-called "consultation."

'The key question is how will the nation honestly deal with the old and the legitimate grievances that are felt by Aboriginal people? That are honestly held and for good reason? Until that's dealt with it's never going to go away. And dishing out a ten-point plan to us is not an honest confrontation of that past. It's not dealing fairly. It's not attempting to deal with the anxiety that many non-Indigenous Australians feel about how they came by this country. And it certainly isn't dealing with the grievance, the legitimately held grievance of Aboriginal people.

'Until you deal with the grievance, you're never going to deal with the problem. And the heart of that is the question of land. Until the nation comes to an honourable settlement over the question of land, the grievance is never going to be settled. One of the things about history is that when you see people who aren't free, they agitate for freedom generation after generation. It took the bloody Irish about eight hundred years ...'

That night, Gerry Adams introduces himself as 'an aboriginal person from Belfast.' He says he feels a natural affinity with all 'native people in colonised situations':

> Whatever we think about other people's culture, their customs or their skin colour, the fact is that they have to be treated on the basis of equality. Their spokespersons have to be respected, dialogue is needed to achieve an end to injustice, and an end to whatever conflict there is has to be done in an understanding way and a process needs to be put in place to achieve it. That was required in my country. It was required in other conflicts, other situations throughout the world.[5]

We went down in the lift with Mick Dodson. He was running late now and apologised again for having to rush the interview.

'Some of my forebears are from Ireland, too. The O'Fagans from County Monaghan.'

— • —

When Aboriginal lawyer Noel Pearson was studying law at Sydney University, the graffiti in the men's toilets read 'Land Rights by '88.' The bicentenary of the establishment of a British colony in Sydney wasn't far off. Someone else had scrawled underneath 'But can fauna own land?'

This was the truth — and the lie — of *terra nullius*. 'We occupied the land, but we were fauna.'[6] It's also the truth — and the lie — of modern racism, that some peoples are closer to animals than others.

Pearson was to become an expert on the finer points of racism. He was brought up at Hope Vale, a Lutheran mission on the east side of the Cape York Peninsula north of Cooktown.

Where Pearson's country meets the sea, the sandhills are up to a hundred metres high and brilliantly striped with the colours of geological time. The place was named 'Coloured Sands' by some white settler whose connection with the land was probably so tenuous that all he could see was what stared him in the face. We bought a permit at the community's office in Hope Vale and camped on the beach. Now that the mission's gone, you are on Aboriginal Land.

Pearson has a lawyer's clarity of thought and a community leader's capacity to express himself simply and eloquently. Behind the hundreds of pages of tortured legal logic in the High Court's Mabo and Wik decisions, and behind the hundreds of pages of wincing attempts at avoidance in the Native Title legislation, there are three simple propositions about Native Title. And these three propositions represent an historic compromise about the events of the past two and a bit centuries.

One. Nobody — not the High Court, not Indigenous community leaders, not the most avid supporters of the principle of Native Title — has ever suggested that the immigrants, the settlers who've arrived since 1788, cannot keep everything they already have. Everything. Unreservedly. Part one of the compromise, Pearson says, involves a recognition of 'colonial history, a history involving the grant of millions of land tenures to the new Australians and their descendants, and the consequent dispossession of the old Australians who once held title to all corners of the continent.' It is also a recognition that 'the new Australians gained their wealth and livelihoods from the land,' that 'they imprinted their own story on the land,' and that 'many of them grew to love the land and, yes, feel indigenous to the land.'

With the benefit of hindsight, it's a generous offer, and one that no settler, or descendant of settlers, should refuse.

Two. Old Australians will be allowed to enjoy their Native Title over whatever land has been left over. They can keep doing what they already do with the leftover bits.

And three. Across the vast pastoral leases, title is to be shared. Pastoralists can keep doing what they have done all along, they can graze cattle as before; while Indigenous people can keep doing what they have done all along, which is live on the land, relate to the land according to their traditional practices, hunt and fish on the land. And this rule applies to the sharing: the new people's title prevails over the old whenever there is uncertainty or disagreement.

It's a more than reasonable set of propositions. As Indigenous communities have said that they will be agreeable to this, you'd think the immigrants would have considered themselves to have done very well indeed.

But the 1998 Native Title Amendment Act, Pearson says, flaunts the spirit of compromise. It 'takes away from the old and gives to the new.' As a consequence, he and his people are left with a feeling of 'bitterness of betrayal.'[7]

'We are in a situation of desperation. We are on the verge of no less than legal apartheid. What I mean by that is we will have a national law that says there are two rights, two titles sitting alongside each other and the Aboriginal title can be extinguished and the other one remain in place.'[8]

'Through tortured moral logic, we're supposed to pretend racially discriminatory property laws do not amount to "racism." We are supposed to refrain from the description of those who advocate racially discriminatory property laws as being "racists."

'The Aboriginal position on the whole Native Title debate has never been discriminatory. We have never urged that the common law or Native Title and legislation dealing with Native Title should result in the reduction of the rights of other citizens.'[9]

— • —

Let's come back to the start of the Native Title story, to one kind of beginning. In 1963 there were no land rights in Australia; no Indigenous people owned land by virtue of their Native Title.

That year, the Swiss aluminium giant, Nabalco, applied for rights to mine bauxite over 362 square kilometres of the Arnhem Land reserve, at its north-east tip. The Yolngu people, who had lived there since time immemorial, called the place Yirrkala.

Yirrkala had been set up as a Methodist mission. A bit like the European carve-up of Africa at the end of the nineteenth century, Christian missionaries had often been the first whites to stake their various ethnic and moral claims over Aboriginal Australia. They were the frontiersmen of white society. The Irish Catholics set themselves up at Bathurst Island. The German Lutherans at Hope Vale. And the English Methodists at Yirrkala; the year was 1934.

When the missionaries came, the Yolngu played a well-considered double game. They accepted the changes but on their own terms. They revealed to the newcomers, and the whole community, some of the images and objects that had been highly restricted secret and sacred knowledge. They put up bark panels of clan paintings in the missionaries' church at Yirrkala. These paintings spoke of another religion, another law, but through a new medium and in a site that was differently sacred. It was a gesture to the missionaries, a kind of gift that they could not refuse, but it was also a gesture through which the Yolngu insisted on a two-way dialogue.

When the Nabalco application came onto the scene, the Yolngu made the same kind of complicated gesture. They could have petitioned the government the way white people usually do, and, if they had, the document would have probably just been ignored and lost to history.

Instead, they sent a bark petition. Written submissions were pasted onto two sheets of stringybark, written in Yolngu — the missionaries had created a written form of the language in order to translate the Bible — and in English translation. The border was made of sacred designs from the two clans whose lands would be affected by mining activities. The submissions asked that the Yolngu's rights be respected and that they be consulted before any land was excised for mining from the Arnhem Land Reserve.[10]

The Yolngu insisted on direct negotiation and, in part, they insisted that this would be on their own terms. They deliberately marked their cultural difference. They said, in effect, something like, 'We have a different kind of claim, so we will express it in a different kind of way, our way.'

In the medium as well as the message, it was a deeply unsettling claim. After all, it was nearly 1966, not long before Australia was to sign the International Convention for the

Elimination of All Forms of Racial Discrimination, and not long before the 1967 referendum that would remove racially discriminatory references from the Australian Constitution.

A Parliamentary Select Committee, which was established to examine the Yolngu claims, visited Yirrkala to investigate the situation at first hand.

Milerrpum, speaking through an interpreter, said that his people wanted to keep their lands. He wanted to know what the hole dug by the mining company would be like. Would it be the size of the shed in which the Select Committee was holding its hearings? And what was this royalty that was to be 'paid into a trust for the benefit of Aboriginal wards in the Northern Territory'?[11] The interpreter spoke for Milerrpum, who spoke for his people:

> They do not want white people to come and dig a lot of holes in the country and take away country which represents wealth to them. Apparently, the bauxite is bringing in money. Therefore, seeing that it is their country, they should share in it. They are the owners of the country and need to be informed as to what is going on. They think it is too vague to have a fund for everybody. When their children grow up they will say 'where is our money from the mining' and they will not be able to point to anything.[12]

Five years later, the mine was well-established, but the Yolngu were still fighting for their rights; through the court system, this time. And once again, they were taking on the Australian system of law and governance, not just on its own terms, but on terms of their own reality. For the first time, the Yolngu reality was recognised, partially at least. In 1971 Mr Justice Blackburn handed down his decision in the case of *Milerrpum v. Nabalco* in the Supreme Court of the Northern Territory. He defined law as 'a system of rules of conduct which is felt obligatory upon them by the members of a definable group of people.' Not often did a case force a judge to go back to principles so fundamental, so basic.

In this definition, he concluded, the Yolngu certainly did have a system of law. Theirs was, indeed,

> a subtle and elaborate system highly adapted to the country in which the people led their lives, which provided a stable order of society and was remarkably free from the vagaries of

personal whim or influence. If ever a system could be called 'a government of laws, and not of men,' it is that shown in the evidence before me.[13]

In English jurisprudence, this is called 'the rule of law.' The judge could see there was an Aboriginal rule of law.

Still, Justice Blackburn could not find something he was able to recognise as property rights. There was nothing resembling a register of titles. There were none of the familiar forms of permission to enter that characterise private property and that indicate 'the right to exclude, the right to alienate.' Ownership represented religious rather than economic interests, and he saw the clan as an indeterminate group of individuals, unstable in its composition. These were the reasons why he found no 'proprietary interests' recognisable in the tradition of English common law.[14]

Blackburn was wrong about Yolngu society in every one of these matters of fact, and by 1992, in the retrospective view of English common law that was presented in the Mabo decision, he was judged to have been wrong in law as well.

The Blackburn decision was handed down late in December 1971. On 25 January 1972 Prime Minister Billy McMahon announced that the Yirrkala people would receive royalties from Bauxite mining, but at a trivial rate.

In the early hours of 26 January 1972, Aboriginal activists set up a Tent Embassy on the lawns of Parliament House in Canberra. Here were the Aboriginal people of Australia, foreigners in their own land, attempting to establish the first diplomatic relations. It was Australia Day, and the one hundred and eighty-fourth anniversary of the establishment of the British colony in Sydney. The idea had been conceived by New South Wales Aboriginal poet and community leader, Kevin Gilbert. Its immediate inspiration was as an act of solidarity with the people of Yirrkala.

The Government called in the police to try to remove the protesters and their tents; it wasn't the kind of unsightly mess they wanted to have outside the front doors of the Federal Parliament. However, the television and newspaper pictures of big cops manhandling Aboriginal protesters over the next few days looked worse. The Embassy has been there ever since.

LAND RIGHTS NOW OR ELSE.

LEGALLY THIS LAND IS OUR LAND. WE SHALL TAKE IT IF NEED BE.[15]

These were some of the placards that went up on that Australia Day back in 1972. Three decades later, there are still signs up around the Embassy that say the same kinds of things.

The tents have since been replaced by an old shipping container and the staff of the embassy now live in caravans. The Embassy has become a site of iconic historical importance, a site that catches, and welcomes, the eye and the interest of tourists.

After the Nabalco case, and after the establishment of the Embassy, the Woodward Royal Commission was set up to inquire into Aboriginal land rights. This was the precursor to the *Aboriginal Land Rights (Northern Territory) Act* of 1976.

And so, the Yolngu eventually won their argument.

CHAPTER 12

A Matter of Unutterable Shame

We'd been doing interviews for this book in Parliament House for most of the day; with Senator Nick Bolkus, who'd led the Opposition case in the Senate against the Howard Government's amendments to the Native Title Act, and then with Bob Katter, who'd been Minister for Aboriginal Affairs in Queensland for six years before he shifted over to the Federal Parliament.

Walking the corridors from one side of this massive building to the other, from the Senate side to the House of Representatives side, you pass some of the treasures of Aboriginal civilization. Haunting Top End bark paintings of skeletal animal-people, safely locked up in the perspex box frames of scientific modernity. Central Australian dot paintings in desert colours, as hugely expansive as the land they were designed to map. And the Yolngu's bark petition of 1963, in a glass case. There's something unavoidable, and unreal, about the presence of these relics, all sacred in one way or another.

After the interviews, we had some time to spare before catching the plane, so we decided to walk down to the Tent Embassy.

On the front cover of the papers that morning there had been images of the police trying to remove the Embassy people from another site they were trying to establish near the new Parliament House. The camera angle was over the shoulders of the police, who looked huge, while the struggling bodies in their hands looked inconsequential. It seemed like a re-run of the images from 1972.

As we walked down the hill, we met a couple of policemen, not far from the new site the Embassy people had tried to set up the day before. Laconic white Australians, who'd been given their instructions from up there, on The Hill, from Parliament House. We joked with them and they were cryptic in reply — just doing a job ... not to be political — but you could tell they didn't like having to be there.

Down at the Embassy, the original Embassy in front of Old Parliament House, the air was full of the smell of the campfires, the wispy blue smoke of eucalypt. The fragrance clears your head.

Two hundred and eleven spears were staked into the ground, one for every year of European settlement. We sat for a while with the folks around one of the fires. Kevin Gilbert's wife, Eleanor Williams, was still there; he had passed away in 1993. She'd drafted a handwritten press release about the events of the day before:

SPIRIT OF FIRE TO DESTROY THE SPIRIT OF THE PREDATOR, SO PEOPLE CAN BEGIN THE HEALING PROCESS TO RID THE EVIL FROM THE LAND.

Howard's Cabinet gave their answer to the Aboriginal Embassy's eight point Declaration of Peace by instructions to Australian Protective Services to move our ancient peaceful ceremonial gathering ... The violent action by Police at 4pm to end the Fire Ceremony with assault and robbery of ceremonial objects has at last made public the silent war that has been raging in this country since 1788.

— • —

Bob Katter told us about the time he had been invited to speak at a big Rotary Club meeting in Canberra.

'And when they introduced me, they said, "You know, Bob Katter was a long-serving Minister for Aboriginal Affairs."

'They all roared laughing. They thought it was a joke, you know, but the interesting thing for me was that I'd been all afternoon here in Parliament with Tracker Tilmouth. One of the ALP blokes in the corridor yelled out when they saw him with me, "Trading with the enemy? Lie down with dogs and you'll get up with fleas."

'Tracker wouldn't have it. He said, "He's family, you'd better wash out your mouth." Tracker married into a family in Cloncurry who are the descendants of one of my forebears.'

'That's not to say that we wouldn't have some violent disagreements on certain things, but, you know, I consider Tracker a real good mate, I really like him, I like his company, I enjoy it immensely.

'And the day before, Sugar Ray Robinson was standing round at the airport, and couldn't get a lift into town, so he yelled out to me for a lift. Now, we've had some ups and downs in the public arena, Sugar and me, but there again, I had spent a significant proportion of both days talking with these blokes on some very, very important issues, national issues.'

Bob Katter is well-known, respected and liked by many of the leaders of Australia's Indigenous communities.

'Yes, what is perception and what is reality, there is a huge gulf between the two.'

The perception down south — and it's a perception which goes as far as a Rotary meeting in Canberra — is that Bob Katter is from North Queensland, that he's a member of the conservative National Party and on the conservative wing of that Party to boot, and that this adds up to being a redneck.

'On my wall over there, there are two pictures. One of them is my football team — I played with Aboriginal people all the time, and it's pretty hard to feel superior to a bloke when he's thrashed you nine times in a football match. And not surprisingly the next picture is me as Aboriginal Affairs Minister giving them land ownership for the first time in history.'

He's very proud of his record as Minister for Aboriginal Affairs.

'For the first time, ownership of the land was handed over to exclusively black groups. And the black groups were the Shire Councils. All the old missions were administered by white State Government administrators. We pulled them out en masse, and Shire Councils were set up. Some would argue that they had a rocky road, and I would agree with that. But, you know, it wasn't a bad sort of an effort. They got self-management, local government and ownership of the land. Totally freehold, vested in the hands of the Shire Council.

'In all, there were 2088 community areas covering seven million acres and more than half of the black population of Queensland. More than thirty per cent of the Aboriginal population is in Queensland, and to a very large degree the Aboriginal phenomenon is a Queensland phenomenon. Whilst there is a population in New South Wales, they are very integrated in the cities and towns into the local community. It's only in the Northern Territory, Western Australia and Queensland you have got vast areas, and people that are totally isolated and sometimes totally alienated.

'Ten thousand people attended the ceremonies and festivities associated with handing over the lands. In the Torres Straits Joh was made father of the islands, Joh Bjelke-Petersen who was Premier at the time.'

We mention John Howard's efforts on Native Title. It's a tricky one, because Katter's party governs in coalition with Howard's and Howard is the Prime Minister.

'John Howard genuinely tries to do the right thing. But I find unless you're really a part of the black community, and feel at home in the black community, you're never going to be able to address these problems.'

A few months after being elected as Prime Minister, John Howard accused Noel Pearson of being a stooge of the Labor Party. It was about the time when Pearson addressed the National Press Club in Canberra, saying, 'Bob Katter dragged Indigenous affairs into the twentieth century.'

Pearson told how Katter's time as Queensland Aboriginal Affairs Minister during the 1980s had inspired him to become involved in furthering self-determination.

'Katter's manic energy invigorated me and many other young Aboriginal people in the community to take an interest in, and play a part in, the new self-management regime he had introduced.'[1]

— • —

Before the nineties, the conversation about land rights had been focused on the Northern Territory side of the Gulf of Carpentaria where the Yolngu peoples live. In the nineties, the discussion became more of a North Queensland thing, a massive wedge of dialogue extending all the way across the map-maker's triangle that is the Cape York Peninsula. At the tip of the triangle, Eddie Mabo's country in the islands of the Torres Straits almost touches Papua New Guinea. One side of the triangle extends south from here all the way down the Pacific side of the Cape, through Hope Vale and as far south as Townsville where Mabo lived, fought his fight, and died. Another side stretches north-west to the south-east corner of the Gulf of Carpentaria. The third side of the triangle takes us back to the Torres Strait, along the Gulf coast where the Wik people live.

It has always been, and still is, a place of multiracial, multicultural engagement. Aboriginal peoples often spoke a dozen or so different languages. Some of these peoples were so distinct as to be racially distinguishable; they actually looked different, as peoples. The Torres Strait Islanders, who spoke two languages of their own, had contact with neighbouring peoples both in what is now Papua New Guinea and Aboriginal groups on the Australian mainland. And later, white settlers, from the various, and often not so happily connected, ends of the British Isles. And immigrants from Asia, mainly Chinese, Japanese and Malay. And South Sea Islanders who had been brought out in large numbers as almost-slaves to work on the sugar plantations of the north. And immigrants from just about everywhere else, but particularly Afghanistan, Lebanon, Italy, Malta, Greece. This was before White Australia began to bite, and insofar as it failed to wipe the colour from the North, despite the policy. Today, when you stand in the main street of Thursday Island, the Queensland number plates on the cars are just about the only clue as to where you are. The place is just so racially, and so culturally, mixed.

So there's little wonder that North Queensland has been at the cutting edge of creating solutions to the greatest challenge of the post-Cold War era, the challenge of peacefully accommodating differences of history, culture and experience.

Eddie Mabo was one of the people who spent his life pushing the frontier — the historical, political, legal, moral frontier.

Born in 1936 on the island of Mer, Eddie Koiki Mabo was a member of the Meriam people. Mer is one of a small group of islands called the Murray Islands by the white explorers. It is the biggest island of the group, and the place where most of the Meriam people traditionally lived, 2.79 kilometres at its longest and 1.65 kilometres at its widest. Before colonial times, five to seven hundred people lived there. Eddie Mabo could recount his genealogy back seventeen generations.

Since colonial times, many people have left. Eddie Mabo left as a young man in 1957 to take jobs in the canefields of North Queensland. Working near The Gardens, a South Sea Islander settlement near Halifax, he met his wife, Bonita, whose family had originally been brought to North Queensland from Vanuatu. After they married, Eddie got a job as a ganger on the railways in Townsville; hard and hot work it was in those days. They saved up, bought a house, had seven children.

Then his life, and work, turned to Indigenous politics. In 1962 he became secretary of the Aboriginal Advancement League in

Townsville, later named the Aboriginal and Islander Advancement League. He established and became the Director and Principal of the Black Community School, and stayed there for as long as it existed, from 1973–1985. Eddie had no formal qualifications, and people who visited the school were amazed by his energy and what had been achieved. Eddie earned nothing from the position at the school, so he took a part-time job as a gardener at James Cook University to make ends meet.

There he'd start conversations with the lecturers, people like Henry Reynolds and Noel Loos. He'd go to the library and pore over Alfred Cort Haddon's six volume *Reports of the Cambridge Anthropological Expedition to the Torres Straits* — Haddon and his team had worked in the Straits in the 1900s and recorded what they had seen with a white man's eye. Later, Henry Reynolds and Noel Loos would get Eddie to give guest lectures about the Torres Straits. Eddie was not your average gardener.

One day, Henry Reynolds and a colleague were talking to Eddie, who was adamant that Mer was his, that it was owned by his people. Henry said no, it belongs to the Crown.

'He stared at us for a long time. He couldn't believe it. He was horrified. It was as if I had punched him in the face.' This is how Henry tells the story.

Eddie Mabo and Henry Reynolds were both embarking on journeys that would change Australian history and Australia's understanding of itself.

Eddie's journey was a ten-year legal battle. It began in 1982 and reached the High Court twice. By this time, it had become an all-consuming struggle, so Eddie had to go onto unemployment benefits. He'd catch the bus and the train to Canberra, $40 for a trip of over 2,500 kilometres, and then he had to be careful he had enough money to afford meals.

His battle culminated in the Mabo decision of 4 June 1992. Eddie, however, had succumbed to cancer five months earlier.

Henry Reynolds's journey covered millions of words of historical records and a succession of books that opened Australian eyes to aspects of their past that had slipped out of view: *The Other Side of the Frontier, Frontier, The Law of the Land, Dispossession, Fate of a Free People, Aboriginal Sovereignty, This Whispering in Our Hearts, Why Weren't We Told?* It is hard to think of any historian, anywhere in the world, whose retelling of the past has been so influential upon the present or the future of a nation. Certainly no other Australian historian has ever been so influential.

The paradoxical thing about both Eddie Mabo and Henry Reynolds is that they contributed to a revolutionary change, but they did it by the most conservative of means. They decided to take the British Empire at its word, to take the colonists at their word, to take the English common law at its word. And they decided to hold them all to their word. Then it was just a matter of recovering that word.

Surely the colonists couldn't have been entirely serious about *terra nullius*, Henry thought. Searching through the archives he found an 1836 instruction from the Colonial Office in London to the South Australian Commission that the commissioners were 'to prepare a plan for securing the rights of the Aborigines [including] arrangements for purchasing the lands of the Natives.' The historical evidence came tumbling out. Reynolds's proof that the Empire, the colonists and the colonial law had already recognised Native Title was assembled in his book *The Law of the Land*. It was a reminder of things that had been hidden away and forgotten.

So when the High Court revisited *terra nullius* in the Mabo case, it found that, in other moments of colonisation, property rights had been retained. Justice Brennan mentioned the Tanistry case of 1608, dealing with the conquest of Ireland, the first British colony:

A royal monarch (who) hath made a new conquest of a realm, although in fact he hath the lordship paramount of all the lands within such realm ... yet ... if such conqueror receiveth any of the natives or antient inhabitants into his protection and avoweth them for his subjects, and permitteth them to continue their possessions and to remain in his peace and allegiance, their heirs shall be adjudged in by good title without grant or confirmation of the conqueror, and shall enjoy their lands according to the rules of the law which the conqueror hath allowed or established, if they will submit themselves to it, and hold their lands according to the rules of it.[2]

These were the ancient truths of English property law, the ancient honour of English colonialism. People who have been invaded are not beneath any form of recognition; they can still own their land.

The judges also turned to international law in their judgement, where the concept of *terra nullius* had been completely discredited. Justice Brennan again:

> If the international law notion that inhabited land may be classified as *terra nullius* no longer commands general support, the doctrines of the common law which depend on the notion that native peoples may be 'so low in the scale of social organization' that it is 'idle to impute to such people some shadow of the rights known to our law' ... can hardly be retained ...

He was quoting a 1919 Rhodesian case here, at one of the high points of European racism.

> ... If it were permissible in past centuries to keep the common law in step with international law, it is imperative in today's world that the common law should neither be nor be seen to be frozen in an age of racial discrimination.[3]

These are strong words for a judge of the highest court in Australia.

The words of the joint judgement of Justices Sir William Deane and Mary Gaudron are even stronger:

> We are conscious of the fact that, in those parts of this judgement which deal with the dispossession of Australian Aborigines, we have used language and expressed conclusions which some may think to be unusually emotive for a judgement in this Court. We have not done that in order to trespass into the area of assessment or attribution of moral guilt. As we have endeavoured to make clear, the reason which has led us to describe, and express conclusions about, the dispossession of Australian Aborigines in unrestrained language is that the full facts of that dispossession are of critical importance to the assessment of the legitimacy of the propositions that the continent was unoccupied for legal purposes ... .
>
> The conflagration of oppression and conflict ... over the ... century [following the establishment of the British settlement] ... spread across the continent to dispossess, degrade and

devastate the Aboriginal peoples and leave a national legacy of unutterable shame ...

As political power in relation to domestic matters was transferred from the Imperial Government in England to the European Colonists on the other side of the world, the Aborigines were increasingly treated as trespassers to be driven, by force if necessary, from their traditional homelands ...

The acts and events by which ... dispossession in legal theory was carried into practical effect constitute the darkest aspect of the history of this nation. The nation as a whole must remain diminished unless and until there is an acknowledgment of, and retreat from, those past injustices ...

For the reasons which we have explained ... re-examination [of the legal propositions which have been used to justify the dispossession] compels their rejection. The lands of this continent were not *terra nullius* or 'practically unoccupied' in 1788. The Crown's property in the lands of the Colony of New South Wales was, under the common law which became applicable upon the establishment of the Colony in 1788, reduced or qualified by the burden of the common law native title of the Aboriginal tribes and clans to the particular areas of land on which they lived or which they used for traditional purposes.[4]

Henry Reynolds was working through archival material at the National Library down the road from the High Court while the Mabo case was being held. He came and sat with Eddie Mabo and they observed the court proceedings together.

After the Mabo decision had been handed down, Sir William Deane sent a card of appreciation to Henry. There were those words again, handwritten this time: 'national legacy of unutterable shame.' Deane was later to become Governor-General of Australia.

Noel Pearson says that Henry Reynolds exerted a seminal influence on the Mabo and Wik decisions.

Mick Dodson agrees. 'What strikes me about him is his honour. There is something enormously courageous about his writing.'[5]

Eddie Mabo, however, did not live to see the fruits of his life's work.

— ● —

Three and a bit years after his death, Bonita Mabo and the Torres Strait Islander community in Townsville finally got together enough money to erect a memorial stone over his grave.

An all-day ceremony was held to coincide with the third anniversary of the High Court's Mabo decision, first in the centre of Townsville — speech upon speech, the white man's way. Then the unveiling of the tombstone at the cemetery, with singing and wailing, the black man's way. The cemetery is at a place called Belgian Gardens. Its name used to be German Gardens, after the first settlers there, until the First World War when the name was changed.

That night, the black granite tombstone was spraypainted with red swastikas and the word 'Abo.' And the life-sized bronze sculpture of Eddie's face was prised off and stolen.

Superintendent Warren Hansen told the *Townsville Bulletin* that the desecration was 'merely a case of wilful damage.' The police, he said, would make every endeavour to apprehend the culprits. 'I said that, as far as the police service is concerned, they will be charged with wilful damage — you cannot make any more than that out of the law.'[6]

Zita Antonius, the Race Relations Commissioner with the Human Rights and Equal Opportunity Commission, didn't see it the same way. She'd been receiving a steady flow of complaints about the presence of racist groups in the north, and the Mabo grave desecration showed all the usual signs indicating that it was the work of one of these groups. The letters 'KKK' and other racist graffiti had been sprayed on other Aboriginal monuments; meetings of white-robed and hooded people had been reported; gangs of young white men had been invading Aboriginal homes and threatening occupants; a monument to the Kalkadoon people on the Barkly Highway had been blown up.

'Because of the swastikas, because of the derogatory term "Abo" and the use of red paint, which seems to be a feature, one is probably safe in assuming that there is a racist motivation,' Antonius said.[7]

Later in the week, the police announced that three Indigenous youths had been interviewed in relation to the desecration of the Mabo grave in the Belgian Gardens Cemetery. The three were alleged to have escaped from a nearby detention centre on Saturday afternoon. They were picked up in Cairns three days later.

This was a nice turn of events for the police in the hand-to-hand combat of race politics, to which Roger Griffith of the Townsville and District Aboriginal and Islander Legal Service responded with a simple bit of detective work of his own.

'It's highly unlikely that two Aborigines and one Islander would have committed this offence.' They had escaped at 2.10pm, and 'it's highly unlikely they would have hung around — especially when you consider that the cemetery is right next door to the (detention) centre. And they would have to go away to get spray cans and then walk back past the detention centre.'[8]

No charges were laid against the three youths.

The next weekend, a group of us decided to organise a Rally Against Racism. It was an attempt to express in the local community a version of the 'unutterable shame' that Justices Deane and Gaudron expressed in the Mabo decision. Our sense was that the racists were few and the people of goodwill many, and that this was something that needed to be given public expression.

The local officials were edgy at first. No, we couldn't use the stage in the mall in the centre of town. Mayor Tony Mooney wasn't sure if he would come — the event might bring more bad publicity to Townsville. The police were less than enthusiastic.

An organising committee was formed more or less overnight. Invitations were sent out to Australia's political leaders. Then the acceptances started flowing in. Brian Howe, the Deputy Prime Minister, would be there. Local politicians would be there, including Senator Margaret Reynolds.

The telegrams of support flooded in. And then, even the Mayor, who'd attracted criticism for his continued attempts to remove the 'park people' from the camping place they'd used since colonial settlement, decided he'd come too. That's when the Council finally gave us a venue — the sound shell on the southern edge of town.

A local band, The Happy Valley Six Pack, started up a quarter of an hour before the advertised starting time. The band members were New Guinean, Indigenous and Fijian; a very Townsville kind of group, singing a hybrid of blues, rock and gospel. 'Happy Valley' is the name local Indigenous people have for a town camp near the airport — a muddy, mosquito-infested squatter settlement on the edge of swampland that's been there for over a century.

Of course, we were anxious that the event would not backfire by showing a lack of support. The band had started playing to an empty amphitheatre. Then, wave after wave of people began to come over the grassy hill at the back of the amphitheatre; more than five hundred eventually. And they all stayed to the end, sitting through the reading of the pile of telegrams from the country's leaders, through the speeches by the community leaders and politicians, through the presentations by local school children. All the national media turned up and the event was a lead news item on every television channel that night. It was a small but important corrective: a message that racism was completely unacceptable.

Bonita Mabo sat quietly in the middle of the crowd. Under the circumstances, she wasn't up to public speaking.

'I haven't any idea who [did] it, but whoever [did] it is very low down. How could they do this? I just wanted something nice for Eddie. It's like starting all over again. [The burial] was the official end of the mourning and coming so quick, [the desecration] is really hurtful.'

Eddie Mabo Junior had words that sounded like his father's.

'He struggled through life and now even in death. There's no peace for the family. The struggle continues.'

The tombstone was repaired, and the Mabo family decided to move it, together with Eddie's remains, to Mer.

'At least if it's taken up to Murray Island I know it will be left alone and looked after up there. Nobody would do this kind of thing up there,' Bonita said.[9]

On 18 September 1995, Eddie Mabo was reburied at Las, his village on Mer, on the sacred hill of his ancestors where legend says that Malo the sacred octopus lives.

CHAPTER 13

New Law, New Land

The Native Title Act received Royal Assent on 24 December 1993 and commenced operation on 1 January 1994. The Act included four practical responses to the challenge Eddie Mabo had taken to the High Court.

First, the law recognised and protected Native Title.

Second, it established procedures for dealing with Native Title questions in the future. The National Native Title Tribunal was created to determine Native Title rights and assess compensation.

Third, the Act provided a 'right to negotiate' with miners. Here, the law allowed for a period of negotiation — but not a right to veto — new mining activities. If there was no agreement between miners and Aborigines within six months, the matter would go to independent arbitration; and if the arbitration process favoured the Aboriginal claim, it could be over-ridden by the relevant Commonwealth, State or Territory Minister.

Fourth, the Act validated past acts extinguishing Native Title. As these clearly had been racially discriminatory, the law provided a right to compensation for actions undertaken since the establishment of law against such discrimination — the *Racial Discrimination Act* of 1975.

A fund was also established to purchase land for Indigenous people who could no longer make legally valid Native Title claims.

The Act did not extinguish Native Title on pastoral leases. It only dealt with Crown lands. The preamble did, however, state the law's presumption that Native Title had been extinguished by leasehold, although a preamble does not have the force of law. In drawing up amendments to the *Native Title Act* after the *Wik* decision, the Howard Government was to return repeatedly to the preamble in the 1993 Act. Paul Keating, who had been Prime Minister at the time of the enactment of the original Native Title legislation, responded that he had always expected the question of the coexistence of Native Title with leasehold would have to be determined later, in the courts.

And, sure enough, the matter did find its way into the courts, in the case of *The Wik Peoples v. The State of Queensland*. It was no small matter, because there are ten thousand such leases covering 42 per cent of the continent. The High Court handed down its decision on 23 December 1996.

— • —

The Wik peoples live on the west side of the Cape York Peninsula, near Aurukun and Wiepa. Their traditional country surrounds the Archer River, extending south almost to Pormpuraaw and inland to the centre of the peninsula.

The Wik have been living in their country for so long that their oral histories still include accounts of the time when the rivers ran across great plains to a vast inland lake, and how that lake was filled with sea water and the plains flooded when the oceans rose.

Much more recently, they tell of a ship that sailed down the coast, and its crew that tried to abduct their women, and how the Wik warriors drove the sailors away with their spears. The story takes three days to tell. It is told in the first person, for it is a recent enough event, and the names of the kidnapped women are still suppressed so as not to 'shame' their families.[1]

Western accounts locate the same events by numbers. The ship was the *Duyfhen*, a Dutch ship which passed by in 1605. The flooding of the Gulf of Carpentaria took place during the Ice Ages, about fifteen thousand years ago.

By comparison, white people have very short historical memories. They only know about the events of 1605 because they have been written down as history and they can look them up, although their records can't identify the Aboriginal women involved, nor the Dutch sailors. They know about what they call the 'Ice Age,' not because they have any way of remembering it or because they have any historical records, but through the processes of retrospective conjecture they call 'science.'

If you want a stark lesson in history and its absence, visit Stonehenge, that most ancient and sacred of places in the indigenous lands of the English colonialists. Dutifully, the tourists put on headphones that tell the story of the stones. You can walk from viewing point to viewing point, listening hard to the tape of the history-man with the authoritative voice, but there is no history to tell. The only truths are the blindingly obvious kinds of sums we can do in a world where only numbers and the next day matter. A circle three hundred feet in diameter. Stones eighteen feet tall, weighing however many tons; the facts are meaningless, instantly forgettable. But whose place was it? Nobody really knows. How did the stones get there? By dint of geological guesswork, it is known they must have come from Wales, a hundred kilometres away or more. We can only guess what the structure was for by the fact that the sun does seem to strike across the stones at the summer solstice in such a way as to indicate that the builders had a calendar of sorts. History is a circle of blank stones. The past is speechless. We are left mute. When we visited, the farmer next door had stacked his bales of hay to look like the henge; his motives, at least, were legible.

The Wik peoples, together with Australia's other Indigenous peoples, have histories longer than any others on earth. The laws of the land of the Wik peoples are more ancient than any English law. They have the living proof that they have owned their place for a remarkably long time. Their country resonates with age-old meanings. They know its every feature and what each feature truly means. They have words for all of it, explanations for everything.

Nobody knows who built Stonehenge. Faced with its palpable presence, we're lost for words. Our explanations are purely hypothetical. But the Wik people know they have owned their lands at least five, ten thousand years — and probably fifty or even a hundred thousand years — before Stonehenge was even built. White people don't have memories so ancient, even of their own indigenous places.

Then the pastoralists came to the Wik peoples' country. Their claim was decidedly thin by comparison; their argument in the High Court was about two areas of leasehold land.

The Mitchellton lease was for 1385 square kilometres. It was issued in 1915, but forfeited for non-payment of rent in 1918. This lease had never been occupied. Yet, from the Queensland Government's point of view, this was leasehold land, not Crown land, and thus not open to a Native Title claim under the terms of the Federal Government's 1993 Native Title Act.

The adjoining Holroyd River Holding lease was issued in 1945 for 2830 square kilometres, and was extended for another 30 years in 1974. An inspector who visited the lease in 1984 reported that the lease was 'not permanently occupied,' and that there were no fences and no buildings. There were just one thousand head of cattle on the property at the time. Another inspection in 1988 found that a shed had been built, but the only cattle on the property were feral.

As far as the Wik people were concerned, the leases amounted to little more than 'the signing of some documents by people in Brisbane.' This is how they put it in their case to the High Court. Justice Kirby summed up the situation as follows:

> Those facts ... demonstrate the very limited occupation of the land which was expected and regarded as normal under pastoral leases. They show how Aboriginal law and tradition could readily survive in such an environment because of the very limited contact which was inherent in these pastoral leases, between Aboriginals and those connected with the lessee ... In pastoral leases of the kind described in the evidence in this case, talk of 'exclusive possession' or 'exclusive occupation' has an unreal quality.[2]

By a majority of four to three, the High Court found that the grant of a lease does not extinguish remaining Native Title rights. But where there is a conflict of rights, the rights of the leaseholder prevail over Indigenous rights.

The majority judges explained that, as a matter of law, pastoral leases were never intended to extinguish Native Title rights. They were a unique form of land tenure invented for Australian conditions by the British Colonial Office in the middle of the nineteenth century. These conditions were a product of the squatting rush of the 1830s and 1840s. When the Imperial government faced a land grab it could not stop, it decided the next best thing it could do was regulate the process. The instrument invented to achieve this end was the pastoral lease.

To explain the peculiar character of the pastoral lease, Justice Kirby turned to the words of Earl Grey, the Colonial Secretary, and a dispatch he had sent to the Governor of New South Wales:

> [I]t should be generally understood that Leases granted for this purpose give the grantees only an exclusive right of pasturage for their cattle, and of cultivating such Land as they may

require within the large limits thus assigned to them, but that these Leases are not intended to deprive the Natives of their former right to hunt over these Districts, or to wander over them in search of subsistence, in the manner to which they have been heretofore accustomed, from the spontaneous produce of the soil except over land actually cultivated or fenced in for that purpose.[3]

These words were from records that Henry Reynolds, by way of historical reminder, had brought to light through his archival research. Reynolds's work is referenced five times by the justices in the Wik judgement.

Earl Grey's legal interpretation, Reynolds also showed, was underpinned by moral scruples of Empire, scruples that were often to be disregarded on the Australian frontier. 'In assuming their territory,' Earl Grey said, 'the settlers in Australia have incurred a moral obligation of the most sacred kind, [and that is] to avert the destruction of the native race as a consequence of the occupation of their territory by British subjects.'[4]

It was an sacred obligation that the law had forgotten, too — until the Mabo and Wik judgements.

— • —

Anne Warner followed Bob Katter as Minister for Aboriginal Affairs in Queensland when the Goss Labor Government came to power in 1989. She remained Minister — 'Family Services and Aboriginal Affairs' was the full title of her portfolio — until the 1995 elections, when she retired from Parliament. These were turbulent years in Aboriginal Affairs, to be sure: first the Mabo decision in 1992, then the 1993 Federal Native Title Act, and then, not long after Anne had left Parliament, the Wik decision. The land rights argument in these years was very much a Queensland thing, although at each step in the story it quickly became a national issue.

'One thing I have to say about Bob Katter is that he did break the absolute patriarchy that existed in Aboriginal Affairs in Queensland, by setting up the Deed of Grant in Trust for communities.

'And I still don't know how he got rid of Paddy Killoran, who had been the Director-General of Aboriginal Affairs in Queensland since the 1960s and was a real patriarchal icon. He was responsible for some of the most extensive removals and movements of Aboriginal people against their will in Queensland.

'He was still there when Bob Katter became the Minister, and somehow he got rid of him. Killoran was a mate of Joh's [Joh Bjelke-Petersen, the Premier at the time], so how Bob did that, I just don't know. It was the best thing Bob Katter did in his life.

'You see, the Aboriginal Affairs Department in Queensland used to be a very powerful department. With this guy in charge, it was actually the spearhead for the settlement of Queensland. The continuing white settlement of Queensland.

'The department's job was to get Aboriginal people out of the way, to promote the interests of the incoming settlers. And in order to do that, you had to round them up, put them in missions, incarcerate them and put walls around them.'

We're talking to Anne in her home, an old Queenslander in an inner-city suburb of weatherboard houses captured by one of the huge, snaking bends in the Brisbane River. Queensland is almost another country sometimes, and there's something sensuous about its difference: the smell of the humidity, the swish of the ceiling fans, the sway of the palms outside the window, the shade of the latticed verandah.

Anne and her husband had seen a vision of this difference from afar and accepted the calling to a new way of life. But was it the Australian — or the Queensland — way of life that they entered?

'There was this lovely picture in the paper with these palm trees, and it said, "Come to Australia and earn three times as much as you earn in Britain." My husband was a teacher, and we said, OK, three small kids on a teacher's salary in Britain is not much fun, and the weather's lousy. So we came. It was January 1975.

'We only came for two years. My husband got a contract for two years. We thought we'd give it a go. A bit of travel, a bit of sunshine, wouldn't hurt.

'It's funny, actually, because I went to this very conservative Catholic girls' school in Birmingham. I had done all the usual sorts of things that a young person does. I travelled. I became marginally involved in a number of far-left parties. I never actually joined any of them, because I couldn't quite get one that suited perfectly. There were always so many slight differences between them, slight variations in dogma. You know, the sort of brawls there used to be between the Stalinists and the Trotskyists and the State Capitalists. The typical Monty Python debate about the Judean People's Front.

'I remember I was given this exercise at school to write a speech as a victorious candidate. So I imagined myself to be a Communist Party candidate, and gave a speech about how we were going to do this, that and the other. I ended the speech by, "And anybody who doesn't agree with the propositions that we're putting forward, they may like to take themselves down to the Tilbury docks where there will be boats departing for Australia."'

She laughs.

'... Because Australia had the White Australia Policy and an international image of gross conservatism. It stood for everything that was most despicable about Britain.

'But Gough Whitlam changed all that. Gough Whitlam actually made it sound like Australia was somewhere to go.

'And when Edward Heath surprisingly won the British election, I thought fascism was around the corner. Little did we know, because the next conservative leader was to be Margaret Thatcher.'

So this is why they came to Australia; or Queensland, to be precise.

'Now we didn't know anything about Queensland. We didn't hear about Joh Bjelke-Petersen until we got into the taxi as we left the airport. The taxi driver said, "Oh, Joh, a lot of people don't like him, but I don't think he's that bad." We'd decided on Queensland because we knew nothing about the importance of State politics in Australia. I thought Australia was like Britain — a nation.'

Whitlam was sacked at the end of the year Anne and her family arrived in Australia, so she joined the local branch of the Australian Labor Party. Seven years later she was a member of the Queensland Parliament.

'It's a very funny story, really. Our candidate in 1980 was a guy called Morrie Dwyer. He was nice and an entertaining sort of bloke, an economics lecturer. But he got a job in Rocky, so he was moving and we didn't have a candidate. The seat hadn't been held by Labor for 25 years. It was Vince Gair's old seat.'

Gair had been one of the Catholics who left the Australian Labor Party in the fifties to form the Democratic Labor Party. 'The Split' kept Labor out of government for a generation as the DLP consistently supported the conservatives.

'There was a working-class area in the seat, around here.'

Anne still lives in her former electorate. Since they moved in, the streets of timber cottages have steadily been gentrified.

'Then there were the flash houses along the river, where they all voted conservative. And there was the DLP area of Annerley, with the red brick Catholic church on the hill. You could always tell where the DLP was strong because there were always red brick churches on hills.

'We hadn't had the seat for a very, very long time. So it was still an academic exercise, being a candidate. There was no expectation that you could win. So our branch — we'd set up a new left-wing branch, and we'd become the movers and shakers in the area — sat around and said, "One of us has to be the candidate, otherwise the right wing will get the candidacy." There was no way we were going to let that happen. "So it's got to be one of us."

'We all sat round and said, "You do it," "No, you do it." One woman said, "No, I know I can't do it. I've got a child out of wedlock and the electorate's not ready for that yet." Another woman said, "My husband's on social security, and the electorate's not ready for the unemployed or their families to go into Parliament yet." A bloke who was sitting next to her said, "No, no, I won't do it. It's not a safe seat. It's a waste of time. I've got better things to do with my life." And the next woman said, "I'm studying to be a lawyer. It takes a lot of work, a lot of effort, and you're not going to win it in the end."

'We'd gone around the room. And then it came to me.

'"Don't look at me," I said. "I'm black."'

She laughs. Anne had been born in Lucknow, India, and her family had migrated to England when she was a child.

'But as a mum who wasn't working, I had more time on my hands. I undertook it on the grounds that we didn't think we were going to win.'

It was 1982, and the Commonwealth Games were about to be held in Brisbane.

'One of the first things I did was become involved in the Commonwealth Games protests. They were about land rights. Aboriginal people used the Games as a forum. And if you protested in Queensland at the time, you could predict that Joh Bjelke-Petersen was going to arrest you. He'd banned street marches and public protests.'

'So I went out and got arrested. The headline was "Queensland Labor Candidate Arrested."

'It was part of the strategy. You'd get footage in the media of police bashing people. Story after story after story. That's how you'd get your issue up. I mean, that's what the conservatives don't understand about this oppression business. If you oppress people you just give them a platform. The Commonwealth Games was our big chance. The whole world was watching. The BBC even did a documentary on it.

'People see it as putting your life on the line by being in a rowdy demonstration. Before the Games protests, I had already been arrested three times in civil liberties demonstrations. It's a tactic that we used over and over again — to get arrested and then clog up the gaols and refuse to pay the fine. They've got to think again before the next time they decide to take you on. Each time, they had to get eight hundred police in from the country to control a couple of thousand demonstrators in Brisbane who simply wanted to walk down the street.

'Anyhow, I made sure there was very strong Labor Party participation. I wanted the Labor Party to be seen to be aggressively opposing Bjelke-Petersen.

'So my campaign manager put out this press statement saying what I had done in the Games protest and why I had done it. And of course, because I was a left-winger and a woman, large numbers of people showed up to work on my campaign.

'A woman also came up who'd recently been elected in the Victorian elections, in 1982 when John Cain became the Labor Premier. She knew all about campaigning, so she showed me how to do it. She kept saying, "Oh, it's easy. You just go onto the street and you just talk to people." And I'm saying, "Can I talk to them about civil liberties? Can I talk to them about industrial issues? Can I talk to them about land rights? So what will I talk to them about?"

'She led me out there, and accosted all these poor passers-by with, "I'd like you to meet the next member for Kurilpa, Anne Warner." And I'd sort of shrink into shop doorways and behind lamp posts. I found that level of campaigning very, very hard. Very hard indeed.

'I also happened to have a very able campaign director, Kath Ratterly, who took no notice of the view that we couldn't win the seat. She had me doorknocking the electorate for eighteen months before the election.

'Every weekend for eighteen months before the bloody election. And I hated it with a passion. The idea of going up to somebody and saying "Please vote for me" scared me to death. It wasn't a political argument as far as I was concerned. It was sort of begging.'

She laughs again.

'But I ended up winning the seat in the 1983 elections, against a former Liberal Attorney-General, Sam Dumarney. He'd had the seat for quite a long time. We needed three-and-a-half per cent to win. I got four per cent. The overall swing to Labor that election was just two per cent.

'And the other funny thing was this. Sam, poor man, was of Lebanese origin. My campaign workers told me that when people saw my name, they said things like, "Well, we're voting for Anne Warner, the real Aussie, rather than Sam Dumarney, the wog." My picture was up around the place, but they mustn't have noticed. They went for the Anglicised name.

'Sam used to have this little slogan saying "Sam's the Man," which, you know, made the point that he was standing against a woman. And so my supporters went round and graffitied it to say "Sam's only a Man."'

In the Labor Party's long history in Queensland, Anne Warner was just the second woman to be elected to Parliament. For her first two terms, she was the only woman.

'And then, after two terms in Opposition, we finally won Government and I became a Minister, the first ever woman Minister in a Queensland Labor Government.'

We ask whether she was surprised to win the seat back in 1983.

'Oh, staggered.'

And we ask what the win did to her life.

'Destroyed it.'

A grimmer laugh, this time.

'No, I found it very difficult to come to terms with, being a Member of Parliament. The parquet floors bothered me, and the sense that I'd been projected into a position that an ordinary person shouldn't be in.'

She's anxious, edgy, waiting for the phone to ring. Five years out of Government, she's still being hounded for actions she took as Minister. Allegations from a person who's the Director of the Enterprise Council, some nefarious organisation that nobody seems to know anything about, but who also writes speeches for the leader of Pauline Hanson's One Nation Party in the Queensland Parliament. When she'd come to power in 1989, and on the advice of the Crown Solicitor, she'd ordered documents destroyed from a strangely constituted inquiry that the Bjelke-Petersen Government had conducted into a youth correctional centre. A decade later, the issue was still in the media, and the allegation was that she had ordered the documents destroyed to cover up paedophilia. The current Labor Government had, contrary to the thirty-year rule, taken the highly unusual step of re-opening Cabinet documents.

The phone rings. It's the media again. After the call, Anne curses the right-wing forces that will never let someone like her rest. It's in the nature of her business, her calling.

'Family Services and Aboriginal Affairs. I always said that anybody who had any reason to believe that they were excluded unfairly from the community was a client of my department. There were people with intellectual disability. There were women who were victims of domestic violence. There were abused children. There were homeless youth. I suppose child care was the only respectable service that we provided, the only service that was not for dysfunctional people or people who were seriously disadvantaged.

'We created the department from a number of smaller ones. I also had Ethnic Affairs. We pulled together Ethnic Affairs, Aboriginal Affairs, Child Protection and Juvenile Justice. I think, in size, we were something like second or third after Primary Industries and Education.'

Anne was also a key player in the huge changes in Indigenous affairs that were going on at the time, working away at the State level at the same time as the new Native Title laws were being made in the High Court and by the Federal Government.

'In the Indigenous area, one of things I tried to do was to get rid of the old patriarchy. My view was that the department had to move from being the mother and father of all Aboriginal people, which it had been historically, to providing a service in the same way as everybody else provides a service.

'Then there was the question of land and local self-government. Aboriginal people want to maintain different structures to white society in terms of the way they govern their communities. Remember they're not rate-based. There's no revenue on those communities. They basically started off as prisons. And often they're still bloody prisons, and simply dysfunctional. Aboriginal people didn't choose to go there. They were sent there.

'Under the *Aboriginal Land Act*, which we introduced in 1991, there was the capacity to disperse those communities by giving back appropriate parcels of land to people who have historical links with that land or who have traditional interest.

'We started this by setting up outstations like the one at Gregory, which is out from Doomadgee in the Gulf country. I would argue, and this is controversial, that the township of Doomadgee is probably the most depressing Aboriginal community there is. The Plymouth Brethren went there in the 1920s and set it up as a mission. It's a very poor community. It's ridden by alcoholism. And it's in the middle of bloody nowhere. If the Nicholson River dries up, it has no water. Bob Katter built a weir, so the water is actually collected a little bit, but there is still a water problem there because it's such dry country and we've had drought for all these years. My view was that we should try to hand back parcels of land out of town as quickly as we possibly could and allow people to build their own communities in their traditional homelands.

'This, and the Port Stewart outstation — I am very proud of these achievements. They were an important part of getting the Homelands Movement going.

'Port Stewart particularly, on the coast near Coen. A group of Aboriginal people were living there in the 1960s, and the local pastoralists at Silver Plains complained that they were stealing cattle. Then in 1962, one of the young Aboriginal women, a sixteen-year-old, got pregnant to the pastoralist's son. He'd been writing to the Department of Native Affairs to try to get them moved off for a long time. So, the Department of Native Affairs sent in a boat, and the officers told the Lana Lana people who were living at the mouth of the Port Stewart River at the time, "Get on this boat. You're going for medical examinations in Bamaga." As they were leaving, they saw their houses being burnt down and all their dogs shot. They were simply dumped in Bamaga.

'This was how Paddy Killoran operated. He had this view that you had to herd them all up. There were already five communities that had been moved to Bamaga, at the very northern tip of Australia. They'd been sent almost to the point where they could be pushed off the edge. There's Bamaga itself, which is an Islander community. Seisia, which is another Islander community. Injenu, which is where the original Aboriginal inhabitants live. New Mapoon, which is where the people live who were moved when the huge Comalco bauxite mine was set up on their lands down the Gulf at Mapoon. And there's Umagico which is for the Lockhart River people. All squeezed in at the top of the Cape. And then the Lana Lana people were sent there as well.

'From about five years prior to us getting into government, maybe a bit longer, they had been going back to their old stomping ground, their old land, and set up a camp there. They desperately wanted title.

'So we gave it to them. It was one of our handbacks. And now there's a flourishing community there again.'

And after Wik and the 1998 Native Title Amendment Act, where are things going now? we ask.

'I think the stupid part about it is that Howard and a number of State Governments seem to be hell-bent on going over the top with their levels of oppression and their levels of disregard. The problem is their complete inability to find a middle way. That's the only way to defuse radical action.'

'It's really silly politics on their part. But I'm not in the business of advising the right. It's pathological. The zero-tolerance kind of mentality.'

She laughs again.

'They're like the rigid and narrow-minded school teacher who stands in front of the class and who says, "If we allow you to do that, we don't know what you will do next."

'Of course what you will do next is to behave like a human being, and when they try to stop you, then you just do something more extreme.'

CHAPTER 14

Extinguishment by the Bucketful

After the Wik decision, the Howard Government set out to redefine Native Title rights generally, and particularly on pastoral leases. Their answer was the so-called 'ten-point plan.' The problem was that if the plan was to become law it had to be passed by a Senate in which independents and minority parties held the balance of power, and they were generally sympathetic to Native Title. A wrenching public debate was to go on for a year and a half until, in July 1998, the Native Title Amendment Act finally passed through the Senate and received Royal Assent.

As his contribution to the public discussion, Prime Minister John Howard appeared on national television holding up a map of Australia with the parts coloured in brown — more than three quarters of the continent — where Native Title claims could potentially be made. Peering over the top of the map, he said:

> Let me just show your viewers that this shows 78 per cent of the land mass of Australia — coloured brown on the map. Now, the Labor Party and the Democrats are effectively saying that the Aboriginal people of Australia should have the potential right to veto over 78 per cent of the land mass of Australia.[1]

Deputy Prime Minister Tim Fischer said on the radio that 'There are bucketloads of extinguishment in the ten-point plan.'

According to ATSIC, the true figure is closer to 12 per cent, as full Native Title ownership claims are only possible on vacant Crown land. These are mostly in remote Western Australian desert country, and even there claims could only be successful if traditional connections had been maintained. Another 15 per cent was already in Aboriginal hands under land rights legislation, leasehold or reserves — so these were hardly under threat, and even there, no right to veto resources development exists. As well, of course, there is the 42 per cent of the land mass subject to pastoral leases; here, nobody has ever suggested that Native Title can displace existing economic interests, or prevent future economic activities. So the development potential of the nation was never facing the kind of dire and immediate danger suggested by the brown expanses on the Prime Minister's map.

A rush of community support for Native Title followed. A sea of sixty thousand plastic hands was planted in the grounds outside Parliament House, each signed by a supporter of Native Title. Meetings and rallies around Australia were organised by organisations like DONT (Defenders of Native Title) and ANTaR (Australians for Native Title and Reconciliation). Church leaders roundly criticised the ten-point plan.

The Native Title Amendment Act was introduced to the Senate in December 1997. It was tossed back and forth between the Senate and the House of Representatives for six months. No law in the history of the Commonwealth had been debated for so many hours — 109 hours in the Senate alone.

Then, in June 1998, Pauline Hanson's One Nation Party won nearly a quarter of the vote and eleven seats in the Queensland election. Her party's policy on Native Title was as simple as the concept of 'one nation' itself. She had a 'one-point plan': blanket extinguishment of native title. In the world of metaphorical quantities, a blanket is greater than a bucket.

Prime Minister Howard kept pressing on. If the Senate would not pass his ten-point plan, he would take the country to a double dissolution election. In constitutional terms, this meant that all members of both Houses of Parliament would be up for re-election, simultaneously, and if the ten-point plan still failed to pass the Senate, it could be taken to a joint sitting of both Houses of the Commonwealth Parliament, where it was likely Howard could muster a majority. However, the thing about a double dissolution as opposed to the usual half-Senate election was that the entry point for Pauline Hanson's One Nation candidates into the Upper House was reduced from about 14 per cent of the vote in each State to about 7 per cent. A double dissolution would most likely hand One Nation the balance of power in the Senate.

Even after the Queensland State election, Howard said he was willing to pursue this course of action if necessary. His advice to Queensland National Party leader Rob Borbidge was that he should, if he could, form a Coalition with One Nation.[2] This was indicative of Howard's own thinking about how he might govern if One Nation won the balance of power in the Senate.

With Labor, the Democrats and the Greens holding strong in the Senate, it was now up to Independent Tasmanian Senator Brian Harradine. He had vowed not to give way on Native Title.

After the shock of the Queensland election, however, and Howard's obvious willingness to go to a 'race' election, he caved in. 'I blinked,' Harradine said.[3] But he did manage to secure another 88 minor amendments to the legislation, which brought to a total of 314 the amendments to the original ten-point plan. The overall framework of the original plan remained nevertheless more or less intact.

The main outcomes of the final legislation were a reduction in the Native Title rights granted in the 1993 legislation, and a much narrower definition of Native Title rights over pastoral leases than those granted by a majority of the High Court Justices in the Wik case.

First, there was to be a higher 'threshold test.' Proof of regular physical access to the lands under claim was now required, and not just a traditional connection. The only exception was where a person or their parents were forcibly removed from their country — the 'locked gates–stolen generation' exception.

Second, the right to negotiate was removed entirely for all private infrastructure projects other than mining. In the case of mining, there would no longer be a right to negotiate at the mining exploration stage. There would be no right to negotiate mining infrastructure and mining lease renewals. And even when it was decided that mining should go ahead, although there was to be consultation with Native Title owners, this was without the requirement for negotiation in good faith. Finally, the Federal Minister and the States could, at their discretion, override arbitrated outcomes that favoured the Native Title claimants.

Third, a large range of other titles were now deemed to extinguish Native Title, even though such titles may not extinguish Native Title at common law — for instance, agricultural, commercial, residential and community-purpose leases. These include scheduled interests such as Queensland's Grazing Homestead Perpetual Leases, which cover 12 per cent of the State and for which, at common law, there was an even stronger case for the existence of Native Title than there had been for the kinds of pastoral leases the Wik decision examined. Native Title was deemed extinguished by any of these titles, even the titles which lasted for just a short time or were issued a long time ago. Any such 'confirmation of extinguishment' is sufficient even to deny Native Title claimants access to the courts.

Fourth, the law provides for a substantial expansion of pastoralists' rights to include higher intensity 'primary production activities.' Until the new Native Title Act, pastoral leases were restricted to grazing animals and infrastructure incidental to grazing, such as building fences and dams. The Native Title Amendment Act upgraded all of these leases to include agriculture, forestry, horticulture, aquaculture and farm tourism. Clearly, all of these extra activities have a far greater potential to affect Native Title rights than pastoral activity. Also, as Native Title gives way to the interests and rights of the leaseholder and as there is no requirement for consultation or negotiation, these activities can and will extinguish Native Title at the whim of the leaseholder. Native Title owners are entitled to compensation for any impairment to their property rights, but they have no right to challenge or prevent that impairment.

So, here's the outcome: all of a sudden, ten thousand pastoralist leaseholders are handed sweeping property rights they didn't have before. Some of the leaseholdings are simply enormous, and so is the scale of their Native Title windfall. Among the corporate leaseholders, the largest are S. Kidman and Co, which holds 11.7 million hectares (117,000 square kilometres), and Stranbroke Pastoral Company, which holds 10.1 million hectares (101,000 square kilometres). Each of these holdings is considerably larger than Ireland, Portugal or Austria. The two largest private leaseholders were closely connected to the Howard Government. Ian McLachlan, a significant leaseholder, was the Defence Minister when the Native Title Amendment Act was passed. His cousin, Hugh McLachlan, is the largest private leaseholder: 4.7 million hectares or 47,000 square kilometres, a holding larger than Denmark, Holland or Switzerland. The family of the President of the National Party, Donald McDonald, owns 3.1 million hectares, the second largest private leaseholding. Whilst the ten-point plan was being debated, Donald McDonald paid $4 million for a Queensland pastoral lease which was subject to a Native Title claim. With the passing of the legislation, the McLachlans and the McDonalds were to be made considerably wealthier overnight. And, if and when there are any successful claims for compensation by the Native Title holders, Australian taxpayers will have to foot the bill.[4]

Fifth, and this, perhaps, is the most important point: the Racial Discrimination Act was effectively suspended when it comes to matters of land ownership. Where the Native Title Act was clear in its intent, it is to override the Racial Discrimination Act. The presumption in the very drafting of the Native Title Amendment Act is that it is discriminatory in the terms of the legal definition spelt out in the Racial Discrimination Act. This alone is an admission that it will, in fact, do things to one group's property rights that would not be done to another's.

But herein lies the biggest problem with the Native Title Amendment Act of 1998: the Racial Discrimination Act is no ordinary law. Constitutionally, it was enacted under the Commonwealth's external affairs power. And in international law, the Racial Discrimination Act meets Australia's obligations under the International Convention for the Elimination of All Forms of Racial Discrimination. But now, we've suspended the operation of the Racial Discrimination Act in the case of property rights.

The Committee for the Elimination of All Forms of Racial Discrimination concluded in March 1999 that 'The amended Act appears to create legal certainty for governments and third parties at the expense of indigenous title.'

The conclusion is couched in the diplomatic language of international law, but the 'early warning and urgent action' procedure the Committee set in train means one thing only: that the provisions of the Native Title Amendment Act of 1998 constitute something that would, in international law, be defined as racial discrimination.

— • —

Bob Katter fumes about the ten-point plan and the Native Title legislation.

'It's unworkable, hypocritical, Mickey Mouse. The people who came up with the Native Title legislation have absolutely no understanding at all.

'Native Title, who knows what it means? Nobody knows what it means.

'I mean quite frankly — and you know the black leadership would never admit this, but they know it as well as I do — you've got to have private ownership. But, I've got to defend them, you know, if they were to give up on Native Title, then they've got no leverage at all.

'And you know, some of these mining companies, their actions are just appalling, absolutely appalling. They just ride roughshod over people. They're going to use this road, and then this road is going to be destroyed. Then they're going to take the water out of the river and there's no water left in the river. Then you find out that they're going to employ no locals at all. Century Zinc is a classic example of that. The original proposal was to employ no locals. No blacks, no whites, nobody. Just fly people in from the coast, five days on, five days off.

'So I went and negotiated with them. At least some of the locals got something, you know, I mean the black locals, at least someone locally got something. But without Native Title the locals would have got nothing.

'So you know, I can see the black leadership's point of view.

'But with Native Title, nobody owns anything. You have these sort of mythical nobodies owning everything. Nobody can make a decision on anything. No money can be raised for improvement.

'Now, of all people, I know that Aboriginals can run a cattle station. I've had cattle all my life. I've lived with Aboriginal people all my life. And I know that they can run the cattle stations. But the reason that they're not running them is, it's not their station. When the stations change over into Aboriginal hands, they end up belonging to some mythical land council. And whenever I go to talk to anyone about the station, I end up talking to a white bloke. The Aboriginals have no sense of ownership over those stations at all. All that happens is more and more money is taken from black people, and it's effectively put into white pockets.

'I was up at Yarrabah the other day, and one of my Aboriginal friends there was banging his fist on the table saying, "This is the only place in the world where a person cannot own his own home." This is Yarrabah, an Aboriginal community, and this is Australia.

'Then I was taking to another woman I know there, and the grocery store is falling down. She pulled me up and said, "How about helping us do something about getting it fixed? The council has condemned it."

'And I said, "They had to condemn it. Get some money and buy it and do it up." She said she'd tried that, but she can't get title. And I said, "You know the reasons you can't get title."And she said "Yep."

So I said, "What can I say?"

— • —

Mick Dodson doesn't like the way Native Title has turned out either. It's a title that is just so much weaker than any other. He says that the Howard Government has passed a law that is clearly racially discriminatory, a law in which one group's property rights are easily dispensed with, and another group's elevated.

But he doesn't agree with Bob Katter that freehold is the best solution to the land rights problem.

'Bob's well-meaning, and a lot of blackfellas vote for him.

'But the problem is that freehold is a commodity that you can trade, that you can buy and sell. It's a fair thing to say you can't raise money on that, and that's a problem. But look what's happened overseas, where the business people have come in and bought up the land from indigenous people. The most recent example is in Alaska where they set up land tenure for the Native Americans in such a way that in a space of twenty years they have lost most of their bloody land.'

— • —

We ask Charlie Perkins to sum up the land rights situation after the Native Title Amendment Act.

Part of him is despairing.

'We've lost. We've lost. Lost. We have lost with this Government on the land rights question.'

Another part of him recognises genuine progress.

'But we have gained a lot as well. The decisions of the High Court still stand. They can't be entirely got around. We have got Native Title in a form that we are not happy with, but at least we have got it there on the books. We have gone some of the way. It's a sort of incremental thing. On the battleground between us and the Government, we are gaining ground all the time. But it is not the great leap forward we should have had.'

— • —

The British colonists of the eighteenth and nineteenth centuries, and then the Australian nationalists of the twentieth century, thought the problems they were having in their relationships with the original Old World inhabitants of Australia would, in the course of time, go away.

They haven't. In fact, with time they seem to have got worse. The relationship of Indigenous and settler peoples over the question of land has become all the more difficult.

So what do we do? Where do we go from here? How do we prevent things from getting worse?

A conservative approach, an approach which has half a chance of practical success, would be built on three foundations:

Firstly, let's be true to the original terms of the colonial settlement. Here, of course, we need to be selective. One aspect of that settlement was illegal brutality, callous dispossession and post-event moral and legal rationalisations such as the doctrine of *terra nullius*. However, that settlement also included important moments of shame and regret, of good faith, of decency, of compensation and of legal accommodation. The conservative point here is this: that the community of settlers has the resources within its historical and legal traditions to do what is just and proper. They have the capacity to imagine and act in a way that recognises the Indigenous claim to the land and restores dignity to Australian Indigenous peoples and their civilizations. The High Court's Mabo and Wik decisions, and the struggles of Eddie Mabo and Henry Reynolds, represent this conservative tradition, the tradition of taking the settlers at the best of their word. Justice does not have to be a radical act.

Secondly, let's also obey international law. Racial discrimination is a serious political crime in the new, globalised moral community of nations. The Committee for the Elimination of All Forms of Racial Discrimination has told Australia that, under the terms of the International Convention for the Elimination of All Forms of Racial Discrimination, the provisions of the Native Title Act of 1998 constitute racial discrimination. We leave this legislation on the books unchanged at our moral and legal peril.

And thirdly, let's build accommodations which have been arbitrated in a way that is fair, and set up procedures that are equitable from the point of all parties involved. Here the parties are two: the Government of the majority of Australians on one hand and the Indigenous interest on the other. The Indigenous interest may not be happy with the final result of negotiations, but there must have been negotiations, and if the consent of both parties is not achievable, the outcome must have been arbitrated in such a way that both parties respect the fairness, the neutrality and the justice of the arbitration process. The difference is between the procedurally fair High Court process and the complete failure to negotiate in the process of enacting the 1998 Native Title legislation.

If we were to build on these unexceptionable principles, it does not seem that agreement between the parties should be so difficult. The settlers' titles should remain intact, except that Native Title exists where Indigenous people have a traditional and continuing connection over 'waste' lands; and pastoral leasehold land should be mutually held.

Part of the process of accommodation must include finding ways to ensure that Native Title and the settlers' titles are as strong and as useable as each other. In practical terms, as the law stands land held under Native Title is not easy to use in ways that are other than traditional. Native Title does not have the economic value and social useability of other titles. If land is to be the basis for social and cultural autonomy, it needs to be useable in any way people might choose.

If these things can be achieved, we as a society will have found a practical way to address what has become the most fundamental political problem in the post-Cold War era: the peaceful accommodation of the interests of different peoples within one nation, peoples whose histories, cultures, experiences, laws and claims to sovereignty are fundamentally different, but whose homelands overlap geographically.

If we could achieve this, we would be able to call ourselves a truly pluralist democracy.

CHAPTER 15

Our History and Our Geography

— • —

And now to the third of the difficult relationships between land and people in Australia: the relationship between who we imagine ourselves to be as a people and where we are located on the earth.

— • —

In the nineteenth century, the motto of the rabidly nationalist *Bulletin* had been 'Australia for the White Man and China for the Chows.'

When it came to staking a claim over the continent, Aborigines did not even rank a mention. They weren't so much as noticed when it came to making the nationalist case for who the Australians were, for whose land it was. Those were *terra nullius* days.

But the Chinese were worth a mention. Australia was a place exclusively for the White Man, and this meant, by way of what seemed at the time to be the most obvious of contrasts, it was not a place for the Chinese. Nor was it a place for any of the other coloured people of the region.

Australia for the White Man. This was the moral project of Australians for the first half of the twentieth century.

In many respects it was a new moral project. During the colonial era, the men of Empire, people such as Colonial Secretary Earl Grey, had recognised that Australia was a place where Aboriginal people should also be able to live out their lives with a modicum of human dignity. That's why Earl Grey took the stance he did on the issue of pastoral leases. Later in the century, the same class of men of Empire strenuously resisted the White Australia Policy, because they oversaw an Empire most of whose subjects were coloured, an Empire that was racist in the effect of its actions but which nevertheless felt it had to express some kind of formal respect towards all its various subjects. Until the end of the nineteenth century, Australia's borders had been open, and many of the people who had come to live and work in the colonies were neither white, nor even necessarily British subjects. This included the tens of thousands of Chinese who came during the gold rushes of the second half of the nineteenth century.

The *Bulletin* was one of the clearest and most influential voices of late nineteenth-century Australian nationalism, one of the cultural influences that shaped the new Australian nation as it developed the Federation compact. Among the first laws of the new Federal Parliament were the *Immigration Restriction Act* and the *Pacific Island Labourers' Act*, which ordered that the Queensland Kanakas be deported by 1906.

— • —

When Donald Horne became editor of *The Bulletin* in 1960, the motto had been refined somewhat. The reference to 'the Chow' had already been removed and now it was just 'Australia for the White Man.' He removed the rest of the slogan immediately.

'I was editor of *The Bulletin* twice, first at the beginning of the sixties, and then from 1966 through to 1972. People today forget how recently we had a White Australia Policy, and they forget how much things have changed. It was not that long ago that married women weren't allowed to work in the public service. The sixties were a period of profound change.'

Donald and Myfanwy Horne had invited us to lunch. He's working on another book, part autobiographical, that focuses on the sixties.

Donald is a public intellectual, and a defender of such a role in public life. Indeed, he's led the life of a public intellectual — as editor of *The Bulletin* and *Quadrant*, as Chair of the Australia Council for the Arts, as Chair of the Ideas for Australia program, as a Professor at the University of New South Wales and then Chancellor of the University of Canberra, and as the author of a dozen or so seminal books about Australia.

In 1964, Donald wrote one of the most important books of the Australian century: *The Lucky Country*. It's still in print three and a half decades later, and the title is so often repeated in the public discourse that the words have turned into a kind of national mantra. Unfortunately, some of the irony intended in the title has since been lost.

Here's the original meaning of the title, as explained on the opening page of the last chapter:

> Australia is a country run mainly by second-rate people who share its luck. It lives on other people's ideas, and, although its ordinary people are adaptable, most of its leaders ... so lack curiosity in the events that surround them that they are often taken by surprise. A nation more concerned with styles of life than with achievement has managed to achieve what may be the most evenly prosperous society in the world. It has done so in a social climate largely inimical to originality and the desire for excellence (except in sport) ... According to the rules Australia has not deserved its good fortune.[1]

Donald Horne was expressing a frustration that comes with living in a place of such enormous possibility where some opportunities we have stumbled upon and others we have lost. The problem, he argued, was a failure of imagination, a failure to progress mentally beyond the most obvious aspects of our colonial past.

'When I wrote *The Lucky Country*, I used the expression "identity crisis." I said Australians couldn't act unless they could refer what they were doing back to something in Britain. They saw Australia as an island in the Irish Channel, half way between Ireland and Britain, rather than as a place between the Indian Ocean and Pacific Ocean.' Three and a half decades later, he's reflecting on the book and its times.

This lack of a sense of location, and the sense of being out of place, is one of the recurring themes of *The Lucky Country*. With the end of colonialism from the Indian Ocean to the Pacific, it was essential to put a final end to the White Australia Policy. This was not just an issue of immigration. It also related to the peoples who were colonised by the British takeover of Australia. Throughout Asia, Donald warned back in 1964, 'the Aborigines are taken to be the victims of the "White Australia" policy and the policy is often described as Australian "apartheid."'

Back then, his identity prognosis was clear:

> We are all Asians now. [I]t is up to Australians to seek for similarities in Asians and mutual interests. To take our ideology of fraternalism seriously and apply it to Asians could lead to a creative awakening among Australians.[2]

And this was where Donald Horne's optimism took him, on the last page of *The Lucky Country:*

> One can only hope that events will liberate what is good and progressive in Australians, not perpetuate what is bad ... [and] that the ideal of fraternalism will gradually extend to include the Asian races ... so that ultimately ... Australia's population problem will be solved in what may be the only way it can finally be solved — by large scale Asian immigration ... [To achieve this,] the qualities of Australians should be described and admired and brought into play. Their non-doctrinaire tolerance, their sense of pleasure, their sense of fair play, their interest in material things, their sense of family, their identity with nature, ... their fraternalism, their scepticism, their talent for improvisation, their courage and stoicism. These are great qualities that could constitute the beginnings of a great nation ... [Through this, a] nation will be created with values that have some relation to ordinary human aspiration.[3]

— • —

Decades later, the question of whether 'we are all Asians now' had become a matter of incessant conversation. In 1995, when Labor Foreign Minister Gareth Evans addressed the Asia–Australia Institute, he spoke of:

> an important truth about our relations with the countries to our north, and that is that there is something more distinctive about our emerging relationship with them than is the case about our relationship with most other parts of the world, including Africa and Europe and even North America. Partly it is a matter of geography: we may not be part of the Asian land mass geographically, but we are closer to it than anyone else, and longitudinally we share broadly the same time zones as East Asia.

He mentioned that Asia was the destination for sixty per cent of Australian exports. Seven of our top ten export markets were countries in Asia. Asia represented six of Australia's top ten tourist sources and destinations, two-thirds of our overseas students, half the immigration intake, the majority of foreign languages taught in school. And five per cent of the Australian population was now born in Asia:

> None of these linkages may be enough to make Australia an Asian nation in any comfortable use of ordinary language. But they certainly give some force to the idea that we are an East Asian Hemisphere nation ... Thinking of ourselves occasionally ... as an East Asian hemisphere nation, and having others in this region think of us in this way, can do nothing to harm, and much to advance, Australia's longer term efforts to engage and integrate with this part of the world in which our future so much depends.[4]

When we spoke with Evans's Liberal Party successor, Alexander Downer, he said the same kinds of things.

'Well, inevitably Australia is going through a transition in which it's accommodating itself more comfortably to its regional circumstances. The changes are unavoidable.

'You can see it in the most obvious manifestation of culture, in what people eat. Australia has moved away from the meat and three vegetables, a middle-class English cuisine, to a kind of Eurasian cuisine which is actually quite unique.

'It's more than a metaphor. It's indicative of the kinds of changes we are going through. In my lifetime, and I'm 47, I've seen an extraordinary transformation of the cuisine of the country. It's extraordinary how that's changed and, of course, it reflects the southern European influence on originally northern European cuisine which in turn has now been overlaid with Asian culture.'

— • —

Just before he was elected Prime Minister, John Howard also addressed the Asia–Australia Institute. What he said, however, was in a subtle way quite different to Evans and Downer. His theme, then and since, is that we should not have to trade 'our history' (British, Christian, European) against our geography (Asian, Western Pacific, Indian Ocean):

> [The coalition parties] do not believe that Australia faces some kind of exclusive choice between our past and our future, between our history and our geography. Such a choice is a

phoney and irrelevant one proposed by those with ulterior motives. We do not have to abandon or apologise for our heritage to contribute to Asia and to welcome Asia's importance to our future.[5]

When Pauline Hanson burst onto the Australian political scene in 1996, she made it abundantly clear that she was opposed to 'Asianisation.' As for Asian immigration, 'we are in danger of being swamped by Asians,' she said in her maiden speech of September 1996.

The speech created a furore. For the next six months, Prime Minister Howard decided to stay silent. His silence simply inflamed the furore, not just in Australia, but throughout the region.

'Howard's silence endorses racist fringe.' This was the headline of an editorial in the Bangkok newspaper, *The Nation*. The editorialist pointed out that 'Australia's future is tied to Asia. Howard, however, seems intent on tying himself to a small band of backward-looking political elements.'[6]

Also in Bangkok, the Thai language paper, *Matichon*, commented that, 'as the leader of the Australian Government, Mr Howard cannot escape criticism for failing to condemn racist remarks by an Australian member of Parliament.'[7]

Soon, reports of an increase in racist incidents were circulating in the region. Hong Kong's *South China Morning Post* ran an editorial on Howard's failure to condemn Hanson. It pointed out that 'reports of Asians being spat on in the streets, and their homes damaged, are earning the country a bad press.'[8] The Chinese Ambassador complained of the racist incidents, including attacks on the Chinese consulate in Sydney.[9]

Howard responded by attacking Asian newspapers for misrepresenting him, to which a *Bangkok Post* editorial replied that Mr Howard had 'shot himself in the foot' by failing to distance himself from anti-Asian views. 'Rather than get to the heart of the matter — the bashing of Asia and Asians in Australia — he took aim at his critics.'[10]

On the eve of the 1997 APEC summit in Subic Bay, Malaysian Foreign Minister Badawi said that 'anti-Asian feeling' in some sections of the Australian community was 'a big issue.' 'First, we get the feeling that Australians are not going to be friendly with us, and that's bad. We already have a history of hiccups in our bilateral relations, and then this is done, then we can't help getting that kind of feeling. Two, parents of students studying in Australia too begin to get worried about the safety of their children, especially if this anti-Asian feeling will be widespread, and that's not going to be good.'[11]

Malaysian Prime Minister Mahathir was even more strident in his comments:

> The Aborigines of Australia were granted citizenship, the right to vote and full recognition as human beings only in 1967. But there still survive a few who, even now, believe that the new attitude towards Aborigines and indeed the abolition of the White Australia Policy are mistakes.[12]

Howard finally spoke out against Hanson in May 1997, eight months after the maiden speech, after eight months of silence on the matter. When he did, the *Bangkok Post* ran a front-page story and there were two other stories on Howard and Hanson inside. The paper's editorial said that, given its timing, Howard's attack on Hanson was insincere. It said that Mr Howard had decided to speak out only hours after two Australian polls revealed the Federal Government was losing popularity as a result of the Prime Minister's long silence.[13]

Foreign Minister Downer had shown no such equivocation, publicly stating just weeks after Hanson's maiden speech that:

> If we are to be successful in engaging with our own region — and we have to be — we must absolutely reject old-fashioned, racist, elitist attitudes. It would be deeply destructive to this country if we adopted those sorts of values.[14]

Downer, however, had a very different view of the connections between Australia's history and geography to that held by the Prime Minister.

— • —

'We both went to the same school, by the way,' Donald Horne tells us. John Howard and Donald Horne both went to Canterbury Boys' High in Sydney's working-class inner west; Mary went to Canterbury Girls' High. We laugh.

'I think that John Howard is a freak, I really do.

'When Hanson got up and started saying what she did, it wasn't good for Australia's image.

'It wasn't even a question of idealism. Even if you saw it just as a question of self-interest . . . But he couldn't understand that.

'He created Hanson. If he'd put her down in a courteous twenty-point response, with each point explained, that would have been the end of it.

'Most of his fellow Cabinet members are people who are capable of reacting to circumstances, either out of belief, or opportunistically, or both. But with Hanson, Howard did neither. He seems to have absolutely embedded, stubborn ways of looking at things. Any other conservative Prime Minister, I think, would have handled Hanson entirely differently. Tim Fischer, Alexander Downer . . . '

Downer had been Opposition Leader until he was rolled by Howard in a palace coup in January 1995.

The issue, Donald says, is really one of leadership.

'The change, the abolition of the White Australia Policy, was successfully conducted at the time partly by concealing what was happening. I think politicians could have spoken more positively about what a great achievement that was, and they still could. Also, the transformation in the way Aboriginal people are talked about.

'In one way, I think they have failed us. One thing that a good political leader can do is praise people as they succeed to change, as they make transitions. But too often, they are inclined to look to nothing other than the prejudices of Australians. That's what we have seen lately.'

— • —

Anne Warner's an Australian now, although she comes from another place too, on the other side of the Asian equator.

'Well, I do think that we have to shift the focus to Asia. I think we have to shift the focus to the whole of Asia and not to just South-East Asia. When we talk about Asia, when we think about Asia, we absolutely, mercilessly exclude India.

'India has a population of nine hundred million people. And we don't take any notice of it. We can put our hands on our hips and start jumping up and down about their nuclear devices, which are abhorrent. But we're not doing ourselves any favours if that's all we do.

'It's so close. I happen to have been born there.

'The only time we take notice of what happens there is when Australia plays India in the cricket. I was there last year when Australia was playing India, and the best we could do was have that absurd Shane Warne being sent all these tins of baked beans because he couldn't eat the local tucker.

'It was completely dysfunctional. This is one of the few ways Indians find out about Australia.

'You see, these populations are just so huge. They are just so vast compared to our population. The idea of isolation is nonsense. Absolutely crazy. If you really want to set us up as a target, well go for it. If you really want Indonesia to invade, well then let's pretend that we can have no dialogue, no debate, no trade, you know. Let's just pretend that we're bigger and better than they are, even though we're minute.

'This communist guy I met when I was a young person living in England, an Asian from East Africa, he told me that China was the best bet for communism because it's such a large, vigorous country. So I asked, won't Australia have some ways of keeping communism at bay in that region? Even then I realised that Australia did have a geographical part to play. I was sixteen years old.

'He turned around and said, "If every Chinese just spat into Australia, the whole continent would sink."

'That's the sort of pressure that we're under. Now, you can respond to that with isolationism or you can respond to that by saying, "Well, we'll take our part in this region."

'And it's more than economic rationalism that we need to do. Economic rationalism has been responsible for the bloody collapse of Asia. I think we have to start talking about real partnerships. Not just this trade for trade's sake, but a real relationship based on cultural exchange and understanding of common goals and common benefits.

'It's more about being an open-minded country rather than a closed-minded country. Unfortunately we've started to close the shutters again recently. They have to be prised open again.'

CHAPTER 16

Ending White Australia

In March 1966, Immigration Minister Hubert Opperman issued a statement lifting the formal ban on non-white immigration that had begun with Federation:

> Applications for entry of well-qualified people wishing to settle in Australia will be considered on the basis of their suitability as settlers, their ability to integrate readily, and their possession of qualifications that are in fact positively useful to Australia.'[1]

This was the kind of diplomatic language that was used to signal the end of the White Australia Policy without making it too obvious a public issue, and without meaning to allow immigration that would change the reality of white Australia.

A succession of Immigration Ministers in the fifties and sixties presided over a gradual shift away from the old framework of White Australia and immigration restriction. The aura of Anglo-Tory conservatism exuded by the Menzies Government of the period was deceptive. Moves were afoot that would eventually change the character of Australian society.

During the Ministry of Alexander Downer Senior, the new 1958 *Migration Act* abolished the Dictation Test. Under the 1901 *Immigration Restriction Act*, all prospective migrants to Australia were to be subjected to a fifty-word dictation test, which could be in any 'prescribed' language. The test would not necessarily be in English, as some ably English-speaking — but non-white — subjects of the British Empire might slip through an English test.

Very many considerations lead to the conclusion that life began on sea, first as single cells, then as groups of cells held together by a secretion of mucilage, then as filament and tissues. For a very long time low-grade marine organisms are simply hollow cylinders, through which salt water streams.[2]

This was an English version of the test from 1908.

In practice, the test served its purpose very well. A government memorandum in 1914 reported that all 'Asiatics' sitting for the test happened to have failed.

Alexander Downer's successor, Hubert Opperman, was a person who professed a particular empathy to immigrants and, particularly, to non-Anglo-Saxon immigrants. After all, his grandfather came from Germany; being of German descent could not have been a comfortable thing in Australia between 1914 and 1945. As he told his Parliamentary colleagues:

> We have discussed [immigrants] in newspapers and in this Parliament, at times as though they were not human beings at all … as though they were a new breed of cattle, oblivious to human treatment. Sometimes I wonder that they do not betray more resentment at the parochial treatment that they encounter from some people in this country.[3]

Opperman was a man of openness, a man prepared for change, but he still deported Nancy Prasad, a six-year-old Fijian girl. Nancy had been living with her sister, who was married to an Australian.

Charlie Perkins was at Sydney University at the time. He and a group of students went out to Sydney Airport to protest. Their placards said DON'T DISCRIMINATE AGAINST RACE and A PERSON'S COLOUR SHOULD NOT MATTER.

'Then a group of students got together in one corner and said, "This is not going to do much good. There are dozens of Commonwealth Police around. They will be able to bring her in by some side door and that will be it. It will be all over. We should do something much stronger than hold up placards."

'Then someone suggested, "What if we kidnap her?"

'This did not seem a bad idea.

'In true student style, the family was advised with great speed, and so were a few sympathetic media people.'

Some of the students had taken part in the Freedom Ride. They'd learnt to be bold in their actions.

'Nancy and her uncle got out of the car and I walked up to him and said quietly, "I'll take her now."

'There was one great, hefty, seemingly immovable Commonwealth policeman outside and no reporters or photographers. If you could have seen his face. His jaw dropped.

'All hell was let loose. As the car departed along the airport road, I watched seventy or so policemen, a hundred students, about twenty-five photographers and cameramen all trying to get out of the miserable swinging doors at Mascot at once, whilst students outside were pushing them backwards.'

Charlie took Nancy back to her home.

'Anyway, the police found her immediately and the whole thing was over.'[4]

'We felt it was wrong for the little girl to be thrown out of the country because of her colour,' Perkins told the press. To which Opperman retorted, 'It's a laugh that Perkins screams his head off about the conditions of coloured people in Australia, but tried to keep Nancy here.'

Nancy's reprieve was shortlived. She was still deported.[5]

When Opperman announced in 1966 that people were to be admitted on the basis of their suitability as settlers, he still said that the goal of the immigration policy was to maintain an homogeneous society. He announced that non-Europeans resident in Australia on temporary permits could now apply for citizenship after five years. Previously this period had been fifteen years.

He also pointed out that Australian immigration policy was not written into legislation. 'Instead, the law has been drafted to give the Minister power to admit such persons as he thinks fit and ... Cabinet decides broad policy issues for administration by the Minister.'[6]

Opperman's 'abolition' of the White Australia Policy meant something like, 'We never should have had it; we wish we had never had it; we never really had it because the Dictation Test and other forms of restriction were not explicit about their intent; but we are white, and we have managed stay white, and we will more or less stay white.' Deporting Nancy Prasad was the sort of thing you did when you've no longer got a White Australia Policy, and when you think you never really had one.

Labor's Immigration spokesman, Fred Daly, knew exactly what Opperman meant. He wanted to confirm his understanding of the

1966 changes. 'We expect a firm assurance from the Minister and the Government regarding the protection of our established policy after these changes are implemented.'[7] 'Established policy' meant he was seeking a guarantee that, even though the policy had changed in name, it would not change in practice.

— • —

Neville Roach is Managing Director of Fujitsu Australia and Chair of the National Multicultural Advisory Council.

Fujitsu's Australian headquarters are in Sydney. The company is typical of the IT industry — the more cutting edge and advanced the industry, the more cosmopolitan the corporate culture. In one moment we were entering a foyer with an indoor Japanese garden, black granite and raked stones: references to a Japanese past. In the next, from the foyer to the CEO's office, we were taken through thumb-print access points. Even grubby bodily traces can be turned into the same stuff as words and music and pictures, the zeros and ones which are the lowest common denominator of digital 'convergence.' Past a bevy of workers of every colour and language. Past images and icons of digital triumphalism. If you could call this a science-fiction experience of sorts, you could also call it a culture-fiction experience. And then into another version of the Australian present, a vast CEO's office with views down to the Lane Cove River, high-tech industrial park modernity in the foreground, the city skyline in the background.

'When we were married and we'd just had our young son, my wife decided to do something, a bit of work, and so she became an Avon person. It was 1965.'

Neville starts with a personal story.

'We lived in a fairly affluent area in Adelaide, and she went knocking on doors. And people would slam the door in her face. Certainly, they wouldn't ask her to come in. She was really quite put out by it.

'I said to her, "I have never experienced that kind of treatment, there's something wrong here."

'You see, she wore skirt and blouse, or a Western-style dress.

'So I said, "I think they must think you are Aboriginal, because I have never experienced anything like that. Why don't you wear a sari?" That is what she normally wears anyway. "Let's see what happens."

'From then on, it was "Please come in, please come in and have some tea." People were effusive and friendly, and it became a great social outlet for her.'

'She's always worn a sari throughout her working life, whether it was with Citibank or the Council for Adult Education, or whatever.'

'One of the good things about Australia in those days was that there were so few non-whites that we really had, I don't like to use the words, "celebrity value." We certainly had curiosity value.'

Neville Roach came to Australia in 1961. He didn't mean to migrate, because at the time he didn't think it was possible.

'I came to Australia on a transfer, I came here on a temporary assignment. And at that time there was the White Australia Policy.

'I worked for an Indian insurance company that had established itself here in Australia as its first foray into a Western country. It wanted to try out Australia to see if things would be viable in other Western countries. And I was sent out here on a four-year assignment.

'The business here in Australia was running into quite serious difficulties with local management. They couldn't understand how our people could be of great value because Australians were so much better. Ironically, of course, the insurance industry was one of the least-educated industries in Australia, whereas everyone working for the company in India had to be honours graduates to get selected. I was selected out of twelve hundred applications for a group of sixty or so people. If anything, you know, we had more skills and knowledge, but you had to convince local management to accept us. And the Immigration Department thought we were coming here to be trained and to learn, you know, from Australia, and then take those skills back.'

These were the decades of the Colombo Plan. For the first time this century, significant numbers of Asians were being admitted to Australia on student visas. This was to be post-war Australia's contribution to the development of the region.

'We took White Australia as a given. When I came here, I simply didn't think of migrating. There was no option of migrating here. I couldn't even think of myself as living in Australia.

'The company's difficulties increased, and they were beginning to review whether they wanted to continue doing business here or not. So I thought I would use it as an opportunity to change careers. And computing was an area where things had already started happening over here. I enrolled in an associate diploma in computer science at the University of Adelaide.

'In a place like Adelaide, we were able to get to know anyone who was anyone. If someone wanted to run a panel on international affairs, the Australian representative would be a Minister in the South Australian Government, or someone significant in the community, and then if you wanted another perspective — and there weren't that many other overseas people available with good English — they got guys like me. So, the opportunities to get to know people were phenomenal.

'We were very, very happy in Adelaide. We did not experience discrimination. We were aware that there was severe discrimination against Aborigines, but people really welcomed us.

'Then IBM was interested in offering me a job. So I told them, "I will work for you for two or three years, then I will go back and work for you in India." That was the only option.

'The IBM people said, "No, that is not how we operate; each country's operation is separate." There was a culture in those days that if I invest in your training, I have to recover my investment.

'So I said, "Well, that is fine, so you would offer me a job if I could stay? So why don't you tell me how long I would have to stay for you to recover that investment?"

'They wrote this letter to me saying, "We are offering you this job provided you are allowed to stay in this country for seven years in total."

'I wrote to Senator Laught, who I had met in Adelaide, and he sent the letter on to the Immigration Minister, and lo and behold — it's one of my favourite letters — the Minister, Hubert Opperman, wrote this letter back to Senator Laught agreeing to this extension. He said, however, that it needs to be clearly understood that under no circumstances will this be extended. In fact, it is hoped that Mr. Roach will return to India before the completion of this period, so he can apply over there the knowledge he has gained in this country.

'So, that is how it happened.

'The only place where I experienced discrimination in that time was in the Immigration Department, because they were enforcing what was in fact a racist policy. When I went to convert my visa to a student visa, I was standing in the queue and in front of me was someone who was having great trouble speaking

English. I could see what was happening. The guy at the counter was doing everything in his power to persuade this person that it was a good thing to become an Australian citizen. And I am standing in the same queue, and I can speak English perfectly, and of course, when he got to me he tried to persuade me that I shouldn't stay here. So you had this situation where you had someone who was thoroughly integrated, assimilated if you like, someone who was comfortable living here, effectively being told we think you should be going home.

'Then things changed, and the policy started being dismantled in 1966. And we stayed.

'I never made the big decision to migrate. I just came and just drifted into staying here.

'In fact, I took a long time to become a citizen, because that White Australia thing remained in my mind. We had never made a decision to migrate, and I was a voter and I was a taxpayer, so there didn't seem to be the need, you know.

'Then my wife came to me one day and said, "Look, this is ridiculous. There is no question, we are not going to return to India. This is our home. We are happy here."'

So the Roaches decided to become Australian citizens.

But to become a citizen was one thing. Under the circumstances, becoming Australian by persuasion was not such an easy thing.

'One of the things that I was unable to do from very early on was to support an Australian sporting team. It's particularly ironic, because in India everyone is interested in cricket, and Test cricket at the time was almost entirely between England and Australia. And so everyone in India who loved cricket either supported England or Australia as if it was their own country. And I always supported Australia, fanatically.

'Within a month of my coming here, Australia won an amazing Test in England, with Richie Benaud; it was one of the great matches in history. And I suddenly found that I wanted England to win. For the first time, I wanted Australia to lose.

'I guess I could not support the Australian fan. Then I couldn't support Australian players, because I observed their behaviour on the field. Gradually I found that there was nothing in sport that I could support Australia in.

'After some time I decided that it didn't make sense because why would I want England to win or New Zealand to win? And at the time South Africa had a white team, so why would I want them to win? Eventually I narrowed down to supporting any team from the Indian subcontinent opposing Australia.

'I have got over that phase. But I still feel Australians play the game very, very hard. Sledging was invented in Australia.

'And look at this incident with the Sri Lankan team. This is a terrible, terrible situation which has done enormous damage to Australia's relations with Sri Lanka, and probably with the whole sub-continent.

'Australia always points the finger at other people. They complained that the Pakistani captain offered a bribe to them to throw the match. What they didn't tell us at the time was that these guys had taken money from a bookmaker.

'Then we are upset because Ranatunga, the Sri Lankan captain, is given a suspended sentence. But what do we do with these guys? We give them a small fine and make them captain and vice-captain.

'The fact is that the very game you say you were offered a bribe — a game you are on the verge of winning by the way — you actually lost the game. In India, they believe the problem was not whether the bribe was offered. They are saying it definitely was offered. The problem, they say, is that it was accepted and carried through. But then, Salim Malik didn't pay them. They waited for three months and that's when they squealed. That's the Indian story.

'I told this story to Australians the other day at a Citizenship Council meeting. And it was like smacking them in the face. I said, now you know how terrible it feels when our boys accuse the Pakistanis of bribery.'

Drawing broad generalisations from the sporting metaphors, we ask Neville about his general sense of where Australia is going.

'I have to say that a few years ago I was much more optimistic about everything. But now I have come to this other conclusion. I think we should not be as self-congratulatory as we have been. My basic view now is that Australia is yet to be tested.

'What we have put ourselves through is very radical compared to the White Australia Policy. But before we start thinking that we have created a model society, we need to understand that we have in fact been quite cautious. We have taken very limited risks.

'I keep coming back to the sporting analogy: just look at the Australian cricket team and the English cricket team. About six of the eleven cricketers playing in the test for England were either coloured or were born in another country ...'

He knows them all, rattles off their names.

'. . . and they play for England, and this is routine. We are going to take fifty or a hundred years before this happens in Australia.

'But I think it is inevitable that we will be tested. Because I really think that the current policy is not sustainable — and I'm talking about the policies of both sides of politics. We need to bring in greater numbers of immigrants, mainly because of our skills shortages, and we will need family reunion to support that. We have tens of thousands too few IT people. If we have decided to train the people we need, it will take five years. But we have the need now.'

The bulk of these people will, inevitably, not be white. Neville Roach is saying that, for all the progress made since the abandonment of the White Australia Policy, and for all the fears that we have already been 'Asianised,' Australia is on a journey that has only just begun.

'I feel very strongly about it, personally. And I also try to come at it from a business perspective.

'I mean, would we have Asian tourists here if we still had a White Australia Policy? Would Asian students be here in numbers if we still had White Australia?

'And here I am living in the community. It is in all our interests that the community is happy I am here, that the community is comfortable with whatever I do that is different.

'No, as a nation, we simply haven't been tested yet.'

The interview took longer than we had planned. Neville was off to catch a plane to the Gold Coast; he was doing a graduation speech the next morning. He does one public speech after another, and the Fujitsu management in Japan actively supports the public role he has assumed in Australia. It's in the interest of their business to have a person with his profile as their CEO.

Driving to the airport together, we found the streets of Sydney were clogged — another kind of a test, for which immigrants are regularly blamed by the gutter press and senior politicians alike.

In the car, the conversation drifted on to the National Multicultural Advisory Committee Report, to which he had devoted an enormous amount of time and energy. He'd been to see the Prime Minister, and told the story of how they'd managed to convince John Howard to stick with the word 'multiculturalism.'

Neville had been upset when we wrote a newspaper article criticising the Committee's terms of reference, which included 'to review nomenclature.' What that really meant was that the Committee had been asked to consider dropping 'multiculturalism.' He was a little defensive, explaining how he had always believed in working within the system.

The final report recommended that 'multiculturalism' be retained, and the Prime Minister came along to launch it.

The traffic test came to an end at Sydney airport. Neville missed his plane. Fortunately, there was still one more that night.

CHAPTER 17

Opening the Door to Asia

In 1988, during his first stint as Leader of the Opposition in the
Federal Parliament, John Howard expressed his concerns about
Asian immigration to Australia in no uncertain terms:

> I believe that Asian migration is in the eyes of some of the
> community too great; it would be in our immediate-term
> interests in terms of social cohesion if we could slow down a
> little so that the capacity of the community to absorb this
> would become greater.

He was speaking on ABC Radio, explaining why he would run 'very
strongly' on the concept of 'One Australia' at the next election:

> I do ... think that the pace of change brought about by the
> migrant intake is an issue that any government has to keep in
> mind.[1]

He was deposed as leader of the Liberals the following year,
and when he returned as leader in 1995, he apologised for the
views he had expressed in 1988:

> I obviously used clumsy language. I obviously didn't handle that
> thing with the right degree of sensitivity and I've dealt with that. I
> don't intend to go on repeating what I've said previously.[2]

Every now and then, Emeritus Professor Charles Price also
expresses views similar to those Howard espoused back in 1988.
And he has the weight of experience and expertise, it seems, to
back up his claims. Until he retired, Price was for many years the
Professor of Demography at the Australian National University in
Canberra.

I am one of those people who think there should be a debate about the direction of our immigration program. Many people are concerned about the trends in immigration not because they are racist but because they are worried about rapid social change. They don't want ethnic change to be too rapid.[3]

By 2040, he claims, 26 per cent of the population of Australia will be Asian. That's the change he thinks we need to 'debate.'

It's the sort of thing that makes good media, except for two things. The first is the assumption that this would inevitably be a terrible thing. By way of immediate comparison, US population projections show that barely a majority — only 52 per cent — of the people of the United States will be white in 2050; the rest will be Asian, black or Hispanic.[4] Australia is not the only country where people are living through a time of significant demographic change, and there is no reason why that change has to be a bad thing. It's not a matter of warning people, scaring them that they won't be able to adjust. Rather, it's a question of finding ways to adjust.

The second thing is the way Price uses statistics. When you examine the Professor's figures, they seem to add up perfectly well, except that 'Asian' includes 'white' people from Turkey and the Middle East, as well as first-language English speakers from the Indian subcontinent. They also include anybody who has as little as one-eighth 'Asian' ancestry.[5] If, in 2050, you have one great-grandparent who was born in his version of 'Asia,' Charles Price would be calling you 'Asian.' Hence the 26 per cent. Mind you, given that Asian immigrants intermarry at a greater rate than preceding waves of immigrants, we might equally be witnessing an insidious 'Anglo-Celticisation' of that 26 per cent, as a very large proportion of them will be of partly mixed Anglo-Saxon and/or Celtic ancestry. Of course that's only if you thought it necessary to assure Price's readers that the 'ethnic change' won't be so enormous, and you were happy to use unwieldy race concepts to do it.

Price's numberwork betrays another huge difficulty in the concept of 'Asian' which underlies the process of 'Asianisation' that could, allegedly, afflict Australia. 'Europe' is a concept which has a human as well as a geographical meaning. 'Racially,' the people of Europe are white and look reasonably similar. Europe's climate does not vary too wildly, from one end to the other, nor do the lifestyles of its peoples. Apart from a few exceptions, such as

Hungarian, it is a place of related languages. Its writing is in three similar alphabetic scripts. Apart from a few small historically Muslim regions, it is mostly a Christian place. The Roman Empire, and later the Byzantine and Catholic empires of Christendom, covered large swathes of territory at various times and created a partially common heritage. The Industrial Revolution and economic development proceeded across its geographical extent much more evenly than has been the case across the world.

'Asia,' by comparison, is an idea that is almost meaningless beyond simple geographical description. It is a European word, a word that has no basis or meaning in local traditions and languages right across the continent. No language of the continent has any way of expressing or imaging such a concept. 'Asia' is also meaningless because there is no such single thing in a human sense. There is more racial variation here than in any other continent. From tundra to tropics, the climate changes as much as is possible on this earth. There are a dozen or more unrelated language groups, scripts and even script types. All the world's major religions are massively represented. Empires have come and gone across Asia, but none has ever covered more than a small proportion of the land mass. Economic development, as well, has been enormously uneven, and the types of political and economic regime extremely varied.

The nice irony is that there's so much variation in Asia — the geographical phenomenon — that Australia could easily, humanly, be 'Asian.' That's if we stopped using the word in its original European sense, to denote a kind of distant otherness. And if we wanted to be clearer, if we wanted to be more specific about the kind of Asians we were, we might revive that now strangely unfashionable idea, 'Australasia' — or south Asia.

— • —

Of the 18 million people living in Australia at the time of the 1996 census, 520,000 people were born in South-East Asia, 290,000 in northern Asia, and 46,000 in the Indian subcontinent — a total of 856,000 people. Another 286,000 were those children who have at least one parent born in these three Asian regions. This is what has happened since the end of the White Australia Policy.

Depending on your points of reference, White Australia was abolished in 1949, when Immigration Minister Harold Holt allowed Japanese war brides and a limited number of non-European refugees to enter Australia, in 1958 when Alexander Downer Senior abolished the Dictation Test, in 1966 when Hubert Opperman announced that non-white immigrants could apply to migrate to Australia, or in 1973 when the Whitlam Government ordered that race be disregarded totally in the selection of immigrants. Just as arguably, however, when it comes to the actual mechanics of visa issue, White Australia is still with us.

Probably the most significant step in the abolition of White Australia, however, was the decision to accept refugees at the end of the Vietnam War, as this was the first influx of non-white immigrants in any significant numbers since the nineteenth century.

Michael MacKellar was Minister for Immigration at the time; the Fraser Government had just been swept to power in a landslide election victory in December 1975. In January 1976, MacKellar announced that the first eight hundred Indo-Chinese refugees had been accepted by Australia, and in May he announced Australia was accepting two thousand East Timorese refugees after the Indonesian invasion of the former Portuguese colony. The flow of refugees and immigrants from the region has been continuous ever since. Two decades later, the number of immigrants from these areas, and their children, was well over a million.

We met Michael MacKellar in his little windowless office at the back of the Alfred Hospital in Melbourne. His business card says 'Chief Operations Officer, Capital Campaign, Baker Medical Research Institute.' That means he manages fund-raising. His desk is covered with a clutter of plans of the new building that will be going up, a testament to his energetic salesmanship. Immigration is not a subject he is called to talk about much these days, despite his historic role.

'You have to remember,' he says, 'at that stage that the Department of Immigration had been abolished by Whitlam, who really hated it, yes really hated it. His reaction to the final stages of the evacuation of Saigon, and to the people who had worked for Australia, was that he would just not allow them in. But it's not just that he wasn't very supportive of the Indo-Chinese situation, you have to remember that under Whitlam, the anti-immigration sentiment wasn't confined to Asia. They wound down the whole program.'

This was where Michael MacKellar started as Minister. He re-established the Department and also created a new area, Ethnic Affairs. The Department of Immigration and Ethnic Affairs it was from then on, and that's what it was to be called for the next twenty years.

'I was immediately faced with the two refugee crises. One was the Lebanese Civil War. We reacted pretty quickly to that, and a lot of Lebanese came out. It was a very sensitive issue, because it was really the first time we had non-Christians coming to Australia in considerable numbers, and we had to make a decision as to whether we were discriminatory or non-discriminatory.

'Then, of course, the major challenge was the Indo-Chinese refugee situation, which we really had to address. The story has never been told about the extent of the challenge that we faced, and I'm proud of the way Australia reacted then, because in fact we led the world in our approach. We virtually forced America and the others to join successive UN conferences on how this whole thing should be dealt with and, of course, it involved an enormous amount of consultation and negotiation with the governments of the region. Because, as you know, there were some pretty clear indications that some governments were supplying these boats with maps, petrol and food and telling people, "That's the way to go!" I didn't want the situation where there was an armada of little boats bobbing around the coast up in the north there, and with our navy patrolling the area and shooing them away.

'I had people ringing me up and saying, "You must stop these boats, blow them out of the water." You only had to think about that for a minute to realise what it would look like internationally for Australia, with all this space and all these resources, to be telling people in desperate circumstances, "You can't come here and we are going to shoot you if you try."

'Fortunately, Fraser was absolutely rock-solid. I mean, I had to fire the bullets, but he'd be rock-solid behind me. There was no if-ing or but-ing.

'Of course, people would say to me, "MacKellar, you are destroying the culture of Australia." And I always had anti-immigration candidates standing against me.

'One election, signs went up everywhere saying "YELLA MacKELLAR — WANTED FOR TREASON." I've still got one of the signs.'

Back then, MacKellar was indeed saying things that were, from the point of view of an older Australia — White Australia — treasonable. This is what he said in a major speech back in 1979:

The inevitable effects of our geographical location close to Asia, coupled with a period of low natural population growth, instantaneous communication and rapid and increasingly cheap transportation, are being emphasised in a dramatic way by the Indo-Chinese refugees ... Either we must put up the barricades around Australia and be seen as an isolationist country seeking to divorce itself from the realities of the world scene, or we must maintain continuing immigration at a higher level than at present with a balanced intake ... Indeed, I suggest it may be in our economic interests in the longer term to embark on a new immigration program much as we did immediately after the Second World War.'[6]

Twenty years later, the effects of beginning that new immigration program are abundantly visible. Australia has become a different place.

'We need to keep in mind that we do have, in terms of population, a disproportionate share of the world's resources. We can't be totally selfish in the way we manage that. The Indians talk about the common heritage of mankind. The world belongs to everybody. If we appear to be too selfish in the way we manage our resources, that could lead to trouble down the track.'

We mention the public discussion of immigration in general, and Asian immigration in particular, that has been a more or less constant feature of the Australian scene since Pauline Hanson came along.

'If John Howard had come out very early on and said this is anathema, and developed a totally bipartisan approach, One Nation would not have had the impact it has. I think he has understood that now. And I think, to look at the other side of the issue, there is a justifiable argument that says that people should be able to express a point of view. Now, I'm a small 'l' liberal. I don't think there should be any limit to the discussion. But the PM should have said right from the start that Mrs Hanson is perfectly at liberty to say as she wishes, but the views of my government are such and such.

'I remember standing up in the Party room and saying to John ...' — Howard and MacKellar were both Ministers in the Fraser Cabinet, and Howard had said something about immigration — "... you have got to understand that in these issues, words are bullets and in this area people are extraordinarily sensitive. You can so easily be misinterpreted."'

So what of Australia's future? we ask.

'I still believe what I have always believed, that Australia has the capacity to be an absolutely leading nation in the world, bringing together a whole host of different people. What it needs is a constant reaffirmation. We need a nation-building approach which confirms that these people are good for us, that these people will add to the benefits of our way of life. We want to be a beacon and an example to the rest of the world through our capacity for tolerance, our capacity as a society to develop individual skills, and to maximise every person's human potential.

'But nobody is expressing this today, nobody is saying these sorts of things, and it annoys the daylights out of me.'

— • —

Malcolm Fraser was Prime Minister from 1975 to 1983.

'I can remember Michael MacKellar coming to me and saying, "What are we going to do about all these Vietnamese and Cambodian refugees who've come here?"

'And I said, "For God's sake, we were fighting alongside them, and we led them to believe that we were supporting them. What can we do except say they can come to stay here and become citizens?"

'There was no moral, and I don't think there was any practical, option. Nobody made a fuss about it. And people accepted it once we had made the decision.

'If you'd polled the Australian people at any point, they would have said, "End migration or cut it down." But it doesn't matter, because it's something that you have to persuade people about. You have to assure them that it's going to be right.

'But I think one of the reasons migration has been run down in the last dozen years is because people in positions of authority know that if the numbers go up, inevitably there are going to be more Asian migrants and I don't think they want it.

'And I think they're just wrong. I think that's a discussion that Australia is going to have to have.

'When I was Education Minister, I would get about two hundred letters per week complaining about Asian students in schools and universities taking a place away from "my little Johnny," and I'd write back and say, "Well, this year we are issuing an extra twenty thousand or forty thousand Commonwealth Scholarships and, if little Johnny is good enough, I'm sure he will get one, and I hope he does. But having Asian students in schools and universities is in the national interest."'

— • —

Bob Hawke followed Malcolm Fraser as Prime Minister from 1983 to 1991.

'Why don't they look at the bloody exam results?' he asks when we mention the people who complain about Asian immigration.

Hawke presided over high levels of immigration throughout the eighties, including the acceptance of some thirty thousand Chinese students and their families after the Tiananmen Square massacre of 1989. Was that a decision which was motivated by sentiment or calculation? we ask.

'There was sentiment in it. I can't walk away from that. Of course there was sentiment. But there was mind as well as heart.

'When people criticise that decision, I ask them, why don't they just love their country and say, "Isn't it bloody marvellous that we're getting this talent, because it is going to make our country better?"

'Kids have come here without any English and in no time, bang, look how well they've done. Look how much better it's going to make the country.'

But are we yet a part of Asia? we ask.

'Basically, it's very simple. The fact is that our economic welfare is increasingly dependent on Asia. Sixty per cent of our exports go to Asia. That's a hell of a lot of your bloody jobs. That means the welfare of Australian parents and their kids, so we're part of Asia in that sense.

'And do we dislike Asians because they provide us with jobs — should we?

'We should dislike people who conduct themselves in a racist way, that's what we should dislike.'

CHAPTER 18

Asian Crisis, Asian Futures

On 1 July 1997, the Government of Thailand floated the Thai baht. The next day, the currency fell fifteen per cent against the US dollar. This sparked a series of crises in Thailand: a stockmarket crash, a crash in the overheated property market, and the collapse of many banks and other financial institutions. Soon the contagion spread, to Indonesia, South Korea, Malaysia and the Philippines. This was the beginning of the Asian financial crisis.

When the International Monetary Fund moved in, ostensibly to bail out currencies and economies in crisis, all it did was make the crisis worse, and probably meant to.

The proper role for the IMF, according to Martin Feldstein, former chair of the US President's Council of Economic Advisers and Professor of Economics at Harvard University, was to provide assistance to stem precisely the kinds of currency runs experienced by those Asian economies worst affected by the financial crisis. Writing in the *Wall Street Journal*, Feldstein said that, when these countries came to the IMF for assistance, instead of providing them with the assistance they needed to support their currencies, it took the opportunity to impose conditions that required the radical restructuring of the entire domestic economy — the tax system, the extent and nature of government intervention in the economy, regulation of the banking system, labour laws, corporate governance, and regulations and processes relating to bankruptcy and receivership. These were matters well beyond conditions that would normally be imposed when providing liquidity to handle a short-term financial crisis.

Instead of working to restore confidence in the economies of Asia, Feldstein says, the IMF 'publicly criticised them as incompetent, corrupt countries with fundamentally unsound economies.' IMF Director Michel Camdessus called it a 'blessing in disguise,' as the crisis provided the West with the leverage it needed to force structural economic changes.[1]

In fact, the crisis provided an alibi to impose Western-style free market orthodoxies on economies which had boomed for decades as a result of what were regarded by conservative Western economists as 'anti-competitive practices,' such as substantial government intervention.

The IMF's actions intensified the panic and fanned the flames of financial crisis. The policies imposed on the countries who accepted IMF support produced recession; they forced massive bankruptcies; they created unemployment. This, in its turn, produced civil and political unrest, most seriously in Indonesia. Malaysia's Prime Minister Mahathir saw the IMF conditions as no more and no less than a new way of forcing Western entry into Asian markets.

The IMF 'offers to lend money with which to repay loans to foreign lenders. But the loans come with a string of conditions, principal among which are the opening of the financial sector to full foreign participation. It is likely that this will result in foreign banks eventually dominating the finances of the country concerned. We are facing a serious problem which can take us back to our colonial past,' he said.[2]

The financial crisis also turned into a discussion about Asian values. The IMF's agenda was not just structural; it was cultural as well.

During the extraordinary eighties and nineties boom across Asia — the Japanese economic miracle, the rise of the 'tiger economies,' the rapid transformation of 'underdeveloped' countries like Indonesia, the development of a hybrid capitalist economy in China — the West went looking for the essence of Asia. It went searching for the cultural keys to Asia's success.

And what the West found were 'Asian qualities' such as a work ethic, frugality, family loyalty, company loyalty and tight corporate cultures, high levels of government intervention and investment in technology and infrastructure, heavy investment in education systems that did not allow a long 'tail' of failure. These 'Asian characteristics' served as an explanation in the new economics of cultural difference.

Then the financial crisis came along and the same cultural differences were found to be the root of the problem. This time, they were called cronyism, corruption, governments undermining the beneficial effects of 'market forces,' and authoritarian and illiberal societies which restricted the values of individualism and choice that underpinned the 'free market.'

Malaysian Prime Minister Mahathir listed the 'Asian values' as hard work, respect for authority, discipline, submission to the interest and good of the majority and filial piety. 'Suddenly we find Asian values equated with authoritarian rule, disregard for human and workers' rights [and] political stability and economic success at all costs. We [are told we] must now discard Asian values and adopt so-called universal values as conceived by the West.'[3]

— • —

Prime Minister Howard has never liked the idea that Australia might be a part of Asia.

In part, the 1996 Federal election result represented a repudiation of the stultifying political correctness which had afflicted so many areas of the Australian polity during the previous decade. Many Australians for example, resent the negative view of our history and the Australian achievement which has become so standard in recent years. Those same Australians resent the constant claim that our history has been little more than a litany of racism, sexism and imperial triumphalism. Those same Australians resent the plaintive way in which so many have encouraged us in the past to approach our association with the nations of the Asia-Pacific region. They resent the suggestion that Australia has to change its identity in order to play an effective role in our region.[4]

So, when the Asian financial crisis came along, he seemed to develop an 'I told you so' kind of response to his Labor predecessors, who had been far more inclined to regard Australia's proximity to Asia as an opportunity that must be seized. Howard used the crisis to remind Australians of the need to keep up our links with the English-speaking world and Europe, and thus with places with which we were supposed to have stronger historical and cultural affinities.

On this theory of who we are and who we are like, Australia cast its lot with the people who were perceived throughout Asia as the bullies who had only made things worse. The Howard

Government offered financial support to the IMF; Australia would lend a hand to a Washington-based organisation to help tackle issues that were right on our doorstep.

The alternative, of course, would have been to see the crisis from a regional point of view. The chances are that the crisis will hasten the formation of a regional trading bloc as a response at least in part to perceived Western impositions, in the same way as the European Union had been formed in the decades after the Second World War as a counterbalance to the dominance of the United States. Mahathir said that the response of ASEAN countries to the crisis must be to relate more closely to each other and to trade more with each other. When he said that, he was not including Australia.

However, if a regional bloc does form, Australia needs to be in that bloc, and not outside of it.

We also need to be on the side of post-colonial futures and not colonial pasts — hence, incidentally, the enormous significance of the republican debate to our standing in the region. As the last major nation in the region to maintain the symbolism of its colonial past, we need to demonstrate that we are future-oriented.

Ironically, perhaps, the Asian financial crisis is primarily a cultural challenge, a challenge to shift our cultural focus.

— • —

Malcolm Fraser expresses his disappointment at Australia's failure to take a leadership role in the financial crisis.

'I think we should have taken a much stronger role. We should have openly criticised the International Monetary Fund.

'The IMF in many ways is an instrument of the United States' world economic policy, and when they brought down their first program for Indonesia, it was so intrusive that no Indonesian government could ever accept it.

'But the IMF was trying to get $18 billion out of Congress and Congress was saying "No." The IMF was terrified that they'd be able to point and say, "There, look, you've thrown billions at Indonesia, and it's all been wasted." Now, did the IMF play hard ball with Indonesia because they really thought that was the way to resolve the crisis, or did they play hard ball because they were trying to get money through Congress?

'Well, I think it's an absolute disgrace that we haven't taken a lead. Now people are on the edge of starvation in Indonesia.'

— • —

In Indonesia, economic crisis produced political crisis. President Suharto's government collapsed under the weight of the financial crisis early in 1998. Until new elections were held and a new president elected in 1999, he was replaced by his former deputy, Dr B.J. Habibie. Ethnic brush fires began to burn around Indonesia, in Aceh, Ambon, Irian Jaya — but particularly in the most troublesome of the Indonesian provinces, East Timor. Indonesia had invaded the former Portuguese colony in 1975, and for the next two decades, East Timorese resistance fighters had continued to struggle for an independent East Timor.

At the beginning of 1999, Habibie agreed to allow an independence vote for East Timor. The province was costing the Indonesian Government $100 million per year, and, to use the words of Habibie's adviser, Monash University-educated Dr Dewi Fortuna Anwar, Indonesia wanted to wash its hands of East Timor. Then 'you'll have another Angola on your hands,' she warned a senior Australian diplomat — drawing a parallel with the difficulties the former white South Africa had with its northern neighbour.[5]

A vote supervised by the United Nations was held in East Timor on 30 August 1999. With a 98.6 per cent turnout, 78.5 per cent of East Timorese voted in favour of independence. When the results were announced on 4 September, militias supporting integration with Indonesia went on the rampage, burning the capital city, Dili, to the ground, as well as many of the other towns of East Timor. Hundreds of thousands of East Timorese fled to the hills or into Indonesian West Timor.

Australia was ill-prepared for this eventuality. In fact, Australia had advised the US and the UN that a peacekeeping force would not be needed. Under US pressure, Indonesia then agreed to allow an Australian-led peacekeeping force to enter East Timor. The force entered a devastated Dili on 20 September 1999.

By that time, however, Australia's relations with Indonesia had been dealt an enormous blow. On 16 September, the Indonesians tore up a security agreement that had been signed by Prime Minister Keating and President Suharto in 1995.

Prime Minister Howard saw Australia's intervention in East Timor as a turning point in Australia's relations with Asia. Interviewed on 17 September, the day after Indonesia repudiated its security agreement with Australia, Howard said:

Gee, we were ourselves in Asia over the last few weeks. We were defending the values we hold as Australians. We were willing to be in dispute with our nearest neighbour, to defend those values.

Howard saw himself as deliberately reversing the policies of the Hawke and Keating governments which attempted to see Australia as 'much like the countries in the region.' We were now asserting our differences with the countries of Asia. Regarding Indonesia, particularly, he said:

One of the errors we have made is that we have operated on the basis that we cannot afford to be offside. I would rather turn it around the other way and say it is clearly very desirable to have a friendly relationship, but it has to be built on practical foundations. It cannot be composed of a starry-eyed notion that we can have a special relationship with them. We have had too many special relationships with too many countries over the years.

Australia, Howard said, needed to draw strength from its distinctive characteristics as a Western civilization in Asia. He wanted to create an Australia that did not seek to fashion itself after the rest of Asia, but one that was confident in its own character as a place that represents a civilization geographically distant and culturally different from those of Asia. On this basis, Australia was defending 'right.' It was no longer prepared to adopt the 'please at all costs' attitude it had had to some Asian leaders of the past. Because, in the Keating period, he argued,

We looked as though we were knocking on their door and saying 'please, let us in', instead of realising we were always somebody they would want to have in because of our particular strength, and that [now] has been demonstrated . . . In foreign policy we [used to] spend too much time fretting about whether we were in Asia, or part of Asia, or whatever. We should be ourselves in Asia.

This new, assertive approach to foreign policy he called 'the Howard Doctrine.'

As a defender of 'Western values' in Asia, Australia did, in Howard's view, however, still have some special relationships, and one of these was with the United States. Indeed, Australia was now going to regard itself as the United States' 'deputy in Asia;' the US would be the 'lender of last resort' in matters of regional security. It was not 'reasonable, appropriate or suitable,' he said, for the 'global policeman,' the US, to lead every peacekeeping operation in the world. In East Timor, 'we have displayed our responsibility, shouldered the burden we should have.' We had shown ourselves to be

> a participant on our own terms. Despite the inevitable tensions that are involved and some of the sensitivities, this has done a lot to cement Australia's place in the region. We have been seen by countries, not only in the region but around the world, as being able to do something that probably no other country could do; because of the special characteristics we have; because we occupy that special place — we are a European, Western civilization with strong links with North America, but we are in Asia.[6]

In Asia, the response to the new 'Howard doctrine' was rapid. This was how Malaysia's highly respected *New Straits Times* reported the Malaysian reaction. It was a front page story:

> Malaysia rejects attempts by any nation to install itself as a peacekeeper, leader or commander in this region, Deputy Prime Minister Datuk Seri Abdullah Ahmad Badawi said today. Commenting on Australia's plan to be the US' deputy in peacekeeping in Asia, Abdullah said Asian nations could take care of themselves ... He told reporters that in a way the plan showed a lack of understanding on Australia's part by not being sensitive to the views of Asians. Abdullah said that the 'Howard Doctrine' unveiled this week would not enhance its eligibility to be in the Asian family ... He added that by co-operating with each other to maintain peace, Asia did not need a commander or a deputy commander.
> Opposition leader ... Lim Kit Siang described the Howard Doctrine as 'an arrogant resurrection of the "White Man's Burden" to save mankind.' Lim said it was highly offensive to Asians and would cause the greatest damage to

Asian–Australian relations since the White Australia policy was abolished in the 1960s. It is also completely incompatible with the trend for internationalisation of peacekeeping roles under the auspices of the United Nations rather than under any Big Brother, Superpower or self-appointed international policeman. Asia does not recognise the United States as chief international policeman in Asia. And the question of Australia allocating itself the role of US deputy international policeman for Asia is not only the height of arrogance but also completely misplaced and unwelcome to Asians.[7]

Indonesian political analyst Salim Said commented:

Howard is like a 19th-century European standing on a beach and thinking he will have to watch out for the little brown uncivilized neighbours that lie to the north.[8]

So Howard retracted his 'doctrine'. 'Howard does U-turn Over Regional Police Role' was the headline in the *New Straits Times* three days after the story first broke. 'I want to make it clear that [*The Bulletin* article] does not accurately reflect my position.'[9] He did say, however, that he still thought the Bulletin story was 'a very good article'. And about the word 'deputy', 'words mean different things to different people.'[10] Besides, 'the position that has been taken by the government has won it wide support in the Australian community.'[11]

The News Analysis column in the *New Straits Times* took a longer view of the Howard approach:

John Howard took his time to answer the criticisms levelled at him by Asian leaders over the so-called 'Howard Doctrine' where he had supposedly advocated the Australian Government's new, interventionist foreign policy. It took him a week after *The Bulletin* magazine had printed the interview where he was quoted as saying that the 'Howard Doctrine' saw Australia acting in 'a sort of deputy peacekeeping capacity' in the Asian region to the 'global policeman' role of the United States, to deny the contents of the article.

When fish and chips trader Pauline Hanson went on a crusade to freeze immigration since Australia risked being 'swamped by Asians' and that benefits to the Aborigines be withdrawn, Howard was once again accused of being too slow to act ... In the issues created by *The Bulletin* and Hanson, Howard's lack of swiftness in putting the issues to rest had resulted in strong verbal exchanges and criticisms which could have been avoided. It is hoped that in delaying his reaction and creating long-run debates, the Australian politician had not deliberately planned to benefit politically on the local front.[12]

And a follow-up column a few days later praised Australia, but not without noting a certain irony:

In a land littered with cenotaphs to the white dead in foreign wars, not one stood for the Aboriginal people who fell defending their country ... It is good that Australia's peacekeeping troops are helping the East Timorese to rebuild their lives, their homes and their shattered country. Lessons learnt from the treatment of the Aborigines will be useful. Australia's backyard has now become a bit larger. It is one shared by Indonesia.[13]

Earlier in September, Howard had made his foreign policy stance clear to Chinese President Jiang Zemin. Howard was hosting a luncheon in Jiang's honour in the Great Hall at Parliament House in Canberra, on this first visit of a Chinese President to Australia. Again, he wanted to make Australia's differences with Asia clear, and he wanted to make it clear that Australia had no special relationship with China, just as Australia was making it clear there was no special relationship with Indonesia:

There are special features of the relationship although I don't call the relationship a special relationship ... First and foremost [we] frankly recognise our differences. They are obvious. The difference in population size, the difference in cultures, the difference in history, the difference in political tradition, the difference in our views on some issues of the appropriate geo-political strategy for our respective countries to find ... Australia has a long democratic tradition. We have democratic values that we treasure, which we defend and which we propound. But we recognise that the choices we have made as a nation and as a society are not necessarily choices that every society in the world would want to make or want to follow ... Issues such as human rights are of concern to the Australian Government and to the Australian people.[14]

Australia was standing on its values — democratic values, the values of Western civilization, the values of human rights. That's why we had decided to take a stand against Indonesia in East Timor.

Jiang's response was diplomatic, but firm:

I can understand the concern of Australia over the East Timor situation. But I think there are so many hot spots in the world and these should be resolved through peaceful negotiations and dialogue.[15]

And, as for human rights, the Chinese, the Indonesians and the Malaysians were very well aware of Australia's own record. When the Howard Government dismissed as 'an insult to Australia' the findings of the UN's Committee for the Elimination of All Forms of Racial Discrimination — the UN's oldest and most experienced committee on human rights and the same committee that had been pivotal in formally condemning the apartheid regime in South Africa — Amnesty International's international head office in London issued the following statement:

Like any other government, Prime Minister John Howard's administration must accept the scrutiny of its human rights record by UN mechanisms which were established and promoted through decades of commendable Australian diplomacy. The sweeping dismissal of the committee's findings is regrettably in line with the government's previous negative responses to UN recommendations on Australia's human rights practices. This dangerous trend risks undermining international efforts to allow specialist UN human rights scrutiny in Australia's neigbourhood.[16]

So, Australia stumbled into East Timor, not as an Asian nation but as a nation apart from Asia. As a country which stood on the high moral ground of 'Western values' and human rights, but with its own human rights record under an international cloud. And, along with New Zealand, as the last country in the region with colonial symbolism remaining in its flag and a European-imperial head of state.

Australia also stumbled into a more serious and more profound difficulty. One of the key features of post-Cold War politics has been the breakup of multinational, multicultural states: the Soviet Union, Yugoslavia and now perhaps Indonesia. In each place, the moral flame of self-determination has lit ethno-nationalist fires. It is simply not clear that ethnic self-determination and the creation of small, more of less ethnically homogeneous states is preferable to the democratisation of the larger, polyglot states. In most cases, the human cost of creating these small states has proven enormous. If the process of self-determination that has begun with East Timor were to be completed across the Indonesian archipelago, the consequences would be terrible, and in all probability involve repeating the horrors of 'ethnic cleansing' that have been part and parcel of the break up of Yugoslavia.

— • —

Phil Honeywood was Minister for Higher Education and Minister Assisting the Premier for Multicultural Affairs in Jeff Kennett's Victorian State Government until the 1999 state election.

He was a fellow traveller with Premier Jeff Kennett: a radical economic reformer in the tradition of Margaret Thatcher, as well as a powerful public advocate for multiculturalism, immigration and greater Australian engagement in Asia. Phil Honeywood shares Kennett's ideology, only he has none of his former boss's brashness.

When we spoke with him, his starting point is the generational shift reflected in his own life and work.

'I think my parents' generation saw Australia as vulnerable and isolated. They looked to superpowers like the States and the UK. And they were really motivated by this idea that we should make Australia economically self-sustainable. Australia had to have its own footwear factories. It had to have its own munitions factories.'

Phil Honeywood grew up born in an old Australia in which this kind of self-defensive isolationism permeated the national sensibility.

'I was born into a working-class family, the eldest of six children. We lived in Gosford, on the Central Coast of New South Wales. I can still remember my father went to work on a push bike. He was a carpenter. Life was a struggle in those years. It was also a very Anglo sort of background. My school was completely Anglo. There were no migrants.

'Then, in 1978, I was one of perhaps three hundred Australian kids who were sent to Japan on the Rotary exchange program.

'I found myself living in a totally different culture, not being able to speak the language. Just by living with four different Japanese families, all these misconceptions that I'd grown up with about the Japanese and about Asia, I found that they really were untrue.

'The experience gave me the chance to see Australia's place in the world. I came back totally convinced that Australia is just a little bit of Asia. It was so obvious to me that it was in the interests of our country to see these connections positively. If I hadn't had that exchange student experience, I'm sure I wouldn't understand the values. From my background, and without those formative years, it would have been very easy to become a Hansonite.

'That exchange experience came at a critical time for me. It taught me how to benchmark my own country. Until we get beyond our shores, we often don't understand the good and the bad things about our own culture.

'Then, when I came back, I finished high school and went straight on to the Australian National University in Canberra. The international students program was big there, and I made many friends. I studied Asian politics and Japanese.

'When I finished my degree, I went back to Japan and worked for a Japanese company. There were seven hundred Japanese and me, working in that office. There I was, working in a Japanese workplace, and living the life of a salaryman in a Japanese community.'

Has his life experience been unusual? we ask.

'If you take my family as an example, there's an amazing generational shift. One of my brothers went off to Canada, met a Portuguese-Canadian girl and subsequently married. And my youngest brother was eight years old when I got back from my exchange. I had so many presents and stories about Japan. So what did he do? He went to Sydney University, did Japanese and computer science, and got a job in Japan. He's lived in Tokyo for eight years now and works for Nintendo. He's become a true internationalist.'

This is the story of just three children born into a poor white Australian family from Gosford.

So, what was your mission in government? we ask. What were you trying to achieve?

'We used to say in Australia, "Oh, we're good at producing wool and wheat and mining commodities." But realistically what we want to do today is value-adding, it's the only way to go, and Australia happens to be good at a range of service industries that are only going to be successful if they penetrate the international market place.

'Take environment management. I agree with Paul Keating's argument in the newspaper today about Australia's role in the Asian crisis, which is partly an environmental crisis. Australia of all places should be marketing its environmental technology, its environmental management expertise. Governments need to support the really good Australian environmental protection agencies to develop the sound marketing knowledge they need to put their services, their intellectual property, to work in the region. We could create an industry which cleans up polluted lakes in China and which develops air pollution programs in Vietnam. These are some of the ways that Australia can engage in a particularly productive way in Asia.

'And take education, too. Here we have a service industry where our main markets are in Asia. We've got the highest proportion of overseas full-fee-paying students at TAFE and university level of any state in Australia. We have a competitive product, and we have gone out and been proactive in marketing it.

'Of course, when Pauline Hanson came along, I'm sure a number of families who could afford to make a choice between different countries would have been influenced to choose our competitors — Canada for example, which is seen as a safe haven without the problems and dangers of the United States. Hanson certainly created the image that we were a racist society. There's no doubt that Hanson did a lot of damage over the last few years, taking us back to the time of the White Australia Policy when I was growing up.

'But I think we've turned it round, because every chance we've had to be up there, we've been on the media, and we've really tried to push that we're a tolerant country.

'If Asian students have had a good education experience in Victoria and they return to their country of origin, usually in a leadership position in politics, the military, business or academia, they become great ambassadors for this part of Australia.

'We also teach aspects of Asian culture in school, within the comprehensive Multicultural Education Policy we launched in 1997. You've also got eighty languages to choose from in our schools. The fastest growth is in the Asian languages: Japanese, Chinese, Indonesian.'

— • —

As CEO of Fujitsu Australia, Neville Roach is a senior manager in a company that is based in Japan and which operates throughout the region.

'I think many Australian journalists and politicians who were uncomfortable about the engagement with Asia misinterpreted the engagement as rejecting other markets. If I have Asia as a customer, it doesn't mean I stop having Britain or the US as customers. No one who said we should engage with Asia also said we should give up on those other relationships.

'Now they are feeling "Gee, I told you we were really putting too many eggs into this Asian basket. Isn't it wonderful that they are in trouble now, and we can go back to Europe and America?" That seems to be the underlying message.

'All the supporters of closer relationships in the region ever said was, here is this huge opportunity, this is the first time that there has been an opportunity like this is in our region, so let's go for it.

'And even with the crisis, Asia is still our biggest customer. If we sold sixty per cent of our stuff to Asia before, and that has dropped to fifty per cent since the crisis, and we have replaced that ten per cent by Europe and America, Asia is still hugely important. It just isn't quite as huge as it used to be.

'If we were to interpret the situation now and say we can neglect Asia, that would just be a dumb thing to do, because Asia will recover. It's got the fundamentals. It's got the people. It's got a thirst for education. These countries in our region are going to be hugely important economically.'

— • —

This is how Australians have been grappling with the difficult relationship between a land located in Asia and a people who have found it hard to imagine that they really are part of that location.

The overwhelming logic of place tells us that we are in Asia. On the map, it's so obvious. If we wanted to be more specific, we might revive that old and strangely faded world, 'Australasia' — the Asia of the South.

Clearly we are more like Asia than like Europe in some of the most important of ways.

Our climate is as varied as Asia's, from the temperate places to wet tropical places, to desert places, to places of cold and snow. Europe has no deserts, no tropics. Just under forty per cent of the Australian continent is in the tropics.

Australia is also a place that was, until colonialism, owned by Indigenous peoples. A similar process of colonialism was imposed upon Indigenous peoples across Asia. There are even remnant populations of Indigenous peoples related directly to Australia's, in Japan, India, Malaysia and other places; peoples who share a common past and a common 'Fourth World' experience today.

Australia also shares a common history of colonialism. We have lived through the same dramas entailed in shaking off that colonial yoke, even if in our case this has been more muted and is still incomplete. We have even shared the same coloniser with many countries of Asia, such as India, Hong Kong, Malaysia, and Singapore. In each place, English is a *lingua franca* or language of common interchange. In each place, the law is a local adaptation of English common law. And in each place, local customs, from sport to demeanour, have been influenced by the coloniser. Yet a minority of Australians are descendants of the English, and smaller minorities in the other places.

Finally, we share resources with the region more than we do with Europe: goods and services, tourist destinations, knowledge and increasingly also, given the amount of movement to and fro, even labour forces.

These are reasons why we are more like Asia than Europe.

Even our differences make us typically an Asian place. Our differences are no greater than other Asian differences, between China and India for instance, or between Vietnam and Cambodia. Europe does not have the variety of Asia — of races, of empires, of languages and scripts, of religions. Compared to Europe, Asia is a much more multicultural place. In our difference as well as in our own multiculturalism, Asia is a place were we should feel comfortably at home. The only barrier is whether we want to be here in our difference, or whether we want to imagine ourselves to be linked to somewhere distant in our supposed similarity.

Indeed, our differences make us more valuably a part of Asia than our similarities. We are usefully different: in our natural resources, in our knowledge, in what we can best create and sell and what we are best to buy from Asia. Differences are the basis for establishing productive complementarities, instead of retreating and looking for some other place where we can imagine we are comfortably similar.

This means that we have to regard the challenges facing the region as our common challenges, be they financial crises, environmental degradation or ethnic conflicts. Crisis time is not a time for retreat into distant zones of imaginary cultural comfort. Rather it's a time for forging lasting relationships.

Eventually, it seems inevitably, we will have to share more and more: free trade, open borders, even a common currency. Eventually, an Asian Union may emerge not unlike the European Union. Australia needs to be a leader in that direction rather than to be led or, worse still, to be left out.

— • —

Australia's past and Australia's destiny turns now on how we resolve the three difficult relationships between land and people.

How do we reconcile the size and the environment of Australia with the number of people who live here? How do we reconcile the claims of immigrants and settlers with the continuing claims of those who owned the land before the newcomers arrived? And how do we reconcile our imagination of who we are with our location on the earth?

These are questions which we have been arguing about with increasing intensity and, in recent years, increasing rancour. The next part of this book is about how we have been answering these questions a century after the Australian Federation, and how we might take the next practical steps into the Australian future.

PART 3

GETTING A FAIR GO

CHAPTER 19

The Resistible Rise of Pauline Hanson

What does it feel like to be Australian at the turn of Federation's second century?

The first century ended with Pauline Hanson's certainties. It ended with the political establishment's equivocation. However, it also ended with another, distinctly more solid reality: the reality of who, by and large, we are.

The more solid reality of who we are and how we lead our lives is the least articulate but most reassuring of our national realities. Thankfully, it is likely to be more durable than the wordy 'realities' of either the populists or the equivocators.

After all, what is this more durable reality? It is the solid truth of the Australian people, the truth that most of us live daily.

We are a nation grappling intellectually with the nature of the place and its borders, with the idea of nation and globalisation, with our Indigenous past and continuing immigration from the ends of the earth, with ourselves and our destinies.

Multiculturalism and Reconciliation are two ideas which give at least an inkling of the kinds of solutions we have just been creating. These solutions are so new and so innovative that we are still struggling for words to describe the kind of Commonwealth we are now, and what we could soon be.

So now, in the third part of this book, we take a journey into turn-of-the-century sensibilities, our national disposition, our sense of ourselves and our future.

— • —

Ipswich is an old working-class industrial town in the western hinterland of Brisbane. Once the town supported thriving coal mines, woollen mills and the huge Queensland Railways workshops. By the mid-nineties most of the traditional industries had been shut down, unemployment was high, and many of the shops were empty.

Pauline Hanson was a single mother who ran a fish and chip shop in Ipswich. She became a councillor on the Ipswich Council for a year in 1994–5, then joined the local branch of the Liberal Party in 1995. When she joined she said it was because she felt the Liberals supported small business.

She barely attended or contributed to branch meetings. Some months later, her name appeared at the preselection for Liberal Party candidature in the Federal seat of Oxley. A complete unknown herself, she managed to win the preselection against two other low profile candidates. Oxley was a safe Labor Party seat and, it seemed, there was no chance that a Liberal could win the seat which had been held by sometime Labor leader Bill Hayden until he resigned to become Governor- General.

In January 1996, three weeks before the federal election, candidate Hanson wrote a letter to the editor of the local newspaper, the *Queensland Times:*

> I would be the first to admit that not that many years ago the Aborigines were treated wrongly but in trying to correct this they [politicians] have gone too far. I don't feel responsible for the treatment of Aboriginal people in the past because I had no say and my concern is now and for the future. How can we expect this race to help themselves when governments shower them with money, facilities and opportunities that only these people can obtain no matter how minute the indigenous blood is that flows through their veins and that is causing racism. Until governments wake up to themselves and start looking at equality not colour then we might start to work together as one.[1]

A Labor Councillor noticed the letter and pointed it out to the *Courier-Mail* in Brisbane. Embarrassed, Liberal Party headquarters in Brisbane asked Pauline Hanson to retract and apologise. She refused. So the Queensland Liberals decided to disendorse her. Opposition Leader John Howard was not asked. It was a State matter, and the officials didn't ask Howard because they thought he might say 'No.'

From the point of view of the Liberals, disendorsing Hanson was a symbolic act; it seemed that she had no chance of entering

Parliament anyway. The symbolism was important because the Coalition had other race trouble on their hands. Among their Coalition colleagues in the Queensland National Party, Bob Katter had made his remarks about 'slanty-eyed ideologues.' And on Australia Day, Bob Burgess, the Nationals' candidate for the seat of Leichhardt in Far North Queensland, called the citizenship ceremonies which traditionally occur on that day 'dewogging ceremonies.' Defending himself, Burgess later said: 'John Howard knows there is a silent majority in Australia who feel very much the same way as I do on many issues.'

These race comments by Hanson, Katter and Burgess became the most reported single issue of the whole election campaign, with, on one count, a total of 2603 mentions in the national print media. The Coalition's response was the epitome of political correctness. Katter and Burgess were chastised. Hanson was disendorsed.

But it was too late to remove Hanson's Liberal endorsement from the ballot papers. In effect, she went into the poll as both a Liberal and an independent, and also, by dint of media exposure, a candidate who had made herself suddenly famous right across the country. Those who disendorsed her afterwards regretted their decision. All the major parties are home to people with views similar to Hanson's. Perhaps she might have been kept at bay if she had been allowed to stay within the Liberal Party? they muse. 'The worst decision of my career,' one person says.

The Liberal–National Party Coalition won the election on 2 March 1996. It was a landslide victory, with the biggest landslide of all taking place in Oxley, where Pauline Hanson won the seat with a swing of 23 per cent.

> My success in Oxley was a win for the silent majority of ordinary Australians. For far too long, too many governments have fallen into the trap of listening to, then governing for, a whole hotchpotch of minority lobby groups who have become very powerful because they have been extremely well-funded by taxpayers who have had no say in the matter. Now, the people of Oxley at least, have had their say.[2]

This was what Pauline Hanson said in her acceptance speech at the declaration of the poll. The speechwriter was the first person to join her staff, John Pasquarelli, a former Liberal candidate for the Federal Parliament and still a member of the Liberals at the time.

Once the new Parliament started to sit, Hanson was the last of those newly elected to give her maiden speech. It was 10 September 1996, and the speech was to become one of the most widely reported and most significant in Australian political history.

Again, Pasquarelli was the speechwriter:

> I come here, not as a polished politician but as a woman who has had her fair share of life's knocks. My view on issues is based on common sense and my experience as a mother of four children, as a sole parent and a businesswoman running a fish and chip shop.

This was how she began her first speech to Parliament that day, speaking nervously, in a faltering voice, to an almost deserted chamber. It was a voice of the ordinary White Australia, the voice of an ordinary woman, the voice of the struggling small-business person. Above all, it was a voice and a persona that powerfully resonated as 'experience' and as 'commonsense' to those parts of the Australian population who were ill at ease in a climate of economic restructuring, globalisation and identity politics.

In that speech, Pauline Hanson went on to lay out the framework which would later become the basis of the political movement that was to bear her name. She had 'commonsense' views on all matters of government policy, she assured Australians, which would cut through the nonsense preached by so-called experts.

On immigration and multiculturalism:

> ...I and most Australians want our immigration policy radically reviewed and that of multiculturalism abolished. I believe we are being swamped by Asians. Between 1984 and 1995, 40 per cent of all migrants into this country were of Asian origin. They have their own culture and religion, form ghettos and do not assimilate. Of course, I will be called a racist but if I can invite who I want into my home, then I should have the right to have a say in who comes into my country. A truly multicultural country can never be strong or united and the world is full of failed and tragic examples, ranging from Ireland to Bosnia.

On government programs for Aboriginal people and other minority groups:

> ...We now have a situation where a type of reverse racism is applied to mainstream Australians by those who promote political correctness and those who control the various taxpayer-funded 'industries' that flourish in our society, servicing Aboriginals, multiculturalists and a host of other minority groups.

On the privatisation of government-owned industry:

> ...Mr Deputy Speaker, we have lost all our big Australian industries and icons including Qantas ... Now this government wants to sell Telstra — a company that made $1.2 billion profit last year ... but first, they want to sack 54,000 employees to show better profits ... Anyone with business sense knows that you don't sell off your assets, especially when they are making money. I may only be a 'fish and chip shop lady' but some of these economists need to get their heads out of the text books and get a real job in the real world. I wouldn't even let one of them handle my grocery shopping.

On globalisation and free trade:

> ...If this government is to be fair dinkum, then it must stop kowtowing to financial markets, international organisations, world bankers, investment companies and big business people ... Reduced tariffs on foreign goods that compete with local products only seem to cost Australians their jobs. We must look after our own before lining the pockets of overseas countries and investors at the expense of our living standards and future.

On membership of the United Nations and foreign aid:

> ...Australia must review its membership and funding of the UN ... The government should cease all foreign aid immediately and apply the savings to generating employment here at home.

And, getting to the ideological heart of the matter, on the creation of a nation state that is strong because it is homogeneous:

> ...To survive in peace and harmony, united and strong, we must have one people, one nation, one flag.[3]

A Morgan poll taken six weeks later added 'the Pauline Hanson Movement' to the list of parties in its question about Senate voting intention and repeated to respondents Hanson's public statement that she was thinking of setting up a new political party. Eighteen per cent of respondents said they would vote for her.[4]

The new party was launched in April 1997. It was called Pauline Hanson's One Nation Party.

Just over a year later, on June 13 1998, the party won 23 per cent of the votes in the Queensland election, and eleven seats in the Queensland Parliament. It was a staggering and unprecedented result for a new party, a party of political novices.

On the conventional Left–Right political spectrum, the party went to the people with policies that were a mix of old Labor and new Right. Its political impact, its candidates and its constituency indicated that it was a middle-of-the-road party, sitting between traditional Labor and Coalition constituencies. It took five seats from Labor and six from the governing National–Liberal Party Coalition. Among the eleven winning candidates, there was a motor mechanic, a painter and decorator, a fisherman and part-time Santa Claus, a policeman, an army officer, two vets and several small business people. The people who voted for One Nation tended to be older, male, small-business people or blue-collar workers, and people with relatively low levels of formal education.[5]

With nearly a quarter of the vote overall, the success of One Nation in winning seats was dependent on preferences. The Coalition had decided to direct its preferences to One Nation ahead of Labor in all seats other than one in suburban Brisbane which was being contested for the Liberals by a Chinese-Australian. If the Coalition had put One Nation last, Labor would have won an additional six seats and a clear majority, and One Nation just three seats. Instead, Labor took power with the support of an independent, and later won a one seat majority at a by-election.

Former Liberal Prime Minister Malcolm Fraser criticised his party's decision to preference One Nation ahead of Labor. The racism of One Nation, he said, 'is extreme and, if allowed to gain hold in Australia, would grievously divide and damage this nation.'

> The consequence of the Liberal compromise with race has resulted in One Nation emerging as the third-largest party in the Queensland Parliament, with more seats than the Liberal Party. If Liberal preferences had gone to Labor over and above One Nation, Labor would have won the election and One Nation would be of minor relevance in the parliament itself. That would have been a better overall result.[6]

'The Liberal compromise with race' — these were strong words from the Party's elder statesman.

By the time the Federal election came around in October 1998, the Liberals, although not all of the Nationals, had decided to put One Nation last. Around Australia, One Nation scored 8.4 per cent of the votes. One million Australians voted for One Nation. However, frozen out of the preference deals, they won only one seat: a Senate seat for Queensland. After a change in electoral boundaries, Pauline Hanson stood for the seat of Blair which included some of her former electorate. She won 37 per cent of the vote against the Liberals' 20 per cent and Labor's 25 per cent. Labor won the seat on Liberal preferences.

One Nation's next major electoral test was the NSW State election in March 1999. Here they won 6.3 per cent of the vote and one seat in the Upper House. The man who won that seat was David Oldfield, a former adviser to the Federal Liberal Minister Tony Abbott. Alongside President Pauline Hanson and organiser David Etteridge, he had become one of a powerful party leadership triumvirate. In just nine months, between June 1998 and March 1999, One Nation won more than four million dollars in electoral funding, paid on a per-vote basis: $498,528 at the Queensland election; $3,044,525 at the Federal election; and $552,735 at the New South Wales election. This was enough to set up a formidable party machine, funded by all the taxpayers of Australia.

— • —

'Have you got your bullet-proof vest on?' John Pasquarelli asked us, striding out of his house to open the gate. Bravado with an edge of nervousness. A meeting with known supporters of things multicultural, things politically correct.

Pasquarelli lives in Yarraville, an inner-western suburb of Melbourne, an old working-class area where waves of migrants have settled. Today, the migrants are moving out to suburbs where the houses and gardens are bigger. New migrants tend to settle on the urban fringe where rents and properties are cheaper. Yarraville is rapidly becoming a trendy place to live, full of yuppies and gays.

Like many of his new neighbours, he's renovating too. Houseproud, he showed us around. On the walls were remnants of his years in New Guinea where he had become a member of Parliament: fearsome masks, spears, framed prints of crocodiles he had hunted. A renovation job faithful in its detail to the original style of the house, antique furniture, a cook's stove with six burners, a framed print of that now famous picture of Pauline Hanson wrapped in the Australian flag. They didn't have one, he said, so they borrowed Liberal Minister Tony Abbott's for the photo shoot.

'You created a storm, you and Pauline Hanson?' we start.

Pasquarelli was Pauline Hanson's adviser from the 1996 election until she sacked him at the end of that year. It was a crucial year in establishing her presence on the Australian political stage and building a constituency. He wrote her maiden speech.

'Don't be patronising like that. Of course I take credit, because that is what happened. I also realised very quickly that I was going to have problems with her. But, I thought, I am never going to have an opportunity like this again.

'And after that maiden speech, I have never ever seen anything like it, the mail and faxes and phone calls. It was just mind-boggling. Coming in from all around Australia. Just boxes and boxes. We had to get some extra space up in Ipswich, to move them out of the office, archive them — we had Bill Hayden's old office, which was big. God knows where they all are now. We couldn't even count them, we just didn't have the staff. I think she must have got mail like no other Federal politician in the history of this country.

'For the first time, politics in this country was exciting, if you want to use that word for it. Talkback was absolutely packed all around Australia, whether in Perth, Brisbane, Melbourne, Sydney. You were getting all these people fired up.

'She brought it all to the surface. People could never write letters to their politicians like they could write to her. Because she spoke about things that were unspeakable.

'The bloody mail we used to get from blokes. "I love you. I want to take you away and make mad love to you." A lot of them were quite dippy, but a lot of them were fair dinkum too. She had potent sexual appeal. If she had been Pauline physically, but had DeAnne Kelly inside her, she'd now be the Boadicea of Australian politics.'

He's referring to the National Party's Federal member for the seat of Dawson in Queensland. He's also referring to his estimation of Hanson's ability.

'She just couldn't understand a lot of things. Seriously, it was frustrating. Where I was stuffed with her is that she had no historical background. So I couldn't get a starting-point. No historical background about immigration. No historical background about Aboriginals. No historical background about mining and the environment. Nothing about protectionism and stuff like that. It was all foreign territory for her, and she wouldn't read. I understand some people can't read, then they have got to be briefed and all the rest of it, and I couldn't even win-out there.

'You paint a bleak picture of her,' we say.

'It was frustrating. Here I was presented with this opportunity. It just popped up out of the blue. It was bloody frustrating.'

Pasquarelli nevertheless took on the role of adviser and speechwriter. His greatest triumph was the maiden speech.

'You know, when I got Pauline to talk about how we were in danger of being swamped by Asians, that was just using language. At the time forty per cent of all migrants did come from the general Asian region, so I am allowed to use this elasticity in language. And I still think they should get down to zero net for a while.

'And it's not much different from what Whitlam had thought. Whitlam said "No" to Asians. He said something like — he was talking about the Vietnamese — "I'm not going to have these fucking fascist bastards here. No way." If Whitlam had stayed on we wouldn't have got all the Vietnamese we have got here now.'

It was not until Gough Whitlam's Labor Government fell at the end of 1975 that Australia started to accept refugees from the Indo-Chinese war, and Asian immigrants in any numbers.

'And that Chinese woman in the New South Wales Liberals, I had a confrontation with her in Sydney. What's her name?'

'Helen Sham-Ho.'

'Yeah, I think she is a disgrace, and I told her so. She wanted to be the President of the Upper House, and seriously, it was very difficult for me to understand that woman. Her accent, I mean, have you spoken to her? And she wanted to be the President of the Upper House!

'Same with the bloody Muslims, for God's sake, how can we have anything to do with them? I can see more problems cropping up with this Middle East stuff and the Muslims here. Immigration was OK when it was Anglo-European. I think you are upping the ante too much by introducing Asians, blacks, Muslims.

'And with the Aborigines, now you are having race-fixing. The numbers are growing, but they are not Aborigines. They are white people who are deciding to become Aborigines. I think a lot of smart-arse whites have done it in the last few years because there might be something for them in Native Title.

'This stuff about the stolen children, too, the alleged stolen children, that was all done to get them into the mainstream community, get them mixed up, to get them in quickly. I think it worked. Have you been out on those settlements? They're disgraceful. Have you been to Palm Island? Pauline and I went to there with *60 Minutes*. Palm Island is a disgrace.'

We ask him what he considers racism to be and whether it's a problem.

'This racism business — I don't give a stuff, because the word to me has got no meaning any more. It has been bandied around by so many different people, mainly from the Left, to intimidate other people. Singing out "You boong bastards" doesn't worry me in the least.

'And, if so many people have such a wrong understanding of race and racism in Australia, what do you do?' we ask.

'You have got to teach history, Australian history, properly. That means getting rid of all this bullshit about the whites being these dreadful monsters. Just teach history as it should be taught. Let Geoffrey Blainey do the syllabus.'

Professor Geoffrey Blainey had caused a huge media storm in March 1984 when he told a Rotary function in Warrnambool that levels of Asian immigration should be reduced for the sake of social stability. A Melbourne University history professor, a voice of authority, he followed up his assertions with a book later that year, *All for Australia*. It's a theme he's regularly returned to since, as he preaches against the evils of Native Title and multiculturalism. John Howard later appointed him to the

Centenary of Federation Committee, to oversee the educational and cultural programs leading up to the 2001 celebrations.

'And the problems of society other than race problems?' we ask.

'When you look at it, there are problems all around. We have got the racial problems, we have got economic problems. I suppose I was running the Bob Santamaria line on the economic stuff with Pauline, and she really liked that. Protectionism, and trying to stop the concentration of wealth at the top end of town. The thing that worries me is that the big boys are getting bigger. The big companies — and this is why Hanson was picking up support from the union movement — and the multinationals rip off the Australians through not paying tax. Shit, I'm starting to sound like a communist!'

While he's speaking, we notice a 'Learning Italian' kit on his couch. A do-it-yourself CD-ROM course.

'I'm just brushing up on Italian, because it has never been very good because my father was an Aussie. I mean, he was born in Italy but raised in Ingham. Hopefully, because I got enough Qantas points when I was working with her . . .'

He gestures to the picture of Pauline wrapped in Tony Abbott's flag.

'. . . I've got a fare to Italy. I want to go back to the village, Conzanno, a little village up north. You can piss from one end to the other, it's so small. Never been there. My father was getting ready to go back for the first time when he died, back in 1974.

'You know, I've been very influenced by my father's idea of assimilation. He did really well at school, so well that he got into Medicine at Melbourne University. He was one of the first medicos from a migrant background to graduate in Medicine. Assimilated properly, he did.

'He left behind two sisters in Ingham. They'd also been born in Italy, but grew up in Australia. They had a big blue and the sisters and my father never spoke to each other again.

'I didn't realise one of the sisters was still alive till I went back to Ingham in '87. She was in a home in Ingham with Alzheimer's, gibbering away in Italian. They had lived what I would call a narrow migrant life.'

Mind you, we suggested, they never had their brother's extraordinarily unusual opportunity to be assimilated — from a school in Ingham to a medical degree at Melbourne University is an amazing social and cultural leap.

'My father was very different to his sisters. He was always preaching assimilation. He said to migrants, "You can't come here and sit in your little ghettoes and expect to sort of ... "

As the end of the sentence drops off, he expects we know what people do in little ghettoes.

'Now I am doing a family history for my two nephews and nieces. My brother died unfortunately when he was 38; he was a doctor too. They have all got Italian names: Maria, Sofia and Sergio.'

We ask him some more about his own life story and what he was turning up in the family history.

'You know, I should have been Labor. Actually, I would have been Labor if my grandfather had not been persecuted by the AWU. If you know anything about Ingham and the AWU, which was Anglo-Irish or Anglo-Saxon, they were always shitty with the Italians and the Maltese canecutters. They said, "These bastards are going to come in and bloody well destroy our standard of living." My grandfather used to have to run the gauntlet. The AWU regarded them really as blacks or, I suppose, as yellow labour. That's how we became Liberals.'

The Queensland Labor Party has been dominated for most of its history by the powerful Australian Workers' Union.

'My father got out, by getting into Medicine at Melbourne University. Once he came down to Melbourne, he met people like Bob Santamaria who was at Newman College, too.'

Santamaria was a powerful force in post-war Australian politics, a leading light in the Movement, a conservative Catholic group which precipitated 'The Split' of the Democratic Labor Party from the Australian Labor Party, and prevented Labor from winning national government for a generation.

'Bob took my father home to meet his parents, who were running a fruit and vegetable shop in Coburg, and I don't think they spoke very good English then. Bob took Dad home and said, "Here's this bloke from Queensland, Joe Pasquarelli, and he speaks Italian."

'Then the war came. A lot of dad's friends up in the North went to prison camps. Italians, you know, they were interned. Some of them were Australian citizens.

'Then he went back to Brisbane for a while. I went to school in Brisbane, just after the war, and I mean, shit, to have a name like Pasquarelli just after the war was not the bloody best thing. I can remember being called "dago."'

We move on, asking him to reflect on the impact Pauline Hanson has made on Australia.

'So have you and Hanson, if you want to take the credit for it, made this country a better place?' we ask.

'Yes. Hanson, she has helped unlock the handcuffs. All that political correctness stuff. There was a hell of a lot of it around. And it's still here. It is not going to suddenly disappear.

'But now there are more people in Australia who can get onto talkback radio and say: "I am not a racist but..." They have confidence now, they are willing to give and take and say, "I want to talk about this," "I am concerned about that." I think that is a positive.'

'And where do you think the One Nation Party is going now?' we ask.

'Well, I think she is dead meat. 'Cos she's a stupid woman. Bear in mind that prior to the Queensland election, based on the figures, reputable polling figures, she had about two million people ready to vote for One Nation nationally. By the time election night came around, October 3rd 1998, she and Oldfield had chased away 800,000 of them and they ended up with only 1.2 million. David Oldfield replaced John Pasquarelli as Pauline Hanson's chief political adviser early in 1997.

'They chased them away with all that mad stuff. The two per cent tax. The stuff about "I'm your mother."'

Hanson had proposed a flat two per cent tax on all financial transactions, designed to capture tax from flighty global capital and prevent multinationals from reducing their profits in Australia by transfer pricing. The Greens have a similar policy. And, in a moment of nationalist excess, Pauline Hanson said she considered herself to be the 'mother of the nation' and the Australian people to be like her children.

'And Oldfield with his hands up the girl's dress. That did a lot of damage. Didn't you see that one?'

He searches around for a copy of a glossy women's magazine with the offending photograph. He also finds a printout for us of a porn website called 'Fun Nation' with pictures of Pauline in bondage.

'Remember, many of the blue-rinse brigade supported us. This cost them a lot of votes in Queensland.'

He's flicking through the magazine.

'There, he has got his hand right up her crutch. And then it was on the front page of the *Courier-Mail* in colour, the front page of the Sydney papers in colour, the front page in the Western Australian papers.

'We are also talking about a bloke who said on national television, "I am a national socialist."

'All she had to do was stay on that road that I had her on. I would still have a job, she would have a job, she would have been a Senator, and I think she would have had the balance of power in the Senate.

'The last time I spoke to her was on the night of the Federal election. I had a big blue with her on the phone and just told her what a stupid, hopeless person she was, running around saying stupid, fuckwitted things like "I'm the mother of the nation." Shit. She's a STUPID woman.

'People feel so betrayed by her. Badly let down.

'Especially in Queensland and New South Wales, a lot of Hansonites, I am being told by my sources, are going to shuffle off back home to the parties they came from. And they won't tell people they ever voted for Hanson.

'Still, at the end of the day, people got the shit off their liver. They got it out instead of bottling it up. She lanced the boil and a lot of the pus has drained out.

'It hasn't gone away, though. These things have a habit of rebounding.'

'So you think that there's still life in the One Nation movement?' we ask.

'Christ, it is still there. You could chop the bloody head off and like a Hydra, it is just going to grow again in another direction.'

We go to leave, and John Pasquarelli keeps talking all the way to the gate. He shows us the vegetables he was growing in the front garden — tomatoes and cucumbers and herbs. We reach the gate, and he gestures to a house across the road.

'When I see what Greeks have done with good houses in Yarraville, and what Italians have done to houses in Carlton ... They've butchered them. And then we have fuckwits like Theophanous and these people saying, "Oh you know, we are the people who brought culture to you."'

Andrew Theophanous is the Federal Member for Calwell and a stalwart of multiculturalism in the Labor Party.

'What's this fucking idea about aluminium? Where did they get this idea of aluminium windows from? And concreting everything in sight? I have just written an article on it. It's architectural vandalism.'

Having vowed not to get into an argument, this is our first.

'Have you ever been to Greece?'

'No.'

'There are no aluminium windows. There are no Greek columns on domestic houses. There is no cement . . . '

'And no balustrades? And where are the big lions at the front gate?'

'No, none, they were invented here. They are uniquely Australian.'

'No, you can't tell me that.'

'They are just assimilating, just like you want them to. They are being modern. They are being Australian.'

'They're fucked. They're not Australian things to do to your house.'

And with that, a cheerio.

'Looking forward to seeing your book.'

He had given us a signed copy of his book, *The Pauline Hanson Story, By the Man Who Knows.*

— • —

In 1941, whilst living as a refugee in Los Angeles, the German playwright Bertolt Brecht wrote *The Resistible Rise of Arturo Ui.* It's about a small-time gangster who sets up a protection racket for Chicago greengrocers, the Cauliflower Trust. The play is an allegory for the rise of fascism. Arturo Ui is Adolf Hitler and the cauliflower market is Germany. At each point in the rise of Arturo Ui, eminently resistible thuggery could have been resisted, and wasn't.

One Nation is an archetypical fascist party. Its rise could have been resisted more effectively by a Prime Minister who, for a long time, refused either to confirm or deny the party's ideological claims. One Nation's rise could even have been forestalled had governments through the eighties and the nineties managed to assure people that the system would protect them against the vagaries of economic restructuring and globalisation, that they did not need One Nation 'protection.'

To describe One Nation as a 'fascist' party is purely to use the term as a technical description of a system of politics. In its classical forms, in the Europe of the Great Depression or Peron's

Argentina, fascism responded to economic anxiety with bigger government and increased state control of the economy, flavouring this with a potent patriotism that put national ahead of international interests and national ahead of minority interests. More than anything else, fascism speaks the intoxicating language of nationalism — of the pre-eminent need to protect the national 'us' against dangerously subversive outsiders, both beyond and within the borders of the nation.

On the night of the Queensland election, Pauline Hanson's supporters sang 'Advance Australia Fair' as she entered the tally room. She spoke as a 'proud Australian' and a 'proud Queenslander.' The One Nation election posters featured the now famous picture of her wrapped in the Australian flag. Pauline Hanson's patriotism represented a nostalgic regret for a world in which we imagined that we were simply 'one nation,' and in which we needed to protect ourselves from hostile outsiders. She showed all the qualities of endurance and vulnerability in the face of the enemy that one would expect of that other female persona: the persona of the mother country.

The One Nation Party was aptly named indeed. For it is through the prism of old-style nationalism — and this prism alone — that all her policies are refracted: tariffs, foreign ownership, the sale of publicly owned enterprises, overseas aid, immigration, Native Title. Monocultural patriotism is her response to the burning anxieties of our time. It is both the heart of her message and her message of the heart.

Most dangerously and most effectively, however, hers is a politics built on resentment. It speaks to and for the little people who feel stranded by economic restructuring, by globalisation, by job insecurity, by the growing irrelevance of traditional work skills, by the increasing inability of unions to defend workers, by economic rationalism and the decline of the welfare state, by cutbacks in government services, by economic decline in regional and rural Australia, by the breakdown of community. These aggrieved people are the old white working-class and lower middle-class, small farmers, small-business people.

It's not that their resentment can't be explained, even justified. It's that the groups they choose as the primary targets of their resentment certainly do not deserve the blame heaped upon them. Aborigines and immigrants can no more be accused of creating the anxieties that beset people as a result of changes in work and community life than the Jews could be blamed for the hardships people experienced in Weimar Germany.

The resentment is levelled both at the elite cosmopolitans, the global businesspeople who are doing very well in the new economic environment, and at the historically poor and marginalised groups who have managed to reframe their claim to social resources around identity politics, the politics of cultural difference. Nor is the resentment doled out in equal measures; the latter are the object of most of One Nation's resentment. The end result is a potently racist identity politics. This is the territory into which Pauline Hanson's One Nation Party took its white Australian supporters.

So, despite the best intentions of politicians who would rather talk about balanced budgets or tax reform, the rise of the One Nation Party has shifted the whole focus of Australian politics towards questions of identity and belonging. Race is one of the big issues now, an issue that seems never to go away. Even economics is now refracted much of the time through the prism of race and nation.

'But it's really just a Queensland phenomenon,' the politicians and commentators say in the other states.

Nothing could be further from the truth. Not only are a large and growing proportion of Australians resident in Queensland, but Queensland is also a typically Australian place: a place of cosmopolitan cities; of international tourist destinations; of global investment; of large-scale and diverse immigrant settlement; of sizeable Indigenous presence. Nor are the underlying stresses and the strains of globalisation and restructuring different in Queensland to anywhere else in Australia. Since the Queensland election, One Nation has also been successful in New South Wales, where they won 6.3 per cent of the vote and a seat in the Upper House in the March 1999 State election.

Hansonism has its basis in real fears and the real difficulties people feel in their daily lives, even if the Hansonites themselves are misguided in their choice of the objects of their resentment, and even though their patriotism is dangerously anachronistic in an era of increasing local diversity and global interconnectedness.

Theirs is a patriotism which can only be fought with patriotism. A counter-patriotism, for this reason, must be of a very different kind, a patriotism that will take pride in our diverse and peaceful local communities, and our achievements and potential in the global economy. It must be an inclusive patriotism of belonging which actively embraces all Australians regardless of their race or background, and which firmly includes multiculturalism and Indigenous reconciliation at the centre of the national ethos of the 'fair go.' It must be cosmopolitan and outward-looking.

During the One Nation crisis, no such alternative patriotism was articulated by Australia's political leaders. One Nation's resistible rise was not resisted.

CHAPTER 20

Gathering Resentment

When the Australian people changed their Federal Government on 2 March 1996, it was for only the fourth time in half a century. Such changes are usually truly defining moments, but this particular moment was, at least at first, eerily ambiguous.

The Opposition went into the March 1996 Federal Election with what the media dubbed as 'me too' policies. On the basics of the Labor Government's agenda, the Coalition seemed to disagree barely at all. Medicare would be maintained; support for the ABC and SBS would continue at current levels; there was no fundamental disagreement about Mabo and Indigenous Reconciliation; immigration levels would remain the same, and bipartisan support for multiculturalism would continue; relations with Asia would grow stronger; and even the issue of the Republic was to remain an open question, the main difference being the process through which the question would be put to the Australian people. With little to differentiate the parties, swinging voters could, reasonably it seemed, opt for a change for not much more than change's sake.

By apologising for the comments he had made about Asian immigration back in 1988, John Howard had cleared the way to take over the leadership of the Opposition in 1995 for a second time.

> If they (my remarks) were seen by Australians of Asian descent as suggesting that I regarded them in any way as lesser Australians, then I regret that very much.[1]

Having put that particular aspect of his past behind him, Howard followed up with strong support for immigration and multiculturalism.

Journalists who followed the 1996 election closely say that Howard's speech at the launch of the Coalition's Immigration,

Multiculturalism and Settlement Policies at the Heidelberg Town Hall on 9 February 1996 was his best of the campaign. The audience was a carefully selected mix of party faithful, ethnic community leaders and the ethnic press. Howard spoke warmly, positively and without notes.

This is what the policy he held in his hand had to say about racism:

> All Australians have a fundamental responsibility to stamp out racism wherever it may appear, in ways consistent with the maintenance, preservation, and strengthening of the basic values and institutions that are the cornerstones of our multicultural society, and our way of life ...
>
> The Coalition yields to no-one in the intensity of its abhorrence, and unequivocal rejection of, all forms of racism. The Coalition's record on this issue is exceeded by no other political party. In particular, it was a Coalition Government that led the way in the abandonment of the obnoxious and racist White Australia Policy ...
>
> The basic cause of racism is ignorance. Education is the only viable long term approach which will eradicate racism. To this end, the Coalition will commit $10 million to a two year extensive multi-pronged education campaign directed towards schools and other educational institutions, as well as the wider community.[2]

The Coalition's stand could hardly have been worded more strongly. Clearly also, the Coalition planned to follow through its words with actions.

And this is what the policy Howard launched that night said about immigration:

> The Coalition does not consider that there should be any significant variation in the immigration intake at this time. Family reunion and humanitarian immigration will remain central parts of the immigration program, together with the skilled category.[3]

The actions that followed the election of the Howard Government, however, were to speak larger than these words of policy. Indeed, the new Government's actions spoke even larger because they seemed to be a kind of echo to the dramatic rise of Pauline Hanson and the foundation of her One Nation Party.

Having gained office, the Howard Government abolished the Office of Multicultural Affairs in the Department of the Prime Minister and Cabinet and then also the Bureau of Immigration, Multicultural and Population Research. It moved the Immigration portfolio out of Cabinet, cut immigration and shifted the balance of the reduced immigration program away from a family reunion policy in favour of skilled migration. It instituted a two-year waiting period for migrants to receive even the most basic of social security benefits. It massively reduced funding to the Human Rights and Equal Opportunity Commission and the Aboriginal and Torres Strait Islander Commission. It cut foreign aid. It cut Radio Australia's non-English language broadcasts and Australia Television Asia. It announced a tariff pause. Taken together, these actions speak to a new kind of race politics.

As for the promised first half of the $10 million anti-racism education campaign, a year and a half after it was due to commence, Minister Ruddock said the government had cut the budget in half and postponed it because they could not decide what racism was and what causes it. 'If you blow $5 million on an ad campaign, which you could easily do in a month, will that have any impact on attitudes?' Mr Ruddock's spokesperson said. 'The answer at the moment is, we don't know.'[4]

'They tell you I'm simplistic, that I have no ideas,' said Pauline Hanson around the time of the 1998 Queensland election. 'But isn't it funny that over the last couple of years things that I say, you can start to see them implement as policies.'[5]

Howard's public words also soon started to match his Government's actions. As Pauline Hanson's voice became more shrill, Prime Minister Howard credited his government with raising the veil of 'political correctness.'

Twelve days after Pauline Hanson gave her maiden speech, Howard was not to be found explaining how her ideas were incorrect or dangerous. This is what he was saying instead:

> One of the great changes that have come over Australia in the last six months is that people do feel able to speak a little more freely and a little more openly about what they feel. In a sense a pall of censorship on certain issues has been lifted. I think we were facing the possibility of becoming a more narrow and

restrictive society and that free speech could not be taken so freely for granted as we might in our calmer moments have assumed. I think there has been that change and I think that is a very good thing ... I welcome the fact that people can now talk about certain things without living in fear of being branded as a bigot or as a racist ... The election of the new Government has done something to make that kind of neo-McCarthyist, zealous, prejudiced reaction against something that you don't agree with, made that a little less acceptable and I think that is a great thing for healthy democracy in Australia.[6]

Tackled directly by radio talk show host John Laws about his response to Hanson, he said:

I think part of the difficulty of this whole debate is that there has been a tendency over recent years that if anybody has criticised or challenged the prevailing orthodoxy on immigration or multiculturalism, they have been branded as intolerant and bigoted.[7]

Hanson, for her part, was willing to give Howard credit where credit was due. Things had changed for the better since the One Nation Party had come onto the Australian political scene.

'Listen, there is freedom of speech, we're not governed by all this political correctness any more,' she said.[8]

Howard steadfastly refused to condemn Hanson, ostensibly in order to deny her the credibility that a reply would have implied. He said that if she was ignored, she would go away.

However Pauline Hanson did not go away. The more John Howard refused to condemn her, the bigger she got. The more he tacitly approved of what she was saying under the rubric of free speech, opening up debate, and lifting the pall of political correctness, the more Pauline Hanson became a kind of rhetorical challenge to him, and to the country.

The key question was, to what extent did Howard disagree with the 'one-nation' view? Here are some of his public pronouncements:

On Indigenous policy and Native Title:

The whole Aboriginal policy area has been hijacked by the social engineers, the politically correct and other sundry groups more intent on dividing than uniting our community ... The actions we take must be within the framework of one undivided Australian nation with a common respect for the one body of law, to which all are equally accountable and from which all are entitled to receive an equal share of justice.[9]

On Australian history and identity:

[The] challenge [is] to ensure that our history as a nation is not written definitively by those who take the view that Australians should apologise for most of it. This 'black armband' view of our past reflects a belief that most Australian history since 1788 has been little more than a disgraceful story of imperialism, exploitation, racism, sexism and other forms of discrimination. I take a very different view. I believe that the balance sheet of our history is one of heroic achievement and that we have achieved much more as a nation of which we can be proud than of which we should be ashamed.[10]

On minority interests:

...Labor ... governed essentially by proxy through interest groups. Identification with a powerful interest group has been seen as the vehicle through which government largesse is delivered. Increasingly Australians have been exhorted to think of themselves as members of sub-groups. The focus so often has been on where we are different — not on what we have in common. In the process our sense of community has been severely damaged. Under us, the views of all particular interests will be assessed against the national interest and the sentiments of mainstream Australia.[11]

On the need to return to the values of 'mainstream Australia':

There is a frustrated mainstream in Australia today which sees government decisions increasingly driven by the noisy, self-interested clamour of powerful vested interests with scant regard to the national interest ... Many Australians in the mainstream feel utterly powerless to compete with such groups, who seem to have the ear completely of the government on major issues. This bureaucracy of the new class is a world apart from ... the Australian mainstream.[12]

Howard's language created a series of great divides, a series of opposing groups in which he clearly supported one side over the other: those advocating the politics of difference versus those who would want a united community; the social engineers of the multicultural and Aboriginal 'industries' versus advocates of 'equality' (by which he meant the pretence of sameness); those who would want to take a 'black armband' view of our history versus those who regard it as a story of heroic achievement; noisy interest groups versus the national interest; those who consider themselves members of sub-groups versus those who identify with the sentiments of 'mainstream Australia'. Clearly, the members of the subgroups — the noisy interest groups, the proponents of 'black armband' history, the multiculturalists and the supporters of Aboriginal rights — are all opposed to 'mainstream Australia.' As such, they are not considered to be a part of 'mainstream Australia.'

Here Howard was perfecting the techniques of wedge politics developed by the Reagan–Bush Republicans in the United States. Labor's electoral success from 1983 to 1996 had been based on a cross-sectional alliance between the old working class, the new middle-class cosmopolitans, migrants and Indigenous people. Labor had developed an elaborate interest group politics — just as, for that matter, the Coalition had when it was in power from 1975 to 1983. Upon the foundation of this interest group politics an alliance was built, an unholy but for a while highly successful mix of multiculturalism, recognition of Indigenous rights, economic globalisation, Asian regional integration, support for trade unions and workers' rights, and large-scale training and transition to work programs for the unemployed. Most of all, it was a politics of inclusion, a politics which tried to pull together interests that were not identical. The problem was that many of the old white working class, white farmers and small-business people felt they had been left out of the new alliance.

Howard tried to strike a wedge into these constituencies in order to bring some over to the Coalition, even if it was at the risk of permanently alienating others.

Nowhere was this clearer than at one of the most subtle and powerful points of difference between Labor and the Coalition in what was in most other respects the 'me too' election of 1996 — the Coalition's primary election slogan, 'For All of Us.'

Reflecting on the slogan six months after winning the election, Howard said:

> Our slogan 'For All of Us' brought together in a very effective fashion the mood and the gathering resentment of the Australian people.'[13]

This is the key point. Not only was the resentment gathering, but Howard's government would gather that resentment in order to build a broader political constituency than the traditional conservative base of businesspeople and the wealthy.

At the time of the election, the then Prime Minister, Paul Keating, railed against the slogan:

> It is cynical and it is bad to play on intolerance and discriminatory motives, in word games, in coded language, like the Liberal Party's slogan 'For All of Us', which really means for some of us. As Noel Pearson said this week ... the American Republican Party, in doing its research, came up with this slogan 'Enough is Enough' ...Enough of pandering to minorities. Enough of the majority carrying the weight of minorities. Enough is enough. That's what it really means. 'For All of Us' is a wink and a nudge slogan. So when the extremists in the Coalition make their intolerant remarks ... and when the Liberal and National Party leaders then say that they won't accept that their remarks are unacceptable, they know they put the shading in which makes the subtext more readable for all of us, and enough is enough. I mean, it is cynical and it is bad.[14]

On face value, the 'For All of Us' slogan was consistent with the 'me too' politics which assured the Australian people the Coalition supported Multiculturalism, Reconciliation and other inclusive agendas. On another reading, it also implied that the 'silent majority' of 'mainstream Australia' would be remembered once again by a Coalition Government. Howard named these people 'the battlers.'

Here, he was building on lessons he had drawn from long-serving Liberal Prime Minister, Sir Robert Menzies. Menzies' name for the critical middle ground of swinging voters was 'the forgotten people.' This is how Howard described his view of the Menzies legacy:

Menzies' political success lay in building an enduring and broadly-based constituency that supported Liberalism's values and priorities. At the heart of that constituency were 'the forgotten people' of that era — the men and women of the great Australian mainstream who felt excluded from the special interest elitism of the Liberal Party's immediate predecessors and from the trade union dominance of the Labor Party ... Liberalism faces the ongoing challenge of building an enduring and broadly-based constituency across the great mainstream of our rapidly changing society. Over recent times, a new constituency has galvanised around new issues and in support of Liberal priorities. It includes many of the 'battlers' and families who are struggling to get ahead ... It includes all those who do not want their national government to respond to the loudest clamour of the noisiest minority ... Liberalism now has an opportunity, unparalleled for almost fifty years, to consolidate a new coalition of support among the broad cross-section of the Australian people. It will only prove enduring if Liberalism continues to relate its fundamental values and principles to the concerns and aspirations of the Australian mainstream, rather than the narrower agendas of elites and special interests. This means building a genuinely shared sense of national purpose rather than an amalgamation of special interests.[15]

Howard was saying that Labor had given special treatment and privileges to immigrants, Aborigines, the environmental lobby and cultural elites. These would be taken away and handed back to 'the battlers,' who truly deserved them. In the context of restructuring and an industrial accord which had provided most people with few real benefits, this message now resonated particularly with the white working class and the lower middle class. 'For All of Us' meant no more than redressing the special favours that had been bestowed on 'them.' But this particular message, of course, was not really targeted at all of us.

You've read the book *The Revolt of the Elites*, haven't you? It was written by Christopher Lasch, an American social commentator. His theory is — and I think he's right and I certainly find it here in Australia — that a lot of, for want of a better expression, mainstream people resent the fact that there's a bit of the ruling elite ... who, in effect, are saying that there are certain issues that you, the public, are too stupid to be trusted even to talk about. We'll decide it for you and we'll tell you what's good. A lot of Australians find that issues related to immigration and multiculturalism fall into that category.[16]

Howard said this late in 1996 in answer to a question specifically about his response to Pauline Hanson. Taking up the issue of immigration, for instance, he said:

If you're a blue-collar working or living in a regional centre of Australia and you've lost your job and you don't have any prospect of getting another one, you naturally will think, 'Well, if you stop immigration I might get my job back.' I don't think that's a racist thing.[17]

Yet one piece of research after another, one economist after another, has shown that immigration creates a greater number of employment opportunities than the number of new immigrant entrants to the labour market. In the words of the old political catchcry, immigration creates jobs; it doesn't take jobs. Repeating rather than contradicting a commonsense fallacy — is that racism?

And, this is the reason Howard gave when explaining why he had not come out strongly on the issues Hanson had raised:

I think a leader on some issues has got to get out in front and defy people to run him over. On other issues he's got to stay back and listen.[18]

When it came to Pauline Hanson and her One Nation politics, he had decided to be a leader of the latter variety rather than the former.

Even after the Queensland election when the question of preferences was being pressed on him over and over again by the media, Howard said that having One Nation with the balance of power in the Senate was no worse than having the Australian Democrats. The Liberal Party machine finally forced his hand, and One Nation was put behind the Liberals in every seat in the 1998 Federal election.[19]

For all his wanting to be compared to Menzies, Howard's wedge politics were very different from the kind of politics

Menzies had practiced. Menzies' injunction to win over 'the forgotten people' meant that the conservatives needed to focus on the middle ground of swingers neglected both by Labor with its trade union focus and the conservatives, who focused on business interests. The difference is that Menzies managed to win the swingers whilst keeping a steady hand on the national tiller. Despite and against the inclinations of the majority of the 'forgotten people,' he presided over high levels of immigration culminating in the end of the White Australia Policy in 1966, gradual progress in Indigenous affairs leading up to the 1967 referendum, and increasing integration of Australia into the Asian regional economy. Yet he still managed to assure 'the forgotten people' that their interests were being looked after.

Howard thought he understood Menzies, but the mistake he made was to take the cues from One Nation and the 'battlers' literally. So, his approach was not one of inclusion but a politics of division. His was not a politics which brought more people into the mainstream, but a politics which defined the mainstream narrowly as 'the battlers' and then set their interests in opposition to those of 'special interest groups.' Hence the insinuations about immigrants and Aborigines rorting the system and getting an unfair advantage, hence all the talk about political correctness and free speech, hence the equivocation in contradicting Pauline Hanson.

One Nation only said — honestly — what the Prime Minister in his own convoluted, coded way often seemed to mean. The 'battlers,' however, might as well buy the real thing rather than John Howard. And, once One Nation appeared on the scene, with more confidence than ever before, they did.

— • —

'With John Howard, you have seen the national consensus being broken down.'

We're speaking with Nick Bolkus, who had been Minister for Immigration and Ethnic Affairs in the Keating Government from 1993 to 1996.

'He's been corrosive and negative. This is how the Hanson factor took off, when he became Prime Minister. But the real damage had already been done, even before he became Prime Minister. He put the brakes on Liberal Party policy. If Kennett was Prime Minister, if Kennett had been Liberal leader for the last ten years, the national consensus would not have been broken.

'John Howard thinks the rest of the world is only there to play cricket against. And, as for political correctness, he would probably call the Lincoln Memorial in Washington DC politically correct. What he calls political correctness is basically a matter of decency.

'It's a terrible turn of events for Australia. If almost any other person had been Liberal leader: Hewson, Peacock, Downer ... '

'And what was the consensus that Howard has broken down?' we ask.

'The thing that strikes me about the whole of the last quarter of a century in Australian leadership is that, until now, the language from the leadership on both sides of the political fence was inclusive. It made you feel as if you had a right, and an equal right. And I think that's changed enormously. Howard, won't even use the word "multicultural."'

'So what drives you? Why do you do what you do?' we ask?

'Why do what I do? When I was growing up in decaying inner-western Adelaide in the early sixties, I soon realised I had to be able to defend my rights. I could see that, as a "wog," I was a second-class citizen. I spent a lot of time in those days wishing I had straight blonde hair and that my nose was straight.

'The stimulus to join the Labor Party came from Don Dunstan who was advocating the end of White Australia at the time, and preaching the benefits of diversity. He actually made me, and I know my parents, feel as if we were welcome and that we would be treated as human beings rather than just economic fodder.

'It was the days of Vietnam, it was the days of enlightenment on the campuses. I actually went on my first demonstration when I was in about third or fourth year at high school. From then on I embarked upon another kind of war, based on the conviction that Australia needed migrants and migrants needed to be respected. Diversity was something we should be proud of.

'When I decided on a political career, I also came to the conclusion very early that if I ever ran for a seat, it would not be a seat on the coastline because that was very much White Australia territory. The irony is that I actually live down by the beach in Adelaide now; so much for that. But essentially what has always motivated me is the politics of race and respect.

'And the best thing that has happened to me in my career was to be Immigration Minister for three years. I got to appreciate the extent of the diversity in the community. And, by living through other people's migration experiences, I got to appreciate fully and enjoy my life, and the things in my past and my parents' past.

'For instance, I spent last Sunday night in Perth at a Kazzie function ...'

Nick Bolkus's remembers that his family came from the Greek island of Kastellorizo, many of whose inhabitants were among the earliest waves of Greek migrants to Australia.

'There were three old guys there, the Kakulas brothers, and we sat for about an hour or so as they talked about how they came over. I discovered that my grandfather came over with one of them. It was June 1923. The boat fare cost £16 if you were not to be fed, and £20 if you were to be fed. These guys paid £16 because they couldn't afford the extra money. They brought their cans of oil and camp fires, and they cooked their own meals for thirty-four days on the boat. I was able to relive that experience with them.

'It's the same kind of story, whether it's Vietnamese or Cambodians or Muslims from the Middle East, or people from Europe, or the Jews; the experiences are often so similar wherever people come from. So similar. How they get here. The acts of courage.'

We're sitting in his office in Parliament House: a Senator for South Australia and Shadow Minister for the Environment. Another migrant success story.

'So what does it feel like to have succeeded? What does it feel like to have come to this point in the cross-generational story of migration?' we ask.

'You can be here for forty, fifty, sixty years and you could still see yourself as foreign.'

'... But you were born here, right? And you still feel that?'

'That's right. If you look at me you wouldn't think I felt that way. You know, I used to get letters when I was Immigration Minister telling me to go back where I came from. The trouble is they didn't know I was born here, and they didn't know where my family came from, so I got told to go back to Turkey, Lebanon, Greece, Italy, everywhere.

'I think many of us are lost between our roots and where we are today. We can't go back to where we came from. It's a long way to go back in many ways. We have a huge commitment here and we appreciate what this place has to offer, but there is always something about being a migrant or a son or daughter of a migrant in a new country.'

Despite his success, Nick Bolkus is not a person who is comfortably at home in the country of his birth.

'Look at the United States. We haven't yet embraced our migrants in the way America has. It's got problems, for sure. But in terms of appreciating, celebrating its diversity and the contributions of migrants, it leaves us for dead. The US doesn't just celebrate it, it's always got it on show. You look at kids' programs like *Sesame Street*, and you see the full breadth of the American society. You look at the *Today Show*, the breakfast show, and you've got Asian-Americans, you've got white Americans, you've got Latinos, and they're all up front. But switch to Channel 9 in Australia, and what do you see?

'The problem in this country is that you live a lie. Australian history as recognised by most Australians is based on some fundamental lies. Based on the lie that Aboriginals weren't human beings. Based on the myth that the Brits were the first ones here. If you can't really accept the truth of your origins ...'

We mention Geoffrey Blainey's notion of 'black armband history,' as repeated frequently by John Howard.

'Black armband history is just a way of dismissing and denigrating the past. It comes from a very dark, paranoid mind. It is an idea propagated by paranoid leaders.

'Mention the word "race" in Australian politics and you get into trouble, unless it's about horses. That's how it goes. I carried the Wik debate in the Senate, and we did it without blood on the floor. I think there are benefits in having a debate about race.

'Howard doesn't want to talk about race when it's what he regards as "black armband" history. Then he says this is "the era of free speech," and what we have next is slanging matches led by Hanson. That's his version of debate, acceptable debate about race.

'I think one thing Keating said was spot on, and that is when you change the government, you change the whole face and structure of your society.'

We ask him for a vision of an alternative, for a new kind of politics that deals with the phobias which drive the One Nation Party, the politics of resentment upon which John Howard bases his wedge politics.

'The truth about governments now is that their economic sovereignty is much more limited than it ever was. You have to recognise that. And once we recognise that, the real battle is the social.

'People are seeking out their roots, wherever they are living. It is something that is happening in all Western societies like ours. I don't know what it all means. I suppose there is a gradual assertiveness of ethnicity and culture, and governments have to accommodate it.

'Governments need to celebrate our diverse backgrounds, and in doing so they send out a very important message of inclusion. It is now just a responsibility for Government to do this. I don't think it has completely sunk in yet; it is sinking in now. Governments need to get mobilised to pursue, not just the identity agenda, but also the social agenda.

'This means that the people Howard calls "the battlers" will have to include the migrant kids of Cabramatta and Bankstown, adults who can't speak the English language very well, and not just middle-aged white Anglo-Saxons.

'This way, we'll all find that we are as a nation becoming something new, something that we are still creating, something that reflects the complete reality here in Australia. Not integrating into the white Anglo-Saxon society of the fifties and sixties, but becoming something much more diverse and larger, and much more relevant to all of us.'

— • —

Meanwhile, other parts of the Labor Party were inventing a 'new Labor' — or is it reinventing an old Labor? — that can take on John Howard and win back the 'battlers' who might otherwise be inclined to vote either for the Coalition parties or for One Nation. Because the One Nation voters are the people in the middle of the old Right–Left political spectrum and because they are the swingers, they have become as much the focus of attention for Labor as for John Howard and the Coalition.

'Hansonites Force Labor Call to Cut Migrant Intake' — this was how the headline in the *Australian* reported on the first major speech made by Martin Ferguson after he became Labor's shadow Immigration minister in 1997.

'Labor needs to focus its attack on the real source of Pauline Hanson's temporary support, which is unemployment and job insecurity,' Ferguson told the NSW Young Labor Conference. 'The intake of skilled migrants should always be undertaken in the context of local employment policy.'

It all sounded very like the way John Howard 'understood'

how people were concerned about the negative impact of immigration on unemployment, even though no economist could be found to show that there is any such impact.

This is how Ian Henderson, the *Australian's* economics correspondent, interpreted Ferguson's statement:

> Mr Ferguson's immigration policy shift is bound to attract significant attention, with its direct appeal to voters attracted to Mrs Hanson's anti-immigration pitch.[20]

Ferguson's very appointment — as Shadow Minister for Immigration, Training, Population and Immigration, to give him his full title — was itself symbolic, given that he was well known as an opponent of immigration. He was also an icon of Labor's bad faith when it comes to the representation of ethnic communities and women in Parliament. With support from key unions, he forced his way into the seat of Batman in 1995, against the preselectors who were in the process of choosing from an array of local women and immigrant candidates who more closely reflected the character of the electorate.

And collapsing Employment and Immigration portfolios meant that immigration was now to be considered a subset of unemployment. This decision repeated one of Labor's greatest political mistakes. After the 1974 election when Immigration Minister Al Grassby lost his seat, Immigration was integrated into Clyde Cameron's Department of Labour. With immigration reduced to its lowest levels in the post-war era, Cameron's reaction to the prospect of taking refugees from the Vietnam war was 'We won't have Vietnamese Balts.' Meanwhile, Malcolm Fraser, Michael MacKellar and Liberal staffer Petro Georgiou were deliberately tailoring their message to ethnic communities. This was a crucial factor in Fraser's electoral success, and later became the basis for his highly successful policy of multiculturalism.

Adding 'Population' to the shadow Immigration portfolio for the first time ever in 1997 compounded the problems generated by the Ferguson appointment. It was a gesture to the line of discussion opened in the Labor Party by Barry Jones in the *One Nation — Two Ecologies* report, which suggested that population growth should be halted in Australia. At the same time, Multicultural Affairs was deleted from the shadow portfolio title, even though the Howard Government had a full Department of Immigration and Multicultural Affairs.

So, it was hardly surprising that, when Ferguson made his first speech in Parliament in his new role, there was no mention of multiculturalism, although there were plenty of mentions of Australian decency to migrants and the sixties concept of 'integration.' So much so that anti-immigration, anti-multiculturalism Independent MP Graham Campbell took the opportunity to congratulate Labor for choosing him.

— • —

When Bob Carr's Labor Party won the New South Wales election in March 1999, independents won the balance of power in the upper house. Peter Wong won a seat for the pro-multicultural Unity Party. David Oldfield won a seat for Pauline Hanson's One Nation Party.

Within days of winning the election, Premier Carr announced that the Government was to change the name of the Ethnic Affairs Commission to the Community Relations Commission. 'It is an important signal that people with migrant backgrounds don't want to be typecast or categorised as ethnic Australians. They are Australians with a full entitlement to all that citizenship means,' Carr said.[21]

By 1999, every other State in Australia as well as the Federal Government had changed the name of its Ethnic Affairs portfolio to Multicultural Affairs. The change wasn't because 'ethnic' had become an unacceptable word, because it is still used extensively to describe the cultural identities of immigrant groups — except, now, in New South Wales. The shift to 'multicultural' indicates a broader agenda, about creating social cohesion through recognising and respecting differences of experience and identity, and in this agenda, 'ethnic' is still an important descriptive term. But, clearly, Bob Carr was as uncomfortable with elevating the word 'multicultural' as he was with using the word 'ethnic.'

One Nation's David Oldfield wholeheartedly approved of the Labor Premier:

Bob Carr is to be congratulated ... Listening to the voice of people who support One Nation ... they were very clear in saying that the word 'ethnic' was divisive and they were quite clear in questioning how long it has to be before someone is no longer an ethnic and are now accepted as being an Australian ... It was an interesting speech to listen to [Bob Carr's], because it was one that you know quite frankly I could have written for Pauline Hanson or she could have written herself. It's one of the impacts that One Nation has certainly had that we're at least starting to get people to describe things differently and we are breaking down some of the political correctness. I applaud those people in Labor who came out and said that 'ethnic' is a divisive word.[22]

Furore ensued among ethnic communities. They knew what David Oldfield, and Bob Carr, were saying. Ethnic community leaders, even longtime Labor supporters, publicly expressed their disgust.

A motion of condemnation was put to the NSW Legislative Council on 3 June 1999. After a heated debate, the motion was passed, Ayes 24, Noes 15. The fifteen Noes were made up of a new and very revealing political alignment: Labor joining forces with One Nation.

— • —

Mark Latham is new Labor personified, a sign of Labor revival, is also interested in John Howard's 'battlers' and the people who vote for One Nation. Taking what he sees as the battlers' perspective, he agrees with NSW Premier Carr, who agrees with John Howard on the issue of immigration. But John Howard has kept a portfolio which uses the word 'multicultural,' and here Mark Latham would disagree with Howard and agree with Carr.

'A big part of the dissatisfaction with migration is the evidence that unskilled migration has been a social disaster. You know, bring people to Australia to leave them on the dole. People see these things with their own eyes and they draw the commonsense conclusion that unskilled migration doesn't work. If the new arrivals are unskilled and not able to get into work, there's a lot of public resentment about that.'

We point to the evidence that immigration increases employment. We ask why migrants should be blamed for structural problems in the economy.

'I don't blame the migrants. I blame the fools who created an unskilled migration program in the eighties.'

'But they were your people, Bob Hawke and the Labor Party,' we say.

'They put too much emphasis on family reunion. I don't blame the migrants for a moment. They're innocent victims of bad public policy.'

'So you think you can have skilled workers here without their families? And that this kind of labour is a sustainable commodity?' we ask.

'I don't think, having made a decision to leave one country to go to another, that the new country is really under any obligation to reunite the family that they, in the first instance, disunited. They made the decision to disunite the family when they moved here.'

Besides, we point out, this is precisely what the Coalition has done, cut family reunion.

'Things have improved a lot. The policy settings are pretty good now.'

'And the other restraint on migration is urban environment,' Latham continues.

'Sydney is the main destination for migrants. And it's bursting at the seams. I mean, the congestion, the pollution, the overcrowding of this city, of this whole Cumberland Basin. It is at crisis point, and I think the size of the migration program needs to be a function of those environmental constraints.'

The facts are that Sydney's population is growing more slowly than the Australian average, and the Australian population itself is slowing down as a result of a declining birthrate and a smaller immigration program. Infrastructure and environmental problems are just that.

Then the conversation moves on to multiculturalism.

'Well now, unfortunately and I don't know whether this is by accident or by design, multiculturalism has been understood by the Australian people as a policy that says we should be a nation of many cultures. This has been understood by many in the public to mean that the Government wants people that I don't know to have a different culture, a culture that I can't necessarily relate to, and here they are, living in my country. In some cases, they're utilising taxes that I've paid for multicultural programs. And I'm struggling along, worried about job security and street crime and the like. I don't think that process is fair. It has led people to resent what some people have described as social engineering.

The impression is that certain cultural groups get money that's not available to others.

'As soon as the Government starts distributing grants — there's the Italians in their groups and there's Lebanese and there's Asians — you start to encourage people to think about their identity in those terms.

'I don't think Government should mandate or direct people on how they should be Australian. When the Government is running a top-down process of mandating or engineering outcomes in society, then there's the feeling that the process is not inclusive.

'I'll give you an example of when a Government goes too far in its efforts to manipulate outcomes. We've got a policy in Australia of universities having quotas for non-English-speaking background applicants. Yet a lot of the research shows that among non-English-speaking backgrounds, people from a Korean, Chinese and Japanese-speaking background have actually got better university participation rates than people from an English-speaking background.

'The problem with positive discrimination programs is that for those who miss out on university entry, those who weren't the beneficiaries of positive discrimination, they effectively are being discriminated against for something that they can't influence — where they were born.'

As a matter of fact, no Australian universities have quotas. Many universities have highly generalised equity policies and specialist student support programs, but never entry quotas.

Until the 1998 elections, Mark Latham was Labor's Shadow Minister for Education.

— • —

We asked Bob Hawke about Mark Latham.

'Well I would simply say to Latham, "Look, you stop giving bullets to the other side. Stay in the tent and piss out, instead of going outside the tent and pissing in. Or you're out." I just wouldn't muck around with him.'

And we bring up with him the way you'll find the same kinds of difference of opinion on both sides of politics. Like the difference between John Howard and former Victorian Premier Jeff Kennett. This identity stuff is not a simple Left–Right thing.

'Yes, you've got to say about Kennett, he's such an amazing mixture of elements. There are some things about Kennett which are just beautiful. He hasn't got a shred of colour prejudice, or any sort of prejudice based on race. None at all. And he's passionate about it.'

As the century closes, Howard, Hanson and now the 'new' Labor are all vying for one small, scared and diminishing ethnic group, the 'battlers.' It's not just that in their obsession with this small, shrinking patch of electoral territory, all three have come up with the same kinds of ways of viewing the world. The larger problem is that in so doing they are losing touch with a far broader and growing expanse of electoral territory: a diverse, cosmopolitan, consciously immigrant and outward-looking Australia.

Worse still, those politicians who scrape the bottom of the populist barrel are doing the 'battlers' themselves a disservice. These are complicated people, who have worked with migrants, lived next door to migrants, and over the decades learned to get on. They are more unsure of immigration and multiculturalism than dead against it.

As we face the maelstrom of change and uncertain futures, the 'battlers' need to be convinced of the benefits of globalisation, immigration and multiculturalism, rather than egged along by the politics of recidivist localism and retreat from the world. The parochial and racist turn in Australian politics will do the 'battlers' no good at all.

Less than four per cent of Victorians voted for One Nation in the 1998 Federal election. We mention this figure to Bob Hawke. Kennett, we suggest, has to take a fair deal of the credit for One Nation's relatively poor showing in his state.

'Yes, leadership makes all the bloody difference.'

This was Bob Hawke's parting remark to us.

CHAPTER 21

New White Australia

Ian Macphee was Minister for Immigration and Ethnic Affairs in the Fraser Government from 1979 to 1982. Following Michael MacKellar as Minister, he was responsible for the management of continued large-scale Asian immigration and the implementation of the idea of multiculturalism, as articulated in the 1978 Galbally *Review of Migrant Programs and Services.*

'You see, for all of the talk of the White Australia Policy having been abolished by Al Grassby and the Labor Party, the fact is that the procedures and many regulations which continued the White Australia Policy remained in place when I became Minister. They hadn't dismantled it.

'It was one of the tragedies of the Whitlam Government. We know that they had these grand visions, but not enough competent Ministers to deliver. And they weren't all committed to them anyway. Many of those Ministers from the New South Wales Right were not committed to abolishing the White Australia Policy. So, despite all the grandstanding by Grassby, the structures hadn't been changed. Things like Assisted Passage, which of course I didn't like, because it only applied to Europeans.'

'So how did it happen, how did you get rid of the last vestiges of the White Australia Policy?' we ask.

'Fraser came and said to me, "Look, this is really crucial." And I just did what I believed I had to do. We shared a great rapport. Many of the big decisions I made were within my scope under the Immigration Act and I didn't take them to Cabinet. He thanked me several times for not taking things to Cabinet that were difficult. He wanted to avoid people running for cover and finding it all too hard. I'm not talking about major decisions like the size of the intake or even decisions that varied the law, but decisions that varied procedures.

'Now, I knew that if we'd had a debate, if we'd had a referendum asking "Will we in fact abolish the White Australia Policy?" the answer would have been "No." Or "Do we want Asian migrants?", it would have been "No." But if you asked, do you want to build a fortress at the southern end of the world, "Yes," they'd have said, "Yes, now."

'In my three years in the portfolio, I unravelled a great many procedural and legal obstacles to the implementation of non-discriminatory policy. Now there was nothing duplicitous about that. If you were committed to abolishing a racist policy, you had to do it. We found that health checks, criminal checks and so forth were not being carried out in Asia and therefore nobody could get a clearance. We also hadn't put immigration officials in the embassies. So you couldn't process applications. People didn't know that they even could apply to migrate. The system had remained entirely geared to the White Australia Policy.

'We even had the Assisted Passage scheme still continuing. Now if someone couldn't afford their fare in the late 1970s, we didn't want them. If they were unemployed in Britain, or wherever else, we didn't want them because they'd be unemployed here, too. Our economy had moved on. The factory-fodder policy had outlived its usefulness. The whole economic basis of the migration had changed.'

'So what motivated you to take on this kind of a public role,' we ask, 'a role that helped change the very nature of Australian society and redirected the whole drift of Australian history since Federation? Tell us about yourself.'

'My mother migrated from Scotland when she was fourteen. My grandmother with whom I was very close — she was a gorgeous person and told me interesting things about the Scots — had not the slightest desire to go back to Scotland. My father's family had come from Scotland in 1856, I think.'

A name like Macphee is a bit of a giveaway.

'But from a very early age I couldn't comprehend why people looked at a place on the other side of the world as being home. When you looked at the map and it was just so obvious that we had Asia and South America as our neighbours. I remember as a kid of eleven looking at the map and saying, "Why do people call England home?"

'Also, I grew up in a time of great sectarianism between Catholics and Protestants. If you went to a State school, as I did, then there was always the school down the road that you were supposed to dislike. I just could not comprehend it.

'Now, as time went on and I read of Australian history, which of course wasn't taught in schools, the more I just couldn't comprehend the White Australia Policy, or the blackbirding of the South Sea Islanders, or the mistreatment of the Indigenes. I was appalled by it. But, of course, it's only in recent years that I realise how little I knew.

'I ended up doing my law degree part-time at Sydney University while working in Legal Aid in the Public Solicitor's Office. I stayed in the Office for eight years in total. I just felt comfortable around a Legal Aid office and not in a major corporate firm.

'And then I went to Papua New Guinea, in the Legal Aid Office again. So I had two and a half years there. I travelled all over the country in little court houses representing people accused of various crimes: sorcery, clan killings, cannibalism even. We had to introduce anthropological evidence to explain the cultural context. You couldn't address how things happened — questions of self defence and motivation — except through culture and identity. So I learnt a lot. I ended up getting a scholarship to study at the East–West Centre in Honolulu to further the understanding of Asia I had begun to develop. I learnt Bahasa.

'Then I ended up involved in a huge arbitration case arguing for equal wages for Indigenous public servants in New Guinea. I came down here to Melbourne and met Bob Hawke, who was then advocate for the ACTU. He gave me huge assistance.

'Later I was to move to Melbourne as Director of the Chamber of Manufactures. The employer organisations wanted me because of my capacity to work with Hawke. It was a very effective relationship.'

'And what motivated you to join the Liberals?' we ask.

'Everything about the Liberals made me feel they were a broad-based party, a party where it is possible for people of conservative and liberal persuasions to work together.

'I might say, to the credit of the Liberal Party, when I first stood for preselection in 1969 in Sydney, I had unequivocally answered questions about my opposition to our involvement in Vietnam. It resonated with a great many people in the Liberal Party branches. So all that gave me heart to think that the Liberal Party was indeed what I'd hoped it was, a broad-based party.'

'And where do you believe the Liberal Party is now?'

'Howard can't rebuke Hanson, because after all she's only saying what he said himself in '88. He's a recidivist really. He just simply stands with his feet facing the past. Within his circle of friends he wouldn't have an Indigene or an Asian migrant. His problem is just a lack of social awareness.'

1988 was a turning point in Ian Macphee's political career. The then Opposition Leader, John Howard, made public his view that Asian immigration should be slowed.

'Hawke had skilfully drawn up a Parliamentary statement in terms which were exactly the same as our policy, about non-discrimination. It was straight from our Cabinet papers when we were in Government. How could Howard expect me in particular, who had helped to formulate the policy, to vote against it? You can't do that. I tried to plead with him not to maintain his position. I also pleaded in the Party room not to vote against the statement.

'I had to cross the floor, and vote with the Labor Government. So did three others, including Philip Ruddock, courageously and properly.

'Ruddock has never caused any ripples since. Whereas I was a bit of a ripple-maker. But I thought Liberalism was about that. It was effectively the end of me.

'Ruddock's survived because he's been quiet. But it was still a courageous thing for him to do, because there were plenty of other people who wanted to get rid of him. His seat was adjacent to Howard's and he had certain enemies from Howard's electorate in his branches.

'I would have kept my branch numbers, too, if the seat had not been redistributed. I lost all of the Jewish branches, which would have always supported me, because you know, if there's a race issue around, they're the ones who are the first to support the non-racist position. Four of my branches which were dominated by Jewish people went to the Melbourne Ports electorate. And the other branches I inherited were from the seat of Henty, which was abolished. They were elderly. The old bluebloods.

'I probably could have won them over if I hadn't crossed the floor. I only lost [preselection] by about three votes but it was the crossing of the floor which was the damaging thing.'

— • —

Two decades after Ian Macphee's term as Immigration Minister, Labor's Andrew Theophanous is still fighting procedural racism, struggling against the White Australia policies still seemingly in place long after the White Australia Policy was supposed to have been abolished. The theory may have been consigned to the dustbin of history, but what of the practices?

Theophanous sits on the House of Representatives Joint Committee on Migration. Here he is questioning Mr Christopher Brown, Chief Executive Officer of the Tourism Task Force in March 1999:

> **Dr Theophanous** — I understand ... that you are concerned ... that [the current tourist and business visa system] is discriminatory. Are you aware that the Department of Immigration in evidence before this committee denied on five occasions that this system is in any way discriminatory? What would you say to that?
>
> **Mr Brown** — No matter what way you look at it and how many rosy ways you can dress it up ... it is impossible to totally remove the spectre ... that without a doubt Asia is the part of the world on a racial basis most targeted, and the less-developed parts of the world which are the most targeted ... It is unfortunate timing that we are decreeing countries unsuitable for doing business with Australia, we are decreeing populations as less-suitable candidates to come here for a holiday ... I do not think that sits well with the proud tradition of an Australian open culture and society.[1]

The Department of Immigration has two visa systems for tourist and business entry to Australia: Electronic Travel Authorities for twenty-nine countries considered to be 'low risk', and a paper visa system for countries considered to be 'high risk.' 'Risk' means the likelihood of people overstaying their visas or becoming illegal immigrants. Most countries in Asia are considered to be 'high risk' and every country that is not in the developed world is considered 'high risk.'

An ETA visa is issued within minutes and without charge by travel agents in the twenty-nine 'low risk' countries, whereas for all other countries paper visas cost $50. They involve complicated form filling-out, and, in many cases, the application process includes interviews of up to two hours which, in great detail, go into many aspects of the potential tourist's private life: their marital status, their assets, their employment status and job security, the amounts of money they have in the bank. Supporting documentation is often required such as a letter from the applicant's employer, bank statements, and a marriage certificate; this, even for the shortest of holidays; this, even to attend somebody's wedding.

The rejection rates for ETAs in Britain, according to the company that is subcontracted to administer them, is 'probably less than half of one per cent.'[2] However, if you are visiting from China on a paper visa, the rejection rate is 25.5 per cent, from Vietnam 19.5 per cent, from Turkey 31.7 per cent or from Lebanon 46.5 per cent.

Here is Theophanous questioning Mr Laurence Stroud of Inbound Tourism Australia:

> **Mr Stroud** — It is pretty appalling. I do not know whether you have looked at the form 48R that people are required to fill out if they are seeking a paper visa —
> **Dr Theophanous** — Yes, I have ...
> **Mr Stroud** — The questions are pretty intrusive and if they are not used to actually reject applications, the immigration officer can ask for a whole heap of additional information which has the effect of turning people away. We are hearing more and more stories about the tougher attitude being adopted at overseas posts in countries where a paper visa is required ... I heard the other day from a Member of Parliament whose friend of his has a law firm in Thailand and one of the junior partners there, a female aged about 28, had sought a visitor visa to come to Australia, and that application was rejected. It would appear it was rejected simply because she fell in the profile of 'Asian female between the ages of 18 and 30' so obviously she was coming to Australia for but one purpose. I cannot quantify how many genuine visitors are being rejected because of this sort of approach.[3]

Theophanous himself told Parliament of the case of an Australian citizen who, following an accident at work, needed an operation on her back. Her sister in Turkey applied to the

Department to come to Australia on a visitor's visa. The sister had a house, a job, and sufficient other evidence that she wouldn't be likely to stay in Australia illegally beyond the duration of her visa, but the application was rejected. She put in a second application, explaining the circumstances and appealing on compassionate grounds, and Theophanous gave his personal assurance as to her bona fides. She was rejected again.[4]

Short-term business visas are also routinely rejected from non-ETA countries. In one case, the managing director of a firm in Australia, travelling from Asia to attend a board meeting, was denied entry.[5]

The Immigration Department in Hong Kong processes all business temporary entry and business-migration visa applications for China. Applicants are all held up in long queues and, as a matter of course and unlike anywhere else in the world, every applicant is sent an extra form requiring more detail.[6]

Then, if business or any other immigrants from Beijing want to bring a spouse, the Department takes 66 weeks to process their application, 92 weeks in Ho Chi Minh City and 47 weeks in Hong Kong — that's before they are put onto the end of a queue which is years long, if they are lucky enough to be accepted. The processing period in London is 18 weeks, Bonn 8 weeks and Vancouver 6 weeks.[7]

The effects of the visa system and other business and migrant entry procedures are to discourage tourism from new and rapidly growing markets, to discourage business relationships with the region, and to discourage business migration from the region. No other country treats potential tourists, temporary business entrants or business migrants in the way that Australia treats entrants from non-ETA countries. The tourism and business beneficiaries are other countries such as Canada or New Zealand.

Here Andrew Theophanous continues his questioning, this time cross-examining Mr John Broome, Chairperson of the National Crime Authority:

> **Dr Theophanous** — Is it not true that because of the ETA/non-ETA system you can have a lot of information about whether, for example, a kid in China has been arrested for shoplifting, whereas you have no information about whether somebody might have robbed a bank or killed somebody in Britain or other European countries?

Mr Broome — It is certainly true that with the electronic system and the way it is processed, you will not, by definition, have provided by the applicant the same amount of information ... There is obviously an inconsistency which is, as I understand it, in large part one based on assessments that have been made about low-risk countries, as they have been described. I understand that, although I am not sure that you can categorise a whole community as high or low risk.[8]

And how is a community classified 'high risk'? The Department determines 'high risk' by the rate of visa overstay. It says that the rate of overstay for Chinese is 14.6 per cent, for Vietnamese 19.5 per cent, for Turkish 17.3 per cent and for Lebanese 25.5 per cent. But in order to come up with these high figures, it includes two categories of legitimate non-returnees: 'legal departure on a new visa' and 'remaining in Australia on a new visa.' If these two legitimate categories are deleted, the actual figures of illegitimate overstay are only 3.2 per cent for the Chinese, 3.3 per cent for the Vietnamese, 2.9 per cent for the Turkish and 3.7 per cent for the Lebanese.

And what are the figures for the 'low risk' countries? The highest number of overstayers of all is people from the United Kingdom, or 11.8 per cent of all overstayers, followed by the United States, 9.9 per cent — two ETA countries. By comparison, 5.4 per cent of all overstayers are from China; and Vietnam, Turkey and Lebanon do not even appear on the list of the top ten overstaying countries.[9] Clearly 'risk' and the whole ETA/non-ETA system do not really have much to do with rates of overstay. It is based on something else.

In his response to the questions Andrew Theophanous put to him, the National Crime Authority's Mr Broome was less than clear about what that something else was:

Mr Broome — There has been for a long period of time a great deal of debate around government — certainly, that I am personally aware of, it has gone on for the last 15 years — where these issues have been thrown backwards and forwards. I think it is fair to say that no-one has come up with the answer that satisfies all competing interests. What we have at the moment is a compromise.[10]

— • —

'I came to Australia as a child of eight ...'

Andrew Theophanous is beginning the story of how he got into politics and why he became such a strident advocate for migrants and of multiculturalism.

'My mother was from Greece. She went to Cyprus during the Second World War to escape from the bombing and ended up marrying my father. There was enormous poverty after the war, so we came to Australia. Half of our village came to Australia.

'After we came out, I learnt English very quickly. I was the eldest son, which is very important in our culture. I became the eyes and the ears of the family. I couldn't speak a lot of English, but I had the advantage of being a child. By the end of the first year here, I was top of the class.

'I grew up in the electorate that I represent. It was a working-class area, Broadmeadows, and I was forced to grow up very quickly. We lived in a Housing Commission house. It was a struggle, and I had to make a lot of decisions on behalf of the family at a very young age.

'But I did have the opportunity to get an education which my father was denied. He never had that opportunity in the old country.

'I went to one of the worst schools in Victoria, Glenroy High School. It was tough. Although I was dux of the school, I barely scraped into university. There were six of us that got into university from sixty in the final year.

'The other thing that was tough was having to put up with the fact that I was a little Greek boy who kept coming top of the class. That wasn't very much appreciated, even by some teachers, I regret to say. It was not uncommon to be abused and called a "wog," and lots of terms of that sort. And quite frankly, by the time I finished sixth form, the pressure was so enormous, the fact that I was Greek and had a pointy nose — I realised that my background was something which would never be fully accepted in this society.'

Andrew went on to study politics and philosophy at Monash University.

'It was during the time of the Vietnam War. Monash was a radical hothouse and I became part of the radical leadership of Monash. But I was not as radical as some of them. I believed in the idea of a parliamentary Left.'

He was awarded a first-class honours degree at Monash, went to Oxford, then went to the United States to teach political philosophy and social theory at the University of Nevada, and then came back to teach at Melbourne University. It was a long journey for a boy born in a dirt-poor village in Cyprus, via Broadmeadows.

'I worked at Melbourne Uni for a couple of years and then, to everyone's absolute and utter amazement, I gained Labor preselection for the then seat of Burke. I mean, who would have thought then, that an academic of migrant background would be preselected from the Left of the Labor Party when it was totally dominated by the union movement? It was the same day as Bob Hawke. He was on the front page of every newspaper and guess what, so was I! I mean, not as big as him, you know, a big picture of him and little picture of me. "Bob Hawke Gains Preselection." Beside, "Unknown Academic Gets Federal Seat."'

He laughs, and goes on to explain the accidental intricacies of the branches, the other candidates, the numbers.

'So, what impact do you think you have had?' we ask him. He had been Parliamentary Secretary to Labor Prime Minister Paul Keating, with responsibility for Multicultural Affairs.

'Well I've changed some things I think, but the problem is, in a democracy you change things but they change back. In the area of Multicultural Affairs, many of the things that I was involved in were reversed within a year by the Howard Government, in particular, things like the Access and Equity Program, Special Services for Ethnic Communities, the Ethnic Aged Program, all those sorts of things. I mean, it's devastating to the people it affects, and it's devastating because of the meaning of your own life. I mean, when you work for all these things ...'

We ask him to evaluate the work of Philip Ruddock, the Howard Government's Minister for Immigration and Multicultural Affairs.

'Ruddock has skilfully managed to reduce the immigration program. His actual achievements, his concrete outcomes have been terrible, and he gets up in Parliament and he brags about it. He brags about the number of people he arrests as illegal immigrants. He brags about the fact that he's been able to make immigration more acceptable to the Australian people.

'You know, now you can't sponsor your brother or sister in any reasonable way and hope that it will be approved. Because the program has been so slashed, even the closest family reunions aren't possible.

'Then there's the situation with visitors' visas. Effectively, you're saying first, "Your family can't migrate." Then you say, "But you can't see your brother or sister either." Why? "Because if your brother he comes over here, he might apply to stay here." Therefore because he might apply to stay here, he can't even come near you. So you can't see your relatives.

'I mean, it's inhuman. The policy's racist. It's shaming Australia.'

— • —

Frequently these days, the media shows images of boats which have been smuggling illegal immigrants run aground somewhere or other along the coasts of Northern Australia. Frequently too, the media shows images of illegal immigrants being caught — in one case, a group of fruit-pickers who had been tied together with ropes by police and Immigration officials because they had run out of handcuffs.

To stem the supposed tide, Prime Minister Howard and Immigration Minister Ruddock held a press conference together to announce that an additional $124 million would be spent on coastal surveillance to stem the tide of illegal immigrants, that a 'central intelligence committee on people-smuggling' would be set up, and that compliance officers would be deployed in Shanghai, Guangzhou, New Delhi, Colombo, Nairobi, Pretoria and Ankara.[11] It wasn't mentioned that there would be no new compliance officers in the UK or the US, although these countries represent the largest sources of illegal entrants. Nor was it mentioned that these funds simply replace funds removed when the Immigration portfolio faced savage cutbacks after the election of the Howard Government, or that although about 700 boat people were picked up in 1998–1999, there is no evidence that a single boat person succeeded in making their way to Australia without being intercepted and detained.[12] In fact, the flow of boat people and illegal immigrants has been constant at a relatively low level for years; it's just that today, the arrival of every boat has been turned into a media circus.

Ian Macphee preferred to handle illegal immigration quite differently when he was the Minister.

'I unhesitatingly expelled two Boeing loads of illegals one year. This was one of those cases I didn't even take to Cabinet. Two

Boeing loads of bogus refugees from Taiwan. They had flown from Taiwan to Hong Kong, then to Bangkok. There they discarded their good clothes, got into the boats, took on refugee status and pretended they came from Vietnam. They landed in Darwin.

'They were imprisoned there and when their origins were determined, I said we had to deport them. It took us three months to negotiate with the Taiwanese Government.

'Now, if we'd made a song and dance … If I'd done what Ruddock is now doing … That was one case when Malcolm rang me and said, "Thank goodness you did it." I did it on Boxing Day so it wouldn't be noticed.'

We ask Malcolm Fraser his view of the publicity now given to illegal immigration, to the crooks and the rorters. The interview had taken longer than we had originally planned, and we had gone with him in the car to his next appointment.

'Ruddock says that, by being tough and by being seen to be tough, he is restoring public credibility to immigration,' we say.

'Every time he gets rid of a Vietnamese crook, he will publicise it and add to the problem. Why don't you ask him if he is going to send back the Anglo-Saxon WASP crooks?'

We tell him we will be seeing Philip Ruddock the following week.

'Then ask Philip Ruddock how his views have changed since he began as a Member of Parliament. Did he like the policies of multiculturalism when they were introduced when I was in government? And does he accept today's political correctness? In my time he would have been even to the left of me on these issues. Has he forgotten it, or just been silent because he doesn't want to offend somebody?'

— • —

Andrew Theophanous came to our house to do the interview for this book.

He parked out the front of the house, and then insisted on sitting near the window so that his car stayed in full view. He was under constant surveillance. His phones were being tapped — and had, as it turns out, been tapped for a long time.

Just days before, the National Crime Authority, acting on behalf of the Department of Immigration, had raided his house and his office at dawn and seized documents relating to a number of immigration and visa cases that he had been pursuing — mostly Chinese, but also including the case of the Turkish woman who had had an industrial accident and who wanted her sister to come out from Turkey for a short while.

'I'm under investigation for being too pushy in immigration matters. I've been making too much of a fuss in recent times.

'They're after me, and I think they're going to try and set me up. I hope that I will have the opportunity to bring out to the public in some way just how the Immigration Department treats people, the inhumane and unfair way they behave.'

He drops a jangle of coins onto the table, a pocketful of annoyance. If he wants to make a phone call and be confident it is not being tapped, he has to stop at a public phone box.

'Federal MP to be Charged' — this was the front page headline of the *Age* when the story of the National Crime Authority investigation finally broke.[13]

On the same weekend that Howard and Ruddock announced their new offensive against people smuggling, Channel 9's *Sunday* program featured the Theophanous case as its 'cover story.'

The *Sunday* program included a recorded interview with 'journalist' Ah Zhong, reviving a 1993 story that Theophanous had taken money from the Chinese students' organisation which had campaigned for the students and their dependents to be allowed to stay in Australia permanently after the Tiananmen Square massacre. 27,210 students were subsequently granted visas as a result of this decision. Theophanous had been instrumental in winning their right to stay. He had been cleared of all allegations of impropriety back then.

The Channel 9 program also showed how the National Crime Authority had given a 'Mr X' $22,000, to give to a Mr Yau, to attempt to bribe Andrew Theophanous. It was an entrapment operation that went wrong. No evidence was presented to suggest that the money found its way to Theophanous.

As it turns out, Ah Zhong is now dead, although the Channel 9 program didn't reveal he was a convicted drug dealer, or that the 'Mr X' the NCA employed for their attempted entrapment was also a drug dealer who the NCA did not think to put into the police because he was doing useful work to help them catch a Member of Parliament.

Other potential witnesses were subjected to intimidatory tactics by NCA operatives. The NCA turned up at the house of one

Chinese man at nine o'clock at night and then interviewed him for six hours. He repeatedly denied Theophanous had done anything wrong. Then he was taken outside, threatened with having his resident status cancelled and told he would be sent to gaol. After this, he was asked to give new evidence which suggested that Theophanous had taken money from him.

'I was very frightened, tired and stressed and I agreed to whatever they wanted.'[14]

NCA Chairman, John Broome, had said that he would neither confirm nor deny that Theophanous was under investigation, but somehow Channel 9 had managed to get its hands on the police tapes of the entrapment operation; the key actors in the drama had tape recorders strapped to their bodies.

Speaking to Channel 9, Broome had no hesitation in saying that the very investigation he could neither confirm nor deny had been conducted in a proper way by the Authority. He was 'absolutely confident' about that.[15]

It was the same John Broome who, when cross-examined by Theophanous on the House of Representatives Joint Committee on Migration, had agreed there were 'inconsistencies' in the ways visa eligibility was determined in 'high' compared to 'low' risk countries.

CHAPTER 22

Politically Correct

Margaret Reynolds's office is in a distant corner of the enormous Parliament building in Canberra, with a nice aspect over the gardens. It is full of the books and pottery and posters of a woman who has an eye for the sometimes forgotten corners of Australian life: women's Australia, Indigenous Australia, immigrant Australia. As the middle-class girl from Tasmania who became a Senator for Queensland and ended up living most of her adult life in Townsville, Margaret Reynolds reflects on the kind of person she is and the kind of politician she has been as she nears the end of her political career.

'I was always regarded as different, but not different in the usual sense. I was a predictably middle-class Anglo. So they sort of understood me, even though I was a feminist and took up unpopular causes. I probably had the advantage of having at least a toe in the camp of those who were the power brokers.

'Perhaps I got away with being an outspoken advocate because I came from North Queensland, and because I wasn't a careerist. So I wasn't really seen as a threat. I mean, I did get into the Ministry for three years' — she was Minister for Local Government in the Hawke Government — 'but I think people knew that I was just as happy to move on and do other things. My life didn't revolve around that sort of prestige. So I think, especially in the Hawke and Keating era, there was a great sense of live and let live, and if Margaret wanted to carry on about land rights at a time when land rights was not really a part of Labor Party policy, she could. Nobody ever rang me up and said, "What the so and so are you on about? This will damage our reputation." I've been doing it for so long, I suppose people just came to accept it.'

'So what were your formative influences? What led you to make the contribution you have?' we ask.

'I'd have to say that living in North Queensland from the 1960s was incredibly influential in shaping how I respond to the world and to issues of social justice and equity and fairness. It's not something I just thought about all that much prior to the age of twenty-four, when I went to North Queensland. I suppose I'd grown up in a fairly comfortable, not affluent, but comfortable environment in a little town in Tasmania, where there weren't too many challenges.

'When we arrived in Townsville in the sixties, as a woman you were defined more than anything else by your marital status, and I was a young wife. And you were also defined by the work that your husband did. So when I arrived, you know, about a month after Henry arrived' — Henry Reynolds, the historian of Indigenous-settler relations — 'there was a formal welcome for me and all the wives were there. Everyone wore stockings and linen dresses, hats and gloves. And I turned up in a mini-skirt and sandals. No hat even, not even a sun hat, and with our eldest child wearing only a pair of tartan pants. The women were so proud of the fact that they were university wives. Whereas I wasn't. That was enough for me to think "I'm not going to make any friends in this circle."

'I guess I've always been a fairly activist sort of person even when I was just a youngster, probably doing things I shouldn't have done. I've always been someone who wants to get out there and get involved. And just being a wife, whose husband happened to be at university, didn't appeal to me as a way of life.

'I don't think I knew what the word "feminist" meant in 1965. But I did know I was my own person, and that I was going to continue teaching and doing things that I enjoyed doing.'

So, she started working in an Indigenous preschool.

'I had never lived with Indigenous people before and I was just shocked at the way they were treated. I just had to keep reminding myself that I was living in Australia.'

She got a job as a lecturer at Townsville Teachers' College, then stood and was elected to the Townsville City Council. Then, in 1983, she won a seat in the Senate. For all these years, she's been a dedicated fighter for services to North Queensland, on women's issues, on Indigenous issues, on human rights.

By contrast, when Pauline Hanson was elected to the Federal Parliament in 1996, she declared publicly that, as a local member, she would not represent Aboriginal people. Margaret Reynolds tells the story of one of the repercussions of Hanson's stance.

'A group of Indigenous women from Ipswich came to me in Canberra, asking if I would help them organise a demonstration against Hanson when she was sworn in. And although I'm an old demonstrator from way back, I sort of said, "Look, it's up to you of course, but these occasions are very formal. I can't help you organise anything like that. This is in the Parliament and it would be totally inappropriate."

'"What you need to do is find some way to highlight the problem you have with her. I can arrange a press conference for you, and then you can make the point in the media."

'So they came to Parliament in that first week when she was sworn in. They had a press conference and called on the Parliament to adopt a Code of Race Ethics. It was their idea.

'I then took the idea into the Parliament. Now when I first started on it, I talked to a few people in the Party about it — who of course shall remain nameless — and they said, "Oh, yeah, yeah, Margaret. It's probably a nice idea, but it won't go anywhere."

'There wasn't much enthusiasm. In my first effort I think I got about thirty-six signatures, and that included the Democrats and the Greens. So it wasn't a lot, on either our side or the other side of politics.'

The wording of the code was unexceptionable:

As a Member of the Federal Parliament I agree:
1. To act in a manner which upholds the honour of public office and the Parliament;
2. To respect the religious and cultural beliefs of all groups living within Australia in accordance with the Universal Declaration of Human Rights;
3. To uphold principles of justice and tolerance within our multicultural society, making efforts to generate understanding of all minority groups;
4. To recognise and value diversity as an integral part of Australia's social and economic future;
5. To help without discrimination all persons seeking assistance;
6. To speak and write in a manner which provides factual commentary on a foundation of truth about all issues being debated in the community and the Parliament;

7. To encourage the partnership of government and non-government organisations in leading constructive and informed debate in the community;

8. To promote reconciliation with indigenous Australians.[1]

'So then I thought, this is ridiculous. The whole country is galvanised around this race issue and people saying what a problem it is. And I can't even get politicians to sign these fairly standard statements. I mean there's nothing very revolutionary about them. They're just basic good sense.

'I thought, I have to have another go. So I went to Beazley and I said, "Look, I've been working on this, but I don't seem to be getting as much support as I'd like. I really think it's a good initiative. If all the Labor Party signed it and all the Democrats, it would really put pressure on the other side."

'Beazley, to his eternal credit, said, "Yeah, Gareth is working on a statement to be debated in the Parliament. This complements what Gareth is doing."

'So he made an announcement at Caucus that I was working on this and Gareth was working on his, and that everyone should sign my Code of Race Ethics. And so suddenly, nearly everybody in the Labor Party did.

'With persistence, we also got a lot of Liberals and Nationals to sign, as well as support from the Premiers in the conservative States. Deputy Prime Minister Tim Fischer was one of the first to sign. But, no matter how hard we tried, John Howard would not sign. I didn't use that politically, as I could have, because I was trying to maximise the number of signatures.'

'So, where are we now?' we ask. 'Where has the public debate on race taken us?'

'We had our race debate and it was very nasty and many of us would have rather not lived through it. But the thing that the Labor Party has to learn is that when the going gets tough, you don't hide from the debate. If you're a public policy advocate, whether you're a politician or a bureaucrat or an academic, you've got to argue the case. You've got to have some passion about defending your beliefs. And the problem with Hanson was that nobody, or very few, in the political leadership was prepared to take her on. They had one eye on the polls and one eye on the fact that any simplistic argument is very persuasive. And we all know, it's very easy to say, "Oh, the problem with unemployment rates is not government policy, it's all these immigrants." It's nice and simple. It's a simple argument, instead of people being prepared to come out and use the facts and figures and be persuasive about the truth. It might take a little bit more time and energy to counter some of these simplistic, populist arguments, but that's the job.

'I think in a strange way the race debate, the Wik debate, the bilingual education debate, the public discussion of all these issues, has been a good thing. There are a lot of people who probably didn't take much notice of Indigenous policy or human rights three or four years ago. They just vaguely thought that reasonable things were happening and they really didn't concern themselves, but suddenly they've been so shocked by some of the events of the last couple of years that they're really mobilising.'

— • —

In the weeks after Pauline Hanson's maiden speech, anti-racism protests were held all around Australia. On the last weekend of November 1996, two thousand attended a rally in Brisbane, and five hundred in Ipswich. There were two separate events in Sydney. In one event, on the Saturday, five thousand people marched on John Howard's office in Phillip Street. In another at Darling Harbour on the Sunday, organised by the Young Liberal Movement, Philip Ruddock said that the Coalition was serious about combating intolerance and would begin the national education campaign that it had promised at the last election early in 1997. He was the first Minister to address an anti-racism rally since Pauline Hanson came to prominence on the Australian scene.

It was these protests that roused John Cook to action. He made his decision as Managing Director of Berri Australia to produce his company's 'intolerance in fruit' advertisements:

INTOLERANCE IN PEOPLE IS JUST AS STUPID. CELEBRATE AUSTRALIA'S DIVERSITY. BERRI.

'The thing that turned my mind so aggressively against this whole One Nation thing was the protests. I was genuinely moved by the behaviours of the kids in Brisbane who decided to walk in protest at the views of Pauline Hanson. And then to have this David Oldfield turn the discussion around and say that one of the leaders of the demonstration was "a contributing member of the Communist Party of Australia which is trying to despoil the flower of the youth of the country." That was the end for me. These were kids who were trying to make a statement.

'Just look how much airtime this woman got. Unfortunately, it's what sells newspapers and gets audiences for TV programs. I was very worried that things we wouldn't have allowed to be said in polite company before, were getting into everyday phraseology and discussion. If we were not careful, it could have led to a change in the wrong direction for the broader society.'

The idea of 'polite company' is a nice one, and old-fashioned in a way. Yet in another way, it's very modern. It's another way of John Cook saying he's a believer in political correctness.

The label of 'political correctness' — anti-political correctness, that is — was imported to Australia from debates that began in the United States late in 1990. By May 1991, President George Bush was using the term in normal public conversation. Speaking at a commencement day ceremony at the University of Michigan, the President complained that the 'notion of political correctness ... declares certain topics off limits, certain expressions off limits.' It 'attempts to micro-manage casual conversation,' to 'crush diversity in the name of diversity.'[2] He was referring to injunctions to use non-sexist and non-racist language.

John Howard introduced the notion of political correctness into the Australian political lexicon in 1996. It was the same year that, in the country in which the idea was born, Microsoft apologised for 'grave errors' when the latest Spanish version of its *Microsoft Word* thesaurus suggested 'maneater' or 'savage' as alternatives to 'Indian,' 'pervert' for Lesbian, and 'Aryan' or 'civilized' for 'Western.'[3] These would have been perfectly reasonable synonyms in an earlier age. Now they were just plain bad for business. For this reason, as the Atlanta Olympics opened, newspaper headlines around the world proclaimed 'Let the Politically Correct Olympics Begin.' There were to be minimal references to the Atlanta of *Gone with the Wind*, the Atlanta of racism and prejudice.

Of course, there are politics to words just as there are politics to the ideas that words express, and if it's all political, why would you not want to be, in a certain sense, correct? Correct in this sense might mean apt, relevant, pertinent or usefully insightful. Or just plain polite.

John Howard soon found himself fiddling with words. Early on in his Government, an edict went out from Howard via the Department of the Prime Minister and Cabinet that the spelling of 'program' should be changed to 'programme.' Within weeks, the new back-to-the-future spelling had become near-universal in officialese right across the public service. In the Australian Government Publishing Service Style Manual, the spelling is 'program' — Australian spelling is a hybrid of English and American usages — but we were now to do it the English way. Then the *Sydney Morning Herald* reported that 'the Prime Minister, Mr Howard, has taken the first step towards dismantling the former Labor government's politically correct grammar, decreeing that the gender-neutral title "chairperson" is out and "chairman" is back in' and that M/s was to be preferred to Ms.[4] Clearly, these new correctnesses were as political as any of those they supplanted.

After all, Howard had a broad cultural vision of his own. He reminded a gathering of Liberal Party faithful in Sydney that 'government is not only about dollars and cents and economic goals and economic objectives but government is also about values, and government is also about the way we think about ourselves.'[5] In a 1996 interview with *Business Review Weekly*, he said that, being in government, 'you've got an opportunity to change the culture, you've got an opportunity for there to be a flow-through benefit and you've got an opportunity for the Government to really take root in the community.'[6]

Clearly, for all Howard's talk of 'political correctness,' he didn't mean we were going to be less correct. It just meant that we were switching conventional wisdoms; we were changing the basis of the political order. One political correctness was to be replaced by another. A new culture was to replace the old.

Head of the NSW Anti-Discrimination Board former Liberal Senator Chris Puplick described such attitudes in this way:

> What is objected to is not political correctness as such, what is objected to is other people's political correctness, [and in particular] the emergence into the Australian political debate of the heretofore marginalised and ignored — women, indigenous Australians, gays and lesbians, the poor, people with disabilities, non-native English speakers, those concerned with economic agendas which are not about economic growth, making money, distributing wealth or rearranging the

deckchairs on the financial *Titanic*. Their emergence is a potential threat to those who ... have done very nicely, thank you, out of the status quo of exclusionism ... The recent attacks on what somewhat nebulously has been called 'political correctness' signal a retreat by our entire society from fundamental notions of tolerance ... If we seek to strengthen the moral fabric of society, what we need then is not less 'political correctness' but more.[7]

Politically correct and proud of it. Why, after all, would anyone set out to be wantonly, wilfully politically incorrect?

The Berri campaign was an exercise in deliberate political correctness, just as Margaret Reynolds's Code of Race Ethics was also such an exercise.

Anthony Helou, the Mayor of the City of Moreland in Melbourne, also faced up to the issue of political correctness when National Action, a far-Right group, set up a bookshop in the municipality. As it turned out, it was a shopfront for their political activities.

'Actually, they did have a permit for a bookshop, but then they became involved in something else. They moved into an area which was the most Anglo part of the municipality. I think their rationale was to move into a low socio-economic community and mobilise.

'There was enormous pressure from the community to have them moved away. There were spontaneous pickets against them. And in the Council, we were trying everything to cancel the permit. So they left.

'We didn't say "It's freedom of the individual." It was not just a matter of free speech. We thought the bookshop was something that might damage and divide. They were neo-Nazis.'

— • —

John Cook explains that it was his basic faith in people, his faith in Australians, that led him to initiate the 'intolerance in fruit' advertisements.

'In deciding to do the advertisements, we took a judgement, and admittedly it turned out to be right, that the great majority of Australians would identify with our very simple, positive message. We were assured by the polls, the public opinion polls, that we were right about Australians.'

A Newspoll in June 1996 had asked the question:

Australia has had for more than 20 years an immigration policy that selects migrants on such things as their work skills and reunion with family, BUT NOT on the basis of their colour, religion or country. How strongly do you agree or disagree with this policy?[8]

77 per cent said they agreed; just 16 per cent disagreed.
Another question asked:

Successive Australian governments have adopted a policy of multiculturalism. This involves encouraging migrants to become Australians without having to give up their own culture. Do you agree or disagree with this policy? [9]

61 per cent agreed; 34 per cent disagreed.

And when the same kind of question was asked in 1997, eight months after the Hanson maiden speech and shortly after the formation of the One Nation Party — 'Has multiculturalism been good or bad?' — 78 per cent thought it had been a good thing, and just ten per cent thought it had been bad.[10]

John Cook continues:

'So, our assessment turned out to be right. Looking at the sort of mail I got once the ads went to air, for all the hundreds of great letters I got — and I got hundreds — I got only about fifteen bad ones, and these were from the One Nation people saying we were responsible for their loss at the Federal election and, by the way, we now boycott your product. But, overall, they were very few.'

We suggest to Malcolm Fraser that the great majority of ordinary Australians are both ahead of the media and ahead of their political leaders on these issues.

'You know, there is a lot of optimism in the way people lead their lives, their everyday interactions with different people from different communities and different countries.'

We're speeding along in the car, and his hand sweeps along the rows of houses that line this particular street in suburban Melbourne. He means these people, these streets, these families whose life histories and backgrounds are different from house to house; people who for a generation and more have managed to live together peacefully, productively.

'And, you know, it's not a bad idea, the idea that the community is a million yards ahead of the Government. And ahead of the Opposition.'

— • —

The community education program that had been promised by the Coalition before the 1996 Federal election went to Cabinet the week before the 1998 Queensland election in which One Nation won 23 per cent of the vote and eleven seats. Philip Ruddock argued hard for a program he'd been promising was just about to start for the past two years, only Cabinet said 'No.' Just after that election, the submission went back into Cabinet and was accepted, ten million dollars for a 'Living in Harmony' campaign.

Finally, too, the National Multicultural Advisory Council chaired by Neville Roach was convened and allowed to complete its work. Its final report strongly recommended that the term 'multiculturalism' be retained. John Howard launched the report in May 1999, and was even able to utter the word.

CHAPTER 23

A Voice for Multicultural Australia

Tonight, the new face of Australian politics. This is a regular Labor Party branch meeting. All over the country traditional ALP supporters are being elbowed aside in a ruthless ethnic numbers game. And now the never-ending struggle for control of branches has taken a dangerous new turn. Right and Left are staging mass recruitment drives among the close-knit migrant communities, shamelessly exploiting some of the traditional ethnic tensions simmering in multicultural Australia.[1]

This was the introduction to a 1994 ABC Television *Four Corners* program, entitled 'The Big Stack.'

During the program, local Party member, Lyle Allan, was interviewed:

Melbourne TAFE teacher Lyle Allan ... lives in the heart of Deputy Prime Minister Brian Howe's seat of Batman.

Q: How have the Greeks fared in their numbers?

A: Very well. The Greeks are experts at recruitment. They are very good at it. If anything they are brilliant.

Q: Have they got people into Parliament as a result?

A: Yes. There are four Greeks in the Victorian Parliament and one Greek from the electorate of Calwell from Victoria in the Federal Parliament — Dr Andrew Theophanous. His brother Theo has just had a large group of Greeks enrolled into a branch at Westgarth balancing the Right's new Filipinos in another branch nearby.[2]

When we spoke with him, ALP President Barry Jones explained his objection to 'branch-stacking.'

'Because, what happens is this — somebody comes along and says to a powerful figure in the party: "If you do this for me, I can deliver five Hispanics in branches in Geelong, and that will guarantee your preselection," or something of the sort. That does create a very adverse reaction. There is tremendous bitterness being created down in the Geelong region by branch-stacking by the Hispanics.'

Besides, he's worried about multiculturalism generally.

'There are several things that have always worried me about multiculturalism. One of the firmest opponents of multiculturalism in the Caucus when I was there was Dick Klugman. Klugman's argument was that for a whole variety of reasons people came out here from their home country. Then what happens when you get here is that you get some local big-shot in the Greek community who says "I'm the boss of the Greeks around here, and nothing really happens in the Greek community without me giving my approval."

'Dick thought that was an intolerable situation. And of course your kids would go to Greek school, how dare you suggest otherwise? And naturally, if you are a Greek boy, we take it for granted you will marry a nice little Greek girl. He thought that could really be quite repressive. Once Greek, always Greek. You have got to act in a Greek way out here. I remember how passionate Klugman was on that issue.'

Mark Latham, when we spoke to him, even suggested there was a connection between branch-stacking and Labor Party policy.

'I'll leave it for others to judge the connection between the ethnic branch-stacking and the Party's migration policy in the eighties, but rationally you wouldn't expect an ethnic branch stacker to be against family reunion migration, would you?' asks Barry Jones.

Jones mentions all the Greeks who have been preselected in Victoria, one of the supposed byproducts of branch-stacking.

'But', we ask, 'what about targeting women candidates, which is also a form of stacking, a deliberate attempt to shift the Party's culture, to change the Party against the weight of institutional inertia?'

'I wouldn't say it was stacking in the case of women, because it's harder to conceive of a larger, more important group, fifty per cent of the population. But I draw the line at ethnic groups.'

Forty-four per cent of Victorians have at least one parent who was born overseas. More than eight hundred thousand people, or twenty per cent of the population, speak a language other than English at home.[3]

— • —

We meet Lindsay Tanner in his Melbourne electoral office. Along with Theophanous and Latham, he's a recent Labor author. He is billed on the cover of his book *Open Australia* as 'Labor's rising star.' The book discusses Australia's future: new technologies, economic transformation, national identity, multiculturalism, globalisation.

'I'm a classic example of a person who's grown up in a small country town, the usual Anglo-Irish mix, of relatively recent migrant background. Spent six years in a country boarding school. Came to the big city to go to university. Got caught up in politics.

'Then, marrying into a Greek family meant that, in all sorts of subtle ways, my world view expanded. It's hard to put a finger on it but it's just the experience of becoming part of something that's quite different from my own past experience.'

He discusses the enormous cultural changes that have occurred in the Australian community and his own life.

'I grew up with a different form of political correctness. And it was far more rigid and far more intrusive and far more unfair than any of what is now called political correctness. It was a set of social norms which excluded large numbers of people, which devalued large numbers of people and which seriously restricted social behaviour. The people who flouted it weren't elected to Parliament like Pauline Hanson. They were ostracised.

'Take swearing, there were men's swear words that wouldn't ever leave the public bar. And now you hear these words on TV. But at the same time, other kinds of words have lost social acceptability, because people were becoming conscious that they represent certain things that we find unacceptable.

'Neo-Nazis desecrating Jewish graves, or people in the supermarket tearing off a Muslim woman's head scarf, or people being attacked because of their external cultural manifestations — that's not freedom of expression. It's an attack on freedom of expression.

'At the time when Howard made his famous 'free speech' comments about Hanson, it took a while for the real seriousness of what he was saying to sink in for me. As I thought about it in the ensuing weeks, I realised the true enormity of it. When you think about it, it was just extraordinary. To say that your primary response to what was ultimately a rabid assault on specific groups of people based on their race, to say that this was a victory for freedom of speech, it was just unbelievable. It was a landmark event in Australia's history.'

We shift the focus of the conversation to the question of branch-stacking.

'You've got to be a bit careful about drawing conclusions, because the critical question is whether this is being done to provide numbers for one group of the Party to win battles against other groups in the Party. If you're just looking at cannon fodder so that Person X can win a preselection against Person Y . . .

'If however, the idea is simply one of, "We've got to broaden the Party's base because we don't just want to be an Anglo party," if that is the motivation then it's entirely legitimate.

'In my electorate, I've got a Chinese branch of about twenty people which is genuine, and I've got a Latin-American branch with seventy people and an Italian branch of twenty.

'And the Greek branch. I go along and speak Greek at that branch. There are some members of that branch who have got good English, and there are others whose English is pretty ordinary. The branch provides a focus for participation. It suits these members' needs. It means also that there is a vehicle for pursuing issues that are specific to them as well as pursuing issues that affect everybody, whatever ethnic origin they may be. So that's a very positive thing. Yes, these·branches became power bases. Yes, in some instances they contributed to people from those communities getting elected into Parliament.'

'So is branch-stacking such a serious problem?' we ask. 'Is it as corrosive of the Party as some people suggest?'

'The problem is that the highly legitimate and desirable objective of genuinely diverse participation in a major political party is being brought into disrepute by what has occurred or what has been occurring inside the Labor Party. And that is, by and large, being driven by — I'll have to be careful how I say this — leading Anglos.

'The only reason this stuff's happening is because you have got very small membership, which means anybody who could come along with a group of people, organised around anything, can sort of take over, can suddenly exert a disproportionate influence. So the real problem is that there's not enough members, and there's not enough of the membership involved. That's the issue.

'What people forget is that Labor Party branches are essentially nothing more than local voluntary community organisations, with immensely variable quality. It's particularly difficult for new members of ethnic background to join in. They get ignored. In a lot of branches you can literally see people front up as new members and in the coffee break they stand there talking to nobody for ten minutes. You wonder why people join and then leave after going to two meetings.'

— • —

After half a century of migration, only eight per cent of the 224 members of the Federal Parliament voted in at the 1998 election were from a non-English-speaking immigrant background. This compared with twenty-three per cent of the general population.[4]

For all the talk of the virulence of branch-stacking, Labor is even less representative than the conservative parties. More than twice as many Liberal Party MPs were born in a non-English-speaking country than Labor. Thanks to the intervention of Jeff Kennett against the Party establishment — his own grandfather was German-Jewish — the Federal Parliament now has its first Asian member, Tsebin Tchen. And the Democrats have only the second Aboriginal MP ever, Aden Ridgeway; the first, of course, was the Liberals' Neville Bonner.

What's more, for all of Labor's good words about increasing the number of women representatives, the Party still lags behind the conservatives there, too.

Michael MacKellar, Immigration Minister in the first Fraser Government, tells how and why he established ethnic branches in the Liberal Party, during the time of the Whitlam Labor Government at the beginning of the seventies.

'When I became Shadow Immigration Minister our support among ethnic groups was minimal. They were traditionally Labor Party supporters.'

So he helped establish ethnic branches.

'I was a strong supporter of ethnic branches within the Liberal Party on the basis of the belief that people of a particular background, should, would, feel more comfortable with members of their own group, and this should be recognised and be part of the political process.

'I also wanted to develop policies that reflected the views of migrants as well as non-migrants.

'Before that, our guys never used to go to ethnic functions. So I set up within the Parliamentary Party groups that had responsibility for going out and establishing and maintaining contacts with the ethnic communities. Philip Ruddock was one of them. And he still does it.

'The communities said, "This is the first time we have really been asked, by anybody, what we really think." I wanted to make contact with people who were influential within the various migrant groups — Lebanese, Greek, Italian — and that had not necessarily ever been Liberal Party supporters before. What I said was, we want to develop a good policy that will benefit your people and Australia. And they responded well to that.'

Andrew Theophanous has a number of ethnic branches in his electorate of Calwell, in the northern suburbs of Melbourne. Forty-three per cent of the people who live in Calwell speak a language other than English at home.

'Now, of course, the argument you'll get is that the ethnic branches create division,' Theophanous tells us. 'My electorate is an example of the opposite. I mean, I have a Kurdish branch, a Greek branch and a Turkish branch. In international terms, these are the three communities that are in pretty hostile conflict at the moment. Nevertheless, these branches relate closely. I've had people from each of those branches come and say to me, "We like the way you actually demonstrate multiculturalism in practice."

'And it works. In 1993 and 1998 we had excellent results, but 1996 was the best result of all because, while the whole Party went backwards, mine was one of the few seats in Australia where we went forward.'

He sees effective representation of the community and ethnic branches as keys to his success, although these are not things that are always acknowledged as valuable by the wider Party.

'From the very beginning, there's been a reaction against the ethnic branches in the Party. The reaction is based firstly on racism. The racists don't want ethnic branches. And they don't want multiculturalism. These are the people who see Labor as a party which represents a narrow base rather than a broad base: essentially white working-class union people and middle-class professionals who believe in left-of-centre policies.

'The fact of the matter is that, if it had not been for the ethnic branches, the Party's base would have been severely eroded. That's not just the ethnic branches, but even in the non-ethnic branches the ethnic membership of the Party is high. In Victoria, ethnic membership is fifty per cent.

'So I mean, what are you going to do? You see, now there is special election funding. If you get a certain proportion of the vote, then you're there, you can get money. Last Federal election, the Party was paid at least $12 million. When you're getting that sort of money, who needs even fifty per cent of your branches? You don't.

'The question really is, and the Labor Party has to decide, does it want to be a mass party or does it want to be a narrow party? And if it wants to be a mass party in a multicultural society, it's going to have to admit people of non-English-speaking background, and if those people wish to speak in the Spanish language or in the Turkish language or whichever other language, why not? In fact, the reason why the ethnic branches are being nipped in the bud is because many Anglo-Saxon people don't want to join the Labor Party any more.

'In particular, there are very few young Anglo-Australians joining the Party. But maybe we should think about what's relevant to them. I'll tell you one thing that's relevant to them, and that's multiculturalism. They believe it. They support it. Maybe the political leaders or their parents don't support it. But they support it, because they've lived with it. They've grown up in it. And what's more, there's dramatic intermixing going on in our society now. Every second person that I meet says, "Oh yes, there's a Greek person in our family, or an Asian person — my daughter-in-law, my cousin's husband ... "

'The danger is that we're going to end up with the politicians at the top moving in one direction while the society is saying, "Hey, that's not really us, that's not really us."'

— • —

We ask Peter and Cyril Wong about branch-stacking. Peter Wong won a seat for the Unity Party in the New South Wales Upper House in the March 1999 election. Until One Nation came with a vengeance onto the Australian scene, he'd been a prominent member of the Liberal Party. Cyril is Peter's brother and a fellow member of the National Executive Committee of the Unity Party.

'There was not much chance of stacking in the Liberal Party. I was a preselector for the seat of Lowe,' says Peter.

Lowe, in Sydney's inner west, is one of the Liberals' most ethnically diverse seats in the whole of Australia.

'Among the two-hundred-odd preselection delegates, there were only about six or seven at the most from a non-English-speaking background, and only three Asians. They were mostly Anglo-Saxon people, usually over the age of sixty.

'We Chinese thought we could get in there and change perceptions within the Liberal Party. But there was a cultural gap which I saw it would be impossible to bridge. It was hard enough to get one preselector up, so there was no prospect of stacking. Anyhow, what about bloody "white stacking"?'

'And if there is branch-stacking in the Labor Party,' Cyril chips in, 'they are singularly unsuccessful.' He's referring to the lack of diversity among Labor Members of Parliament.

We are interviewing the Wong brothers at Peter's house in Strathfield, an affluent and leafy suburb of inner-western Sydney. It's a Sunday afternoon, and Peter's church choir is practising in a big room at the back of the house.

People are coming and going. Some leave their shoes at the door. Others take them off to walk on the shiny white tiles and light-grey carpets. Chinese traditions are optional here.

Clean lines, modern furniture, family photos, Chinese artworks, framed qualifications, photos of marriages, mixed and otherwise, all indicate an easygoing fusion of cultures and a sense of openness.

There is plenty of evidence too, that the house is a centre of activity for Unity, with boxes of how-to-vote cards, piles of posters and brochures strewn about, as well as people fussing around wearing Unity T-shirts, emblazoned with the Unity slogan.

UNITY. A VOICE FOR MULTICULTURAL AUSTRALIA.

Shoes off, we fell into the huge sofas in the lounge-dining room at the front of the house. This was the room in which the first Unity meetings had been held back in July 1998 when, brimming with people sitting on the floor, standing, squashed wall-to-wall, the party was founded. Now Unity has its own offices in the City and Parramatta and the meetings are mostly held there.

'I was born in China and brought up in Indonesia.' Peter starts with his life story.

'Growing up in a minority in Indonesia, we experienced a lot of discrimination. I arrived here in 1961, attended Birrong Boys' High. At the time, I was the only Asian at Birrong High. I went back to Birrong Boys' High a few years ago and it has completely changed since then; it is full of kids of every background.'

He studied medicine, and became a GP. Later, he got involved in ethnic politics.

As did his brother Cyril.

'I have always been a bit of a rebel. I left home at thirteen, did my high school in Hong Kong. Then I came to Australia to do my Leaving Certificate, then on to medical school. And from here I did surgical training in England for a year.'

Cyril is now a leading Sydney surgeon, with an international reputation.

Peter explains how he was drawn into politics.

'I was invited to be a part-time Ethnic Affairs Commissioner. I was appointed by the Liberal Premier of New South Wales, Nick Greiner, as a non-Liberal Party member. At the time what really impressed me about Nick Greiner was I was the only non-Liberal Party member among three nominees, and somehow Nick Greiner picked me, rather than the other two Liberal Party members. It made me think the Liberals were fair.

'Then my good friend Helen Sham-Ho got into Parliament. I was invited to join the Liberal Party, and I did.

'I still really did not know anything about politics. Later I realised that what you see is a facade, and the inside machinery of the Party is quite different. They are very friendly, and project the impression that they are willing to accept other people. But the Party has a very old Anglo-Saxon culture in reality.'

And Cyril recalls how he was drawn into another kind of politics, community politics and the politics of the medical profession.

'I remember when I first set up practice as a specialist, I was working in the western suburbs and I went down to see this guy, a doctor in Seven Hills. I visited him because I needed some referral work. I said, "Look, I am here in this area." And he said, "Why did you come to see me?" I said, "I am a specialist, so I thought I would come and introduce myself." And he said, "There is a Chinese practitioner down the road, why don't you go to see him?" I was shocked, desperately shocked. But anyhow, ultimately I learnt that my referral sources would have to be my friends. And ultimately I learnt that you needed to be organised, to be involved in community politics.

'I helped establish the Australian Chinese Medical Association. People often say that Chinese people are inscrutable, that they do not want to participate in general society. The truth is they are not allowed to speak, they are scared to speak, they feel sort of intimidated. And they have no experience of public life, no experience of organisational processes and things like that. So that is why we formed the Australian Chinese Medical Association. And we found that people suddenly bloomed. In fact now, ACMA is a very important organisation in the medical scene.'

He goes on to explain one of ACMA's current struggles — he's the Association's Chair at the moment — and the reason why organisations like it are needed.

'In the past, something like forty per cent of the medical students at Sydney University were from a non-English-speaking background. That was when it was an undergraduate degree and entry was decided by your Higher School Certificate score. Now they've changed it to a postgraduate course, and you have to face a specially designed assessment process including psychological testing, and face-to-face interviews to assess personal background, communication skills, and so on. The Asians and other ethnic groups are less bubbly, or their English is not perfect, so they get negative points. As a result, the numbers of non-English-speaking background students have now dropped by sixty per cent.

'The hidden agenda is to reduce the number of non-English-speaking background students. One of the key people at the University actually confided to one of his friends that the goal was to reduce the Asian intake. It's racism in disguise. ACMA is currently pursuing the issue.'

'So how did you come to found the Unity Party?' we ask.

'Peter Wong and his group of Chinese leaders — at that time I was not involved — begged, literally begged, John Howard to say One Nation should be put last at the federal election,' Cyril tells us. 'There was no response. They were completely disregarded.'

'So, I resigned from the Liberal Party,' Peter says. 'It became clear John Howard was not going to act on the Pauline Hanson issue. We set up Unity in the weeks after the Queensland election.'

'You see, we had always lived under the protection of a bipartisan agreement not to play the race card,' Cyril explains. 'Now, unfortunately, Pauline Hanson was singing the song. But the Liberal Party was playing the music, if you ask me.'

'When I resigned I called a press conference,' Peter goes on. 'For somebody totally unknown — nobody knew who I was — there was such a lot of interest. At that time I was really very politically naive, and I didn't know how to answer their bloody questions.

The *Daily Telegraph* wrote a very nasty article about me: "This Peter Wong, we don't know who he is, the Liberal Party head office has never heard of this guy." But somehow, the "little Peter Wong we have never heard of" became a prominent issue overseas, in Singapore and even as far as Brunei and Borneo, where my sister-in-law lives — she saw my face on TV and got a shock.

'Obviously my reaction was typical of what many other people were thinking at that time: this thing has gone too far, something has got to be done. I had a meeting with a few of my friends and talked about setting up a party, but we thought that was far too difficult. Number one, you need money, number two, you need structures, number three, you need candidates and we had none. Perhaps I should stand as an independent? But my wife and my children were very upset. They were in tears. They said, "Look, we need a party! Why don't you do it? We must have a party."'

'We had to do it,' says Cyril. 'There are the lessons from the Jews. They might have been well-to-do, they might have been rich, but when you have no political power, you can be destroyed any time. I think the Chinese have had the same experience in Indonesia and in Malaysia, and OK, Australia now is in a prosperous situation. But what happens when there is an economic downturn? What happens to our children?'

'So that is how it started,' Peter says. 'I turned around and convinced all my friends, this Independent thing doesn't work, and we need a party. And they were surprisingly very enthusiastic. The Party began meeting in this room, and every week there were more and more people at our meetings.'

A constitution was drawn up. An Executive Committee was elected. Subcommittees were formed: Media, Strategy, Preselection, Policy, and so on.

Cyril became the head of the Policy Committee.

'We wrote a platform as rank amateurs.'

Our Philosophy
The Unity Party is founded upon recognition of, and pride in, the diversity of the Australian people.

We vary by race, heritage and religion. We vary because some of us are indigenous Australians, some of us are recently-arrived migrants and refugees, and some of us are longer-established settlers. We vary because of our ability to work and to find meaningful and ongoing employment. We vary because of ability and disability, age, gender and lifestyle choices. We vary by citizenship and residency status. We vary because some of us live in cities and others live in country areas. And we vary in many other ways.

This diversity is Australia's strength.

It is therefore incumbent upon this nation's egalitarian and pluralist society to recognise that from this diversity springs crucial individual, group, and democratic rights.

The Unity Party upholds the fundamental Australian value of 'a fair go for all.' Australian society must ensure that opportunities are available so every person can realise their full potential. Australian society must ensure that services and support are available to those who need them.

We don't have to be the same to be equal.

The future of Australia as a harmonious, progressive and prosperous society rests upon the acceptance and practice of these values.

'I think we have shocked the major parties, nearly as much as One Nation shocked them,' Peter says. 'They always thought that these ethnics would never rebel. They thought the Chinese would never rebel. These ethnics are for fundraising, for handing out how-to-vote cards at polling booths. As long as we are nice to them, give them some crumbs from time to time, they will be happy.'

'Look at the corporate culture of the Labor and Liberal parties,' Cyril suggests. 'I don't think they are capable of getting equal representation for minority groups. I don't think, ultimately, they would want the Parliament to look like the rest of Australia. I don't think they are culturally capable of doing that. Helen Sham-Ho and Bill O'Chee were in tune with multiculturalism, and their parties turned against them.'

So, Unity set out to get representatives into Parliament.

Our Vision

The Unity Party calls upon all Australians to work towards creating a society for current and future generations that is harmonious, culturally rich and cohesive in its diversity.

The Unity Party envisages a society that recognises the diverse needs of all its peoples — of all races and creeds; of those who live in the bush and those who live in the city; of women and men — and enables all to reach their true potential and make their own positive and unique contribution to our nation.

The Unity Party calls upon all Australians to embrace the spirit of multiculturalism and reconciliation to create a society that is fully inclusive; where prejudice and division are replaced by understanding, tolerance, acceptance and unity; and in which healthy, informed and truthful debate is promoted.

The Unity Party envisages one nation in which all Australians, including the original inhabitants of this land, have political, educational and social equality, and full legal rights.

The Unity Party seeks to create a progressive society in which all the people of Australia are supported and encouraged in embracing and responding positively to change, to maximise the nation's economic opportunities, its productivity and prosperity.

The Unity Party envisages a dynamic and outward-looking Australian economy that has thriving international market networks, and a nation which is globally engaged and highly respected in the international community.

'If you look at health, the ethnic communities have access problems. They don't get public health education, they have trouble finding specialists who speak their languages, and even in the hospital situation interpreting services are often not available. So, they have a problem accessing public services,' Peter tells us.

'Look at law and order issues. All this stuff about gangs, and drug dealing; who are they trying to blame all the time?' asks Cyril. 'And look at the church in Bankstown that the Muslims wanted to use — a Christian church is a place of worship, but they wanted to use it, and it was suddenly not a place of worship.'

'And we do have a lot of problems. We people have a suicide rate that is higher, we have culture shock, we have intergenerational conflicts, our foreign qualifications are not recognised so we can't do the work we are trained for. The list goes on and on,' Peter says. 'And where are all the politicians? Where are all the Anglo-Saxon politicians who are supposedly representing us?'

'I think Australia has done a lot of migrants a lot of good,' concludes Cyril. 'In fact, the Chinese have been, if I can speak for them, very grateful. We say we are guests in this house, and we do not want to make waves. But ultimately, if we believe in true democracy, then we need to be able to speak for ourselves. If we don't exercise our freedom, maybe one day that freedom could be taken away. Because of John Howard, because of Pauline Hanson, we have been pushed to the stage where we have actually got up and said, "Look, enough is enough." We want our place in the sun, too.'

— • —

In the space of six weeks, Unity attracted two thousand members.

Three months after those first meetings in Peter Wong's lounge room, Unity stood seventy-four candidates in the Federal election in New South Wales, Victoria, Western Australia and Queensland.

David Zyngier, a former principal of a Jewish community school, stood against Federal Treasurer Peter Costello in the blue-ribbon conservative seat of Higgins in Melbourne. At a meet-the-candidates community meeting chaired by a well-known radio personality, he won the greatest applause from the hundreds of people attending for his impassioned plea that a cohesive, peaceful community was far more important any conceivable change to the tax system.

Robbie Thorpe stood for the eastern Victorian seat of Gippsland. Robbie is one of the traditional owners, and has been fighting a series of cases through the courts arguing that Australian governments are guilty of genocide against Aboriginal people. He's not an Australian citizen, and refuses to become an Australian citizen, preferring instead to carry an Aboriginal passport. The Electoral Commission allowed him to stand on the basis of his eligibility to vote in ATSIC elections.

Sarah Kemp, former star of the television series *Sons and Daughters*, stood against John Howard in the seat of Bennelong.

Randa Abdel-Fatteh, an arts/law student at Melbourne University, stood for the seat of Wills. At a public meeting, Randa made an impromptu speech of almost-Gettysburg proportions — short, elegant, profoundly moving — about respect, fairness, belonging, living together.

Mark Rose, cousin of the famous boxer, Lionel Rose, stood for the Senate in Victoria. He spoke at a community meeting in Melbourne's Chinatown; it was the first time most in the audience had heard an Aboriginal person speak, and many said they were very moved.

Wellington Lee, longtime Melbourne City Councillor and later Deputy Lord Mayor, resigned from the Liberal Party to stand for Unity in the Senate. Phong Nguyen, President of The Vietnamese Community of Victoria, also stood for the Senate.

Assyl Haidr, a student at Monash University, stood for the seat of La Trobe. Assyl's family held a function at their house attended by Lebanese community leaders, consular representatives of various Arabic-speaking countries, and leaders from the Muslim community. An uncle orated a stirring Arabic poem he had written for the occasion.

Jason Li, a young human rights lawyer and prominent contributor at the Constitutional Convention, stood for the NSW Senate. Allan Jacobs, former Director of Sydney's Jewish Museum, stood for the Sydney seat of Wentworth. Ted Wilkes, a prominent Aboriginal community leader, stood for the Senate in Western Australia. Diana Wolowski, a well-known member of the Australian Republican Movement, stood for the seat of Melbourne Ports. Harry Fong, a Chinese-Australian barrister, stood for the Senate in Queensland.

These were just some of the seventy-four candidates fielded by the Unity Party, and to compare these candidates — their energy, their raw talent, their grasp of ideas, their ability to express themselves — with the people who actually sit in the Federal Parliament is both a tragedy and cause for hope. There is another Australia out there, bursting to be recognised, talents that are there to be used if anybody were to notice them.

The English-language media took almost no interest in the Unity Party; even SBS barely reported on Unity. This was the same media that had turned Pauline Hanson into a celebrity.

But Unity was headline news in the non-English-language press and the Asian regional press. The world's largest newspaper, Beijing's *People's Daily*, reported a Chinese Ministry of Foreign Affairs spokesperson as saying that 'Australia risked becoming unwelcome in the region if Ms Hanson's policies led to the abandonment of support for ethnic equality.' The Australian Government's attitude towards racism, it said diplomatically, was 'temporarily not clear-cut.' The paper singled out the Unity Party as a driving force among those battling racism in Australia. 'A tide of anti-racism among the Australian people has arisen … which will allow Australia to return to its previous state as an open and free nation.'

Peter Wong had asked us to help Unity. We were attending a function welcoming the new Chinese consul in Melbourne.

The theme of his speech in appreciation was the Three Unities: the unity of the Chinese people in meeting the challenge of the flood disaster; the unity that might one day come with the fusion of Taiwan with China; and the new hope represented by the Unity Party.

Between courses at dinner, the mobile phone rang. It was Peter Costello, saying he was sorry, but he hadn't kept his eye on the ball, he hadn't noticed Unity. He was after preferences. The election was going to be a close call.

'Why did your Party equivocate on One Nation preferences?'

'But I didn't.'

'Do you think they are going to do well in this election?'

'No.'

'Did you expect them to do anywhere near as well as they did in the Queensland election?'

'No.'

'And what about economic matters, what about your portfolio, what about the gap between what you believe and what's actually happened? You're running on One Nation policies: the tariff pause, the decision to stop selling down the wool stockpile, the Nationals' objections to the full sale of Telstra because foreigners might end up part owners. And if you believe in free markets, why would you make one market, the labour market, less free by cutting back immigration? They're all economic decisions, but they're really race decisions.'

Silence.

'Yes, we can talk preferences, but how about getting rid of your boss?'

Silence.

Some of the creative people at J.Walter Thompson offered to donate their skills to create an advertising campaign for Unity:

PLEASE COMPLAIN.
For the sake of our country, make sure your voice is heard all the way to Canberra. By voting for Unity, you can help put an end to the racist and divisive policies of the One Nation Party. Unity was formed to protect and maintain our cultural diversity. So, if you believe in an open and tolerant Australia, complain loudly at the ballot box. Vote 1 Unity.
UNITY. SAY 'NO' TO HANSON.

The reference was to Pauline Hanson's famous response, 'Please explain,' when a *60 Minutes* reporter asked her if she was a xenophobe. She'd never heard of the word.

Unity won nearly 100,000 votes in the 1998 Federal election. In the Sydney seat of Fowler, Andrew Su won 11.5 per cent of the vote and up to thirty per cent of the vote in some booths. The following March, in the State election, he improved his vote to 18 per cent in the equivalent State electorate.

For a party that came from nowhere and had almost no media coverage, the 1998 Federal election result was remarkable. But the result went publicly unremarked everywhere except in the ethnic media.

While the English-language media selectively didn't notice Unity, the operators in the big party machines did. After the election, Philip Ruddock's Immigration and Multicultural Affairs ministry was expanded to include Reconciliation and moved into Cabinet, and Labor created a dedicated shadow Immigration portfolio once again.

Peter and Cyril Wong say that the next task for Unity is to build the party from the grassroots, to give people political experience at the local government level. Unity stood thirty candidates in the NSW local government elections in September 1999, and won five seats. The Mayor of Auburn, the City of the Olympic Games, is a Unity Party representative.

Peter Wong believes Unity has had a real impact.

'After the Federal election, multiculturalism has no longer been a taboo word. Our PM chokes on it, but now at least he knows he has to say it. Even the Nationals put One Nation last in the New South Wales State election.

'And ethnic communities have become more involved. They are participating. Sue Green from the *South China Morning Post* interviewed me only five days ago. She said to me, "I have been around Malaysia, I have been to Indonesia, I have been to New Zealand, and it confirms what people are saying, that Chinese people have no political awareness, they don't care. Except," she said, "when I landed in Sydney, and I said my God, they are aware of politics, this is something I have never seen in the rest of the world."

'What Pauline Hanson has done, and what John Howard has done, is to make the community aware, politically aware.'

CHAPTER 24

Living in the Mainstream

Whether it's the frenzied outrage of the talkback radio hosts, or the populist insinuations of politicians with a nose for white backlash, the refrain is similar: 'Why do Aborigines get all this special treatment?' 'Why do we stand for all the corruption in ATSIC?' 'Why the waste of taxpayers' dollars?' 'Why the race-based lurks, the advantages they get which we don't?' 'Why are more and more people identifying as Indigenous? Because of the benefits that come with identification, that's why!'

353,000 Australians identified themselves as Aboriginal and Torres Strait Islanders in the 1996 Census, a 33 per cent increase since the 1991 census. Despite all the setbacks, all the difficulties, there is a growing pride in Indigenous heritage; but very few material advantages.

Employment: The median weekly income for Indigenous men in 1996 was $189, compared to $415 for other Australian men.[1] 26 per cent of Aboriginal people were unemployed at the beginning of 1998, compared to 8 per cent for the general community. Of those in employment, 32,000 were working on the Community Development Employment Program — a compulsory work-for-the-dole scheme for which, until recently, there has been no equivalent in the general community. Even now, outside Indigenous communities, only young people are expected to participate in work-for-the-dole schemes. If it wasn't for the CDEP, Indigenous unemployment would have been over 40 per cent.[2]

Income: On average Indigenous people earn $14,200 per year, compared to $21,000 for Australians generally.[3]

Health: Life expectancy for non-Indigenous women is over 81 years; for Indigenous women it is 61.7 years. And whilst more than one in two non-Indigenous males will reach the age of 75, more than one in two Indigenous men die before they reach the age of 50.[4] Mortality rates in certain age brackets are simply appalling. Indigenous men between the ages of 35 and 44 are 7.9 times more likely to die than other Australians; Indigenous women 8.2 times. Diabetes is endemic, and Indigenous people are 17 times more likely to die of the condition than other Australians. A survey in 1995 showed that 40 per cent of Torres Strait Islanders over the age of 35 had diabetes. 20 per cent of children under 10 have trachoma, and the rate of blindness among Aboriginal people in rural Australia is ten times that of non-Aboriginal people.[5]

Housing: Indigenous home ownership is 31 per cent, compared to a 72 per cent home-ownership rate for the non-Indigenous population. Indigenous people are twenty times more likely than non-Indigenous people to be homeless. 13 per cent of Indigenous communities have no regular water supplies; 34 per cent have water supply below the standard set by the Federal Government as fit for human consumption.[6]

Education: Fewer than one-third of Indigenous children complete secondary school, compared to the national retention rate of 70 per cent. In the Northern Territory, teenage Aboriginal students complete school with an average educational level of year two to early year three. Their educational progress is hampered, among other things, by hunger and deafness; by the time they begin school, up to 80 per cent of students are hearing-impaired as a result of ear infections.[7]

Justice: 1823 Aboriginal people are imprisoned per 100,000, compared to 99 per 100,000 for the non-Aboriginal population — eighteen times the rate of imprisonment. Aboriginal people are taken into police custody at 27 times the rate of the non-Aboriginal population, or 3539 per 100,000 compared to just 131 per 100,000 for the non-Aboriginal population. One Aboriginal person in seven is arrested annually. One-quarter of all Aboriginal people between the ages of 15 and 44 report that they have been arrested in the past 5 years. Since the mandatory-sentencing law was introduced in the Northern Territory in 1997, it has affected Aboriginal people more than any other group in the population. An Aboriginal woman living in a remote community and with no prior convictions was sentenced to 14 days in prison for stealing a can of beer. The Royal Commission into Aboriginal Deaths in Custody found that even though Aboriginal people were less than 2 per cent of the population, they accounted for about a quarter of all deaths in custody.[8]

It's a sorry tale, a tale of two nations and the great divide that separates them.

Yet the refrain continues. 'Why does all this money go to ATSIC?' The answer is that $1.5 billion of Federal Government funding goes to dedicated Indigenous programs each year, but much of that is to provide services that the rest of the Australian community expects as a matter of course. $374 million goes to CDEP which would otherwise be counted as unemployment benefits. $130 million goes to improve the appalling state of health services. In 1996, this funding accounted for $370 per Indigenous person for primary health care; meanwhile, the balance of Federal health spending amounted to $1034 per annum for each non-Indigenous person in the population.[9] The simple fact is that Indigenous people get far lower levels of government services than the rest of the community. Hence the health outcomes, the educational outcomes, the housing outcomes, the employment outcomes. Indigenous people might get small amounts of special services, but they don't get the mainstream services that other Australians enjoy as a matter of right.

Meanwhile, other sectional interests get their own special favours. Yet the talkback radio jockeys and the populist politicians seem to take less interest in this than the special favours that the government is supposed to be showering on Indigenous people. The diesel fuel rebate alone —which benefits farmers and miners, together about the same size as the Indigenous population — is worth more than the total ATSIC budget. The Department of Veterans' Affairs spends $6 billion annually on people retired from the military, who amount to 2.8 per cent of the population.[10]

Mick Dodson, Indigenous community leader and former Social Justice Commissioner in the Human Rights and Equal Opportunity Commission, summed up the situation when we spoke with him.

'It's just crazy. When you a look at any socio-economic indicator, we're a distant last. You know, it's very difficult to turn around a position that is manufactured by the Government, fabricated by them, if you like, where they seem to have convinced the electorate, or large enough numbers of the electorate, that one group is getting more than another group. Then they complain that it's "positive discrimination." What's wrong with positive discrimination? We do it all the time. I mean, why shouldn't they get a diesel fuel rebate? And, for that matter, remote Aboriginal communities don't get it, and they're in exactly the same boat as the bloody pastoralists and miners.

'This bullshit about Abstudy.' Abstudy is the income support scheme for Indigenous students undertaking tertiary education. 'Abstudy's not that much different to what everybody else gets. It's just got a different name. And it's targeted because of the disadvantage. That's why it's called a special measure.

'People like Hanson say, "Well, I just want everybody to be treated equally." Sure, you can do that if the playing field's level. But if the playing field ain't level, people will be discriminated against because they're at the wrong end of the tilt. You could tax everybody $20,000 a year. That would be equal. But is it fair?

'What they're on about now is going back to more of the same. Cutting back services, trying to mainstream them. I mean, it's the mainstream that's failed us. If they were in private enterprise, these mainstreamers who provide services to Aboriginal people, they'd have been drummed out of business years ago. And you know, in mainstream services, huge amounts of that money gets sucked up in white bureaucracies. 9.8 per cent of the ATSIC budget goes on administrative costs. A bit under 2 per cent goes to running the ATSIC Board and all the regional councils and the zone councils. No-one gets within cooee of that. The going rate for administrative costs in Commonwealth bureaucracies is 24 per cent, more than double what ATSIC spends.

'The most efficient agencies in Indigenous affairs in this country are the community-based agencies. They do bloody wonderful work on a shoestring. They've got to.'

— • —

The Report of the National Inquiry into the Separation of Aboriginal and Torres Strait Islander Children, *Bringing Them Home*, was released on 26 May 1997. It reported that between one in three and one in ten Indigenous children had been forcibly removed from their parents between 1910 and 1970 — 'half-caste' children who were placed in institutional care or fostered out to white families. The report documented gross violations of human rights and a policy whose intention had been the elimination of Indigenous culture, or genocide. It recommended that the Federal Government offer an apology and compensation to the estimated thirty thousand living members of the 'stolen generations.'

In March 1999, the case of Lorna Cubillo and Peter Gunner commenced in the Federal Court in Darwin. They were claiming compensation for having been forcibly taken from their parents by government authorities.

Lorna Cubillo had been one of sixteen children, including breastfeeding infants, who were loaded onto a truck at Phillip Creek on Banka Banka Station, north of Tennant Creek, and taken nearly a thousand kilometres north to Darwin:

> As the truck left Phillip Creek, everyone was crying and screaming. I remember mothers beating their heads with sticks and rocks. They were bleeding. They threw dirt over themselves. We were all crying on the truck. I remember that day. Mothers chased the truck from Phillip Creek screaming and crying. They disappeared into the dust of the track.[11]

It was 1945, and Lorna Cubillo was seven years old. This was the beginning of a two-day journey to Darwin's Retta Dixon Home, a children's institution run by the Aborigines Inland Mission.

Welfare officers had failed to capture Peter Gunner on two previous occasions. He was living with his family at Utopia station, west of Alice Springs, and had run away once and been concealed under blankets by the old people another time. But on this day in 1956, they managed to catch the seven-year-old:

> It was ration day and I was standing not far from the homestead with other people from my family. They were standing about getting rations. I didn't see the welfare blokes and they grabbed me and held me by the arms and dragged me to the truck. I went mad, screaming to my family to help me, but they didn't move. The women were crying. They couldn't do nothing about it. They were yelling and talking. My mother was there. She was crying and so were her sisters.[12]

Peter Gunner was taken 250 kilometres to St Mary's Home in Alice Springs.

Barrister Jack Rush QC told the court that his clients had been 'subjected to a cruelty which is unsurpassed in recent Australian history.'

For both applicants, Lorna Cubillo and Peter Gunner, the years after removal were years of institutionalisation, effective incarceration ... For both, during their time at both homes, they were dealt the blow of having their Aboriginal heritage and culture or the attempt to have their Aboriginal heritage and culture, completely and utterly taken away from them, eradicated ... If they spoke their Aboriginal language, they were assaulted. Both ... were denied any contact with their mother and family.[13]

Rush provided the court with evidence that the government policy of removing 'half-caste' children was founded on the fear that half-castes would soon outnumber whites. The policy was also based on ideas of eugenics, the theory of race-breeding, together with the idea that the Aboriginal race would, and should, eventually be bred out of existence.

C.E.A. Cook, the Chief Protector of Aborigines in the Northern Territory from 1927, and legal guardian of all Aboriginal children in the Territory, made the purposes of the removal policy quite clear:

Generally by the fifth and invariably by the sixth generation, all native characteristics of the Australian aborigine are eradicated. The problem of our half-castes will be completely eliminated by the quick disappearance of the black race, and the swift submergence of their progeny in the white ... The Australian native is the most easily assimilated race on earth, physically and mentally.[14]

This was before the full horrors of Nazism became known, before genocide had become a fundamental concept in human rights, and before eugenics had been thoroughly discredited as a theory and a practice.

The Howard Government rejected the main recommendations of the *Bringing Them Home* Report. There was to be no apology, and no compensation.

Aboriginal Affairs Minister John Herron said that the Howard Government would never apologise:

The apology is an attempt at blackmail and that has to be understood ... What we must recognise is that a lot of people benefited from that [policy of removal]. ... You've got to put the past behind you ... If it was so horrific ... and the churches were the main instrumentalities of doing this, are they going to say it was ill-intent, genocide? That's what turned me off too, when they said it was genocide. I've seen genocide in Rwanda.[15]

The date the *Bringing Them Home* report was released, 26 May, has become National Sorry Day. The first Sorry Day after the report was released was 26 May 1998. In Sydney, Sorry Books containing half a million signatures were presented to Indigenous leaders.[16] Liberal Premier of Victoria, Jeff Kennett, offered a formal apology on behalf of his Government. In Brisbane, Aboriginal people marched at dusk across the Victoria Street Bridge to be met in King George Square by a crowd of ten thousand people. There, they were offered the keys to the city. Earlier this century, Aboriginal people had not been allowed into the city after dark.[17]

Even that ideological backbone of global business, the UK's *Economist*, for a moment turned its mind away from the calculus of the international free market and towards distant Australia. The magazine's editorialist compared Australia to Germany — an appropriate comparison when the crime under investigation, genocide, was the same:

> Postwar Germany's readiness to express remorse for Nazi wrongs has been an integral part of the evolution of a benign German democracy that is respected and trusted both at home and abroad ... [In the Australian case,] an apology to the Aborigines would serve two purposes. First, it would soften the sense of grievance of those people who suffered at first hand the effects of an inhumane policy, which ended only in the 1960s ... Second, it would in a small way, change Australia's sense of itself ... Saying sorry comes cheap ... But for a country, as for an individual, it does involve confronting one's standards of behaviour.[18]

When we spoke to him, former Liberal Prime Minister Malcolm Fraser was just as clear and just as direct. An apology was a fundamental part of the reconciliation process, the process of establishing a settlement between Indigenous and other Australians.

'At the end of the day an apology will have to be part of the settlement process. It means to say that something in the past has happened, and that you regret something in the past happened. Facing our own past is a very hard thing for a lot of Australians who were not taught anything about the truth of Australia's history.'

— • —

The pressure for the Government to apologise reached new heights when Senator Aden Ridgeway took his seat in the Federal Parliament. The second-ever Aboriginal member of the Parliament, and member of the middle-ground Australian Democrats Party, he was willing to talk, and compromise, with John Howard.

Because Howard rejected the concept of 'custodianship' to describe prior Indigenous occupation in the constitutional preamble he planned, Ridgeway suggested that it mention Indigenous 'kinship' with the land. And because Howard refused to apologise, he helped him come up with an alternative statement of 'regret.'

> I move this house:
> - recognising the achievements of the Australian nation, commits to work together to strengthen the bonds that unite us, to respect and appreciate our differences and to build a fair and prosperous future in which we can all share;
> - acknowledges that the mistreatment of many indigenous Australians over a significant period represents the most blemished chapter in our national history;
> - expresses its deep and sincere regret that indigenous Australians suffered injustices under the practices of past generations and for the hurt and trauma that many indigenous people continue to feel as a consequence of these practices; and
> - believes that we, having achieved so much as a nation, can now move forward together for the benefit of all Australians.[19]

Not only was there no apology. There was also no mention of the issue which precipitated the call for apology in the first place — the question of the 'stolen generations.' The treatment of Indigenous people was recast as a mere blemish on Australia's history, together with a riposte to the 'black armband history' people to the effect that, since we had 'achieved so much,' we could surely 'move forward together.'

In fact, Howard seemed to be saying that the sooner we put the past behind us, the better:

> I have frequently said that, and will say it again today, that present generations of Australians can not be held accountable, and we should not seek to hold them accountable, for the errors and misdeeds of earlier generations. Nor should we ever forget that many people who were involved in some of the practices that caused hurt and trauma felt at the time that those practices were properly based. To apply retrospectively the standards of today in relation to their behaviour does some of those people who were sincere an immense injustice.[20]

To all of which, Mick Dodson, lead author of the *Bringing them Home* report that had initially sparked the public discussion of an apology, replied:

> John Howard is not capable of apologising. Let's wait for the man and the hour to come. We have got the hour but the man has not cometh.

And his brother, Pat Dodson, former chair of the Council for Aboriginal Reconciliation, read a statement from nine Land Council heads:

> Do not be caught up in this hasty and disgraceful pretence when members of the indigenous peoples have already suffered so much indignity ... Saying sorry removes a heavy burden that the stolen generations have been carrying and involves giving back something to those who have suffered.

But Pauline Hanson thought John Howard's formulation was about right:

> I think all Australians feel regretful for what has happened in the past to Aboriginal people ... I think the word regret is appropriate.[21]

_ • _

In December 1998, the Northern Territory Government announced that it was phasing out bilingual education in Aboriginal community schools — the simultaneous teaching of Australian languages and English. Costing $380,000 per year, bilingual programs were at the time running in twenty-one schools. Some of the programs had been running continuously since the introduction of bilingual education in the Northern Territory by the Whitlam Government in 1973.

The Northern Territory Minister for Education and Training, Peter Adamson, issued a press release saying that there would be a transition to English-only programs. Teaching English alone, and teaching it using English-as-a-second-language methodologies was 'in the interest of improved outcomes.' Teaching Indigenous languages in schools, by implication, was a waste of time and money.

Former Aboriginal and Torres Strait Islander Commissioner Mick Dodson responded immediately. The move to deny Aboriginal students the right to learn their own languages in school was in breach of Article 27 of the UN International Covenant on Civil and Political Rights, as well as against Article 15 of the UN International Convention on the Rights of the Child.[22] It signalled a return to the assimilation policies of the past.

Raymattja Marika is teacher-linguist at the school at Yirrkala in North-East Arnhem Land. Her father, Roy Marika, had been one of the signatories to the Bark Petition sent to Canberra in 1963 when Nabalco first proposed to set up its bauxite mine and alumina plant in traditional Yolngu country. The petition was a landmark in the long fight for land rights which culminated in the Northern Territory Land Rights Act of 1976.

We met Raymattja in Darwin. She had come to argue the case for bilingual education at a teachers' conference.

'The sort of education we want for our children is an equal education — so that our children can have the same job opportunities as all other Australians. This means that they can be a lawyer, or a professor, a pilot, a carpenter or be whatever they want to be.'

None of this Minister Peter Adamson could disagree with, but he and Raymattja's people, the Yolngu, have completely different ideas about how equality is to be achieved.

'Being equal in education also means being consulted as to what our children are taught and how our children learn. Our community and our school need to plan together to see what our children need in order to get a good and equal Balanda education as well as maintaining our language and culture.'

The Yolngu had a word for white people before white people even knew the Yolngu existed, and even before white people knew Australia existed. Through centuries of trade with the Macassans from the North, they had learnt of the presence of white people — the Dutch, or 'Hollanders,' or 'Balanda' in today's Aboriginal languages — who had colonised Java.

'A good Balanda education is meaningless if we lose our identity.'

In all the arguments about race, culture and difference, one of the most powerful and difficult concepts is 'equality.' In one version of the idea, equality means the same. However, attempting to make people the same is not the way to create equality.

'We believe that our children have a right to know and understand their own cultural belief systems as well as the language and values of mainstream Balanda education. After all, English-speaking children learn in and through their first language. Their cultural knowledge is central to their learning at school. We are asking that our children have the same rights as your children — nothing more, nothing less.'

The same right is the right to be different. The right to be yourself. The right to an education which reflects, values, supports who you are, and not an education which devalues who you are and only encourages you to simply become like another culture: in this case, Balanda culture. These are some of the paradoxes of equality.

Raymattja explains how the school at Yirrkala works, about the School Council of community leaders and elders, about the largely Yolngu teaching staff, and about the 'both ways' curriculum which teaches Yolngu language, traditions and kinship structures alongside the English language and Balanda knowledge.

She tells us about the theory and practice of bilingual education.

'Learning literacy in the children's first language, Yolngu Martha, takes precedence in the first primary schooling years from Transition to Level 3. The focus of their English learning at this early stage is very much an oral one, helping the children become confident speakers of English. Once students have mastered literacy skills in Yolngu Martha, they can transfer to English literacy.'

This is the best way for children who do not know English as a first language to become literate in English, to teach them to read and write in their first language at the start. This is something which has been proven time and time again in the research of leading international literacy experts.

'So, what's the Minister trying to do?' we ask Raymattja.

'It's a direct attack on our rights to teach, and for our children to learn, both languages. We just have to accept that he is a monolingual, monocultural thinker, and that understandings about education are beyond him. But we will not give up and follow his limited assimilationist view of education. We will not allow him to devalue our elders' vision for the future.'

Flying into Yirrkala in a light plane, the first thing we see in the distance are the red scars in the land from the bauxite mine. The Yolngu have managed an accommodation with the mine that works 'both ways,' much like the school's philosophy of learning. Yirrkala Business Enterprises employs more than sixty people from the community and now has a turnover of more than $10 million per year. Its business activities include contracts with Nabalco for bulk ore haulage, earthworks construction, roadworks and also environmental rehabilitation — healing the red scar when the mining is completed. It's a community-run enterprise.

The Yolngu are one of the great success stories of modern Aboriginal Australia. For just 1300 people living in a remote corner of Arnhem Land, without even year-round road access to the outside world, theirs has been a remarkable achievement.

They have produced some of the greatest land rights activists since the beginning of the sixties, and now the Chairperson of ATSIC, Gatjil Djerrkura. They have also produced the band Yothu Yindi, led by former Yirrkala School principal, Mandawuy Yunupingu. The band sings a kind of 'both ways' music, a hybrid of traditional and rock music.

'Living in the mainstream' is the title of one of its best known songs, a song which vividly describes Yolgnu country, and the vision of a new dreamtime in which black and white can share their dreams. Yolgnu and Balanda, living together, learning together, in the mainstream. 'This is Australia,' they say.[23]

The band sells its records, and performs live, in New York, Rome, and Tokyo. Living in the mainstream: 'world music,' it's called by the mainstream music industry. While we were there, a German art dealer picked up a load of artworks to be sold in galleries across Europe: bark paintings, linocuts, batiks.

This is Australia, this is the world market, and Yolngu culture has attracted international interest because the Yolngu have insisted on being true to themselves.

We visited Yirrkala with Harvard University Professor Courtney Cazden, a world-renowned expert on literacy learning and teacher–student 'talk' in the classroom. She was interested in the bilingual program that had begun there in 1974. And here, in Yirrkala, she found educational ideas, and practical innovations in teaching and learning, that are of world significance. She has written up the insights from the Indigenous teachers of Yirrkala and presented them to the academic world in a number of research papers:

> Yirrkala has organised their curriculum and teaching around a metaphor of the contact zone where rivers meet the sea, named ganma in one of the local Aboriginal languages. Literally, ganma is where fresh and salt water meet. Metaphorically, ganma is where cultures meet: fresh water is indigenous Yolngu knowledge and practices; salt water is the white Balanda knowledge and practices; and one place where they meet is in school ... If the two can be kept in balance in the ganma space, then the rich nutrients that come together from the mix of different waters nourishes richly diverse forms of life — biologically in the literal situation, culturally and intellectually in the metaphorical situation of the school.[24]

Education by its nature is a complex cultural thing, a process of mixing the culture of the school and public life with the cultures that children bring to school from their home and community life. The Aboriginal teachers at Yirrkala have recognised this and created a theory of interaction, a theory in which the school values community life and teaches 'both ways.' This is a lesson that schools around the world could learn, Cazden concludes.

— • —

Sitting in another aeroplane, we shared the flight with earnest, grey-suited men, off to do serious business in Canberra. Heads in their newspapers, these people with a sense of nation were more likely to be reading the *Australian* than the Melbourne *Age* or the *Sydney Morning Herald.*

The main photo on the front page of the *Australian* that day was of Aboriginal children kicking a ball in the blood-red desert sands of the playground at the Yuendumu school in Central Australia. 'War of Words: Speaking up for a Culture,' was the headline, and the story was about the end of bilingual education. In the pale grey light of a morning flight, the red picture flashed eerily up and down the aisle each time a suit turned the page of his paper, an image from a world away.

Joe Lo Bianco met us at Canberra airport. His conversation in the car was full of the latest doings of the organisation he directs, the National Languages and Literacy Institute of Australia. He was about to go to a meeting with the Australian Defence College — now a training ground for officers from regional defence forces, forces which, in an earlier era, might have been regarded as the enemy. They are interested in what he, and the Institute, might have to offer: developing training programs in the skills and ideas and sensibilities of multilingualism and intercultural communication, of regionalism and globalism.

Joe wrote the landmark National Policy on Languages in 1987. One of his great concerns is the fate of Aboriginal languages.

Once there were about two hundred and seventy distinct Australian languages. About one hundred and eighty of these have disappeared completely over the past two centuries, and only ten per cent of Aboriginal people still speak an Australian language. Now there are only about twenty languages left that are still passed on to children as the primary language of the community. Fifty languages are on the verge of disappearing; in fact, as the old people die, they are disappearing — entirely disappearing off the face of the earth — at the rate of about one and a half languages every year. Bilingual education is one way of helping to keep the old languages strong.

It's also a way to improve Indigenous students' results at school.

'On the basis of international and Australian research, people began to say, "Look, this continuing lack of success in education for Aboriginal kids might have a lot to do with alienation, and a clear part of this is the languages stuff."

Joe is explaining the rationale for bilingual education, one of his Institute's areas of expertise, and the opposition that it has always faced.

'What's happened really is that ever since they got going, they have been undermined by hostile bureaucracies. A senior officer in the Commonwealth Department of Education once angrily described Aboriginal language support to me as frog shit. Those were his very words. He said, "All this stuff about Aboriginal languages is just frog shit. They need English literacy." This was years ago. And now that's what we've just gone back to in the Northern Territory.'

So, we ask him for his expert appraisal of the value and importance of teaching Australian languages to Indigenous students.

'There are two critical questions. One, what makes kids succeed; and, two, what's the loss to humanity and obviously to any prospect of cultural maintenance when the languages disappear.

'On the first point, the kid's English is actually better off if they begin school in their mother tongue, and then learn English literacy in parallel to literacy in the first language.

'On the second point, languages are absolutely central to culture and identity. I mean, the grammar, the words — the structures of society are in the language. What's lost with the language is a large part of traditional culture. We have also realised from the "stolen generations" report and the Royal Commission into Aboriginal Deaths in Custody that one of the reasons why there was so much turmoil in young people's lives is their distance from the elders and the authority figures in their community. Maintaining the language is absolutely a human rights issue. What we're embarking on in this country is a great violation of Indigenous Australians' human rights, and their rights to maintain their languages and cultures.

'I also think those languages can speak to all of us, give all Australians a relationship with this place which is more ancient than almost any other people in the world. The poetry, the literature, the art of Australia, is all about locating us in this land, even though we don't belong here in some ways, culturally. Well, we can only learn that from people who know it.'

You just don't hear people, or organisations, advocating for Indigenous languages very often. But when there is some rare lizard, or tree, or small desert mouse that is on the verge of extinction, you hear an outcry. One way or another, steps are usually taken to make sure that the treasure of Australian biodiversity is not reduced. But who even knows, let alone cares, that Australian languages are disappearing at the rate of one and a half per year?

And Australian languages are so rich, so complex, so strange to outsiders. Linguists say that some Australian languages are grammatically so unusual that they come close to disproving the most fundamental proposition of the greatest modern linguist, Noam Chomsky. His theory is that language is 'hard wired' into the brain, and that behind any utterance, in any language, is a 'transformational grammar' — a kind of deep logic, linking events and actions and people and things and causes and time, that is common across all languages and all cultures. But, in some Aboriginal languages, the grammar is just nothing like any other human language. There are no individual agents ('I did something to something'); it is as if the world is made up of events that occur in unison with people and places. Some have a kind of perpetual passive voice in which people and their actions are not separable from the cosmos. Instead of proverbial chickens coming before eggs, the world is in a state of chicken-and-eggness. It doesn't translate, and it can't translate.

Some of the languages are just so hard, not even linguists can ever get to the bottom of them. Some languages have up to three hundred pronouns — compared to the half-dozen or so in English — to describe every conceivable human relationship; some have dozens of tenses, to describe temporality far more subtle than our mere divisions of pasts and presents and futures; and there are no neat and simple name-object correspondences, because a word is simultaneously a person's name, a religious totem, a place, or a kind of animal. You have to have a sense of what someone is referring to in order to know what they are talking about, and when you are talking about one thing you are also talking about all the others, because you are represented by your totem and your name refers to the places that are yours. Word by word, life and land and religion are all metaphors for each other.

Then, to make things more complex, your names for things — a place, for instance — will be different to what other kinds of people call the same things. What you call that place tells people about your relationship to that place: your clan, your moiety, whether you are young or old, man or woman. So, among the several thousand people who originally speak each language, there are dialect differences which tell people who exactly you are. Plus different ways of speaking if you are a man or a woman. Plus different ways of speaking once you are initiated; before that you speak a 'baby language.' Then, as you get older, as you grow in wisdom, you learn the ever-more arcane and difficult secret and sacred languages of the elders, the ancient religious texts. And then, when someone dies, their name cannot be uttered again, and everything has to be renamed.[25] English, by comparison, is so simple.

Which brings us back to Mr Adamson, the Northern Territory Minister for Education who wants to take Aboriginal students back to an English-only curriculum.

Schools need to value and support and teach Australian languages if they are to survive. And survive they must. They are a unique part of the heritage of this continent. There is nothing else like them anywhere in the world.

Australian languages represent ways of understanding the land, ways of thinking, ways of seeing, ways of being human, which are fundamentally different to what is possible in English, or any other language. They are Australia's most profound contribution to philosophy, to the world of ideas.

They are a treasure to be guarded and they are a resource for all of us. The biodiversity of rainforests might hold keys to curing all manner of diseases. So too, understanding the nature of Australian languages might help us find solutions to many of the fundamental dilemmas of multimedia communications, global language and dialect differences, and, indeed, to language learning itself.

CHAPTER 25

Nations to be Reconciled

Philip Ruddock was Liberal Shadow Immigration Minister for quite a few years while Labor was in power. He became Minister for Immigration and Multicultural Affairs in the first Howard Government. After Howard's near-death experience at the 1998 election, the Prime Minister vowed that Reconciliation would be high on his agenda in his second term of office. Ruddock was elevated to Cabinet and his full ministry renamed to include Reconciliation. It was a two-edged honour, given that Ruddock and Howard have often been on opposite sides of party-factional divides, and Ruddock had committed the political sin of treason in 1988 when, along with Ian Macphee and two others, he crossed the floor to vote against Howard on the issue of Asian immigration.

He greets us with smiles, kisses, embraces; we have known him for many years, even if sometimes there's an edginess because, as he says, we always seem to be criticising him. He had set aside the morning to talk with us. The people in the Department had prepared a detailed briefing paper about the things he should tell us. He hadn't read it and gave it to us instead. They were the official answers, but he was going to speak personally.

We mention 1988.

'I mean, what I was being asked to do was to vote against a proposition which is self-evident. That is, you cannot discriminate. I could not bring myself to vote against such a proposition. Now, if it was the end of my political career, as far as I was concerned, that was fine. I was in a party which had always prided itself on issues of conscience, and I saw this as an issue of conscience, so I crossed the floor.'

'What was it that led you to work in this area?' we ask. 'What led you to have the views that you do?'

'I went to a typical Anglo-Celtic Protestant private school.'

He laughs, and lists the Labor icons, pillars of progressivism, whose backgrounds are similar.

'I have to say when I go to the school these days, because it's in my electorate, I see it as a cultural experience. Because you go to the chapel, and you have the Anglican minister there in his penguin outfit, and you've got the brass band, you've got the prayers before the school assembly — it's all the old English traditions, and they are all still a part of my life. It's part of my cultural background. I see myself as having a cultural background.'

'My father was a formative influence. A public servant, then the mayor of a municipality, then a Member of the New South Wales Parliament. Askin [the long-serving Liberal Premier of New South Wales] would never have my father as a Minister. My father was too honest.'

After Askin departed the scene, Ruddock's father finally became Assistant Treasurer in the Willis Liberal Government of the early seventies.

'And the kind of person you are? The kind of person who gets involved in immigration, multiculturalism, Reconciliation?' we ask.

'I was never a great sportsman. I had a convergence problem, which means you don't get the depth of vision and so you can't hit the ball. Everybody had to play sport at school. It was one of those schools where everybody played sport. So I was always the twelfth man in cricket.

'I went to university at sixteen. My general sobriety flows from the fact that I never got around with the kids at university, you know, drinking in the pubs. I got involved in the Young Liberal movement at that time. It was a time of causes, issues of South Africa, human rights. The Liberal Party was a broadly based party in which a lot had a very strong social conscience and talked about conscience issues. I was a founding member of Amnesty International in Australia.'

'In the community in which I lived as a child we had Dutch, Italian and Lebanese neighbours, and my father was working with these communities, locally, right from that time. It's still the reality of my community today.

'You can see it even in my own church — and we are talking about the Anglican Church in Sydney, conservative, extremely evangelical. Yet St John's, Parramatta, where we have worshipped for twenty years has Arabic-speaking people in the congregation.

And St Mark's, where I taught in Sunday School, has a Chinese congregation, and the assistant minister is Chinese.'

'I won the seat of Parramatta when I was thirty. And, you know, you do become typecast. There are some people who come into Parliament and they immediately want to be either on the treasury committee, or the public accounts committee, or the foreign affairs committee. These become their interests, their abiding interests, and they want to be on these committees right from the beginning.

'Now I never looked to be on these committees. It was probably because I came in much younger, and I didn't see myself as being a headline hunter. I didn't consider myself to be the answer to the country's problems. You see the Menzieses, you see the Frasers, and you say, is that me? I never really came in with those sorts of ambitions. I just wanted to do what I was competent to do and do it well.

'I came in at a by-election. The committee positions were all taken. They didn't know which committee they could put me on. Then the Aboriginal Affairs Committee came up; the Member for Herbert had retired. It was the first vacancy.'

On the committee, he travelled to Indigenous communities in most parts of Australia, just about everywhere, except the Torres Straits. We ask him how that experience influenced him.

'Do you want to know what really influences me?'

He fumbles with his portable computer. Gets some help from a staffer to get it started.

'This is a village in Rwanda.'

He shows us digital photos of the horrendous consequences of genocide. He and John Herron, the Minister for Aboriginal Affairs, had gone to Rwanda together.

'I guess the point I'm making here is that things like this have had a profound impact upon me. Aboriginal settlements are not like that.'

'So what's your impression of Indigenous communities?' We're referring to the conditions of living that are still often to be found in some remote communities.

'Who's going to tell people how they should live their lives and how and what they should do? You know, we put people in Housing Commission accommodation in the nice leafy green suburbs of Adelaide, away from their family and friends and so on; we removed people. And then we gathered people up and we put them onto mission stations. And now we let them go to the outstations, and then we say the outstation is no good because it's not got all the stuff that you've got back in the Commission housing.

'These days we step back and say, what do you want? We try and give people choices. Some of the Reconciliation groups, you know, are asking, why are we telling them that they should have an education? Why are we telling them they should have a Western health standard? Why are we telling them they should have Western houses?

'Well I mean this is why we had self-determination, self-management. To try to give people a say, and then you find some still end up in the same situation.'

— • —

Jackie Huggins is on the Council for Aboriginal Reconciliation, which reports to Philip Ruddock. We meet her at the airport. She's rushing from one meeting to the next to represent the Indigenous case.

'You know, being a Black for me is a twenty-four-hour-a-day, eight-days-a-week job. You never get any rest from it. People can ring you up any time. Knock at your door. Really, you have your own private self connected with theirs. You're never really free of expectations, those of us who are committed, I guess, to the cause.'

And that cause, for Jackie, began on the old Cherbourg mission in Queensland, where she was born.

'Yes, it's my mum's community. My sister got married last weekend and we went back for her wedding and stayed there.

'My mother was a single mum and my father died when I was two. So she raised four children single-handedly and struggled every inch of the way. On the pension, and we were poverty-stricken, six children to the one room. She resorted to drinking, heavy drinking at times. I guess it was the way she dealt with her grief after my father had died.'

Jackie's story is one of struggle, and survival, and achievement for her community's cause. She also says there is something about her background that influences the way she works.

'It probably extends back to being part of a very vibrant, extended Aboriginal family and household, where one didn't think of oneself as an individual. You were part of a whole, and connected as a fraction to that whole. You weren't anything without those other pieces of the jigsaw puzzle. You could never be someone who operated solely by themselves. So for me it was never an issue of having to decide whether I would be Jackie Huggins, the individual. It has always been Jackie Huggins, the person who would be responsible for a whole number of people in the Aboriginal scene. And so for me I've never really seen myself just as the professional, or the businesswoman, or the historian, or the writer. Whatever education and expertise I have gained throughout my life, I will always in some way, somehow, in some fashion, turn back to the benefit of Aboriginal people. It really pisses me off when I see our people being educated as lawyers and doctors and academics, but when they don't necessarily want to do any real, positive things for their people. They go mainstream. And that hurts me.'

On the Reconciliation Council, she's been working with author David Malouf to draft a Reconciliation statement:

> *Speaking with one voice, we the*
> *people of Australia,*
> *of many origins as we are, make a*
> *commitment to go together recognising the gift of one*
> *another's presence.*
>
> *We value the unique status of*
> *Aboriginal and Torres Strait*
> *Islander peoples as the original custodians of*
> *traditional lands and waters.*
>
> *We respect and recognise*
> *continuing customary laws,*
> *beliefs and traditions.*
>
> *And through the land and its*
> *first peoples, we may taste this*
> *spirituality and rejoice in its*
> *grandeur.*
>
> *We acknowledge this land was*
> *colonised without the consent of*
> *the original inhabitants . . .*

These are the opening words of the draft statement.

'It has to be about three to five hundred words, no more. We have to choose every word carefully, and at the same time keep both sides on board. You can't offend people — words like 'invasion' or 'massacre.' You don't want to make them feel guilty. You've got to write something that everyone will accept, and that's the challenge. It's taught me to eat humble pie, I can tell you.

'We want to come up with a kind of declaration. It's really a ... the word's "treaty," if the Prime Minister is willing to accept that word. In the rounds of consultations, Aboriginal people are telling us on the ground that it's a treaty they want.'

'We've stood very firmly on the apology. The Prime Minister came to see us. Three of our people from the stolen generation spoke to him, told him their stories. And one of them said, "Well sir, after hearing all our stories, we would hope that you would reconsider the apology." He was sitting from me to you away, and I tried to get a sense of his body language. And, you know, there was nothing. He was stiff. He was numb. There was nothing.'

'Everywhere I go, communities are feeling very dejected. They have no faith in political systems. They have no faith in anybody that's even trying to be a messenger or mediator. I've never seen so much mistrust in all my life, and frustration and anger.

'Still, five years ago you wouldn't have had the numbers of people who are openly standing up for Reconciliation today. I really believe that five years ago you wouldn't have had at the one table the mining interests, Aboriginal interests, pastoral interests, conservation interests, all talking about land use. That's what happened with the Cape York Regional Agreement. So I try to be positive.

'But sometimes I ask myself, how gullible am I, wanting the best out of people?

'And it's got to be more than good will. There have got to be actions and we've got to see some real outcomes.

'I hope that in my lifetime, and there's a few more years to go yet, I might be able to do something that will help turn things around. I still live in hope. And fear. I have fear.'

— • —

We ask Mick Dodson what he thinks of the Government's commitment to Reconciliation.

'I think it's a cynical political exercise. The Prime Minister got belted around the ears by his own constituency during the election. They were saying, "Look, we didn't like you not saying sorry to the stolen generation. We didn't like what you did with the Native Title Act. You had better lift your game or we'll seriously consider voting for somebody else." That's what it's all about. It's got nothing about a new heartfelt desire on the part of the Prime Minister to do something about Reconciliation. Anyway, given his track record to date, who would want a bar of his version of Reconciliation?'

'So what do you do?' we ask.

'Governments come and go. But we'll still be here. We'll still be fighting the fight.'

'And if Reconciliation were to come, what would it look like? What does the word mean?'

For a start, it means remembering, 'an honest acceptance of the facts of our shared history.' This was the subject of a speech he had given.[1] Then, having remembered, it means a sense of shame, but not necessarily a sense of guilt for those who are descended from the colonisers.

'Shame is quite different from guilt. Guilt is taking responsibility for what we did: it stems from our actions. Shame, on the other hand, is about who we are: it stems from our character. I can and do feel shame for acts which I did not bring about.

'There is nothing shameful about feeling ashamed. On the contrary, it is a creative and curative emotion.

'Because shame is about identity, an identity which extends beyond my body to my society. It is shame that ignites the healing process, in which our changing sense of who we are changes our relationships with others. It expands the boundaries of our identities. It takes people or groups whom previously we treated as irrelevant to our sense of self, and alters our identity by including them within it.'

This is Mick Dodson's vision for an Australian identity which recognises the truth of the past. It's a vision in which two nations 'become as one in the dreaming of this land.' It is a vision for 'those who dare dream a dream of an Australia that could be.'

'So what keeps you going?'

'Hope.

'I've been able to provide my children with opportunities that sadly, too many other Aboriginal families can't provide for their kids. All the sorts of things I've done in my lifetime or will have done before I expire — I hope they will make a difference.

'I don't know. If they do, that's great. If they don't, it won't be for the bloody want of trying.'

CHAPTER 26

The Multicultural Australian

At the beginning of the nineties, we sat in on Nathan Glazer's classes at Harvard University. He's a conservative social theorist, internationally famous for his pathbreaking work on the sociology of ethnic groups. And he's always been an integrationist — a believer in the American 'melting pot' — rather than a multiculturalist. He wrote a book in the 1980s called *Affirmative Discrimination* which criticised attempts to right historic wrongs through programs of positive discrimination such as affirmative action.

He retired in the mid-nineties to write another book. Published by Harvard University Press in 1997, its title came as a shock to people who knew him and knew his work. It was called *We Are All Multiculturalists Now.*

The book begins with the story of the School Board of Lake County, Florida, which in 1994 passed a resolution reaffirming the purposes of education:

> To instil in our students an appreciation of our American heritage and culture such as our republican form of government, capitalism, a free-enterprise system, patriotism, strong family values, freedom of religion and other basic values which are superior to other foreign or historic cultures.[1]

Just a few words, from an unheard-of white community in the backwoods of rural Florida. Not so long before, these words would have been regarded as unexceptional. But they became a headline story in *The New York Times*: 'School Board Will Recognize Other Cultures, But As Inferior.' It was yet another salvo in what commentators on contemporary American society have called 'the culture wars.'

Within months, the school board was voted out at this last frontier for multiculturalism. It was time to recognise as well the contributions of Native Americans, African-Americans, Hispanic Americans.

By then, Glazer had changed his mind, too. Multiculturalism was a word, and an idea, he had always disliked. He was ready to admit that:

> The expression 'We are all multiculturalists now' harks back to others that have been pronounced wryly by persons who recognised something that was unpleasant but nevertheless unavoidable. 'We are all socialists now,' Sir William Harcourt, Chancellor of the Exchequer in one of Gladstone's Cabinets, was reputed to have said in 1889 [when he convinced] Parliament to accept progressive taxation on estates at death ... 'We are all Keynesians now,' President Richard Nixon is reputed to have said in 1971.[2]

Glazer speaks of a new America to which he is now resigned. It is an America in which people and schools:

> will not, like the old, take it for granted that it is the best of all countries, as well as the strongest and the richest. We will become more self-conscious about making any claim to a distinctive virtue and superiority, and that is all for the best.

And will multiculturalism, now inevitable, undermine the reality of America's successes? Will it produce divisions and resentments between majorities and minorities?

> I believe things will not come to that pass because the basic demand of multiculturalists is for inclusion, not separation, and inclusion under the same rules — stretching back to the Constitution — that have permitted the steady broadening of what we understand as equality.[3]

Multiculturalism and the greatness of the United States are not incompatible. Multiculturalism is now as American as the idea of equality itself. Indeed, the American idea of equality has been broadened by multiculturalism. Fundamentally, it's about democracy and inclusion.

Then, for an Australian reader, comes the most staggering of Glazer's insights. It's something you know if you have worked with the Australian idea of multiculturalism, but from the vantage-point of a small country at the end of the earth it's still hard to believe.

Where did this idea come from, the idea of multiculturalism? Glazer asks. For it is certainly not an American idea. He went to the Harvard University Library and looked up all the books which had the word in their titles. The first mentions are in the seventies, and the only books with the word in their titles for the whole of the 1970s and 1980s are from Canada and Australia.[4]

As Al Grassby pointed out to us, the Australian idea is very different to the Canadian idea. In Canada, multiculturalism is the product of a conflict between two groups, French-speakers and English-speakers. The multiculturalism of equality-through-diversity that Glazer refers to is more like the Australian idea than the Canadian idea.

Multiculturalism is an Australian idea that's become a world idea. Maybe even *the* world idea for the era of globalisation and cosmopolitan local diversity.

— • —

Al Grassby was Immigration Minister in the Whitlam Government. We meet him for lunch in Canberra. He's working on a biography of J.C. Watson, Australia's first Labor Prime Minister, born in 1867 to Johan Christian and Martha Tanck in Valparaiso, Chile. Al's own grandfather, born in Spain, had also migrated to Australia from Chile. His mother had been born in Ireland.

'Where did the word come from?' we ask. 'Where did you first hear the word multicultural?'

'Well, of course there are a lot of myths and legends about the subject, but I first heard the word in Canada. I was terribly impressed with the concept of multiculturalism, but not the Canadian model.

'You see, the Canadian model was launched by the Prime Minister at the time, Pierre Trudeau. But it was based on two dominant races: the English and the French. Now, as far as I was concerned, it was a flawed multiculturalism because there was no mention of the Indigenous people, or of course the million or so

Italian-Canadians in Toronto. Or all the rest. It was not really multiculturalism at all.

'So I took this up with Trudeau, and he said, "It was a ploy which I thought of to try and bring the French and the English together." That was the whole basis of it.

'They started off differently to us, but I brought the word back, I brought the concept back to Australia. I did get suggestions that the word should be polyethnic, which would be Greek, as against multiculturalism, which is Latin, but I thought, well, the Latin seems to be easier.

'Of course, the debate on the word multiculturalism that we've had since in Australia has simply been a device to attack the concept. You've got to recognise what it replaced, and that was Anglo conformism. Before, everything we did was based on assimilation.

'Multiculturalism replaced that. It was meant to give everyone their "place in the sun," to coin a phrase.'

We'd mentioned the title we were considering for this book. What Al Grassby meant by 'multiculturalism' back then, Nathan Glazer is now calling 'inclusion.'

Al didn't get the chance to follow through on the word, or the idea, because he lost his seat at the 1974 election. At the time, there was nobody else in Labor who was willing or able to continue where he had started off.

So the practical business of making multiculturalism a reality — the Australian version of the idea — began during the Fraser era. With the Galbally report, Fraser introduced multiculturalism as a full scale national policy. This is how he explained the term:

> We cannot demand of people that they renounce the heritage they value, and yet expect them to feel welcome as full members of our society ... Multiculturalism ... sees diversity as a quality to be actively embraced, a source of social wealth and dynamism ... The [Galbally] report [has] identified multiculturalism as a key concept in formulating government policies and recognised that Australia is at a critical stage in the development as a multicultural nation.[5]

Al picks up the story again, a story that involves a Labor man giving enormous credit to Labor's political opponents. After Al lost his seat, Gough Whitlam made him Commissioner for

Community Relations. Then Whitlam lost the 1975 election, and Al stayed on in the position to work for the Fraser Government.

'You see, when Whitlam was Prime Minister, we planned to have the first Greek Glendi in Melbourne. There was going to be an international hook-up with Karamanlis, the Greek Prime Minister, in Athens. In the meantime, we'd had the Kerr coup, and Fraser had replaced Whitlam as Prime Minister. So Fraser was going to come to the Glendi. It was the beginning of 1976.

'We thought we might get five or ten thousand people. But in fact between sixty and seventy thousand people had turned up. And of course there had been a lot of bitterness in the election campaign; Greeks at that time were mostly Labor voters.

'The Chief of Police came up to me and said "What are you going to do with the Prime Minister?"

'I said "Well, I've arranged for his car to pull up just behind the Myer Music Bowl. He won't be seen by anybody until he actually gets up to speak."

'And the Chief of Police said "Do you expect any trouble?"

'I said "No. Now, all I would ask you to do is to ask your officers to be friendly. Hold the kids, smile, and everything will be fine."

'Fraser's Department had given him a speech of about four foolscap sheets, you know, the usual thing, the cliches about what the Greeks had done, particularly in fish and chip shops. It was a pretty awful speech, and he knew it. I was worried about how the crowd would react. Then I saw him writing on the back of an envelope. Just a few sentences.

'He got up and spoke. Just four points. But the main point was right at the beginning.

'"The days of Anglo-Saxon dominance are now over," he said.

'I was absolutely amazed, absolutely astounded. The man with the country property, the man from the Establishment. I wouldn't have dared to say that. But he said it. And, you know, he got a very good hearing.'

— • —

Since the emergence of One Nation, a chorus of complaint has arisen against multiculturalism.

'It's divisive,' people say. 'It feeds a bloated "multicultural industry,"' they say. Leading politicians have even said it. 'What do you make of this?' we ask Malcolm Fraser.

'At the most charitable, it is mischievous. And further down the track it is destructive, it is wrong, totally misconceived, totally misunderstanding what the problem is and what we were trying to address with the concept.

'It's like saying that some people can be people but other people can't be people. Or some people can develop their full potential but other people can't. You need an education system, a social structure, that meets the needs and demands of all people in the community, not just some people in the community. And for some people — I mean, forgive me, I've used the phrase often — to be a good Australian you have to be white Anglo-Saxon Protestant, and if you aren't, you'd better pretend to be.'

'And the other accusation is that multiculturalism has gone too far. Too many programs, too much money spent?' we ask.

'No, no, nothing that has convinced me that it's gone too far. I've heard the allegations that money's been wasted, but I have not personally seen any evidence. One way of testing it would be, to ask, is what is being done consistent with the principles set down by the Galbally report? Is it serving a useful purpose, and you could define a useful purpose as assisting a group's capacity to participate in, and contribute to, life in Australia? Because that's really what it's all about. It wasn't designed to give people special benefits not available to other people.

'For example, we were taught to read biased English history at school. Back then, children of Italians and Greeks couldn't have access to any form of teaching about the history of their countries of origin. Why shouldn't they know something about their origins? It's a very natural thing. I mean, why do people go digging up their family tree? They want to know where they came from, they want to know. Why then should they be accused of placing their loyalty to some other country above loyalty to Australia?'

Immigration Department figures show that the Federal Government spent $159 million on settlement, citizenship and multicultural programs in 1998–9. The bulk of this went to the Adult Migrant English Program ($115 million) and the Telephone Interpreter Service ($18 million), which are moving in the direction of cost recovery through the introduction of fees. Just $4.1 million is spent on multicultural programs, including the management of the National Multicultural Advisory Council. In addition, $5 million was spent in 1998–9 on the Living in Harmony initiative. The migration program sets its charges to achieve full cost recovery.[6]

— • —

The Hawke and Keating Governments accepted and extended the idea of multiculturalism as defined by Fraser and the 1978 Galbally report. The landmark 1989 *National Agenda for a Multicultural Australia* described multiculturalism both as a social description and also as a prescription in the form of 'a policy for managing the consequences of cultural diversity in the interests of the individual and society as a whole.'

The *Agenda* had three dimensions. First, 'cultural identity: the right of all Australians, within carefully defined limits, to express and share their individual cultural heritage, including their language and religion.' Second, 'social justice: the right of all Australians to equality of treatment and opportunity, and the removal of barriers of race, ethnicity, culture, religion, language, gender or place of birth;' and third, 'economic efficiency: the need to maintain, develop and utilise effectively the skills and talents of all Australians, regardless of background.'[7]

Neville Roach's National Multicultural Advisory Council was charged by Philip Ruddock with redefining multiculturalism a decade later, and even to review whether the word itself should be changed. These were anti-political correctness days, One Nation days.

Now we are talking to Neville about the work of the Council.

'If you look at what we are trying to do, the biggest objective I had in the first instance was to keep the Council going in an environment where there was a strong belief that it would be disbanded.'

The Council survived. Its report was launched by Prime Minister Howard in May 1999.

'So if you ask me about what the Council was doing, I think we wanted to get a reaffirmation of multiculturalism and to get comfortable public statements from the Government with concurrent bipartisan support from the Opposition. And this is what we managed to achieve.'

'And the Prime Minister's presence ... ?'

'The fact that he came? I am told that on election night Howard — what do they say happens, your life goes before your eyes? — all the polls said they had lost, and he spent several hours facing that. Then suddenly it turned.

'And I think he meant what he said that night, that his new term of Government would be different. He had won again and he could afford to be magnanimous.'

The Council's report was entitled *Australian Multiculturalism for a New Century: Towards Inclusiveness.* It spelt out four principles for an inclusive multiculturalism:

Civic Duty: support for the basic structures and principles of Australian democracy which enable diversity to flourish.

Cultural Respect: the right to express one's own culture and beliefs and the reciprocal obligation of others to do the same.

Social Equity: the right to equality of treatment, free from discrimination.

Productive Diversity: the economic and social benefits of diversity for all Australians.

At the launch, John Howard said 'I can say to you that the essential thrust and the main elements of the report are, of course, endorsed by the Government' — a very unusual thing to say, as Governments usually go away and think about reports before they respond. And 'most importantly, what the Government endorses are the values that are expressed in the report.'

Of the values expressed in the report — he was speaking without notes — he went on to say:

The experiment that Australia represents, if I can call it that, of bringing together, in a quite unprecedented way people from the four corners of the earth ... it really has been a quite remarkable experiment. And Neville is right to use the adjective Australian before multicultural because what he's really putting his finger on is that we have developed an Australian way of doing things.

Howard had used the 'm' word. And he seemed to be meaning what the word meant:

There's no nation on earth that, in this part of the world, in the Asian Pacific region, that has such profound links with the nations of Europe, shares such values in common as we do with the nations of North America, has taken people from 140 source countries. And more recently ... we've taken large numbers of people from the nations of the Asia-Pacific region. And they have made an immense and beneficial and positive contribution to the modern Australia ... It doesn't mean for a moment some newcomers have not been subjected to bigotry, discrimination and intolerance ... I do want to make it very plain on behalf of the Government, without ambiguity, that we stand totally and utterly and uncompromisingly opposed to any form of discrimination of any person in this country based on ethnic background, nationality, race, colour of skin, religious or political convictions ... And I think the values espoused in this report resonate very well with the Australian experience. I warmly thank you Neville, and all the members of your committee for your work. I think it contributes greatly to the ongoing debate about the Australian story and the Australian identity. Thank you.[8]

— • —

'Productive Diversity' is one of the main ideas in the National Multicultural Advisory Council's report. It's an idea that had first been conceived in the Office of Multicultural Affairs before it was abolished in 1996. Put simply, it means that multiculturalism makes good business sense, good economic sense, and good employment sense for the whole country.

John Cook, the Managing Director of Berri, explains to us 'the four business drivers' that will take his company into the future.

'The first is identification with the emerging culture of the new business. The next one is people taking control, developing a sense of confidence and the ability to do what needs to be done. The third thing we are creating is a sense of urgency; there are windows of opportunity, but it's a very competitive world. The fourth thing we are trying to develop inside our business here is entrepreneurialism, the development of a group of people who are going to go out and personally make a difference.'

At first, this sounds like the usual run of corporate-speak, but it's a lot more than that. Diversity is at the heart of John Cook's vision for his company. The culture of the business is one that values the diversity of a workforce which has come from the ends of the earth. That's the only way to bring staff on board, to get them committed, and to bring consumers on board: 'relationship marketing,' it's called. And the urgency is in the world market, particularly considering the company's drive to sell its products into Asia.

'We took the Berri "Tolerance in Fruit" advertisements and showed them to our distributors around the Asian region. We said, "Look, there is probably no better indication of our commitment to our community than what we have just done. So, don't continue to grill us about our motives and what Australia is like. We have just proven that eighty-five per cent of the population identify with this message. That's it. No matter what you read in the damn newspapers about the sensationalism of this idiot woman, this is really what is happening."'

At Berri, the values of multiculturalism make business sense whichever way you look at things.

And at the National Australia Bank, where diversity programs help senior staff develop local niche markets and provide strategies for people to work together in a multinational corporation — Australia's largest company by stock market capitalisation — in which more than half the seventy thousand staff work offshore and across four continents.

And at American Express, which decided to locate its regional headquarters and call centre in Sydney, not because it is a place where English, the language of global finance, is spoken, but because Australia is the only place in the region where you can recruit fluent speakers of every regional language; there's no particular competitive edge in being an English-speaking country. Amex is in Sydney because, language-wise, it's the most Asian city in Asia.

And at Vulcanite, a small Australian manufacturer of something so mundane as brake shoes for railway rolling stock, but which beat a huge Scandinavian manufacturer to a Hong Kong Tramways contract because of the Cantonese speakers on its staff. They suggested that the boxes be labelled bilingually and that the brake shoes be packed in boxes that are small enough to be lifted without a forklift — an essential requirement for the cramped conditions in Hong Kong. Making a cultural difference gave them an edge, over and above the bottom line of price competition.

This is all the basis for a conservative optimism for the future of multiculturalism. Conservative because it's not just about people of goodwill, or minority rights, or migrant welfare. It's about the new business realities, too.

The world of business which is emerging today is built upon the value of the skills of the new, multicultural person, the person who respects and can work effectively with differences. It's the kind of person who can work in global markets, with the language skills, or just the cultural wit, to get international clients on board. And now that the old world of mass-produced, homogenised products has been replaced by a broad range of products customised for niche markets, it's the kind of person who can work out just what the customer's needs are — what's special about their difference. In a business world that has now gone forever, Henry Ford paid little regard to the differences among his customers. 'Any colour you like, as long as it's black,' he said of his Model 'T' Ford. Now, differences and niche markets are everything. Women's markets, and gay markets, and generational markets, and ethnic markets, and different national markets. Markets for every fashion, and style, and enthusiasm, and identity-statement.

Then, having the right stuff for the new corporate culture, being a good team leader or manager, means bringing all the differences into play, in global workforces and local workforces that draw their human resources from diverse communities. Every language people speak at home that could be used with local or global clients, every community network that could provide an entree to new niche markets, every way of communicating and thinking and feeling that might add a creative edge in the development of a new product or marketing concept. The most vibrant and creative corporate cultures are ones that thrive on differences. The most effective organisations are the ones that look and feel as diverse as the local and global markets that are, at the end of the day, the reason for their very existence.[9]

Australia comes to this new world of business with several accidental virtues, several things that give us a competitive advantage. The first is who we are. Migration has made us a microcosm of the new, global marketplace. No other workforce in the world is so diverse and comfortably used to working with its own diversity: one-quarter of the workforce is overseas-born.

And few countries in the world are so geared to the world market — markets which are as diverse as our main regional trading partners; nine of our ten top export destinations are non-English-speaking countries. Few countries are so dependent for their growth, and their futures, on highly culture-sensitive and language-sensitive industries such as tourism (worth $16.1 billion in 1997–8), education (worth $3.2 billion) and human services.

Also, for all the unfinished discussions about multiculturalism and Reconciliation, few societies have become so aware and so skilled in facing the challenge of living with and negotiating cultural differences. We have acquired sensibilities and attributes — or most of us have — which are perfect for the new era of global connectedness and proliferating local diversity.

— • —

'Business Leaders Blast Immigration Cutback.' This was the *Australian Financial Review's* front page headline when the Howard Government cut immigration at the height of One Nation's popularity. It was, the report said, '...a politically motivated decision that flew in the face of the needs of the economy.' The Housing Industry Association called the decision 'extremely disappointing.' Chris Richardson from Access Economics, the influential economics consultancy frequently used by the Government, said there was 'little evidence of a link between immigration and unemployment.' Victorian Premier Jeff Kennett said skilled migration should be immediately increased by twenty thousand.[10]

Professor Glenn Withers from the Australian National University in Canberra, an expert on the economics of immigration, sums up the latest research results as follows. Immigration, he says, creates:

Economic vigour: high migration of one per cent of population will add $600 billion more to Australia's GDP by 2051; without the migration of the past in post-war Australia, our economy would only stand at some $260 billion now, half its present size and a puny thing. Recent research ... shows without qualification that migration not only does not cause unemployment, it actually benefits the locally unemployed.

Social savings: present demographic trends will require almost 10 per cent MORE of GDP for aged support by 2041 — higher and younger immigration can halve this requirement. Recent research ... shows clearly how previous analysis has massively understated the social savings possible with migration.

Global positioning: well-structured migration will sustain our capacity to determine our own directions, underpin technological infrastructure for defence and help usher in the global knowledge economy.[11]

— • —

Rod McGeoch is National Chairman of Corrs Chambers Westgarth, one of Australia's top legal firms, and a former president of the Law Society of NSW. He headed Sydney's successful bid for the Olympic Games in 2000.

We meet him in his firm's palatial offices, where he is a senior partner. Floor-to-ceiling windows and views down Sydney Harbour, all the way to the Heads. Fancy paintings, unobtrusive secretaries, corporate calm.

The Committee for Sydney and the Committee for Melbourne — business-driven lobby groups — have both been pushing for a return to the levels of migration Australia had until the nineties.

'Only those developed countries that have got a positive immigration policy actually have economic growth. Whereas some people might be arguing, "Look, immigration just takes away jobs," the economists will tell you it actually creates jobs. It really is a dollar-driven argument, not an argument over races and cultures. But I believe it. And the statistics are there.

'Then people say, "Australia can't take more than twenty million people. We won't be able to feed them and we'll run out of water," and whatever. Nobody in the business world believes that. Australia produces five times more than it consumes.'

We also ask him about the diversity dividend, the productive diversity effect. Here, he mentions the example of how he led the team that won the Olympics for Sydney. The fact that Sydney is a city of immigrants, a multicultural society — this was the decisive factor in Sydney's victory.

'It was in the original strategic planning. We saw it as an absolute strength. We didn't make a video, we didn't produce a brochure, that didn't have a strong multicultural and Aboriginal message in it. We not only saw it as an immense strength of our own, but we noticed what an unbelievable weakness it was in

Beijing's bid. In fact, in the final evaluation report for China versus Sydney, one of the things that the International Olympic Committee marked China down on very strongly was its inability to cover the languages of all the visitors that were coming — written materials, television broadcasting, you name it. But they just had no mastery of all the languages.

'We were also saying that what makes Australia special is all the cultures living together. We were the absolutely perfect example of the original Olympic ideal — if you brought people from every nation together to play in the games, then they'd go away thinking well of each other and we'd have no war. We're the best microcosm of peaceful living together in the world.'

And with this kind of value set, this sense of Australia and orientation to the world we ask, 'Who are you? What's your background?'

'My background was certainly modest in terms of finances. And my father, he was strongly opinionated. You know, a returned serviceman, anti-Japanese, strongly anti-Catholic, anti-Jewish and all the old ideals of short haircuts, manners maketh the man and that sort of stuff.'

He's talking about an enormous generational shift, from his father's generation to his own.

'Somewhere in all of that, I rebelled against much of what he articulated. He would actually say at the dinner table, "The only bloody problem with Hitler was he didn't get them all." It would just rock me. Even in my formative years I took great exception to racism. I went right to the other end of the spectrum.

'My daughter said to me the other day, "Dad, what do you think of Pauline Hanson?" which is, you know, the kind of question you get from your kids while you're shaving, you're about to race off to work and you've got ten seconds to give them an answer.

'I said, "Anna, there's just one globe and we're all on it. It's a small place. And we've all got to get on together. It's as simple as that."

'And she went, "OK Dad."'

— • —

In July 1998, Philip Ruddock launched *The Charter of Public Service in a Culturally Diverse Society*. It was a document that the old Office of Multicultural Affairs in the Department of the Prime

Minister and Cabinet had begun to develop around the time the Howard Government came to power in 1996. At first glance, its principles seemed self-evident, a re-statement of the obvious:

1. **Access:** Government services should be available to everyone who is entitled to them ... and should be free of any form of discrimination on the basis of birthplace, language, culture, race or religion.
2. **Equity:** Government services should be delivered on the basis of fair treatment of clients who are eligible to receive them.
3. **Communication:** Government service providers should use strategies to inform eligible clients of services and their entitlements.
4. **Responsiveness:** Government services should be sensitive to the needs and requirements of different communities, and responsive to the particular circumstances of individuals.
5. **Effectiveness:** Government service providers must be 'results oriented', focused on meeting the needs of clients from all backgrounds.
6. **Efficiency:** Government service providers should optimise the use of available public resources through a user-responsive approach to service delivery.
7. **Accountability:** Government service providers should have a reporting mechanism in place which ensures they are accountable for implementing Charter objectives for clients.

The *Charter* has since been accepted as a set of operational principles by all State Governments, Labor and conservative alike, as well as the Local Government Association of Australia.

Behind the obviousness of the *Charter*, however, are some ideas that reflect a deeper transformation in the very nature of government and citizenship.

The classical theorists of democracy — Rousseau and his successors — thought of political society as consisting of identical individuals. The State worked on the assumption that there was an idealised universal citizen whose needs were entirely predictable, and fundamentally the same from person to person. The ideal of equality was synonymous with sameness.

With the rise of the welfare state, governments set about developing universal services — in education, in health and social services. Once again, universal meant the same. Mass-produced as if the same service was just as appropriate to everybody.

The problem with generic services, however, is that they work for some people some of the time, and for others they barely work any of the time. The school curriculum that worked in middle-class city schools produced a cycle of alienation and failure in Aboriginal bush schools and in city schools full of migrant kids who came to school without English. The health service that worked in English-speaking urban environments didn't produce even half-reasonable outcomes in Indigenous communities or in hospitals where some of the patients didn't speak English as a first language. Even when the service was there in Aboriginal and immigrant communities (although, often it wasn't), the kids didn't seem to learn, and the patients seemed to get sicker. A lot of the time, resources were simply wasted.

The *Charter* is based on a fundamentally new proposition about how democracy works: the idea that people are different, or the idea of multicultural citizenship. Citizens are all entitled to access but to get comparable outcomes, they will need to be provided different kinds of service.

The solution? Effective communication, including multilingual services, interpreting, translating. Services customised to fit the needs of particular groups in the community. Getting communities involved in service design to make sure that the services end up working for them.

And the outcomes? What are the benefits of thinking of citizens in this new way? It produces services that are more effective, that are more efficient, and that use the public purse to best effect. This is a new kind of public service which moves away from the old bureaucratic 'provider knows best' model to a 'citizen knows best' model, from top-down governance to bottom-up governance, from centralised and uniformly regulated government to more decentralised, informal, interactive relationships between government and communities. It's a new kind of democracy, a new kind of state that we would call 'Civic Pluralism.'[12]

Nor is it so terribly radical, so terribly far-fetched. It's something that we seem to be already doing at all levels of government all around Australia, and we're only just realising that we do it. We're only just starting to describe its principles in documents like the *Charter of Public Service in a Culturally Diverse Society.*

Sixty-one per cent of the citizens of Darebin City Council in Melbourne's north are first- or second-generation immigrants. Darebin also has the largest Indigenous population in Melbourne.[13] The Council is implementing the *Charter*, which now affirms what they have been beginning to do for a long time, and provides a framework for doing it better.

The City offers a meals-on-wheels service for the elderly. It's no longer a just-chops-and-peas menu because not everybody wants to eat chops and peas. So, the service presents a variety of cuisines, to make sure that all elderly ratepayers are able to enjoy the rights of citizenship equally. Even the people who once reliably ate the chops and peas are happier with the new range of choices.

The Darebin libraries have collections in a variety of languages, as well as a specialist Koori collection, because if they didn't do this, they'd be meeting their obligations to a smaller proportion of the ratepayers. The collections are a resource for everybody: people learning another language, school kids doing projects on Indigenous Australia.

The Planning Department at Darebin knows that, at heart, its job is to juggle different value systems in the argument about streetscapes and community — ideas of heritage, or modernity, or amenity, or landscape. The Darebin Indigenous community assists in identifying sites of archaeological significance when decisions need to be made about parks and development.

The Council has also begun building a mausoleum, as above-ground burial has recently been legalised in Victoria. An edifice of concrete and marble, it has been designed to last a thousand years, and they can hardly keep up with the demand. The project is worth tens of millions of dollars and is an enormous commercial success.

Everywhere you look, in everything Darebin City Council does, you can see this new idea of multicultural citizenship working, the idea that you don't have to be the same to be equal.

In fact, the lesson of the old version of citizenship — with its endemic failure to solve many of the problems it set out to address and with its 'welfare traps' — is that providing services which are exactly the same means people will never be equal.

CHAPTER 27

New Commonwealth

Leaving Italy, Franca Arena was drawn to the promise of the Australian way of life. In 1981, she was to become the first woman of a non-English-speaking background to sit in an Australian Parliament.

'I arrived on the 5th of May 1959, on my own, a single girl. I was in search of peace, in search of my destiny. After having had a very difficult childhood, I was looking for a new life, far away from my father, far away from what I had experienced in those days as the pettiness of Italian society.

'At first I felt myself an Italian in Australia. Later I felt an Australian of Italian background. It was a definite turning point in my life. By acquiring this Australian passport, by having two sons born in Australia, I became an Australian of Italian background.'

Franca was one of the founders of ethnic radio in Australia, beginning with 'The Italian Hour' on 2SM in 1961, and later public ethnic radio, initiated by Al Grassby and vastly extended into SBS television and radio by the Fraser Government.

'Don't forget, back in those early days we had to do everything in English as well as Italian, there was this distrust of us speaking our own language, as if we were sending subversive messages. Even advertisements to buy a washing machine.' She laughs at the thought.

'This was a time of enormous change, such as the setting-up of the Ethnic Communities Council.'

She was involved in that, too.

'Now we had our own structures. Whitlam, and Fraser, and the NSW Premier, Neville Wran — they all took an enormous interest.'

And she joined the Labor Party.

'Then one day I was at the Ethnic Communities Council and I got a phone message. "Oh, the Premier rang, he is looking for you."

'I said, "The Premier?"

'So I rang up the Premier's office and his secretary said, "Yes, the Premier's looking for you."

'I spoke to him and said, "Yes, Mr Wran." Because for years and years I could never call him Neville, you know. It was matter of respect, an Italian thing. And he said, "Look, there is a vacancy coming up in the Legislative Council and I want you to take it."'

Franca Arena began her Parliamentary career in 1981.

'I wanted to define my place, and slowly I saw that people were making some room for me, in a way that made me grateful to Australia, and I wanted to contribute. Contribution for me meant showing that I was worthy.

'I wanted to be bilingual, and I wanted to contribute, but as an Australian of Italian background. It was possible for me to have an input, not larger or smaller than other people, but a different input, and that's what was so wonderful about multiculturalism.

'But, you know, when I gave my maiden speech, I spoke strongly about multiculturalism, I spoke about the republic, I spoke about Aboriginal rights. And when I had finished my speech, Johnno Johnson, President of the Legislative Council and one of the powerbrokers in the Labor Party, came up to me and said, "You have done irreparable damage to your career."

'That's what he said. And now he goes around with this 'R for Republic' thing written all over him.'

We ask Franca about her involvement in the founding of the Australian Republican Movement.

'Mark McKenna's just written a history of republicanism in Australia. And you know, in it he says that the Australian Republican Movement was the brainchild of Franca Arena. I nearly cried when I read it. When I thought about it, yes, I did do a lot of the footwork. Then of course, once it got launched, you know, who would think it had been this ethnic woman?

'You see, I used to be a great talker, a guest speaker at Rotaries and Apex Clubs and all these kinds of places. And I also spoke a lot on ethnic radio, and at Ethnic Communities Council functions. Then I started coming out with republicanism, and they all closed the doors because they didn't want to hear it. I was really ostracised. But I felt so strongly about it.

'I mean, I'm from Genoa which has been a city-republic for seven hundred years. Historically, you know, Giuseppe Mazzini was a great republican. I grew up imbued with the idea of the republic, the government by the people. Then coming here — I mean, I came here to be an Australian, and I had to swear allegiance to the Queen of England. My God, it was the most difficult thing in my life.

'Back then, the only person who responded to what I was saying was Neville Wran. And so Neville and I got working. I said, "Look, what we need is one hundred people." You were one, Mary. One hundred people who can put up $100 so we can have a bit of money to register the thing. They had to be prominent people, because every time we raised our heads with the republic issue, people said, "You're just a bunch of ratbags."

'People say the ARM are elitists. It wasn't that we were being bloody elitists. It was just so we couldn't be dismissed by the media as ratbags. And I made sure that there was a Greek, and an Italian, and a Chinese, and Aboriginal people. Plus well-known Australians like Thomas Keneally, Peter Wilenski and Donald Horne.

'So I said, "I'll get a hundred people, Neville, and you get a President. You can't be the President," I said. "We are Labor people, and we don't want it to be a Labor-dominated thing." So we got Thomas Keneally to be the President.

'I'm still on the national committee, but now I take a back seat because I don't want them, in a way, to be tainted. You know the cause is too important for me to be there.'

Towards the end of her Parliamentary career, Franca took up the cause of paedophilia. She revealed high-level cover-ups among the police and the judiciary.

'I could see the rottenness that there was in the system. If you look at the statistics, only ten per cent of paedophilia cases go to court. One girl in four gets abused, and one boy in five. I mean, the figures are just staggering, just staggering.'

In the process, she ran foul of the Labor Party, and resigned. She stood as The Franca Arena Child Support Group at the 1999 New South Wales elections, and lost.

'Do you think you've paid a price for maintaining your values around multiculturalism?' we ask.

'You see, I never had a chance, I never had a chance because I'm not a groupie, I'm not a drinker. I was always out there in the community and wasn't well-connected with what was happening in the party rooms. They knew I had support, they knew I was gaining votes for them, but it was never appreciated. Despite it all, I kept on doing my work. I loved it.

'Yes, I've paid a price. For being myself. For being proud to be an Australian of Italian background. And I was happy to pay it, bugger them. I didn't come here to be somebody else. I am so proud to be an Australian, I love this country deeply. I owe it my allegiance, but my origins are Italian. I can never deny my roots.'

— • —

'Yes, that's right. *The Lucky Country* was the first public affirmation of the idea of Australia becoming a republic. You know, it sparked debates on television; the section on Australia becoming a republic was photocopied tens of thousands of times in schools.'

We're speaking with Donald Horne about his Australian classic, first published in 1964.

> There are many comforts in being provincial, but given Australia's peculiar relationship to the rest of Asia, these are comforts that Australians might not be able to continue to afford ... Australia is sometimes considered to be a half-sovereign state, a weird survival of the colonial age ... This is backwater colonialism, nervous of its final responsibilities ... Is Australia alone in the world in being unable to rig up its own head of state? [Does] Australia not run to the kind of person we could turn into a president? ... Australians are likely to feel increasingly foolish that their Head of State resides in London.[1]

For several decades, Donald Horne was the main public advocate of republicanism in Australia.

'Then Franca Arena had this idea of forming the Australian Republican Movement. I'd first met Franca in the seventies. It was her idea entirely. She went off and put together some people. She's undoubtedly the founder of the ARM.'

'And how does diversity fit into the republican vision?' we ask. 'These were Franca's themes, they were what brought her to republicanism. But in the rush for minimalist change, we seem to have forgotten the original impetus. As you said in *The Lucky Country*, the impetus for the republic comes from where we are in Asia, and from the increasingly obvious fact that we are not just an Anglo-Saxon society.'

'We've been talking about the republic a lot in the past few years,' Donald says, 'and there's been far too much yakka about the Head of State. If you're becoming a republic, what's most important are the principles. What's more important than the mechanics is that we have a Constitution about which we can speak in slightly idealistic civic terms.'

Australia is a country of ideological moderation, a country that shuns highly idealistic statements as often hypocritical, sometimes dangerous. It is a country of ordinary pragmatism.

'So what are the ordinary things about this country that we should be able to describe in a Constitution?' we ask.

'Well, it should proclaim the sovereign independence of Australia, a country in which all power is given to the people. It would talk about prior occupation by Indigenous people. Then it would describe the political system in Australia in a way that school children could relate to.

'You could also make a couple of declarations. There should be a declaration of tolerance, or something like that. I don't think in Australia we've ever thoroughly worked out what we mean by tolerance. It doesn't mean we have to love each other. That's ludicrous. Conflict and difference exist in society. Harmony is based on that recognition. Oppression occurs when the differences are not recognised.'

These, then, are some of the fundamentals Donald Horne says need to be spelt out so that we have a common understanding of our civic virtues and civic ideals.

'And where does "equality" fit in?' we ask. It brings Donald back to one of his key concepts, the vernacular Australian idea of 'the fair go.' We are also referring to the idea, peddled by the populist politicians, that equality means sameness.

'Yes, Pauline Hanson and some of the others are saying the Aborigines are not being treated equally. They're getting extra runs. I mean, when there's a bloody flood, you make a special case and give people relief. War veterans get special treatment. Well, the Aborigines are an absolutely special case in Australia. They were out here, occupying the place. That's what everyone has to recognise. They were in fact dispossessed. And that's not true of anybody else. So they require absolutely special approaches.'

Donald returns to the question of describing Australia, slightly idealistically, for what it is.

'What I'm saying is that we need to create a political definition of Australia, the great things that hold us together. It might be something like ... "A country in which the core beliefs are ...

liberal, democratic ..., accepting the rule of law and equality under the law irrespective of race, creed, background ... a tolerant society ... recognising the place of the Indigenous people and the custodianship of the land we now share ... "

'Now that's what being Australian is. And it mustn't be ethnic. There's no bloody ethnic Australian. The distinction here is between ethnicity and nationality.'

Here Donald Horne is describing a nation whose strength comes from its adherence to civic virtues rather than from having a population with a single ethnic background, a nation which stays cohesive for its democracy, and not because its citizens' historical and cultural experiences are identical, a nation without the ethnonationalisms of many nation-states which insist, in one way or another, that cultural homogeneity is essential in order to maintain national integrity.

— • —

The Australian Republican Movement was launched at The Rocks in Sydney on 7 July 1991. Thomas Keneally was the movement's first President, and standing beside him in the newspaper images of that day were Donald Horne and Franca Arena. Among the nine people posing for the photo was another person who was to become a key player in the ARM, merchant banker and lawyer Malcolm Turnbull.

When Paul Keating followed Bob Hawke as Labor Prime Minister at the end of that year, the focus for discussion about an Australian republic shifted to Canberra. Keating prided himself in having a 'big picture' view of Australia's future: engagement with Asia, reconciliation with Indigenous people, and the creation of an outward-looking multicultural society. And he was the first Prime Minister actively and persistently to promote the cause of an Australian republic.

Keating cast the issue of the republic in terms of his vision of a new Australian identity, as a multicultural rather than an essentially English society, as a society that wanted to project a new, independent image in Asia, and a society that had reconceived the colonial legacy in its relationship with Indigenous people. The response from his political enemies was swift. National Party backbencher Michael Cobb told the Federal Parliament that Keating's support for the republic was his 'bog-Irish coming out;' it was the result of a 'cultural imprint' and of 'certain prejudices' which produced an 'irrational and paranoid dislike of everything English.' Returned Services' League National President Alf Garland said, 'Mr Keating is what one would call an Irish republican bigot' with roots in 'the days when we had convicts here in Australia.'[2]

Keating was re-elected in March 1993, and within six weeks he announced the formation of the Republic Advisory Committee chaired by the Australian Republican Movement's Malcolm Turnbull. The Committee reported, suggesting alternative republican models, in October 1993. From these alternatives, the Keating Government was to select a 'preferred model.'

On 8 June 1995, Keating announced that the Government's preferred model was one that involved 'minimalist' constitutional change. The only change in becoming a republic would be to make the Governor-General the Head of State, and change the name of that position to 'President.' It was to be a 'relatively simple and modest undertaking,' Keating said. The change was based on one idea only, and that was that 'our Head of State should be one of us.'

> In proposing that our Head of State be an Australian, we are proposing nothing more than the obvious. It changes nothing more than what is required to make clear and unambiguous our independence and our responsibility for our own affairs. It is a small step, but a highly significant one. Each and every Australian should be able to aspire to be our Head of State. The creation of an Australian republic can actually deliver a heightened sense of unity, it can enliven our national spirit and, in our minds and those of our neighbours, answer beyond doubt the perennial question of Australian identity — the question of who we are and what we stand for.[3]

The then Opposition Leader, John Howard, responded by saying that, if elected, the Coalition would hold a Constitutional Convention, and that if a consensus emerged from this convention, that consensus would be put to the Australian people at a referendum. The Coalition won government in March 1996, and the Constitutional Convention was conducted over two weeks in February 1998. It consisted half of elected and half of appointed representatives. Although 89 delegates, or 59 per cent of the 152 present, supported the shift to a republic, only 73 delegates or 48 per cent of the convention voted in favour of what emerged as the predominant model — a slightly revised version of the

Keating/Australian Republican Movement minimalist model brokered by the leader of the ARM on the New South Wales ticket, Malcolm Turnbull. The convention also suggested what elements might be included in a rewritten preamble to the Constitution.

— • —

Two propositions were put to the Australian people in the referendum held on 6 November 1999. The first question was 'to alter the Constitution to establish the Commonwealth of Australia as a republic with the Queen and the Governor-General being replaced by a President appointed by a two-thirds majority of the members of the Commonwealth Parliament.' And the second was 'to alter the Constitution to insert a preamble.'

Funding to promote the 'Yes' case was given to a committee that essentially represented the Australian Republican Movement. Funding for the 'No' case was given to a bizarre alliance made up of Australians for a Constitutional Monarchy and a loose grouping styling itself as 'Real Republicans' which had emerged at the time of the Constitutional Convention and which was advocating direct election of the President. Commentators viewed the whole process as crafty politics on the part of monarchist Prime Minister John Howard, splitting the republic vote by attaching republicans who disagreed with the proposed model to the monarchist 'No' vote. Just a month before the referendum, a Newspoll opinion poll published in the *Australian* indicated that 50 per cent of voters preferred an elected president, 14 per cent wanted the referendum's proposed model in which the president was elected by Parliament, and 32 per cent wanted the monarchy to remain, with 4 per cent still uncommitted. However, of the fifty per cent who favoured an elected President, 65 per cent said they would vote 'Yes' to the model presented, and 29 per cent said they would vote 'No.'[4] A clear majority favoured a republic, and although most republicans favoured a directly elected president, the referendum would be decided on whether republicans who wanted more than a minimalist republic would vote 'Yes' in the hope that further change would be possible later, or vote 'No' in the hope of a later vote on the question they really wanted asked.

One effect of this situation was to ensure that the referendum vote would say nothing about either the overall level of republican sentiment in Australia or, if Australia were to become a republic, the model preferred by the Australian people.

Obscurantism was the monarchists' last hope, and with consummate politician Prime Minister Howard firmly at the helm, the monarchists were going to determine the way the republic issue was publicly discussed and decided.

However, one of the nice ironies of the obscurantism and crafty divide-and-rule politics was the increasing support for constitutional change that went well beyond Keating and Turnbull's original cautious minimalism. On the conservative side of politics, leading Liberal frontbencher Peter Reith came out in favour of an elected President — and advocated a 'No' vote. Meanwhile in the Labor Party, which was advocating a 'Yes' vote, Opposition Leader Kim Beazley admitted to Parliament that 'maybe if you scratched all members of my party, most of them would be direct-election republicans.'[5]

But another effect of the obscurantism was that the public debate in the months leading up to the referendum was, at best, convoluted. The republican case was presented as the blandest of Aussie nationalism: 'An Australian President will represent our uniquely Australian identity as we face the world into the future.' The republicans were also at pains to reassure people of the things that the constitutional changes would *not* do. They would not mean we would have to change the flag (as if, on becoming a republic, it would still be appropriate to keep the Union Jack in the corner of the Australian flag). Nor would the new Constitution mean any change in Australia's relationships with Britain. Most disingenuously, 'replacing the Queen with an Australian Head of State is a small ... step', involving 'only minor amendments to our Constitution.'[6] And gone were the relatively clear indications of why change was needed which had been clearly articulated when the idea of the minimalist republic was originally introduced. The republicans were at pains to avoid the impression that, in historical terms, becoming a republic was a truly significant step for Australia.

The 'No' case was even more convoluted than the 'Yes,' if not at times downright dishonest. It was an unholy mix of the arguments of diehard monarchists and 'real' republicans, and they increasingly blurred their entirely contradictory arguments into each other. Senior Government minister and monarchist stalwart Nick Minchin even said that a directly elected president would be preferable to the minimalist model[7] — something that smacked of political opportunism given his own staunchly conservative political principles.

There was not a single mention of the Queen in the 'No' case, which asserted that 'our constitutional head of state, the Governor-General, is an Australian citizen and has been since 1965.' 'All legal links with Britain were cut in 1986 with the passage of the Australia Act through both Australian and British Parliaments.'[8] These claims were hard to reconcile with the text of the Constitution itself, and inconsistent with the argument that it was the constitutional monarchy which should be preserved; if 'monarchy' means kings and queens, the throne is indisputably in London.

So, the choice at the referendum was between republicans who said there was to be very little change, and monarchists who said we were already a republic. It was a choice between no real change (the republicans), and a real change to being a republic that had supposedly already occurred (the monarchists).

Meanwhile, both sides engaged in populist puff about whether their model was likely to produce a President who was either more or less like a politician. 'A President, not a politician,' shouted the republicans:

All Australians will have the opportunity to nominate a fellow Australian for the office of President. These nominations will be considered by a special Nominations Committee made up of representatives from all Australian parliaments and all parts of our community. It will prepare a short list and then the Prime Minister and the Leader of the Opposition will agree on one nominee. That person will then need to be approved by a two-thirds majority of a joint sitting of both Houses of the Federal Parliament. This means that our Australian President will *not* be a politician.[9]

'Vote "No" to the politicians' republic,' the monarchist–Real Republican coalition shouted back:

The proposed republic gives more power to the politicians, at the expense of the people ... The people won't choose the President: the political deal-makers will. Only politicians will be allowed to pick the President. The Australian people will never get the chance to vote for the President. No say! No way! Vote 'NO' to this republic.[10]

— • —

Many of the things that really needed to be spoken of in the debate about the Australian Constitution in 1999 remained largely unspoken. Things unsaid fell into two large categories: symbolic and constitutional.

The symbolic silences were around the reasons why, beyond a bland 'one of us' nationalism, the time had come for Australia to become a republic. One deeply important reason was that the symbolism of the Crown left out Australians of English ancestry who identified less and less with that ancestry, and the fact that post-war immigration had created a society in which fewer people than ever were of English ancestry. The constitutional symbols had to change if they were to be more inclusive, if they were accurately to describe the origins and destinies of all of us. It was the difficulty of having to swear allegiance to the Queen, starkly contrasted with the fact that we were rapidly becoming a multicultural society, that spurred Franca Arena to found the Australian Republican Movement. By the time of the 1999 referendum discussions, this fundamental issue had been all but set aside. A second symbolic reason was our place in Asia. Along with New Zealand, we were the last colonial society in Asia in symbolic-constitutional terms, and this in a region where most countries prided themselves in having spent a good part of the twentieth century shaking off colonialism. And the third reason was the pressing need to redefine the relationship of two centuries of immigrant settlement to the pre-existing Indigenous settlement, and to redefine the relationship in terms that were unequivocally post-colonial. Yet these symbolic arguments had slipped out of the main drift of public discussion.

These were also the symbolic reasons why, despite the protestations of the republicans, the flag would inevitably have to change with the coming of an Australian republic.

The only reference to some of these issues was in the discussion of the second referendum proposition, about the draft preamble. Most republicans chose to ignore the preamble, and regarded it as yet another divide-and-rule diversion created by Prime Minister Howard, who advocated a 'Yes' vote for this question even though he was advocating a 'No' vote for the republic question. Having worked on an initial draft with poet Les Murray which included reference to the blokey Australian quality of 'mateship' and which ended by chiding the perpetrators of political correctness, the Australian Democrats forced a compromise upon Howard. Their leverage was the grip they had on the balance of power in the Senate. So the preamble presented to the people was penned by a couple of politicians, without public consultation. This is why it read like all the Howard compromises; like the ten-point plan on Native Title that had been reduced to seven and a bit points after the Harradine amendments, and the Goods and Services Tax that included cooked but not raw chicken after another compromise with the Democrats:

> With hope in God, the Commonwealth of Australia is constituted as a democracy with a federal system of government to serve the common good.
> We the Australian people commit ourselves to this Constitution:
>> proud that our national unity has been forged by Australians from many ancestries;
>> never forgetting the sacrifices of all who defended our country and our liberty in time of war;
>> upholding freedom, tolerance, individual dignity and the rule of law;
>> honouring Aborigines and Torres Strait Islanders, the nation's first people, for their deep kinship with their lands and for their ancient and continuing cultures which enrich the life of the country;
>> recognising the nation-building contribution of generations of immigrants;
>> mindful of our responsibility to protect our unique natural environment;
>> supportive of achievement as well as equality of opportunity for all;
>> and valuing independence as dearly as the national spirit which binds us together in both adversity and success.

Should anybody be in any doubt as to the intent of the preamble, a new Section, 125A, was to be inserted into the Constitution proper:

> The preamble to this Constitution has no legal force and shall not be considered in interpreting this Constitution or the law in force in the Commonwealth or any part of the Commonwealth.

As a symbolic statement, the preamble had serious limitations from a number of perspectives.

'With hope in God'... it began, with 'God' capitalised. This was to contradict the spirit of one of the very few sections of the Constitution of 1901 which guaranteed rights, Section 116: 'The Commonwealth shall not make any law for establishing any religion, or for imposing any religious observance, or for prohibiting the free exercise of any religion, and no religious test shall be required as a qualification for any office or public trust under the Commonwealth.' The preamble opened by ignoring the spirit of this section, as well as one of the foundational principles of modern democratic societies: that church and state, religion and politics, citizenship and personal faith, are strictly separate. Given that Howard was wanting a 'No'/'Yes' result, it was also worth pondering whether the God he was referring to was that of the Head of State of the 'No' choice (who is simultaneously and by birthright head of the Church of England, the Established Church of the constitutional monarchy), or the Christian God, or some generalised pan-religious (but nevertheless monotheistic, singular) God which a few idealistic theists have struggled in vain to promote for centuries. With any of these alternatives, the preamble's foundational hope included some kinds of believers but not others, and in any interpretation left out believers in Man or Mammon, to stick with just two of religion's stated alternatives to God.

Nor did the preamble start with any words which could define Australia as a republic, should a 'Yes'/'Yes' result eventuate. These are usually relatively straightforward, along such lines as 'government of the people, by the people, for the people.' In fact, the new preamble would sit alongside the old constitutional preamble and its anachronistic setting in the Westminster Parliament of Queen Victoria.

It also mentioned diversity of ancestries, but only as part of a plug for unity. 'Proud that our national unity' — that old fashioned one-nation idea again — 'has been forged from many ancestries.' Our virtue is to have taken so many ancestries and, from them, created unity. It's not that we want to celebrate the richness and the enduring importance of our diverse origins (the multicultural idea); it's the fact that we've created a unity from them which we will celebrate (the 'melting pot' or assimilationist idea which was at its height in the fifties). Put alongside the mention of 'tolerance' (a way of congratulating ourselves for having been so accommodating towards people who are 'different'), and the idea that migrants have made a 'nation-building contribution' (that they can be thanked insofar as they have helped 'us' in the mainstream story of Australian progress), the references to immigration and Australia's cultural diversity were all vintage John Howard, and vintage Australia circa 1955.

Then there was the reference to an Indigenous presence. The word 'Aborigines' is rarely used these days. And the idea that 'their ancient and continuing cultures ... enrich the life of the country' is somewhat patronising when we all know that the relationship of Indigenes and settlers is a difficult and unfinished business. The most contentious issue in the proposed preamble, however, was the word 'kinship'. This was the word used to describe Indigenous relationships to the land in Australia. If it was original occupation that 'kinship' was supposed to refer to, the word is 'sovereignty'. And if it was Native Title it was talking about, the word is 'ownership'. 'Kinship' was the compromise brokered by Australian Democrats Senator Aden Ridgeway. It is a word that only has the most indirect of metaphorical meanings. It's even weaker than 'custodianship,' which is defined as 'the physical holding of, control over, a thing without a right of claim to ... possession.'[11] This was an alternative proposed by some Indigenous leaders — but even this Howard rejected as implying too much.

– • –

The drift of the discussion in the lead up to the 1999 constitutional referendum also studiously avoided significant constitutional issues. The monarchist case had nothing to say other than it was a great Constitution just the way it was — and what else could they say? But the republican positions were disappointing for what could have been said, but wasn't. To move from a constitutional monarchy to a republic is a huge change, the biggest constitutional change in a century. The mainstream republicans, however, were trying to pretend that the change would be minimal, and that minimal was enough. And from the 'real' republicans we heard little more than the beating of the populist anti-politician drum.

Former Prime Minister Keating, originator of the idea of the minimal republic, described 'this surreal debate' to a Labor Party gathering in Sydney a month before the referendum: 'this strange debate headed by a Prime Minister who believes in the monarchy. The monarchists don't even mention the Queen. The love that dare not speak its name.'[12]

But equally, the new draft Constitution presented at the referendum was for a republic that dare not speak its name. In the name of minimalism, the Australian people were being presented with a strange cut-and-paste hybrid of a monarchical constitution — and certainly not a modern constitution for a modern republic. As such, it had five major flaws.

First, there was no mention that Australia was a republic in the whole of the proposed Constitution, let alone a definition of what it meant to be a republic. The old monarchical Constitution spoke of the sovereignty that was vested in the Crown; yet the republican redraft failed to mention that, by definition, sovereignty was now to be vested in the people. The new document also introduced critical concepts that didn't previously exist, such as the idea that there is a 'Prime Minister' and a 'Leader of the Opposition.' These were dropped into the new sections about the processes for the selection of the President, and were included without a definition of what these positions entailed. As well as saying that 'the executive power of the Commonwealth is vested in the President' (and leaving these powers unstated), it might have been useful to indicate that the Prime Minister is the head of government and has to enjoy the confidence of a majority of the members of the House of Representatives. And, if the idea of a 'Prime Minister' was being introduced, it might also have been useful to mention the Cabinet, its relationship to Parliament and its functions, rather than the 'Federal Executive Council,' which for all its constitutional power on paper, never meets as such, and which, in the style of the kings and queens of old who would summon the lords and knights and bishops to the round table at their pleasure, in the words of the new Section 59, 'shall be chosen and summoned by the President ... and shall hold office during the pleasure of the President.'

Second, the draft republican Constitution stood replete with obsolete clauses, some of which were worse than rubbish. Section 25 suffices as one example. It follows Section 24, which states that 'the House of Representatives shall be composed of members directly chosen by the people of the Commonwealth' and that 'the number of members chosen in the several States shall be in proportion to the respective numbers of their people.'

25. Provisions as to races disqualified from voting

For the purposes of the last section, if by the law of any State all persons of any race are disqualified from voting at elections for the more numerous House of the Parliament of the State, then, in reckoning the number of the people of the State or of the Commonwealth, persons of that race resident in that State shall not be counted.

As it happened, Aboriginal people could for the moment vote at elections for the more numerous house of the Parliament of every Australian State, as could citizens and permanent residents of any other race. So the Commonwealth did not have to do the race reckoning which this section would otherwise require. Nevertheless, a clause like this had no place in the constitution of a modern nation.

Third, although we prided ourselves in living in a modern, democratic society, there was nothing in the Constitution — the minimalist republican draft no less than the monarchical one that was in place — which even described the key features of that democracy, let alone assured us that these features were inviolable. One would expect a modern constitution to do both of these things, and in fact most constitutions currently in force in the world, do. There was no definition of the franchise (the secret ballot and the like), nor any guarantees that suffrage would be universal, nor assurances that votes would be of equal value; in fact, Section 25 clearly continued to indicate that the suffrage did not have to be universal, and could even be discriminatory. There were no guarantees of the free speech that is essential to the functioning of a democracy. There was no guarantee of the rule of law, and the separation of the judicial from the legislative and executive arms of government. And there were no guarantees of citizens' rights, even though the monarchical idea of 'subject' was struck from the draft Constitution and the term 'citizen' introduced for the first time. The new Section 127 defined a citizen as 'a person who is an Australian citizen according to the laws made by the Commonwealth' — allowing 'citizen' to be defined elsewhere in any way at all, but not by the Constitution itself.

If the monarchical Constitution did not answer the question of who we are and what binds us in a civic sense, the minimalist republican draft Constitution contributed nothing more to an understanding of what Australian democracy is, let alone an Australian republic. The new Constitution was little better than the old. Neither provided rigorous legal protection for any time of crisis that might arise in the future. And neither provided idealistic statements of the kind that are needed for a robust civic education and public understanding of civics. These are among the most basic purposes of any constitution.

Fourth, the minimalist republican draft failed to define the vast constitutional powers of the President, who would simply assume the powers formerly held by the monarch and the monarch's representative in Australia, the Governor-General. The President was to remain Commander-in-Chief of the armed forces, could refuse assent to legislation, and could 'summon' members to join the Executive Council, who held office at the President's 'pleasure.' And, as occurred at the time of the constitutional crisis of 1975, the President could dismiss a Prime Minister and an elected government. In practical terms, an Australian President would be able to exert these powers at a time of crisis with greater moral legitimacy than the royal House of Windsor in London, a house which now treads the fine line dividing feudal absolutism of the fairytale variety from the soap opera of postmodern media in which the dysfunctional Windsor family now stars. If the 'reserve' powers are not defined, a Head of State lacking legitimacy is much safer than a Head of State — 'one of us' — in whom we are all supposed to have faith.

On the other hand, the minimalist republican Constitution presented perhaps the strangest relationship of a Head of Government to a Head of State in the world. If a Prime Minister wanted to keep a President beyond the prescribed five-year term, or if the Prime Minister could not win the support of the Leader of the Opposition and a two-thirds majority of both Houses of Parliament to support the appointment of a new President, there was nothing in the Constitution to prevent the old President staying on indefinitely. Conversely, a Prime Minister could get rid of the President immediately, without consultation, without due process, without needing to heed even the most elementary principles of natural justice. 'The Prime Minister may, by instrument signed by the Prime Minister, remove the President with effect immediately,' said the proposed new Section 59 ominously. The Prime Minister wouldn't have to have any legitimate reasons for removal — such as a criminal conviction or breaking the Constitution — and would not need to give any reasons. The position of President would then fall to the most senior of the State Governors, and again, should there be an impasse in which it was impossible to win the agreement of the Leader of the Opposition or to find a two-thirds majority to agree on a new President, or should it suit the Prime Minister to leave that State Governor as Acting President, then that Governor could remain as Acting President indefinitely.

Fifth, the minimalist republican Constitution effectively divided one Head of State, one Crown, into seven. In the monarchical Constitution, the Governor-General of the Commonwealth and the Governors of the six States all represented the Queen. The Governor of each State was to be the Head of State for that State, and not somebody responsible to the new Australian Head of State, the President. This represented a strange return to a situation akin to the pre-Federation arrangements, in which each State was in a constitutional sense almost a nation-to-itself. This was all the more worrisome given the weakness of the State Constitutions, which are so feeble that they can even be amended accidentally by subsequent legislation. The States are only democratic insofar as it suits the legislators of the moment to be democratic, and not because there are constitutional guarantees of any description. And the States need only allow the third tier of Australian government, local government, to be democratic insofar as it suits them.

In both the monarchical and minimalist republican alternatives put to the people of Australia on 6 November 1999, Australia was to remain, from a constitutional point of view, an accidental democracy, and perhaps, an accidental republic. Our civic virtues can be attributed to nothing more than the hitherto relatively good behaviour of our rulers, and good luck. Because at the time of the 1999 referendum we had still not been allowed to discuss what a democratic constitution would look like, let alone a republican one, no matter what the result we were going to have to continue to rely on our rulers' behaviour as well as our luck. And our civic vices, such as they are or might be in the future, were to remain constitutionally unchecked.

— • —

On 6 November 1999, a majority of Australian electors, and a majority of the electors in a majority of States, to quote the formula for change in the Australian Constitution, voted 'No' to the proposition that Australia should become a republic and 'No' to the draft preamble. The national conversation about the shape of a republican Commonwealth of Australia could then begin.

'No' and 'No' were the answers when there were only oversimplified alternatives on the table, alternatives which systematically underestimated the intelligence and overestimated the gullibility of the Australian people. Do you vote for the republic you create when we're really not changing anything at all (the minimalist republican 'Yes' position)? Or for the monarchy you have because you're already a republic (the monarchist 'No' position)? Or do you just let out a scream of anti-politician populism (the 'real-republican' 'No' vote)?

With the referendum behind us, it was now time for Australians to start to consider what it would really mean to be a republic, and this had to go well beyond the low-level nationalism of having a President who was merely 'one of us.'

And how might we conduct this discussion about the shape of a new Commonwealth? The best starting point would be to design a constitution that simply describes what binds Australia in a civic sense, the things about which ninety per cent of Australians could not disagree. In the lead up to the referendum, even the monarchists had to concede that Elizabeth II, and her heirs and successors, had been for some time been becoming less and less relevant to Australia in a real constitutional sense.

The starting point for this discussion might be to ask how would we fairly describe our democracy, the things about which almost nobody could disagree? Then, let's agree to write those things down in our Constitution; an unexceptionable proposition, conservative even. Any such discussion would take longer and require more mature consideration than a two-week convention followed by a $15 million media campaign which looked more like a series of go-the-Aussies beer advertisements than the result of a mature national conversation about the ties of democracy that bind us.

It will take a lot of very public mulling over. It might take a long time. But the assumption would have to be that, eventually, most people would have to be able to agree on the things that are obvious — the obvious things about the Australian people, Australian history and Australian democracy.

This is no more and no less than an utterly conservative proposition: to describe accurately who we are and what makes us civil. It the basis for another, more robust but more honest, kind of minimalism.

EPILOGUE

The New Australian Way of Life

After considerable debate, the men who created the Australian Federation which was to commence on the first day of the twentieth century decided to call this place a 'Commonwealth.' It was a contentious decision, smacking of republicanism (Cromwell's Commonwealth, England's only time without a monarchy), and American people's democracy (Revere's Commonwealth of Massachusetts, Jefferson's Commonwealth of Virginia), and socialism (Edward Bellamy's images of a worker's paradise). Queen Victoria didn't like the word, but by the time the drafters of the Constitution of the Commonwealth of Australia found out, it was too late. The word was already in the Constitution and the Australian people had voted for it.

In the words of Alfred Deakin, they were creating a state 'for the common good of its people, for their common-weal'[1] and, in some ways, the new Commonwealth was as good as its word. When in 1902 Australia granted women the right to vote in national elections, New Zealand was the only nation that had gone before. Australia was the first country to introduce old-age and invalid pensions (in 1910) and maternity allowances (in 1912). Australia created an Arbitration Court to settle industrial disputes, which introduced the notion of a living wage in the Harvester judgement of 1907. The Commonwealth of Australia became a kind of laboratory of fairness.

Although, of course, Aborigines were excluded even more thoroughly than before; the South Sea Islanders were ordered home; and Chinamen would never, and it seemed then could never, be allowed to be Australians. In some respects, these other fundamentals in the Federation settlement detract from the achievement, but so does slavery detract from the achievement that was classical Athens, and so it does from the achievement that was the late eighteenth-century American republic.

At the end of the century we can take the idea of a laboratory of fairness and look at its implications in a world that was unimaginable in 1901. Despite moments in which some of those among us anxiously cast their eyes back over their shoulders, and despite our inability as yet to match the robustness of our experience with the symbols and constitutional framework of our nationhood, the Australian experiment in fairness is still alive, in the spirit if not to the letter of what had been intended in 1901.

In one measure of the Australian achievement, we continue to build upon Federation's principles — encapsulated in the idea of the Commonwealth. Even though we do not have a constitution which reflects our progress, by century's end we have in reality embarked on the project of making a new Commonwealth that extended the Commonwealth's original principles.

Now we can go back and retell our history and reinterpret our symbols of nation.

— • —

The Darveniza brothers came to Australia from Dubrovnik, Croatia, and established the Excelsior Vineyards in Victoria's Goulburn Valley. The year was 1871. When the brothers created a trademark for their wine, it was a wine barrel with a kangaroo and emu on either side. The design was a stroke of genius, an insight into the beauty of these strange antipodean creatures. This is something Croatians could see, at a time when the sycophants of Empire could only imagine coats of arms with lions and unicorns.

By the time the Commonwealth decided to adopt the kangaroo and the emu in the Australian Coat of Arms, everybody had forgotten where they had first seen the image. But not Troyano Darveniza. He had a piece of paper which said the right to use the kangaroo and emu insignia had been granted to the Darveniza brothers by 'Her Britannic Majesty Victoria, Queen of the United Kingdom, its Dominions and Colonies, Empress of India.' The Commonwealth offered to buy the trademark but he refused. The government offered to pay a royalty but he refused again. He said instead that the Commonwealth could use it freely, and for his gift he has been forgotten.[2]

Australia is the country of meat pies (invented by a Lebanese immigrant in the nineteenth century), Holden cars (where the American idea of the automobile meets the Australian landscape), and the exclamation 'fair dinkum' (derived from the Cantonese word for 'gold,' a residue of the Chinese contribution to the gold rushes). It is a country whose imagery of place is refracted more and more through Indigenous symbolism — by far our most outstanding contribution to world art.

In the life of communities, here are just a few of the things that people are doing as their contribution to the Federal Government's 'Living in Harmony' program. Lest in the everyday world of Australian people and Australian places, we forget who we are and what we have achieved.

- **Kempsey High School:** Reconciliation Camps Project
- **'A Tale of Two Peoples':** The Australian Arabic Council Project on Arabic and Aboriginal Youth
- **Australian Industry Group:** 'Winning with Cultural Diversity' — Three Steps to a Better Workplace
- **Federation of Chinese Associations:** East and West in Harmony
- **Brisbane Indigenous Media Association:** 'Waanya — It's Time to Talk'
- **Commemorative Cultural Exchange Program — Vietnam, Returned Services' League:** Veterans' Initiative for Living in Harmony
- **Blue Mountains Community Cultural Diversity Project:** Exploring and Creating Harmony
- **Muslim Women's National Network of Australia:** Living In Harmony with Islam and the Law
- **Darebin Community Health Service:** Young People And Cultural Diversity Theatre Project
- **Dreams, Schemes and Ideas, Queensland Police Force:** Police And Harmony
- **Kooemba Jdarra Indigenous Performing Arts:** Many Colours — One Land — Reconciliation Workshops
- **Rockville School Parents and Citizens Association:** Peace Builders

And hundreds of others, all around the country. Under the overall slogan:

You. Me. aUStralian.

— • —

In 1997, the Victorian Multiculturalism Commission ran a campaign for students in Years 10 and 11 at school. They were asked to send in one of two postcards, completing either of the statements 'Being Australian means ...', or 'If I could make a difference I'd ...'. They were encouraged to say exactly what they felt, to speak from the heart.

Nearly six thousand students mailed their postcard responses to the Commission, or six per cent of 15–17 year olds in Victoria. The students represented the whole of Victoria: regional Victoria as well as Melbourne; State, Catholic and Independent schools; students of recent immigrant origin and longer-established Australians.

The results were a foretaste of Australia's future. They also expressed the hopes of a generation whose life experiences had been different from any other in our history. This was the voice of the first generation of Australians to have lived with large-scale Asian immigration for their whole lives. This was the first generation of Australians to have lived with the difficult public debate about Indigenous rights for their whole lives. This was the first generation of Australians to have lived through the vicissitudes of globalisation for their whole lives.

And the results were all the more remarkable for their timing. The campaign was run just as Pauline Hanson's One Nation was rising.

We were asked to look at the six thousand responses, and to analyse what they were saying.[3]

Perhaps the most interesting responses were the negative ones. Even though the postcard activity was open-ended and encouraged an honest response, only 0.27 per cent of responses, or a quarter of one per cent, could be classified as racist, or even mildly intolerant.

Most students (90.0 per cent) responded to Australia's diversity in terms of universal human values: primarily, democratic political values such as freedom and equality; everyday interpersonal values such as openness, acceptance, respect and generosity; and the importance of a sense of belonging, and the personal friendships that come with it.

Almost half the students (45.3 per cent) used specific value concepts referring to the inter-relation of differences. Most important among these was tolerance. But, they were definitely not using the word in the way what they define as the 'older generation' means by the word, with the connotation that it is 'our' virtue to be putting up with 'them.' Rather, for these young people, tolerance is an overarching value, linked closely to respect, acceptance, sharing and the diversity among us all. It is an inclusive concept, rather than an 'us' and 'them' concept which mainly serves to congratulate 'us.'

They also freely used the concept of 'multiculturalism.' For older generations, multiculturalism often seems to be one of those policy ideas invented by governments. But for these young people, multiculturalism is a word that describes something fundamental in their lived reality. It refers to their everyday social being. And it describes everybody's differences, not just the migrants. In a very practical day-to-day way, multiculturalism is a central characteristic of the Australian 'mainstream' of these young people's experience:

> Being Australian means being who you really are inside. Having all the independence each individual needs, whether you're black, white, yellow … Australia is a multicultural country where people accept each other and everyone has their own freedom.

The responses tell us about a new generation, and a new Australia in which we can all live comfortably with our cultural differences. This is the new mainstream that truly includes 'all of us.'

> If I could make a difference I'd put a stop to racial discrimination. The world is filled with different colours and shades, but underneath the frail cloak of colour is a person, a person like you and me, someone who feels and loves and cares.

These were just two of the six thousand responses, two responses that capture the spirit of 99 per cent of the rest. Two voices from the new Commonwealth of Australia.

— • —

How do we account for this new reality, this new Commonwealth of Australia? When the symbols of our nation do not yet match the reality, how do we describe and explain that reality?

As a nation, we are the inheritors of five accidental virtues; five profound aspects of our history and identity. The first is that we are irreducibly an immigrant society. Australia's immigration program has been larger than any other in the world in the past half-century, bar the peculiar case of Israel. No society is more diverse, ethnically, linguistically, religiously. The genius of this place is how well it hangs together. The key has been the always innovative and creatively dynamic government policies that have managed to hold it together: first assimilation, then integration and, in the past two decades, the evolving principle of multiculturalism. A diverse, immigrant society: this is our inheritance; this is our history; this is our identity; this is the Australian mainstream.

The second accidental virtue is our belated recognition of the rights of Indigenous Australians. It may be a matter of shame that this has been so long coming. But in this particular moment there is a new opportunity, and that is the opportunity of democratic pluralism. On the one hand, this means the possibility of genuine cultural democracy, a possibility that is imminent in Indigenous regional self-government, for instance, and an open legal system that is at last able to work in tandem with traditional law such as Native Title. On the other hand, this is a moment when settler Australians are increasingly able to recognise Indigenous symbolism in their own national identity. When a new Australian flag includes some element of Aboriginal symbolism, we will have powerfully brought Indigenous people into the mainstream, not by the refusal-to-see that was assimilation, but by recognition and inclusion.

Our third accidental virtue is that our national life is built upon the foundations of an export-oriented economy in which the growth industries are now highly culture-sensitive: tourism, education and human services. This, as well as the myriad niches in our local market, is the reason why our enterprises must be built on the business principles of multiculturalism, best encapsulated in the idea of 'productive diversity.' In this endeavour, the multiculturalism of our civic life is a resource of immeasurable value. If large corporations are increasingly setting up their regional headquarters in Australia, for instance, it is because the Australian community is a cultural and linguistic microcosm of the new global economy, and because Australian community values are deeply rooted in the generosity and flexibility with which we have learnt to negotiate our differences, in our schools and in our neighbourhoods.

Australia's fourth accidental virtue, paradoxically, is our weak sense of national identity. We were not established by glorious revolution. The battles that have most defined our character are tinged by the irony of loss. In a world where chauvinistic, atavistic, anachronistic nationalisms produce daily-reported obscenities, our lack of nationalism is our strength. It is a strength that makes us open enough to take on the totally different strong identity all nations will need for the near future: that of outward-looking, globally engaged, locally pluralist, cultural democracy. These will of necessity become the non-negotiable core values of the democratic nations of the next century. The time has come for us to describe these values, and inscribe them in our Constitution; modestly, without ideological pretence, but nevertheless 'slightly idealistically', to use Donald Horne's expression.

Our fifth virtue is somewhat less accidental than the previous four. It is the tradition of engaged government: of distributive justice, of great national projects such as the peopling of Australia through mass immigration, and of cultural leadership such as that exhibited by all Australian governments of the past fifty years as they first created assimilation, then integration, then multiculturalism — and always ahead of public opinion. Australian governments have always led, in their characteristic, very low-key, informal, reasonable sort of way. We have thrived on an engaged, carefully interventionary state.

— • —

'What I'm saying ...' — to repeat Donald Horne's point which we reported in the last chapter of this book — 'is that we need to create a political definition of Australia, the great things that hold us together. It might be something like ... "A country in which the core beliefs are ... liberal, democratic ..., accepting the rule of law and equality under the law irrespective of race, creed, background ... a tolerant society ... recognising the place of the Indigenous people and the custodianship of the land we now share..." Now that's what being Australian is. And it mustn't be ethnic. There's no bloody ethnic Australian. The distinction here is between ethnicity and nationality.'

This is quite a fundamental point, ordinary in its truth to Australian civil society at the end of the century, and slightly idealistic. But, deep down, it's a point of profound importance.

Without knowing it at the time, we have been creating in Australia a new kind of nation, a multicultural nation, a nation of the world. We're talking about the third quarter of the century particularly: since the beginning of the Asian immigration which has brought more than a million people here; since the introduction of the theory and practice of multiculturalism; since the reconceptualisation of Indigenous land rights; since the development of the idea of Reconciliation as a way of thinking about our colonial past; and since we have embraced globalisation, especially in culture-contact-intensive industries.

We have been making a nation that is, in its foundational principles, deeply antithetical to the classical idea of the nation state. The modern nation state, the nation state of the recent past, was one in which citizens — by a rhetorical leap of faith — were bound together because their life histories and experiences and interests were supposed to be identical. They were bound together because they were of one ethnos; because they were kith and kin. When they were not identical, there were various ways to make them identical: by expulsion, or by assimilation. 'One Nation, One State, One Leader.' This was the slogan of the highest and most rigorous form of nationalism in the twentieth century, Nazi Germany. And the 'one-nation' people are still wreaking havoc wherever they raise their heads in the world today.

Then suddenly, at the end of the century of horrors, this little country at the end of the earth seems to have found another way to be civil. We have created a nation without nationalism, a community without ethnos. We have built a civic home for all of us, and when it works, it works because we thrive on diversity. It works because it has become our nature to shun the closed culture of conformity. It works because our dispositions as citizens are built upon the civic virtues of tolerance, dialogue, interchange, sharing, borrowing, creativity, synergy.

New ways of living together. New forms of civic association. If we were to stop to think about it, this is an achievement of world-historic proportions, a lesson of global significance for a new century of open borders and cosmopolitan locality. It's why, as Donald Horne says, we should put down words to describe who we are, so we can have a way to reassure ourselves, and tell our children.

Behind all of this is an emerging achievement of possibly world-historic importance. Since the end of the Cold War particularly, the modern ideology of nationalism has become increasingly virulent as a force, and one that daily fills our news with mayhem and murder.

Until recently, the modern nation state answered questions of identity or belonging in relatively simple terms: it consisted of those who are born into the more or less singular kith and kin of the nation, plus, in milder variations of this theme, those outsiders willing and able to assimilate and become culturally the same as those kith and kin. Nations and nationalisms in the modern era have attempted to create imagined communities in which pre-existing cultural differences have been erased.

Since the end of the Cold War, the logistics of belonging have begun visibly to take a new turn. This is the byproduct of an emerging politics of cultural difference in which exclusionist or assimilationist policies have become far less workable. And it is the result of the paradoxical alliance of two forces: globalisation, and the rise of a politics of subcultural and identity differentiation in local communities.

The twentieth century's main political argument was between capitalism and communism, with forms of 'social democracy' and the 'welfare state' representing intermediate, compromise positions. For the preceding century, the political debate about the distribution of resources had been couched in terms of universal economic classes and the redistributive role of the state. The result was the creation of planned economies on the communist side of the argument and the growth of the welfare state on the capitalist side.

By the end of that century, the West had won the Cold War. This great political argument was suddenly 'resolved.' And with the end of the Cold War, the space taken up by this political discourse was precipitously vacated.

Since then, a whole new political framework and language has been emerging, although its precise shape is not yet clear. The American commentator Francis Fukuyama calls our new times 'the end of history,' a time in which there is no fundamental argument against liberal capitalism as a political and economic system.[4] Certainly, there are no economic-system alternatives visibly threatening capitalism, but its fundamental systems dynamism — its tensions and pressure points — have just as clearly not gone away. There is still argument about how resources are distributed, and increasingly this is being articulated through the politics of identity, and the politics of nationally, ethnically or subculturally defined groups.

The triumph of liberal capitalism changes the ways in which the politics of belonging are articulated. All around the world, the contest for social resources is increasingly being expressed through a politics of culture and identity. Many of the combatants represent positions which are fundamentally incompatible with Western liberalism. In some places, the state has all but disappeared, to be replaced by ethnonationalist brigandry. In others, anti-liberal and fundamentalist movements have taken over from states that have virtually vanished. And, in the more stable liberal democracies of the West, we also witness the shrinking of the state and the growth in importance of what has been termed 'identity politics' or group interests. Meanwhile, the question of culture, once the obsessive interest of nation states, is being abandoned to 'market forces,' and, in this context of uncertainty and change, the genie of racism has been let out of the bottle.

As a consequence, nations and nationalisms in their characteristic modern form are fast becoming anachronistic. The forces of change challenge the modern nation-state to its roots: the bases of its sovereignty, its legitimacy and its citizens' loyalty. For the most practical of economic and social reasons, the question of how people belong now has to be answered in a very different way to the neatly homogenising 'one nation' response of the classical nation state.

These are the difficult questions. We in Australia have been struggling to answer them, sometimes falteringly in recent years, but sometimes with ingenuity and flair.

— • —

So what are the lessons? How, as Australians, do we now live? And what is the promise of the Australian Way of Life, the promise of our recent pasts and near futures?

Australia is a country which is struggling to come to grips with its colonial history. And because we are doing this late, we could possibly come up with practical solutions which are more forward-looking and more lasting than most others in the world so far. The High Court's Mabo and Wik decisions were, in retrospect, incredibly late in coming, but they represent a form of legal pluralism: the idea, in this case, that there can be fundamentally different ways of establishing title to land, even the same land. Such a pluralism represents a model for the way in which so many of the conflicting claims over country can be resolved, all around the world.

Australia is also now, incontrovertibly, a country in and of Asia. It's where we do most of our business. More than a million Asians and their children became Australians in the last quarter of the twentieth century. And we are comfortably Asian for being just as different — and in this sense just as similar — as other countries in a region of remarkable differences.

We are a country that is outward-looking, cosmopolitan in our ethos; people of this land and people of the world. We do our business on a world scale. We revel in our productive diversity.

We are a country whose people are of more diverse Indigenous and immigrant origins than any other on earth. We are multicultural in reality and multicultural in spirit: a nation in which the ties that bind simply have to be civic rather than ethnic.

We are a nation without nationalism, a community without a single, overarching ethnos, and this, in a world torn apart by arguments over spaces and identities, is our strength.

These are our virtues. Some are mere accidents of time and place and population. Some are the product of social ingenuity and political design.

However, onto the paradoxes which produced who we are, new paradoxes are now piled.

None of the discussions about the new Australia are happening on the Left–Right political spectrum. The multicultural Australian, the Australian reconciled to our colonial past, is just as easily to be found on the Left or the Right of politics, just as easily among the followers of the Labor Party as the supporters of the Coalition. And just as easily, the enemies of pluralism still try to take their place on both sides of politics.

It is also a time when the new Australian Way of Life is being created through alliances that would have seemed strange indeed until very recently: the business establishment and the ethnic lobby groups who find themselves agreeing on the issue of immigration; the mining companies and the pastoralists who have succeeded in coming to an accommodation with Indigenous people where governments have failed; the anti-racist groups and the large companies who welcome the Asian immigrant presence in Australia and multiculturalism generally.

Most of all, the hope is in the generational shift represented in the people of this book, and the Australians who are struggling to understand our past and realise our destiny.

— • —

Writing this book has been a kind of a journey, a journey into the Australian Way of Life at the turn of this country's first century as a nation.

On that journey, we discovered paradoxes at every turn. A country that is so new, just a century as a nation in the modern sense, yet a country with the oldest living civilization on earth and the most stable and long-lived democracy in the world. A country which at times seems to be tearing itself apart over immigration and the Indigenous presence, yet which shows enormous promise in resolving what, in a practical sense, are the fundamental dilemmas of the new century: the close proximity of differences as a consequence of globalisation, cosmopolitan locality, and identity politics. A country which has the moral fibre needed to invent new, multicultural conceptions of citizenship and ways to reconcile ourselves to a colonial past, but a country which can't yet quite find the words to express these in a confident, public or perhaps even Constitutional way.

Most of all it has been a journey into what our country feels like, the disposition and the sensibility of Australians at the Centenary of Federation.

ENDNOTES

PROLOGUE: *Australian Days at the Turn of a Century*

1 The authors wish to express their gratitude to Maria Katsabanis and Linda Singh who transcribed the tapes of these conversations, as well as Lorraine Murphy and also Maria Katsabanis who provided invaluable research and editorial assistance. We also wish to thank Robin Freeman for the original inspiration she gave to this project; editor, Patrick Carew; as well as Cathy Jenkins and Susannah Burgess at HarperCollins. And for their editorial advice and friendship, we thank George Pappaellinas and Maria Walsh.

CHAPTER 1: *A Place in the Sun*

1 Australian Institute of Political Science, *Northern Australia: Task for a Nation*, Angus and Robertson, Sydney, 1954, p.201.
2 Department of Native Affairs, Western Australia, *A Place in the Sun*, Perth, n.d.

CHAPTER 2: *A New Social Contract*

1 Perkins, Charles, *A Bastard Like Me*, Ure Smith, Sydney, 1975, pp.74–91.

CHAPTER 3: *Great South Land*

1 Ward, Russell, *Finding Australia*, Heinemann, Melbourne, 1987, pp.78–79.
2 *ibid.*, p.70.
3 *ibid.*, p.71.
4 Downer, Hon. A.R., *Australia and Asia: The Case for Our Immigration Policy*, Speech to the Commonwealth Club luncheon, Town Hall, Adelaide, 4 December 1959, p.4.
5 Downer, Hon. A.R., *The Influence of Migration on Australian Foreign Affairs*, The Roy Milne Lecture for 1960, Australian Institute of International Affairs, Sydney, 1960, pp.9–10.
6 Donohoe, James, *The Forgotten Australians: The Non-Anglo or Celtic Convicts and Exiles*, Sydney, 1991, pp.8,33.

7 *Commonwealth Parliamentary Debates*, House of Representatives, 26 September 1901, p.5233.

8 *Commonwealth Parliamentary Debates*, House of Representatives, 25 September 1901, p.5177.

9 Department of Immigration and Multicultural Affairs data.

10 Department of Immigration, *Australians of Tomorrow*, c.1949.

11 Calwell, Arthur, *Australia and Your Future*, c.1946.

12 Calwell, Arthur, *Why You will Feel at Home in Australia*, c.1949.

13 *ibid*.

14 *ibid*.

CHAPTER 4: *Being 'Australian'*

1 *The Age*, Melbourne, 1 April 1981, p.15.

2 *The Australian*, 13 March 1995.

3 Speech by Parkes to the Australian Federation Conference, Melbourne, 1890, in Clark, C.M.H., *Select Documents in Australian History, 1851–1900*, Angus and Robertson, Sydney, 1955, pp.475–476.

4 Department of Immigration and Multicultural Affairs statistics.

CHAPTER 5: *Market Realities*

1 *Commonwealth Parliamentary Debates*, House of Representatives, 25 September 1901, pp.5143–5144.

2 *Sydney Morning Herald*, Australia Unlimited Supplement, 18 July 1966, p.3.

CHAPTER 6: *Creating Security*

1 Quoted in Buckley, Ken and Wheelwright, Ted, *No Paradise for Workers: Capitalism and the Common People in Australia 1788–1914*, OUP, Melbourne, 1988, p.220.

2 OECD, *OECD Economic Outlook No.65*, June 1999, p.252.

CHAPTER 7: *Citizens All*

1 Moreland City Council, *Democracy and Accountability*, Council Plan, 1998–2001; Mayor's Speech, 10 March 1998, 'Democracy and Accountability'; *Reconciliation Policy and Action Plan*, May 1998.

2 Moreland City Council, *Reconciliation Policy and Action Plan*, May 1998, p.5.

CHAPTER 8: *People for a Continent*

1 Instituto Geografico De Agostini, *World Atlas*, Rand McNally, London, 1998, pp.11ff.
2 *The Australian*, 22 May 1997, pp.1,4; *Australian Financial Review*, 22 May 1997, p.1; *Courier-Mail*, Brisbane, 14 May 1997, p.26.
3 *Australian Financial Review*, 22 May 1997, p.20.
4 Opening Speech by the NSW Premier, Hon. Bob Carr, Australians for an Ecologically Sustainable Population, National Conference, Sydney, 30 August 1997.
5 *Telegraph-Mirror*, Sydney, 22 May 1995, p.1; *Newcastle Herald*, 22 May 1995, p.5.
6 *Herald Sun*, Melbourne, 23 May 1995, p.11.
7 *Sydney Morning Herald*, Editorial, 25 May 1995, p.17.
8 *Sydney Morning Herald*, Editorial, 24 May 1995, p.14.
9 Department of Immigration and Multicultural Affairs statistics.
10 Department of Immigration and Multicultural Affairs, *Population Flows: Immigration Aspects*, January 1999, p.2.
11 *ibid*.
12 Hong Kong Census and Statistics Department, 9 September 1999.
13 *New Internationalist*, September 1998, p.19.
14 *Sydney Morning Herald*, 28 May 1997, p.17.
15 *ibid*.
16 Sheehan, Paul, *Among the Barbarians*, Random House, Sydney, 1998, p.109.
17 *Sydney Morning Herald*, 24 June 1998.
18 *ibid*.
19 O'Connor, Mark, *This Tired Brown Land*, Duffy and Snellgrove, Sydney, 1998, p.190.
20 *The Age*, Melbourne, 19 September 1999, p.12.

CHAPTER 9: *The Nature of Australia*

1 Quoted in House of Representatives Standing Committee for Long Term Strategies, *Australia's Carrying Capacity: One Nation — Two Ecologies ('The 'Jones Report')*, AGPS, Canberra, 1994, p.7.
2 Quoted in Fincher, Ruth, *Immigration, Urban Infrastructure and the Environment*, Bureau of Immigration Research, Canberra, 1991, p.xii.
3 *Jones Report*, pp.41,90.

CHAPTER 10: *Sustaining a Life*

1 *Jones Report*, pp.85–88; Sen, Amartya, 'Population: Delusion and Reality', *New York Review*, 22 September 1994, pp.62–71.
2 *Jones Report*, p.87.
3 *ibid.*, p.65.
4 *ibid.*, pp.41,90.
5 CSIRO, *Towards a Sustainable Agriculture*, 1997, pp.1,10.
6 *Jones Report*, pp.54,22,24,29.
7 Population Issues Committee, National Population Council, *Population Issues and Australia's Future*, AGPS, Canberra, 1991, p.25.
8 *The Australian*, 22 May 1997, p.1.
9 Department of Immigration and Multicultural Affairs, *Population Flows: Immigration Aspects*, January 1999.

CHAPTER 11: *The Lie of the Land*

1 Goodall, Heather, *Invasion to Embassy: Land in Aboriginal Politics in New South Wales, 1770–1972*, Allen and Unwin, Sydney, 1996, p.106.
2 *Townsville Bulletin*, 1 March 1997, p.1; *The Australian*, 8–9 April 1995, p.33.
3 ATSIC, Press Release 18 March 1999, 'Indigenous People of Australia Welcome CERD Findings'.
4 *ibid.*
5 *The Age*, Melbourne, 23 February 1999, p.4.
6 *Sydney Morning Herald*, 31 May 1997, Spectrum, pp.1,4.
7 *The Australian*, 3 July 1998, p.13.
8 *Townsville Bulletin*, 24 Nov 1997, p.12.
9 *Courier-Mail*, Brisbane, 5 November 1997, p.3.
10 Morphy, Howard, '"Now You Understand": An Analysis of the Way Yolngu Have Used Sacred Knowledge to Retain their Autonomy', in Nicholas Peterson and Marcia Langton (eds), *Aborigines, Land and Land Rights*, Australian Institute of Aboriginal Studies, Canberra, 1983, pp.110–133.
11 *Commonwealth Parliamentary Debates*, House of Representatives, 9 April 1963, pp.481–483.
12 Commonwealth of Australia, *Report from the Select Committee on Grievances of Yirrkala Aborigines, Arnhem Land Reserve*, 1963, Part II, Minutes of Evidence, pp.31–32.
13 Reynolds, Henry, *Aboriginal Sovereignty*, Allen and Unwin, Sydney, 1996, p.37.

14 Williams, Nancy, 'Yolngu Concepts of Land Ownership', in Nicholas Peterson and Marcia Langton (eds), *Aborigines, Land and Land Rights*, Australian Institute of Aboriginal Studies, Canberra, 1983, pp.94–109.

15 Goodall, Heather, *Invasion to Embassy: Land in Aboriginal Politics in New South Wales, 1770–1972*, Allen and Unwin, Sydney, 1996, pp.338–339.

CHAPTER 12: *A Matter of Unutterable Shame*

1 *Courier-Mail*, Brisbane, 27 June 1996.

2 *Mabo and Others v. Queensland (No. 2)* (1992) 175 Commonwealth Law Reports, LR 1 F.C. 92/014, Brennan Judgement, para. 52.

3 *Mabo*, Brennan Judgement, para. 41.

4 *Mabo*, Deane and Gaudron judgement, paras. 78, 50, 51, 56.

5 *Sydney Morning Herald, Good Weekend*, 13 June 1998, pp.14–21; *Sydney Morning Herald*, 23 August 1997, p.8s; Loos, Noel and Koiki Mabo, *Edward Koiki Mabo: His Life and Struggle for Land Rights*, University of Queensland Press, Brisbane, 1996.

6 *Townsville Bulletin*, 7 June 1995.

7 *ibid.*

8 *Courier-Mail*, Brisbane, 8 June 1995, p.7.

9 *The Australian*, 5 June 1995, p.1.

CHAPTER 13: *New Law, New Land*

1 Dodson, Michael, 'The Practicalities of Reconciliation', Speech by Aboriginal and Torres Strait Islander Social Justice Commissioner, 27 March 1997.

2 *The Wik Peoples v. The State of Queensland and Others*, High Court of Australia, Matter No B8 of 1996, Kirby Judgement.

3 *ibid.*

4 *The Australian*, 18–19 May 1996, p. 22.

CHAPTER 14: *Extinguishment by the Bucketful*

1 Quoted in Brennan, Frank, *The Wik Debate: Its Impact on Aborigines, Pastoralists and Miners*, UNSW Press, Sydney, 1998, p.61.

2 *Sydney Morning Herald*, 22 June 1998, p.7.

3 *Sydney Morning Herald*, 22 June 1998, p.1.

4 Bachelard, Michael, *The Great Land Grab*, Hyland House, Melbourne, 1998, pp.131–134.

CHAPTER 15: *Our History and Our Geography*

1 Horne, Donald, *The Lucky Country: Australia in the Sixties,* Angus and Robertson, Sydney, 1965 edn, p.217.

2 *ibid.,* pp.100, 105–106.

3 *ibid.,* p.230.

4 *The Australian,* 25–26 March 1995, p.24.

5 Speech by Opposition Leader John Howard to the Australia–Asia Society, 'The Coalition's Asia Focus', Sydney, 12 October 1995.

6 *Sydney Morning Herald,* 2 Nov 1996, p.8.

7 *The Australian,* 2–3 November 1996, p.8.

8 *Courier-Mail,* Brisbane, 15 October 1996, p.4.

9 *Australian Financial Review,* 8 November 1996, pp.1, 12.

10 *The Australian,* 31 October 1996, pp.1, 6.

11 *Courier-Mail,* Brisbane, 17 May 1997, p.5.

12 Speech to Malaysian Institute of Strategic International Studies, quoted in *The Australian,* 22 November 1996, p.4.

13 *Courier-Mail,* Brisbane, 17 May 1997.

14 *Australian Financial Review,* 8 November 1996.

CHAPTER 16: *Ending White Australia*

1 Opperman, Hon. H.F., *Immigration Policy Affecting Non-Europeans,* Statement by the Minister for Immigration, 9 March 1966, Commonwealth of Australia, *Parliamentary Papers,* Volume VIII, 1964–1966, p.377.

2 Willard, Myra, *History of the White Australia Policy to 1920,* Melbourne University Press, Melbourne, 1923, p.126.

3 *Commonwealth Parliamentary Debates,* House of Representatives, 19 February 1959, pp.132, 131.

4 Perkins, Charles, *A Bastard Like Me,* Ure Smith, Sydney, 1975, pp.92–96.

5 Quoted in Franklin, Margaret Ann, *Black and White Australians: An Inter-racial History, 1788–1975,* Heinemann Educational Australia, Melbourne, 1976, p.183; McGregor, Craig, *Profile of Australia,* Penguin Books, Melbourne, 1968, p.315.

6 Opperman, Hon. H.F., *Australia's Immigration Policy,* Paper delivered to the Youth and Student Seminar on International Affairs, Canberra, 28 May 1966, p.5.

7 *Commonwealth Parliamentary Debates,* House of Representatives, 24 March 1966, p.576.

CHAPTER 17: *Opening the Door to Asia*

1 *Sydney Morning Herald,* 1 August 1988, p.1; *Sydney Morning Herald,* 27 January 1995, p.1.

2 *Telegraph-Mirror,* Sydney, 31 January 1995, p.4.

3 *Sydney Morning Herald,*12 May 1990, p.1.

4 *The Australian,* 6–7 May 1995, p.27.

5 *The Australian,* 1 November 1996, p.17.

6 Address by Michael MacKellar to the Quarterly Luncheon Meeting of the Australian Chamber of Shipping, Sydney, 27 June 1979.

CHAPTER 18: *Asian Crisis, Asian Futures*

1 Syndicated to *Australian Financial Review,* 8 October 1998, p.20.

2 *Sunday Star,* Malaysia, 14 December 1997, p.19.

3 *The Australian,* 22 November 1996, p.4.

4 Speech by John Howard to the Australia–Asia Society, 'Australia and Asia: An Enduring Engagement', 8th May 1997.

5 *The Bulletin,* 12 October 1999, p.26.

6 *The Bulletin,* 28 September 1999, pp.22–24.

7 *New Straits Times,* Malaysia, 25 September 1999, p.1.

8 *The Australian,* 25 September 1999, p.1.

9 *New Straits Times,* Malaysia, 28 September 1999, p.1.

10 *The Age,* Melbourne, 28 September 1999, p.15.

11 *The Bulletin,* 12 October 1999, p.30.

12 *New Straits Times,* Malaysia, 30 September 1999, p.2.

13 *New Straits Times,* Malaysia, 2 October 1999, p.10.

14 Speech by John Howard, Great Hall, Parliament House, Canberra, 8 September 1999.

15 *The Age,* Melbourne, 13 September 1999, p.15.

16 Amnesty International Press Release, London, 19 March 1999.

CHAPTER 19: *The Resistible Rise of Pauline Hanson*

1 Pasquarelli, John, *The Pauline Hanson Story, By the Man Who Knows,* New Holland, Sydney, 1998, pp.30–31.

2 *ibid.,* p.23.

3 *ibid.,* pp.119–126.

4 Goot, Murray, 'Hanson's Heartland: Who's for One Nation and Why', in Davidoff, Nadine (ed.), *Two Nations,* Bookman, Melbourne, 1998, p.53.

5 *ibid.,*p.57.

6 *The Australian,* 22 June 1998.

CHAPTER 20: *Gathering Resentment*

1 *The Australian*, 7–8 January 1995, p.1; *Telegraph-Mirror*, Sydney, 31 January 1995, p.4.

2 Coalition's Immigration and Multiculturalism and Settlement Policies, 1996, launched at the Heidelberg Town Hall on 9 February 1996.

3 *ibid.*

4 *Sun-Herald*, Sydney, 19 August 1997.

5 Quoted in Kingston, Margo, 'On the Campaign Trail with Pauline Hanson', in Davidoff, Nadine (ed.), *Two Nations*, Bookman, Melbourne, 1998, p.104.

6 Address by Prime Minister John Howard to the Queensland Division of the Liberal Party State Council, 22 September 1996, p.4.

7 John Laws, Radio 2UE, 24 October 1996.

8 Quoted in Kingston, *op. cit.*, p.105.

9 Speech by Opposition Leader John Howard, 'The Role of Government', The Menzies Research Centre, Canberra, 6 June 1995.

10 Speech by Prime Minister John Howard, Menzies Lecture, 'The Liberal Tradition: The Beliefs and Values Which Guide the Federal Government', 18 November 1996.

11 Speech by Opposition Leader John Howard, 'The Role of Government', 6 June 1995.

12 Speech by Opposition Leader John Howard, 'The Role of Government', 6 June 1995.

13 Address by Prime Minister John Howard to the Queensland Division of the Liberal Party State Council, 22 September 1996, p.5.

14 Address by Prime Minister Paul Keating, Immigration Policy Statement 1996, National Gallery of Victoria, 24 February 1996.

15 Speech by Prime Minister John Howard, Menzies Lecture, 'The Liberal Tradition: The Beliefs and Values Which Guide the Federal Government', 18 November 1996.

16 Interview with Prime Minister John Howard in *Who Weekly*, 30 December 1996, p.34.

17 *ibid.*, p.34.

18 *ibid.*, p.35.

19 Grattan, Michelle, 'Pauline Hanson's Hijack of John Howard', in Davidoff, Nadine (ed.), *Two Nations*, Bookman, Melbourne, 1998, p.87.

20 *The Australian*, 29 August 1997.

21 *Australian Financial Review,* 9 April 1999, p.7.

22 David Oldfield speaking on the Mike Carlton show, Radio 2UE, Sydney, 6 May 1999.

CHAPTER 21: *New White Australia*

1 *Commonwealth Parliamentary Debates,* Joint Committee on Migration, 3 March 1999, pp.M214–215.

2 *ibid.,* M170.

3 *ibid.,* M195.

4 *Commonwealth Parliamentary Debates,* House of Representatives, 17 February 1999, pp.2774–2775.

5 *Commonwealth Parliamentary Debates,* House of Representatives, 2 December 1998, p.1129.

6 *Commonwealth Parliamentary Debates,* House of Representatives, 3 June 1998, p.4778; 17 February 1999, p.2775.

7 Senate Legal and Constitutional Committee documents, September 1998.

8 *Commonwealth Parliamentary Debates,* Joint Committee on Migration, 3 March 1999, p.M203.

9 *The Australian,* 26 June 1999, pp.19,22.

10 *Commonwealth Parliamentary Debates,* Joint Committee on Migration, 3 March 1999, p.M203.

11 *The Age,* Melbourne, 28 June 1999, p.6.

12 *The Australian,* 26 June 1999, pp.19,22.

13 *The Age,* Melbourne, 24 June 1999, p.1.

14 *The Age,* Melbourne, 27 June 1999, p.1.

15 *The Age,* Melbourne, 28 June 1999, p.1.

CHAPTER 22: *Politically Correct*

1 Parliament of Australia, *Code of Race Ethics,* 1997.

2 Kalantzis, Mary and Bill Cope, 'An Opportunity to Change the Culture', in Adams, Phillip (ed.), *The Retreat from Tolerance: A Snapshot of Australian Society,* ABC Books, Sydney, 1997, pp.57–85; Cope, Bill and Mary Kalantzis, 'White Noise: The Attack on Political Correctness and the Struggle for the Western Canon', *Interchange: A Quarterly Review of Education,* Kluwer Academic Publishers, The Netherlands, Vol.28, No.4, 1997, pp.283–329.

3 *The Australian,* 17 July 1996.

4 *Sydney Morning Herald,* 3 June 1996.

5 Speech by Prime Minister John Howard to the Business Council of Australia, The Regent Hotel, Sydney, 26 March 1996.

6 Forman, David and Robert Gottliebsen, 'Taking Care of Business: Interview with John Howard', *Business Review Weekly*, 5 August 1996, p.100.

7 Puplick, Chris, 'Truth Marching On: Equity, Political Correctness and A Fair Go For All', Address to the Equity in Vocational Education and Training Conference, Sydney, Anti-Discrimination Board of New South Wales, 27 May 1996, pp.17, 15–16, 45, 17.

8 *The Age*, Melbourne, 19 June 1996.

9 *The Age*, Melbourne, 19 June 1996.

10 *The Australian*, 3–4 May 1997.

CHAPTER 23: *A Voice for Multicultural Australia*

1 *Four Corners*, ABC Television, 12 July 1994.

2 *ibid.*

3 Department of Immigration and Multicultural Affairs statistics.

4 *Sydney Morning Herald*, 16 January 1999, p.13.

CHAPTER 24: *Living in the Mainstream*

1 *The Age*, Melbourne, 14 August 1999, News Extra p.7.

2 Aboriginal and Torres Strait Islander Commission, *Aboriginal and Torres Strait Islander Peoples and Australia's Obligations under the United Nations Convention on the Elimination of All Forms of Racial Discrimination: A Report Submitted by the Aboriginal and Torres Strait Islander Commission to the United Nations Committee on the Elimination of All Forms of Racial Discrimination*, ATSIC, Canberra, 1998, p.115.

3 ATSIC, *CERD Submission, op.cit.*, p.114.

4 *The Age*, Melbourne, 14 August 1999, News Extra p.7.

5 Aboriginal and Torres Strait Islander Commission, *As A Matter of Fact*, ATSIC, Canberra, 1999, p.16; ATSIC, *CERD Submission, op. cit.*, pp.109–110.

6 ATSIC, *CERD Submission, op. cit.*, p.111.

7 *The Bulletin*, 22 October 1996, pp.24–5.

8 ATSIC, *CERD Submission, op. cit.*, pp.90, 91 ,98, 96, 85.

9 *Courier-Mail*, Brisbane, 5 March 1996.

10 Aboriginal and Torres Strait Islander Commission, *As A Matter of Fact, op. cit.*, p.17.

11 Manne, Robert, 'Stolen Lives', *The Age*, Melbourne, 27 February 1999, Saturday Extra, p.1.

12 *ibid.*

13 *The Age*, Melbourne, 2 March 1999; *The Law Report*, ABC Radio National, Tuesday, March 9, 1999.

14 National Inquiry into the Separation of Aboriginal and Torres Strait Islander Children from Their Families, *Bringing Them Home*, Human Rights and Equal Opportunity Commission, Sydney, 1997, p.137.

15 *The Weekend Australian*, 5–6 October 1996, p.1; *Daily Telegraph*, Sydney, 18 October 1997, p.10.

16 *The Age*, Melbourne, 27 May 1998, p.1.

17 Peel, Pauline, 'One City, Many Cultures: Brisbane City Council — Building a Tolerant and Inclusive Community', paper presented to the Negotiating Frontiers Conference, Canberra, March 1999, p.7.

18 *The Australian*, 23 June 1997.

19 *The Age*, Melbourne, 27 August 1999, p.1.

20 *ibid.*, p.15.

21 *ibid.*, p.6.

22 *The Australian*, 11 December 1998.

23 'Living in the Mainstream', Yothu Yindi, Mushroom Records.

24 Cazden, Courtney, 'Four Innovative Programs', in Bill Cope and Mary Kalantzis (eds), *Multiliteracies: Literacy, Learning and the Design of Social Futures*, Routledge, London and New York, 2000, pp.321–332.

25 Cope, Bill, 'The Language of Forgetting: A Short History of the Word', *RePublica*, Issue 2, 1995; reprinted in Fraser, Morag (ed.) *Seams of Light: Best Antipodean Essays*, Allen and Unwin, Sydney, 1998, pp.192–223.

CHAPTER 25: *Nations to be Reconciled*

1 Dodson, Michael, 'The Practicalities of Reconciliation', Speech by Aboriginal and Torres Strait Islander Social Justice Commissioner, 27 March 1997.

CHAPTER 26: *The Multicultural Australian*

1 Glazer, Nathan, *We are All Multiculturalists Now*, Harvard University Press, Cambridge USA, 1997, p.1.

2 *ibid.*, p.160.

3 *ibid.*, p.20.

4 *ibid.*, p.8.

5 Fraser, J.M., 'Multiculturalism: Australia's Unique Achievement: Inaugural Address to the Australian Institute of Multicultural Affairs', Melbourne, 30 November, 1981.

6 National Multicultural Advisory Committee Report, *Australian Multiculturalism for a New Century: Towards Inclusiveness,* Canberra, 1999, p.119.

7 Office of Multicultural Affairs, Department of the Prime Minister and Cabinet, *National Agenda for a Multicultural Australia, . . . Sharing Our Future,* Australian Government Publishing Service, Canberra, 1989, p.vii.

8 Speech by Prime Minister John Howard at the launch of the National Multicultural Advisory Committee Report, *Australian Multiculturalism for a New Century: Towards Inclusiveness,* Canberra, 5 May 1999.

9 Cope, Bill and Mary Kalantzis, *Productive Diversity: A New, Australian Approach to Work and Management,* Pluto Press, Sydney, 1997.

10 *Australian Financial Review,* 22 May 1997, p.1.

11 Withers, Glenn, 'Immigration: The Australian Way', speech to the Federation of Ethnic Communities Councils of Australia Congress, Brisbane, 20 November, 1998.

12 Department of Immigration and Ethnic Affairs, *The Charter of Public Service in a Culturally Diverse Society,* Canberra, 1998; Cope, Bill and Mary Kalantzis, *The Charter of Public Service in a Culturally Diverse Society: Principles and Practice,* Centre for Workplace Communication and Culture, Sydney, 1997.

13 Darebin City Council statistics.

CHAPTER 27: *New Commonwealth*

1 Horne, Donald, *The Lucky Country: Australia in the Sixties,* Angus and Robertson, Sydney, 1965 edn, pp.89–92.

2 *Sydney Morning Herald,* 9 June 1992, p.13.

3 *The Australian,* 8 June 1995, pp.1,5.

4 *The Australian,* 9–10 October 1999, p.1.

5 *Commonwealth Parliamentary Debates,* House of Representatives, 28 June 1999.

6 Australian Electoral Commission, *Official Referendum Pamphlet,* Canberra, September 1999, pp.8,10.

7 *The Age,* Melbourne, 14 October 1999, p.3.

8 *Official Referendum Pamphlet,* pp.15,19.

9 *ibid.*, p.12.

10 *ibid.*, pp.23,13.

11 *The Australian*, 14–15 August 1999, p.26.

12 Hon. Paul Keating, Life Membership Acceptance Speech, ALP (NSW Branch), Annual Conference, 3 October 1999.

EPILOGUE: *The New Australian Way of Life*

1 Irving, Helen, *To Constitute a Nation*, Cambridge University Press, Melbourne, 1997, p.77.

2 Darveniza, Zon, *An Australian Saga*, Southwood Press, Sydney, n.d. , pp.21–22.

3 Cope, Bill and Mary Kalantzis, *'The Frail Cloak of Colour': Young People Speak About Identity and the Making of a New Australia*, Victorian Multicultural Commission, 1998.

4 Fukuyama, Francis, *The End of History and the Last Man*, Penguin, London, 1992.

INDEX

CLAIMING A CONTINENT
A New History of Australia
David Day

A new and challenging narrative history of Australia by acclaimed historian, David Day, *Claiming a Continent* takes a fresh look at the events which shaped Australian history from invasion to the present day. Placing race at the centre of his narrative, Day explores the broader Australian story of possession, dispossession and proprietorship, contributing to a debate that still splits Australia today.

Written in an accessible and easy-to-read style, this book will appeal to anyone interested in discovering for themselves the real story behind contemporary Australia.

David Day is one of Australia's most respected historians. Among his many books, he is the author of *Reluctant Nation, Menzies and Churchill at War* and *The Great Betrayal*.

'In a bold reinterpretation of the major themes of European settlement in Australia, Day's provocative synthesis of historical writing is every bit as jolting to the status quo as was Germaine Greer's The Female Eunuch *more than two decades ago. It is a powerful, moving and extremely convincing study that every Australian at all interested in where we have come from, what we have done and where we are going, should read.'*

Canberra Times

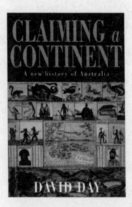

ISBN 0 207 19670 2

PULSE OF THE NATION
A Portrait of Australia
Mark Day

Mark Day sets out to explore his land and distil the essence of what it means to be Australian — who we are, where we're from, and where we're going in the 21st century. He travels from the bustling and energetic cities by the sea to the vast and utter desolation of Lake Eyre; from the pristine wilderness of Arnhem Land to wave at a train on the Nullarbor; from the place where the land rises from the ocean in the south to the tip of Cape York in the north; and from the awesome Bungle Bungle Range in the Kimberley to the desert death camp of Burke and Wills. His vivid descriptions of these remarkable journeys bring to life the places, the characters, the mysteries and the moods of a unique and beautiful land.

He raises questions about the dreams and the paradoxes of Australians: the search for unity in diversity as 150 nationalities meld into one; the struggle to define an identity beyond the belief that 'this is the greatest nation on earth'; and the yearning of modern Australians to reconcile their legitimacy as the new custodians of a previously owned land. For a year, and across 75,000 kilometres, he took the pulse of the nation.

ISBN 0 7322 5863 4